D0812111

THE DOTCRIME MANIFESTO

THE dotCRIME MANIFESTO

How to Stop Internet Crime

Phillip Hallam-Baker

♦♦Addison-Wesley

Upper Saddle River, NJ • Boston • Indianapolis • San Francisco
New York • Toronto • Montreal • London • Munich • Paris • Madrid
Cape Town • Sydney • Tokyo • Singapore • Mexico City

Many of the designations used by manufacturers and sellers to distinguish their products are claimed as trademarks. Where those designations appear in this book, and the publisher was aware of a trademark claim, the designations have been printed with initial capital letters or in all capitals.

The author and publisher have taken care in the preparation of this book, but make no expressed or implied warranty of any kind and assume no responsibility for errors or omissions. No liability is assumed for incidental or consequential damages in connection with or arising out of the use of the information or programs contained herein.

The publisher offers excellent discounts on this book when ordered in quantity for bulk purchases or special sales, which may include electronic versions and/or custom covers and content particular to your business, training goals, marketing focus, and branding interests. For more information, please contact:

U.S. Corporate and Government Sales
(800) 382-3419
corpsales@pearsontechgroup.com

For sales outside the United States, please contact:

International Sales
international@pearsoned.com

Visit us on the Web: informit.com/aw

Library of Congress Cataloging-in-Publication Data:

Hallam-Baker, Phillip.

The dotCrime manifesto : how to stop Internet crime / Phillip Hallam-Baker. — 1st ed.

p. cm.

ISBN 0-321-50358-9 (pbk. : alk. paper) 1. Computer crimes. 2. Computer crimes—Prevention. 3. Internet. I. Title.

HV6773.H35 2007

364.4—dc22

2007041798

Editor-In-Chief
Karen Gettman

Acquisitions Editor
Jessica Goldstein

Senior Development Editc
Chris Zahn

Managing Editor
Gina Kanouse

Senior Project Editor
Kristy Hart

Copy Editor
Gill Editorial Services

Indexer
Lisa Stumpf

Proofreader
Williams Woods
Publishing Services

Publishing
Coordinator
Romny French

Cover Designer
Chuti Prasertsith

Composition
Gloria Schurick

ISBN-13: 978-0-321-50358-9
ISBN-10: 0-321-50358-9

Text printed in the United States on recycled paper at RR Donnelley in Crawfordsville, Indiana. First printing December 2007

This Book Is Safari Enabled

The Safari® Enabled icon on the cover of your favorite technology book means the book is available through Safari Bookshelf. When you buy this book, you get free access to the online edition for 45 days.

Safari Bookshelf is an electronic reference library that lets you easily search thousands of technical books, find code samples, download chapters, and access technical information whenever and wherever you need it.

To gain 45-day Safari Enabled access to this book:

- Go to www.awprofessional.com/safarienabled.
- Complete the brief registration form.
- Enter the coupon code 8ZLI-ZR2J-WHIH-4DJR-PXV5.

If you have difficulty registering on Safari Bookshelf or accessing the online edition, please e-mail customer-service@safaribooksonline.com.

Dedicated to the memory of Linda Franklin,
1955-2002.

Contents

Preface

For more than a decade, surveys of Internet users, administrators, and developers have consistently ranked "security" as their top concern. Despite the advances in Internet security technology, the problem of criminal activity on the Internet has only become worse.

As Nicholas Negroponte, founder of the MIT Media Lab and the One Laptop Per Child association observed: *bits not atoms*. As the world goes digital, so does crime. Only the venue is new in Internet crime. Every one of the crimes described in this book is a new twist on an ancient story. Willie Horton robbed banks because, "That's where the money is." Today, the money is on the Internet, and so are the criminals trying to steal it.

People not bits: Internet crime is about people. Money is the means; technology is merely an end. Some Internet criminals are world-class technology experts, but rather fewer than you might expect. Most Internet criminals are experts in manipulating and exploiting the behavior of people rather than machines.

Internet crime is caused by the criminals, but certain limitations of the original design of the Internet and the Web have encouraged its growth. To change the behavior of people, we must change the environment in which they interact. Paradoxically, understanding the *problem* of Internet crime as a social process leads us to *solutions* that are primarily expressed as technical proposals.

If we are going to beat the Internet criminals, we are going to need both strategy and tactics. In the short term, we must respond tactically— foiling attacks in progress even if doing so costs more than accepting the loss. In the longer term, we must change the infrastructure of the Internet so that it is no longer a lawless frontier but do so in a way that does not compromise the privacy and liberties that have attracted people to the Internet in the first place.

We must pursue both courses. Unless we can bring Internet crime under short-term control through a tactical response, it will be too late for strategy. If we don't use the time bought by the tactical approach to advance a long-term strategy, we will eventually run out of tactical options.

The Internet has more than a billion users. It is a complex and expensive infrastructure. Changing the Internet is difficult, particularly when success requires many changes to be made at the same time and the people who must bear the cost are not always the ones who will see the benefit.

I am currently a participant in six different working groups tasked with changing a small part of the Internet. I have interactions with and occasionally appear at 20 more. Taken individually, none of the groups are likely to have a significant effect on the level of Internet crime. The best that can be hoped for is to move the problem from one place to another. Secure the e-mail system, and the criminals will start infiltrating Instant Messaging; secure Instant Messaging, and they will attack blogs or voice communications.

Taken together, the groups are working toward something that is much larger: a new Internet infrastructure that is a friendlier place for the honest person and a less advantageous environment for criminals.

The purpose of this book is to show how these pieces come together. In particular, it is an argument for a particular approach to Internet security based on *accountability*.

This book is arranged in four sections providing a rough narrative from problem to solution and from people issues to technology issues.

Section One: People Not Bits

Before we start to look at solutions, we need to understand both the problem we want to solve and the reasons it has not been solved before. What might surprise some readers is that technology only plays a minor role. *Money is the motive; people are the cause.* You don't need to be a technology expert to understand how these crimes work; the typical Internet criminal is not a technology expert.

The first two chapters deal with the problem. Chapter 1, "Motive," looks at the crimes themselves, every one a new twist on an ages-old scam, and Chapter 2, "Famous for Fifteen Mouse Clicks," looks at the criminals behind the scams. The common theme running through both chapters is that these crimes are due to the lack of accountability in the design of the Internet and the Web. To combat Internet crime, we must establish an accountable Web.

The next three chapters consider the problem of changing the Internet infrastructure to make it a less crime-friendly environment, and how to make the changes necessary to establish accountability. Chapter 3, "Learning from Mistakes," looks back at the reasons that the Internet is the way that it is. Chapter 4, "Making Change

Happen," looks forward and sets out a strategy for changing the Internet that is driven by pain and opportunity. Chapter 5, "Design for Deployment," describes an engineering approach based on that strategy: design for deployment.

Section Two: Stopping the Cycle

Having looked at the problem, we can begin to look at solutions to specific types of Internet crime, such as phishing and measures to limit the use of the criminal infrastructures that support them.

At this point, we are looking at measures that can be deployed in the short term with minimal changes to the existing Internet infrastructure. As a result, the measures tend to offer tactical rather than strategic advantage. Although tactical measures are valuable in the short run, we must accept that the respite they offer is temporary and use the time that they provide to deploy strategic changes to the Internet infrastructure that bring lasting benefits that the criminals find much harder to circumvent and make a profit from their activities.

Chapter 6, "Spam Whack-a-Mole," looks at previous efforts to control spam and the reasons that they have failed. Chapter 7, "Stopping Spam," describes more recent efforts to control spam by establishing an accountability infrastructure for e-mail use.

Chapter 8, "Stopping Phishing," examines the problem of phishing. Although phishing is not the only form of bank fraud on the Internet, it is currently the one that causes the most widespread concern.

Spam is one of the two principle engines of Internet crime. Chapter 9, "Stopping Botnets," looks at ways to disrupt the use of the other principle engine of Internet crime: networks of captured computers known as **botnets**.

Section Three: Tools of the Trade

Before looking at how to change the Internet infrastructure to make strategic changes, it is necessary to describe the technical tools available, in particular the use of cryptography.

Chapter 10, "Cryptography," presents a brief introduction to modern cryptography. Cryptography is a powerful tool but must be used with care. Security is a property of a system. A program can employ the most advanced cryptographic techniques known and still fail to control real risks and thus provide security in the real world.

Chapter 11, "Establishing Trust," describes mechanisms that are used to establish trust in the online world today and some of the recent developments in the state of the art that will help us to establish the infrastructure we need to meet our future needs.

Section Four: The Accountable Web

The final section of this book presents the actual technical architecture of the accountable Web. Each chapter focuses on a particular layer of security infrastructure, beginning with those where work is already well advanced.

Chapters 12, "Secure Transport," and 13, "Secure Messaging," describe work that is currently underway to create the next-generation transport and messaging layer security infrastructures. In particular, the design of Extended Validation certificates and Secure Internet Letterhead are examined.

Chapters 14, "Secure Identity," and 15, "Secure Names," address the issues of identity and naming. This area is currently hotly contested with OpenID, CardSpace, and SAML all competing for position. I believe that in the long run, all of these technologies will develop complementary niches within a common Identity 2.0 ecology.

Chapter 16, "Secure Networks," looks at the network layer and describes Default Deny Infrastructure, an architecture designed to meet the challenge of deperimeterization. Chapter 17, "Secure Platforms," describes some of the work currently underway to develop a secure operating system and the use of next-generation code signing.

Chapter 18, "Law," examines the use of the legal system to reduce Internet crime, ensuring that law enforcement and prosecutors have the tools they need to do their job. Chapter 19, "The dotCrime Manifesto," sets out a plan of action for stopping Internet crime.

A Note on Jargon

Most technologists (sometimes including me) use rather too much jargon. After 25 years in the technology business, I have come to the conclusion that the more jargon a person uses, the less he is likely to know what he is talking about.

While preparing to edit this book, I reread a book on a related topic that was also aimed at a general audience written some years ago. I was somewhat surprised to find it somewhat heavy going even though I had found it a light read at the time. The field has moved on in the years since the book was first published, and so has the language. Will anyone remember what a "Joe job" is in ten years' time? I hope not. I hope we have made both the attack and the jargon name for it obsolete.

To avoid this problem, I have adopted the following principles.

- Where a term has been used as a term of art for many years in the field, I use it. The term **social engineering** has been used in the security field to describe obtaining information from a person through some form of confidence trick.

- Where a jargon term is widely used in the establishment media, I use it. The term **phishing** is widely used to describe the theft of credentials through a social engineering attack.

- Where a term has been recently introduced and is either self-explanatory or readily remembered after explanation, I use that term after giving an explanation. The term **capture site** is used to refer to a Web site used to collect credentials stolen in a phishing attack.

- Where a term is used with different meanings inside and outside the field or is otherwise ambiguous, I avoid it. Even though the term **hacker** is commonly used to refer to computer criminals, it is often used in the field in the original sense of an expert trickster.

- Where a term is not widely used outside a specialist clique and is not self-explanatory without reference to other jargon terms, I avoid it. In particular, I make a point of avoiding the hacker jargon **leet speak**. The point of leet speak is that it allows cliques to show each other how clever they are through use of a private code.

Word games can be fun, but we won't beat the criminals if we allow them to choose the rules and the game. I was recently in a meeting where a speaker had a cute term for every Internet crime imaginable. The next morning they were all forgotten.

Acknowledgments

This book is a personal account, not the result of a committee process. Many people have helped me write this book, an even larger number have helped to shape the ideas presented.

I first became interested in computer networking as an undergraduate at Southampton University where Denis Nicole my third year project supervisor and Professor Tony Hey got me interested in massively parallel processing systems and the Transputer.

My interest in the Transputer and the formal methods on which its design is based took me to the Nuclear Physics Laboratory at Oxford University. Large scale physics experiments need large computers. Working with my thesis supervisors Ian McArthur and Robin Devenish on the ZEUS experiment taught me a lot about the way that large scale computing projects fit together.

A major influence at Oxford was my college tutor Tony Hoare. He convinced me that the pursuit of simplicity in systems designed to address complex problems was not only possible, but essential if the system was to be feasible.

Digital Equipment Corporation sponsored my work at Oxford. At the end of which Chris Youngman took me on at Zeus, where the interesting sequence of events that brought me into the world of network security began.

High Energy Physics, a world dominated by FORTRAN, was considered to be about as far from the leading edge of computer science research as could be. Two people rescued me, first Paolo Palazzi who persuaded the European Union to award me a fellowship and more importantly persuaded the CERN management to hire me despite opposition. Secondly, Tim Berners-Lee, inventor of the Web, who asked me to take on the security brief in the Web design and later the secure payments portfolio at the World Wide Web Consortium (W3C).

During my time at CERN/W3C I worked with many people whose ideas have shaped the Web in ways that affect us daily. Some moved into the commercial world like I did but many stayed at W3C to work on the next generation of the Web. I am indebted to them all but in particular Dave Ragget, Dan Connoly, Henrik Frystyk Nielsen and Rohit Khare. I am also indebted to many people who joined W3C after I left, in particular Danny Weitzner and Thomas Roessler.

Working at CERN and W3C brought me into the world of commercial cryptography. Many thanks to Alan Schiffman and Eric Rescorla of EIT/Terisa, to Taher Elgamal, and Jeff Weinstein

Huge thanks are due to Jock Gill and Tom Kalil for making the Whitehouse Web site happen and to Al Gore for telling them to make it so. In 1992, Jock took the time to listen to me when I told him that the Web was the future of political communication despite the fact that we had no more than a hundred users at the time. Thanks also to John Mallery and Roger Hurwitz at what was then the MIT AI lab Political Participation Project and became the Intelligent Information Infrastructures project, which I joined after leaving W3C in 1996. MIT is an amazing place to be and John and Roger are amongst the people who helped me learn the most. I must also thank Ron Rivest and Butler Lampson for helping me to understand the difference between cryptography and security protocol design.

In addition to his many valuable technical and philosophical contributions I must thank Roger for introducing me to Karen and for marrying us some years later.

After leaving MIT I joined VeriSign where I have now worked as Principal Scientist for a decade. Thanks to Michael Baum for hiring me and for teaching me more about the law than I had ever expected to want to know but now find essential, for Warwick Ford for being both my mentor and my boss but most importantly my friend and for Jim Bidzos and Stratton Sclavos for starting the whole thing.

During my time at VeriSign I have worked with many extraordinary people, both inside and outside the company. At VeriSign, Anthony Maccario, Jack Biggane and Quentin Gallivan taught me about the sales process, Stephen Wu, Mark Silvern and Tony Berman some of the complexities of a Certificate Practices Statement works, to Chris Babel, Fran Rosch and Tim Callan in marketing. On the technical side huge thanks to Ari Balogh, Jay Patel, Alex Deacon, Jeff Burstein, Joe Adler, Thomas Hardjono, Nico Popp, Hemma Prafulchandra, Sidharth Bajaj, Rick Andrews, Casey LaRose, Tim Mather, Paul Meijer, Hans Granqvist, Gary Krall, Gabriel Swift, Sue Todd, Sean Wilcox, David M'Rahi, Mike Olsen, Ram Moskowitz, Matt Larson, Mark Kosters, Andy Newton, and Michael Aisenberg.

Thanks also to my public speaking coach, Marc Chodorow from Chodorow Associates, Brendan P. Lewis at 463 Communications, and all the people at Weber Shandwick.

Outside VeriSign there are thousands of people I should thank; a hundred will have to suffice.

At the IETF, in particular Russ Housley, Tim Polk, Stephan Santesson, Sam Hartman, Pat Cain, Derek Atkins, Jeff Schiller, Steve Bellovin, Carl Ellison, Andrea Doherty, Philip Hoyer, Stuart Vaeth, Jim Fenton, Barry Leiba, Dave Crocker, Steve Crocker, Harry Khatz, Tony Hansen, Nathaniel Borenstein, Eric Allman, Jon Calas, Mark Delaney, Miles Libbey, Larry Masinter, Hannes Tschofenig, Magnus Nystrom, Stephen Whitlock, and Lisa Dusseault.

From the W3C XKMS group, my co-authors, Brian LaMacchia, Barbara Fox, Blair Dillaway, Jeremy Epstein and Joe Lapp and to Stephen Farrell and Shivaram Mysore for chairing it.

From the W3C Web Security Context Working Group, Tyler Close, Mary Ellen Zurko, Bill Doyle, Maritza Johnson, Brad Porter, Johnathan Nightingale, Rachna Dhamija, Serge Egelman, Audian Paxson, and Yngve Nysaeter Pettersen.

From the OASIS SAML working group Prateek Mishra, Eve Maler, Jeff Hodges, Hal Lockhart, Bob Blakely, Joe Pato, Heather Hinton, Maryann Hondo, Frederick Hirsch, and Ronald Monzillo.

From the OASIS WS-Security working group, Anthony Nadalin, Kelvin Lawrence, Chris Kaler, and Merlin Hughes.

At the Anti-Phishing Working Group, Dave Jevans, Peter Cassidy, Foy Shiver, Lance James, Craig Spiezle, Joanthan Rusch, Bill Harris, and from the banking world Rhonda Maclean, Mack Hicks, Dave Solo, Dan Houser, Todd Inskeep, Dan Schutzer, Michael McCormick, and Richard Parry.

From CAB-Forum, Tim Moses, Mike Beltzner, Gervase Markham, and Steve Roylance.

In addition there are many people who have influenced me, either directly or through their work whose input I would like to especially acknowledge. These include Burt Kaliski, Adam Shostack, Kim Cameron, Dick Hardt, Michael Froomkin, Simson Garfinkel, Linda Franklin, Judith Spencer, Peter Alterman, Stefan Brands, David Chaum, Esther Dyson, Brian Behlendorf, Hans Peter Brøndmo, Join Praed, Meng Weng Wong, Ben Laurie, Amir Herzberg, Clifford Neuman, Richard Guida, David Berlind, Dan Farber, John Aravosis, Joshua Marshall, Bruce Schneier, and Ross Anderson.

That my manuscript turned into this book is due to my agent Ming Russell at Waterside productions, my editor Jessica Goldstein, her assistant Romny French, and project editor Kristy Hart. Thanks are also due to my reviewers, some of which have already been mentioned, others of which are anonymous.

Most importantly I thank my family for supporting this project and for tolerating the many weekends and evenings when family commitments were neglected to complete it. In particular Karen for her unstinting support and for being at times the only person who believed this would ever be completed.

About the Author

Dr. Phillip Hallam-Baker has been at the center of the development of the World Wide Web, electronic commerce, and Internet security for more than a decade. A member of the CERN team that created the original Web specifications, his list of design credits has few rivals and includes substantial contributions to the design of HTTP, the core protocol of the World Wide Web.

A frequent speaker at international conferences with more than 100 appearances over the past four years and numerous media interviews, Hallam-Baker is known for his passionate advocacy of what he calls *technology for real people*. His mission is to democratize technology, making technology serve the needs of the ordinary person rather than interest technologists or an artificial business model. *The dotCrime Manifesto* serves this mission by reaching out beyond the field of network security specialists to provide a firsthand, accessible account of the measures needed to control Internet crime.

Dr. Hallam-Baker was also responsible for setting up the first-ever political Web site on the World Wide Web and worked with the Clinton-Gore '92 Internet campaign, correctly predicting that the Web would change the future of political communication, a prediction that led to the creation of the Clinton Presidential Web site, whitehouse.gov. While at the MIT Laboratory for Artificial Intelligence, Dr. Hallam-Baker worked on developing a security plan to allow deployment of the groundbreaking Internet publications system at the executive office of the president.

VeriSign Inc. was founded in 1995 to provide a trust infrastructure for the Internet that would allow people to buy and sell over the Web without worrying that a criminal might be able to steal their credit card number. This trust infrastructure was the key technology that allowed the development of online retail stores and banks. Dr. Hallam-Baker joined VeriSign in 1998 and became its first principal scientist in 2000. His first commission as principal scientist was to design a second-generation trust infrastructure for the Internet. This research work led to the design of XML Key Management Specification (XKMS), a protocol that reduces the number of lines of code necessary to connect to a trust infrastructure from more than a quarter of a million to less than two thousand. This research was also a major influence on the development of the Security Assertion Markup Language (SAML) protocol, which Dr. Hallam-Baker also edited. Both XKMS and SAML have been adopted as industry standards, and SAML was chosen by the Liberty Alliance as its key infrastructure protocol.

Since 2002, Dr. Hallam-Baker has increasingly focused on the problem of how to stop Internet crime. He played a leading role in the fight against spam and was one of the first researchers to argue for the authentication-based approach to spam control that has since become the Industry standard. In 2004, Dr. Hallam-Baker testified at the Federal Trade Commission workshop on authentication-based approaches to stopping spam.

Dr. Hallam-Baker holds a degree in electronic engineering from Southampton University and a doctorate in computer science from the Nuclear Physics Lab at Oxford University. He has worked at internationally respected research institutions such as DESY, CERN (as a European Union Fellow), and MIT. He is a member of the Oxford Union Society and a Fellow of the British Computer Society.

Motive

Have you ever seen a bank robbery? Before the Web, the chance that you would have seen an actual bank robbery was quite small. Today, though, if you have e-mail, it is almost certain that you have been targeted by bank robbers.

By the last count, I receive more than 2,500 criminal e-mails a day. These criminals want my money; they want your money. How are we going to stop them?

The first step toward finding an answer is to understand how the crimes work. Knowing how Internet crimes work will do little to reduce the number of victims: it will only take a little longer for the criminals to find them. It is, however, the best way to make sure *you* do not become the victim.

Internet crime is real. It's organized. Internet criminals have stolen hundreds of millions of dollars and caused billions of dollars' worth of damage. The number of attacks and their sophistication is on the rise, and this trend is expected to continue for the next several years.

In the early years of the Web, Internet crime was mostly the actions of teenage vandals looking for a way to pass time. Attempting to make money from hacking was considered too risky, too likely to attract the attention of the authorities. Today it's all about the money.

One consequence of this change is that Internet crime has become much easier to predict. Only the most obsessive vandal would attempt the same crime in the same way, again and again for long enough for investigators to build a profile. The professional criminal does not become bored so easily and will keep doing what he is doing until the act no longer makes money or he is caught.

The Internet criminal changes his tactics frequently. The techniques that Internet criminals used to perform bank fraud three years ago simply do not work today. The techniques they are using today are not likely to be as profitable or as safe in three years' time. But the goal of the professional Internet criminal remains the same—to take money from other people—and so do the three basic strategies that he uses to achieve this goal: extortion, impersonation, and persuasion.

- **Extortion**—Criminals have operated extortion rackets for millennia. The Internet is a major engine of the global economy. Many companies cannot carry out their business when their Web site is down. A criminal who can make a site unreachable may find businesses willing to pay for protection.
- **Impersonation**—The money that the criminals are after is mostly stored in banks. Taking the money from the bank directly is far beyond the capabilities of most Internet criminals. Instead, they attack the system at its weakest link: the customer. The customer has access to his bank account through the Web. All the attacker needs to do is to cause the customer to divulge his account name and password.
- **Persuasion**—The most pervasive type of Internet crime is the confidence trick. The larger the pool of potential victims that the attacker can reach, the less credible the story needs to be. The Internet allows a criminal to reach an audience of more than a billion.

Internet crime is a mile wide and an inch deep. What appears at first glance to be something new invariably turns out to be a new way to perform an old scam.

The Tools of the Trade

The tools of the Internet criminal are chosen for effectiveness rather than sophistication. The Internet allows the criminal to contact a vast audience of potential victims, to communicate in ways that are difficult to trace, and to collaborate with other criminals. Criminals have always done such things but on a smaller scale. The Internet gives the criminal enterprise global reach and the whole world to hide in.

The Internet also gives the criminal a new capability: the ability to spy on the activities of people who are not in their immediate vicinity by taking control of their computer.

Of Bots and Botnets

Traditional criminals use stolen cars as getaway vehicles. Cyber criminals cover their tracks using stolen machines but do one better—the real owner continues to pay for gas.

Many Internet users believe that they are not at risk from Internet crime because they have nothing of value on their computer. But the computer itself has a value to the Internet criminal. The thief can steal the use of the machine without taking the physical machine, but the owner continues to provide the necessary space, power, and network connectivity.

In hacker jargon, there are many names for a machine that has been taken over. News reports often use the terms **bot** or **zombie;** within the field, the term **owned machine** is sometimes used.

Control of one bot gives the criminal a getaway vehicle. Running an Internet crime from your own house using the network connection you (or your parents) pay for is risky. Channeling communications through a bot allows the Internet criminal to lay a false trail.

The sophisticated criminal hides his activities through a constantly changing series of machines carefully chosen so that the trail passes through as many jurisdictions as possible.

Bots are also used to perform the crime itself. A bot can be used to attack other machines, to send spam, and to create other bots, forming a **botnet.** The more bots an Internet criminal controls, the more crime he can perform. Most worrying of all, perhaps, a bot can spy on the owner of the machine and watch as he logs in to his online bank or enters his credit card number.

Some years ago, taking over (**cracking**) machines was a bespoke industry. The attacker would select a machine and work on ways to break into it until something worked or he decided to give up and move to another target. Today it is easy to obtain hacking tools that probe thousands of machines at a time.

Botnet management has become a commodity, a low-skill, low-return Internet crime. Skilled professional criminals often prefer to "rent" the use of bots. A bot is priced on the black market according to the utility to the criminal: the speed of the Internet connection, the speed of the processor, and whether the network management is likely to shut it down quickly.

An attacker can gain control of a machine in much the same way that an army can capture a walled city: by direct assault or by subterfuge.

A direct assault requires the attacker to find an exploitable vulnerability in the defenses of the machine. Computers have no common sense; they just follow instructions. If a program is written properly, the only instructions that the computer will execute are the ones the programmer writes. If a program has a specific type of programming error, the computer might end up executing instructions that an attacker supplies.

A direct assault is unlikely to compromise a "securely" configured machine with every nonessential service turned off and every security fix installed. With a billion users and a billion-plus machines, there will never be a shortage of vulnerable targets.

Every machine that is connected to a network and has some form of processing capacity is a potential point of compromise: every router, every wireless gateway, every cable modem, every printer.

The vandals competed to crack the machine in the most ingenious ways they could. The professional Internet criminal is only interested in results and accordingly attacks the system at its weakest link: the user. Why bother working out how to bypass the computer defenses when the user can run any program you want? All you need to do is to persuade him to run it.

A program that has a hidden malicious purpose is called a **Trojan** after the Trojan horse of Greek legend. Mistaking the horse for a parting gift, the Trojans wheeled it into their city and left it unguarded while they went off for a feast. During the celebrations, the soldiers hidden inside the horse quietly slipped out and opened the city gates to let the waiting Greek army through.

Computer Trojans work in the same way. The user thinks that he is doing something harmless while the Trojan takes over his machine.

Five years ago, a Trojan attack could be neatly classified as a **virus, worm,** or **spyware.** But the changing tactics of the criminals have rendered the distinction obsolete. The terms **malware** and even **crimeware** have been introduced in an attempt to keep pace.

A true computer "virus" spreads from one infected machine to another as a biological virus does. Today the analogy is obsolete. Instead of waiting for their creations to spread gradually from one machine to another, the criminals pump out Trojan-bearing e-mails from a botnet.

Equally obsolete are the tools based on the assumption that the criminals will continue to respect these distinctions.

By the time the "virus" has been detected and analyzed, and "antivirus" signatures have been distributed, the attack will already have reached tens or hundreds of millions of machines, and the attacker will be busy creating his next attack.

When spyware first began to appear as a significant concern for computer owners, it was mostly ignored by the suppliers of "antivirus" software. It took a new group of vendors offering antispyware solutions for the antivirus vendors to realize that their customers expected to be protected from all forms of harm regardless of cause.

Spam

In the words of FTC Commissioner Orin Swindle,[1] "Spam is killing the killer application of the Internet." But spam is no longer merely a nuisance that threatens to make e-mail unusable; spam is one of the primary vehicles for Internet crime. Virtually every Internet crime involves spam at some point, and most spam is sent to further a criminal end.

Spam frauds range from simple consumer frauds such as peddling quack medicines and bogus get-rich quick schemes to sophisticated confidence tricks. The vast majority of spam products are fake, stolen, or nonexistent. Spam is cheap, difficult to track, and provides access to a billion potential victims.

Stopping spam is widely considered to be an intractable technical problem. That's true: The cause of spam is social, not technical. Spam can, however, be controlled and to a large extent "solved" by a social solution, and technical measures can be designed to support that social solution.

There is no "technical solution" for graffiti either. The problem of graffiti has existed for thousands of years, as the remains of Pompeii attest. But as New York City Transit Police Chief William J. Bratton demonstrated, control of graffiti is entirely practical given the necessary determination and resources. Bratton's "policy" of erasing the work of vandals within 24 hours of its being created coupled with a zero-tolerance policy toward fare-dodging and other types of vandalism had a noticeable effect. Technical measures such as graffiti-resistant paint are not by themselves a solution, but the right technical measures can make a social solution possible or more effective.

The problem of spam is caused by the lack of accountability in the e-mail system. The social solution to the spam problem is to establish accountability. How this is done is the topic of later chapters.

Like graffiti, the problem of spam was largely ignored as a nuisance until people decided that the problem mattered. Users who complained that their electronic Inbox was full of junk were told not to worry about such a trivial matter; just don't respond to it.

The catalyst for the New York subway graffiti crackdown was the "broken windows" theory[2] that tolerance of minor crimes creates an environment perceived to be permissive of crime that leads to major crimes.

Whether the broken windows theory is true and whether the zero-tolerance policy is the main cause of the reduction in crime is open to debate. Social change almost never has a single cause. If we wait for absolute certainty before we act, we can be certain of only one thing: Our actions will come too late.

Internet Crime Markets

The term **organized crime** suggests a single group of criminals organized in much the same way as a business. Al Capone and his fellow bootleggers organized their criminal enterprises using the principles of modern business management then being developed by Alfred Sloan and others. Professional Internet criminals continue the tradition, applying the organizational principles of the "virtual corporation" long before the legitimate businesses of the day have fully realized them. A free-market approach is pursued in which individual criminals or groups of criminals specialize in particular tasks, selling their services to others or buying services that they need.

Stolen credit card numbers are traded in numerous criminal venues that are exchanged in chat rooms or offered for sale on bulletin boards. In some cases, the sellers even have Web sites offering their product. Figure 1-1 shows a Web site offering stolen credit cards (referred to as **dumps**) priced according to the card issuer, the region the card was issued, the credit limit, and so on.

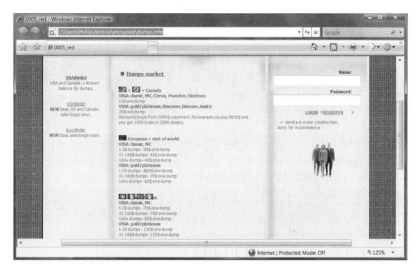

Figure 1-1   *Online trading site for stolen credit card numbers, or dumps*

Criminals with technical expertise sell information and tools to the less expert criminals who do the actual dirty work. Like traditional arms merchants, these experts occupy a gray area of dubious legality. Some of the tools they sell might have legitimate purposes as well as criminal ones. A security scanner, for example, is used to detect the vulnerabilities in a system, but this can be done by a legitimate "white hat" hacker to identify a system needing attention or by a criminal "black hat" hacker looking for a vulnerability to exploit.

To make the situation even more murky; there is more than anecdotal evidence to suggest that some play both sides of the fence. The Internet security world is like a John le Carré spy novel; it is difficult to know the good guys from the bad.

Fortunately, the system works both ways: The bad guys cannot know which of their associates might turn out to be a police plant. This has allowed law enforcement to deal effectively with certain Internet crimes, such as attempts to establish online pedophile rings. A pedophile can never be sure whether the other person in the Internet chat room is really the 12-year-old child he thinks or an undercover police officer.

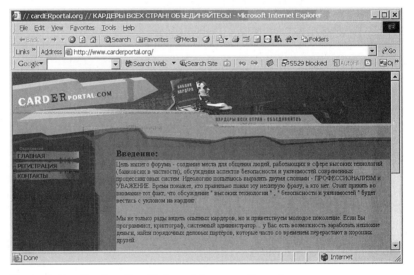

Figure 1-2   *Russian site offering advice on carding crime*

Figure 1-2 shows a Russian Web site (since closed) that provided online forums for various forms of Internet crime, including **carding**—the use of stolen credit cards. The banner on the site logo reads, "Carders of all lands unite." The picture is of Lenin, but the quotation is adapted from Karl Marx's closing lines to the Communist manifesto. The choice is somewhat unfortunate from the carders' perspective because the original quotation continues, "You have nothing to lose but your chains." Anyone who wants to avoid chains would be better advised to steer clear of carding rings, as the U.S. Secret Service and Department of Justice demonstrated in **Operation Firewall,** a multinational investigation of the **Shadowcrew** carding organization, which resulted in 28 arrests, including seven in foreign countries. The Shadowcrew Web site was taken over by the U.S.

Secret Service, who used it to send a message to the carding rings (see Figure 1-3).

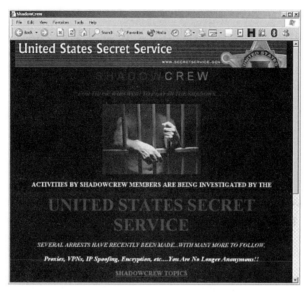

Figure 1-3   *The Shadowcrew Web site after Operation Firewall*

The Internet allows criminals to communicate secretly and anonymously with others of their kind. Payment for services rendered might be made by wire transfer or courier service envelopes stuffed with up to $20,000 in used bills or through more anonymous means such as a gift card bought with cash or an anonymous Internet currency such as e-Gold.

Although it would take an entire book to describe every detail and development of every Internet crime, most are variations of the same basic schemes, which in turn are adaptations of much older schemes. The crime is old; only the context is new.

The existence of Internet crime markets is probably the single most important factor behind the recent explosion in Internet crime. Making money from stolen credit cards is a complex undertaking requiring a lot of different skills and knowledge. To perform every step in the process himself, a criminal must be a computer operating systems expert, a computer networking expert, a confidence trickster, a money launderer, and a handler of stolen property (**fence**).

The crime markets allow the criminal who has only one skill to make money, and the would-be criminal with no skill to quickly learn one. It is not in a criminal's interests to teach his own special expertise; it reduces the value. But teaching another criminal's expertise lowers the cost.

The Crimes

Money is the motive: Internet criminals change their tactics frequently and their strategy rarely. Their goal is constant.

Phishing

At one time, spam was used to advertise products. It is possible that some spammers of the old school still exist, and they actually intend to make good on their offer to sell penis potions, fake Viagra, ink-jet cartridges, or whatever. Or the spammer might just take note of your credit card number and billing address and sell it to another group of criminals who will run up as many charges on your account as they can before the credit card company blocks it.

Stealing credit card numbers or other personal information—in hacker lingo **phishing**—was the first form of professional Internet crime to gain widespread notice. The complacent belief that professional Internet crime was a myth propagated by Internet security companies quickly evaporated as people's Inboxes started to fill up with fake e-mails from banks they had never heard of telling them that their account details had been compromised.

The gangs are after any type of personal information they can use to obtain money: usernames and passwords for financial sites such as online banks, stock brokers, payment schemes, and so on. In some cases, the gangs are attempting to perform **identity theft**—applying for credit using the identity and credit history of someone else.

Phishing attacks are not unprecedented. Almost as soon as credit cards appeared, so did ways of stealing card numbers. Each card has the account number clearly printed on the front of the card to be seen by every shop assistant, waiter, and hotel clerk who accepts the card for a purchase. Fraudulent mail order companies are also set up. These usually operate legitimately for some time until they suddenly saturate their advertising channels with an offer that is too good to be true. The perpetrators charge the cards, take the money, and run.

Some phishing e-mails are easy to spot, but many are not. The criminals impersonate anyone they think people might give their credit card number to: banks, merchants, charities, and even politicians. An attack in 2004 sent e-mail that appeared to come from a presidential campaign. In 2005, many phishing attacks solicited money on behalf of charities to support victims of the Asian tsunami and the Katrina hurricane within hours of the event.

Phishing e-mails use a wide range of techniques to fool the victim. Obscure Web browser features are used to conceal the address bar showing the user which site is being visited. In some attacks, the user is directed to the real Web site of the brand being impersonated, and the phishing attack page appears separately in a pop-up window.

Click Here for the Egress

You are in a crowd listening to a carnival barker describing the attractions you are about to watch. He warns the audience to make sure they know where their wallet is, as pickpockets have been operating. The pickpockets watch as hands instinctively reach out to wallets: now they know who might be nervous about carrying a large amount of cash and where they keep it. The barker gets his cut later.

Security problems lead to the call to "raise public awareness." But merely raising awareness of a problem without telling people *how* to protect themselves is counterproductive.

Phishing attacks frequently use concern for security against their victims. Attack messages often contain detailed instructions describing how users should protect themselves against phishing spam, which would clearly identify the message as a fake. The phrase "Protect your security: Verify your account" has become a criminal cliché.

A legitimate e-mail was sent out providing Australians with ten tips to prevent identity theft. Within hours, criminals were sending out the same e-mail with tip ten changed to "Click here to verify your account."

User education is useful only when the advice can be acted on. Telling people "Beware" does no good. Telling people what to beware of is better. Telling people what to do is best.

Unfortunately as you will see later in this book, the state of Internet security is so poor that we cannot provide the concise and understandable safety instructions today that as we would wish. In 2004, the U.S. Federal Trade Commission began an online safety campaign with the advice Stop—Look—Ask. "Look" would be good advice if consumers could be expected to look at a typical Internet e-mail and determine if it were genuine. As of 2007, this is a difficult task that an expert might be unable to answer with confidence.

We must work to change the Internet infrastructure so that any user can tell if an e-mail is genuinely from a trusted source, without the need for any special expertise. Until that is achieved, the best user education we can give is to tell users about the scams the criminals are using to try to steal their money and to tell them to stop, think and ask (see Figure 1-4).

Fact: there is no reason to ever give your credit card number to anyone unless you are making a purchase and certainly no set of circumstances that would lead to your bank forgetting your username and password.

A good procedure to follow whenever receiving any unexpected offer is to **stop, think** and **ask:**

Stop
    The old Quaker advice of counting to ten works well in most situations. Even in the Internet age there are few situations that genuinely require immediate action and none that require an immediate response to someone you have never heard from before.
Think
    Are the claims made plausible? A bank that has a security problem will contact you by paper mail. The chances of winning a lottery are slim, the chances of winning a lottery you never entered are zero. Before buying anything from an Internet merchant ask if they can be trusted.
Ask
    Fraudsters often tell their target not to talk to anyone else. They know that a target who talks to a second person is more than twice as likely to become suspicious. Simply trying to explain a scheme to a second person is usually enough to raise suspicions.

Figure 1-4   *Advice for Internet users: stop, think, and ask.*

User education can help protect against visible danger. Impersonating a merchant, a lottery, or a famous brand is a threat that users can guard themselves against. User education cannot protect when the danger is hidden. A **Trojan keylogger,** a spy in the machine that watches as users log on to their online bank, is a challenge for even the most expert user.

Even this scam is not unique to the Internet. At one time, a gang would set up a fake ATM that would steal the card details of anyone trying to use it. More recently, the criminals have discovered that it is much easier to just attach some additional equipment to an existing ATM.

The problem of Trojan phishing has led some banks to introduce new authentication schemes that use the mouse for input rather than the keyboard. But some phishing gangs have already found ways to bypass this technique.

Stolen credentials are used as currency. A perpetrator needing information might offer five fulls for the first person to supply it. A **full** is a credit card number with the full name and billing address of the card holder. The value of a stolen card number on the black market varies according to the amount of supporting information available. There is little demand for raw card numbers, which are worth only pennies. Most valuable are COB (change of billing) card numbers, with an account username and password that allow the billing address of the card to be changed.

Conversion to Cash

Criminals are not really interested in credit card numbers; they want the money. We have already seen that criminal markets allow phishing criminals to sell stolen credit card numbers. They are only worth money to the buyer if he has a means of turning them into cash. This process is known in criminal circles as **carding**.

When the phishing epidemic began, it was possible for a perpetrator to use his stolen information to create fake ATM cards with PIN numbers that could easily be turned into cash. Today, carding is a much more difficult and risky crime. The crime markets are awash with stolen card numbers, and the prices paid for stolen cards reflect this.

A typical carding scheme was described in the hacker magazine *Phrack*.[3] The perpetrator used the stolen card number to buy goods from a mail order outlet. After the goods were shipped, he would ask the shipper to change the delivery address to a location where he could safely collect them.

This scheme worked (for a time) by exploiting a loophole in the credit card security controls. The merchants would only ship the goods to the billing address on the card, but it was possible to reroute the package after shipping.

Turning card numbers into cash is the most time-consuming and risky aspect of credit card fraud, as many who have attempted to use the *Phrack* carding scheme have discovered. One of the factors that has until recently kept the problem of phishing in check is that supply of stolen card numbers has far exceeded demand. The sudden increase in phishing attacks, therefore, indicates that the fraud rings have discovered ways to turn large numbers of stolen credentials into cash.

Some carding gangs make fake credit cards that are resold to petty criminals. One of the pieces of evidence that points to an Eastern European origin for many of the carding frauds is that many of the fake cards end up being used in German department stores by Eastern European youths.

Making fake cards works, but counterfeiting physical objects is an approach from the age of atoms, not bits and is thus difficult to scale. Each recruit who is brought into the organization represents a risk. As soon as the organization grows beyond a certain size, the risk of detection becomes a certainty. In the real world, there is no honor among thieves, and the chance that a low-ranking member of an organization will be willing to trade information in return for a lighter sentence is good.

Recruitment is a major problem for any organization that has to operate clandestinely. When I was at Oxford, some of my fellow students complained that they were disappointed that nobody had ever asked them to join the Secret Service. But the recruitment problems of the British intelligence services are surely minor compared to those of James Bond's adversaries. Where, for example, do you go to find sufficient hired help to carve out the inside of a volcano without anyone noticing? How does a criminal mastermind go about recruiting dispensable henchmen?

Recruiting through the Internet scales much better. The advertisements do not need to reveal the true nature of the enterprise. The recruit thinks that he is a shipping facilitator, but to the carding ring, he is a dispensable mule.

The carding ring buys goods with the stolen credit card numbers, giving the home of the mule as the delivery address. The mule then calls an international shipping company that offers expedited delivery and sets up a pickup. These companies specialize in shipping goods door to door in a hurry. In most cases, the package is delivered within 36 hours, 48 at the outside. These services are not inexpensive, but the carding rings don't mind; they can pay using a stolen card.

This scheme is called **package reshipping,** and it is a form of receiving stolen goods. There is absolutely no legitimate business of this type. The mule is dispensable and replaceable. The carding rings know that it is a matter of *when* rather than *if* the mule is caught.

The fraud control systems of the credit card companies are designed to quickly identify the possible use of a stolen card. The carding rings use the mule to bypass these fraud control mechanisms long enough for the goods to be shipped overseas.

The carding schemes sometimes involve Internet auctions. The mules are told that a distribution company needs domestic agents for its product because the auction company "will not let them in its system." The mules are told that the distributor is being unfairly excluded; they either don't think to ask why or don't care.

The Last Mile

Communications companies used to talk about the problem of the "last mile." Deploying a new network for long-distance telephone or data communications is relatively easy. The cost of this infrastructure can be shared among thousands or hundreds of thousands of customers at the same time. The biggest expense is cabling the last mile to the customer, where the costs are not so widely shared.

Internet criminals face a similar problem. It is relatively easy for them to endlessly shuffle funds between bank accounts using the Web. Their problem is how to convert their stolen funds into cash without being caught in the process.

A common approach is to recruit **money movers**. These perform essentially the same function as the package-reshipping mules but transfer money rather than forwarding parcels of stolen goods.

Employment advertisements for this type of scheme offer positions with impressive titles such as finance manager, financial consultant, and finance director but turn out to have only one actual requirement: The recruit has to have his own bank account. The real name for these positions, of course, is **money launderer**.

The money mover is instructed to open an account with one or more of the Internet payment services that facilitate anonymous payments. There are (or rather were) several schemes of this type offering an Internet currency backed by either a hard currency such as the U.S. dollar or in some cases a precious metal such as gold, platinum, or silver. The commissions charged by the operators of these services are typically in the range of five percent per transaction, a rate that would generally be considered prohibitive for a legitimate transaction.

It is hard to understand why any legitimate customer would want to invest money in a "bank" that does not reveal its owners, its directors, or even its place of business; is neither licensed nor insured as a bank; and makes no financial reports.

Pump and Dump

One way to cash out that is rapidly gaining favor requires no direct financial route between the accounts of the victim and the accounts of the perpetrator.

In a traditional **pump and dump** scheme, the perpetrator touts a penny stock with false promises of a sure-fire rapid increase in price (the pump). If the stock chosen has a small trade volume, a small increase in demand can cause the price to escalate rapidly. When the price has risen sufficiently, the perpetrator sells all his stock, leaving the investors with worthless stock they will soon find they are unable to sell (the dump).

Pump and dump scams have circulated through spam for several years. In some cases, the e-mails are designed to fool the reader into thinking that he has been inadvertently sent a hot tip by mistake. In others, the spam is carefully crafted to appear to have been sent by a well-known investor information service. But such pitches still rely on the ability to convince people to buy, and the perpetrator has to time his exit from the position carefully; if he waits too long, someone else might unload his position, leaving *him* with a pile of worthless stock.

The solution that some criminals have found to this difficulty is to remove the element of choice on the part of the victim. The criminals gain access to the victim's accounts using a phishing attack and place orders for the junk stock on their behalf.

Premium Service Fraud

Premium rate telephone services allow a service provider to charge people calling their telephone number. Services on offer range from erotic conversation to phone sex. High prices are charged; a single call can cost $5 a minute or more.

From a security perspective, everything that *can* be wrong *is* wrong.

Telephone subscribers have no reliable way of knowing if a telephone number is a premium rate service or not. There is no way to know what rate is to be charged and no way to know if the advertised services will be provided. The result is fraud.

In theory, subscribers can opt to have premium rate numbers blocked, but they are expected to know to ask for it. In practice, they can have access to 900 numbers blocked, which is not the same thing.

A premium rate service is typically set up through a service bureau whose function is similar to that of a book publisher in that it performs the necessary technical functions to provide the service, collects money from the telephone companies, and pays royalties to the service provider less their own (substantial) fees.

In the early 1990s, many bureaus were not particularly diligent in checking the credentials of companies applying to establish an account. Complaints from fraudulently charged customers were a problem for the telephone company or the service provider. Both preferred to consider any problems to be the customer's fault.

The telephone companies understood that fraud was likely. To control risk to themselves, they adopted a rule that payments would only be made to service providers after the telephone subscribers had had the opportunity to review their bills and make a complaint. Dishonest service providers would not be paid.

Paying the service providers late was good for the telephone companies, but a cash-flow problem for the service providers waiting to be paid. Some service bureaus stepped in to solve this cash flow problem by offering to **factor** an account—that is, to pay the service provider as the payments were earned (less a fee).

Factoring solved the cash flow problem for the legitimate service providers but eliminated the only fraud control. The telephone companies did not much care, as they were making big profits from the service, and the only security problem they recognized was the risk of the company being unable to recover money that they had already paid out. This risk had been accepted by the service bureaus factoring the account. The risk to the customer and the potential for criminal profit were ignored.

Con artists quickly developed ruses to trick the unwary into calling the premium rate number unintentionally. Some hackers took a more direct approach and took over the private exchange systems of businesses so that they could make calls to their own premium rate lines.

Premium service fraud reached a completely new level as large numbers of computers were connected to the Internet through modems connecting to the telephone system. The first attack of this type to gain public attention was the Beavis and Butthead incident in 1997. This involved a program whose advertised purpose was to view movies. Two versions of the viewing program were distributed. The version of the program that most victims admitted to having used included cartoons of the MTV cartoon characters Beavis and Butthead. The other version catered to an interest in gynecology. The Beavis and Butthead viewer was a Trojan that reconfigured the victim's machine to silently dial a telephone number in Moldova.

The Moldovan telephone company, like many serving smaller countries at the time, was acting as a premium rate service bureau, splitting the inbound international calling charge with the content providers. Premium rate call blocking had no effect because it only blocked premium rate calls to a 900 premium rate number.

An Accountability Failure

It is easy to get lost in the technical details. The real failure is social, not technical. There were plenty of companies and governments that might have chosen to act. The reason they did not is a failure of accountability. Everyone who could have stopped the fraud pointed the finger back at someone else, leaving the consumer to bear the loss.

The central theory of this book is that the principle cause of Internet crime is the lack of accountability in the Internet architecture, and the solution to Internet crime is to establish an accountability infrastructure for the Internet. Accountability means taking responsibility when our online actions might result in harm to others. Accountability means deterring crime with the prospect of consequences. Accountability means accepting responsibility to protect others from harm.

Wherever possible, the tools chosen to establish this infrastructure are technical rather than governmental. This choice is pragmatic, not ideological. The legislative process rarely works well when forced to move at a rapid pace. Legislative action should be the last resort, not the first. Technologists made the Internet an attractive medium for Internet crime, and technologists must take the lead in making the Internet an unattractive medium for crime.

Premium rate fraud illustrates an important exception. Regulation or the threat of regulation is sometimes necessary to align responsibility with the ability to act. The problem of premium rate fraud was created by the telephone companies, not the consumer. It is the telephone companies that must act.

In the case of international premium rate frauds, the carriers can plausibly claim that regulation prevents them from acting. Payment for international connection charges is an international treaty obligation, and carriers are obliged to pay for charges their customers incur.

There are, however, measures the telephone companies can take, including covering the cost of this fraud with a surcharge on all calls to any country that facilitates it and in extreme cases refusing to carry any calls to that country. In 2004, the telephone regulator in Ireland became the first to take action: blocking calls to 13 countries linked to this type of fraud.[4]

A middle ground would be for regulators to require deployment of a mechanism that would only block automatically dialed numbers. When a person attempted to dial, he would hear a message that told him that because of repeated failure to control frauds, it was necessary to screen calls to that country. The caller would then be asked to repeat a word or phrase to demonstrate that the call was intended. The user experience would be suboptimal, particularly because of language issues. But this would be all the more encouragement for complacent (or complicit) governments to take this crime seriously.

Extortion

Protection rackets have long been a favorite of organized crime. The extortionists approach the owner of a business and suggest that they need "protection" in case trouble occurs. The unspoken threat is that, unless payment is made, the extortionists will create the trouble themselves.

Peter Cook, owner of The Establishment, a London comedy club, once recalled being threatened in this way by the Kray twins, a pair of notorious criminals then waging a campaign of terror in the East end of London. Fortunately, Cook was a quick thinker and replied, "Oh I don't think it's very likely that there will be any trouble, and in any case, there is a police station next door." Cook did not see them in his club again and later named them as gangsters in the satirical magazine *Private Eye*.

Online protection rackets follow the same basic scheme, but the "trouble" in this case is bringing down the victim's Web site and the perpetrators calling themselves "security consultants."

This type of attack is known as a **denial of service** (DoS) attack. Instead of stealing information or using the machine itself, the attacker denies the legitimate owner the use of his system.

New virus releases were at one time frequently followed by DoS attacks against well-known targets. An army of captured machines will send a stream of nonsense packets to the targeted service in hopes of overwhelming it. This is known as a **distributed denial of service** (DDoS) attack.

DoS attacks are relatively easy to perform and difficult to prevent. It is unlikely that attackers expect to successfully extort money from the high-profile targets that result in newspaper headlines. But these attacks still serve a practical criminal purpose: demonstration of a protection ring's ability to take out any system it chooses at a time of its choosing.

DoS attacks often target online betting sites before a major sports event likely to attract many wagers. The online gambling industry is somewhat controversial in the U.S., where it competes for revenues with state monopolies and has been made illegal in most states. As a result, the industry has moved offshore to a number of Caribbean havens where specialist ISPs cater to their needs.

Like many industries that operate at the fringe of legality, the online gambling industry is considered easy prey by organized crime. It is quite likely that, in addition to outright extortion attacks, some attacks are intended to keep a competitor off the net before a lucrative football game or boxing match.

Loss of profits is not as effective as physical violence when it comes to persuading the target not to contact law enforcement. In the UK, betting is a legal and respectable business. When a number of UK bookmakers were threatened by a protection ring, they called the police. A payment was made in a sting operation that led to several members of the ring being arrested as they tried to pick up the money from banks in Latvia.[5]

Advance Fee Fraud

Next to phishing, the most visible Internet fraud is advance fee fraud. Early versions of this fraud often originated from Nigeria, and the Internet version is often referred to as the **Nigerian letter** or **419 fraud**, after the section of the Nigerian criminal code that deals with it. In this version of the scam, the perpetrator claims to be an official or businessperson who needs your help to move a large sum of money out of his country.

As the Nigerian letter version of the scam became a cliché, the fraud rings behind the scam developed endless variations on the same basic scheme. The e-mail may purport to come from practically any country, and the reasons cited for needing to move the money include payment of a ransom, diverting money from dormant bank account, or to prevent seizure of an inheritance. Another common tactic is to tell the recipient that he has won a lottery.

The sum of money is almost always large, usually $25 million or more, and your cut is never less than 10 percent. Some report that if you negotiate, you can increase this to 15 percent.

In a week, I get approximately 200 solicitations of this type purporting to come from Nigeria alone. At an average of $30 million per e-mail, that makes $300 billion a year, about twice Nigeria's total Gross Domestic Product.

In an **advance fee fraud**, the perpetrator offers the potential victim (the **mark**) an opportunity to make a lot of money if he pays some money in advance. When the mark replies to the offer, there will be some "problem" that will invariably require some money to be advanced for an "unexpected" cost: some paperwork to clear, an official to be bribed, and so on. The amounts start small but increase gradually so that each time the victim finds it easier to trust the con men and throw good money after bad rather than accept that their earlier investment is lost.

It is easy to see these schemes as outright frauds when you are alert to the danger and have your full wits about you. But many senior citizens do not, and many prefer not to report the crime in case people start thinking they might be senile.

The money does not always come from the mark. Olsman Mueller & James, a small law firm in Michigan, first found out that it had been a victim of advance fee fraud when a $36,000 settlement check to a client bounced. When the firm checked with the bank, it discovered that the client suspense accounts had been drained—more than $2.1 million in all. Ann Marie Poet, a 60-year-old grandmother who had been with the firm for nine years, was charged with 13 counts of wire fraud.

The charges alleged a Dr. Mbuso Nelson, who claimed to be an official with the Ministry of Mining in Pretoria, South Africa, had contacted Poet in January of that year promising a $4.5 million fee for helping Nelson transfer $18 million from South Africa to a bank account in the United States. Poet then "borrowed" from the firm to pay "expenses" that kept turning up, wiring amounts ranging from $9,400 to $360,000 to pay for fees such as "ecological damages," "currency fluctuation marginal difference" and a "drug, terrorists, and money laundering clearance certificate." Like many embezzlers before her, Poet soon discovered that, once started, she had little option but to keep going and hope that the confidence tricksters were telling the truth.

This fraud is a modern twist on what was known in the 1930s as the **Spanish prisoner** con when it appeared during the Spanish civil war, but the scheme is even older and has been used in various guises since at least the Middle Ages when the story went that a rich knight on crusade had been kidnapped, needed to be ransomed, and would reward any lord handsomely for assistance.

Reliable estimates of the scope of 419 fraud are hard to come by. The thousands of complaints made to the police are likely to be only a fraction of the total, because most victims are unlikely to report that they were conned while engaging in a criminal conspiracy. The Michigan case is not an isolated one:

- A couple in Minnesota lost $2,600 after they wired the money to pay "taxes" on a fake lottery win paid with a forged cashier's check.[6]
- Melbourne financial planner Kerry Francis was jailed for 4½ years for transferring more than $700,000 from clients into a Nigerian letter scam.[7]
- Cuttle and Isaacs, a New Zealand livestock broker, went bankrupt owing farmers $4 million after two directors of the firm embezzled from the firm to participate in a section 419 fraud.[8]

In February 2003, the Nigerian Consul to the Czech Republic, Mr. Michael Lekara Wayi, was shot dead by a 72-year-old pensioner swindled of his life savings in a 419 scheme. The U.S. Secret Service reports that a U.S. citizen was murdered in Nigeria in 1995 while he visited Nigeria in connection with an advance fee fraud and that many more people have gone missing.[9]

Although the fraud is not unique to Nigeria, the vast majority of the advance fee frauds being operated through the Internet come from Nigeria, where the fraud accounts for a significant proportion of the country's income. The Nigerian government has shown little interest in prosecuting 419 frauds, which is not surprising because corruption is endemic, and the country faces many other serious public order problems.

The Nigerian gangs have been linked to several other murders. The major cons often involve enticing the victim to visit

Nigeria, where he will be entirely within his power. The victim is often told that he does not require a visa to visit Nigeria, and the gang often pays off the customs and immigration officials to allow him into the country. As the U.S. Secret Service puts it,[10] "Because it is a serious offense in Nigeria to enter without a valid visa, the victim's illegal entry may be used by the fraudsters as leverage to coerce the victims into releasing funds."

One scam used by the con-men at this point is known as the **wash-wash**. The victim is taken to a hotel room, where he is shown a suitcase of what appears to have been money before it was covered in some sort of chemical dye. The victim is invited to pick any of the bills and take it to a washbasin, where an amount of scrubbing reveals a $100 bill. The bill is actually counterfeit, covered in washable ink or a combination of petroleum jelly and iodine. The money will be his after he pays for the removal agent. It's the same advance fee fraud in a new guise.

After exhausting every means of tricking the victim out of his money, the gang switches to violence. The victim is kept hostage until the gang is convinced it has drained his wallet completely. Only then is the victim released. In some cases, the gang is nice enough to give the victim a lift to his national embassy, where he can apply for a loan to buy an air ticket to return home. Sometimes the victim disappears.

You might be wondering if there are organizations to help the victims of these schemes. There are.

These investigators will call up victims of 419 frauds to report that the Nigerian police have arrested a gang and offer to use their local knowledge of the banking system to reclaim whatever is left of the stolen money in return for a small fee and percentage of the amount recovered.

Of course, the Nigerian police has not arrested the gang, and the real way the "investigator" got the name is that he is part of the same gang who stole the money the last time. This is re-victimization, or **re-vic fraud**. After all, if they fell for it the last time, they will probably fall for it a second time.

Franchising Fraud

The sheer scale of the 419 scams is self-defeating; it makes no sense to bombard a person with 20 messages a week, let alone

20 messages that look suspiciously similar. Even more peculiar is the fact that would-be 419 scam perpetrators seem unable to learn from the tricks played on them by groups such as 419eater.com who make a sport of them.

The people behind the Web site make fun of would-be perpetrators of 419 frauds by "baiting" them with unlikely stories of their own. Each of the section headings on the 419eater.com Web site consists of a person holding a handwritten sign with the heading. Each is a would-be 419 fraud perpetrator who has been tricked into providing the photograph as "proof" that he is genuine. The trophy room contains hundreds of similar pictures, most showing a different perpetrator. Some show the perpetrators posed in embarrassing positions. One even carries a sign saying "Baiting is my favorite sport."

It is not unusual for a con man to be conned himself, but the tactics used by the scam baiters are as scripted as those used by the perpetrators. The tricks would quickly stop working if the perpetrators were talking to each other. This is itself an interesting fact because most of the scams originate from a relatively small geographical region. The scam would not continue if it was unprofitable, yet remarkably little effort seems to be taken to adapt to the publicity surrounding the scam. The vast majority of the 419 letters follow the original scheme.

An intriguing possibility is that there is a scam within the scam. The people sending the 419 letters might themselves be the dupes of an advance fee fraud, paying for the software tools and mailing lists necessary to set themselves up in a "business" they believe will make them a fortune. The would-be scammer might even be allowed to "earn back" some of his initial investment before being asked to forward a much larger sum.

This hypothesis would explain some of the odder features of the 419eater.com site, such as the fact that many of the photographs are taken in front of the same backdrop. The photographer would surely remark on the curious nature of the signs and warn the scammer that he had been fooled. Unless, of course, the photographer was working with the ring running the fraud within the fraud, and one of the ways that the rings extract money from their victims is to sell them photographs, forged documents, and so on.

Regardless of whether the rise in traditional 419 attacks is due to the fraud rings franchising their underperforming scams or some other reason, the fraud rings have been aggressive in developing new variations on the same theme.

One of these new "products" targets the sale of expensive goods such as luxury used cars through online ads. The vendor lists an expensive car such as a Mercedes on an online used car site for say $50,000 and is surprised to receive an offer to pay $6,000 more than the asking price with the proviso that the vendor forward the additional money to another party such as a shipper or a freight forwarder as part of the deal.

The vendor receives a cashier's check for $56,000, which normally clears three days after deposit. The vendor then wires $6,000 to the "freight forwarder" as per the agreement. A few days later, the bank cancels out the credit for the fraudulent cashier's check despite previously reporting it as "cleared." The vendor has lost the $6,000 wired to the "freight forwarder."

Other forms of advance fee fraud include a bogus "National Scholarship Fund" that would pay students scholarships of $2,500 to $6,500 after they had paid a "registration fee" of $100. Loan frauds are also common; the victim is told that he has qualified for a loan that will be paid as soon as he remits his first payment.

Copyright Theft

The one major form of Internet crime I do not try to provide a solution for in this book is theft of copyright work. Theft of copyright works is a major and growing problem. The Internet has led to a major increase in theft of copyright work. If copyright theft continues to grow, it might become impossible to finance the production of feature films costing a hundred million dollars or more.

Copyright is limited by the doctrine of "fair use," and for good reason. Every form of art borrows from others. The tune of *Memories* by Andrew Lloyd Webber sounds remarkably similar to Ravel's *Bolero*. The plot of *The Forbidden Planet* is essentially Shakespeare's *Tempest*. More importantly, the right to earn a living from copyright works is a net benefit to society. The "right" to suppress criticism through control of copyright works is not.

Fair use does not, however, mean that a person who has paid for one copy of a film or an album should be able to share it with the rest of the world for free. Extracting profit due to the content creator by facilitating "exchange" of copyright material is simply not a legitimate business.

I do not deal with the issue of copyright theft because the conditions for success do not exist. Faced with the major threat of Internet copyright infringement, the lobbying organizations for the content owners are still engaged in attempts to obtain retrospective extension of the lifetime of their copyrights. While the representatives of the U.S. recording industry were pleading the need for longer copyright terms and stronger enforcement methods to protect the livelihood of their artists, they slipped a provision into the Digital Millennium Copyright Act (DMCA) of 1999, which effectively transferred rights from the artists to the recording company by retrospectively redefining the status of the work.

The underlying problem here is that the Internet does much more than increase the threat of piracy; it changes the business model for the recording industry. The role of capital is reduced, and distributors will no longer act as gatekeepers. Power has shifted from the labels to the artist. The film industry has already undergone a similar transformation in the 1950s with the demise of the studio system. The recording industry understands that it now faces the same change.

It is not possible to effect a plan to protect against a criminal nuisance without a widespread consensus on the result to be achieved. Such consensus is impossible when neither side of the argument will accept realistic goals. If, however, it is shown that action can be effective against phishing and extortion, there will be much more incentive for both sides in this dispute to come to mutually acceptable terms.

Emerging Threats

Internet crime tends to move from bad to worse. Just as the amateur hackers quickly moved from vandalism to making money, there is always a fringe of crimes where money is not yet the primary motive or the techniques are not yet outright criminal.

Spyware

Spyware is the common cold of the Trojan world. Most spyware will not kill you, but it can make you feel pretty miserable until you get rid of it. And, like the common cold, almost all spyware will make you more vulnerable to more serious forms of infection, and some can ruin your financial health.

The small group of spyware companies clinging to the pretense that they are engaged in an honest business is rapidly dwindling. It is being replaced by worse.

The most benign form of spyware insinuates itself into a Web browser and provides a constant stream of reports on the sites the user is visiting, the pages viewed, and so on. The spyware company constructs a profile of the user from this information and sells it to any buyer willing to pay.

A more intrusive form of spyware called a **cobrowser** or **adware** pesters the user with advertising related to the sites he surfs. If you visit a site on rock climbing, an advertisement for climbing gear or outdoors clothing might appear. If you looked at a TV on one site, you might see an advertisement from a competitor.

The worst type of spyware silently watches the user and reports his most sensitive personal data to the organized crime rings that produced it. This might be used to steal money from the victim directly or to perform an identity theft and apply for a loan in his name.

Today, spyware of the first type has pretty much sunk into the second type, which is rapidly sinking into the third.

The same thing happened with spam. The first spam tried to sell real products. As people stopped buying, the spammers found peddling porn and fake Viagra was the only way to make spam pay. As the second generation of spammers found it increasingly difficult to get legal network access, the gray-market spammers were quickly displaced by the outright criminal.

We could make an effort to distinguish legitimate spyware from the outright criminal, but it is easier to make the propagation of any software intended to resist removal at the direction of the owner of the machine a criminal act. Spyware provides nothing of value to the Internet community.

Like the spammers, the spyware outfits are caught between the pincers of legislative and technical measures, which are certain to obliterate their "industry." Even if they manage to stay ahead of the technical measures intended to make it harder for them to infect machines and easier for users to remove infections, legislative action is inevitable. As with the spam "industry," all that will be left is a hard core of spyware operations whose activities are unambiguously criminal.

Terrorism

The Internet has become an infrastructure that is as critical to the running of the modern economy as the telephone system or electrical power. And just as the Internet is dependent on electric power to run, there are complex and increasing interdependencies between the Internet and the telephone and electrical systems.

The threat of cyberterrorism is usually considered in terms of preventing an attack on critical infrastructure. In a recent TV drama, the fictional cyberterrorists performed the highly unlikely feat of successfully disabling every nuclear power station in the U.S. by hacking into the computer system that controls them. In practice, such an attack would be most unlikely to succeed because the nuclear power stations in the U.S. were designed long before the Internet existed, and there is no reason why the computer systems that are used to control them would need to be connected to the Internet.

Bombs are simple but effective means of creating fear and causing disruption. Cyberattacks require considerably greater resources to perform and are much less likely to be effective in achieving these particular ends.

The history of the Red Army Faction (Bader-Meinhof Gang) and similar groups operating in Europe in the 1970s and 1980s suggests that it is more likely that terrorists will turn to the Internet for funding and propaganda rather than as a means of attack. The Red Army Faction financed its activities by robbing banks. Al Qaeda's primary means of finance was the opium trade. Paramilitary groups on both sides of the sectarian divide in Ireland funded their activities through bank robberies and extortion rackets. We must deny these and similar groups the ability to raise funds through Internet crime.

Most terrorist groups already operate Web sites to further their political program, either directly or through sympathetic groups. These Web sites are often the target of attacks by opposing political groups, in some cases disabling the sites completely, but in other cases posting their own propaganda on their opponent's sites.

Often the attacks come from hacker groups that do not consider themselves as terrorists in the conventional sense. But there is a significant risk that actions by these irregular groups might cause escalation of an international incident at a time when the state actors are trying to diffuse the crisis.

A situation of this kind occurred during an incident in 2001 when a U.S. plane struck down a Chinese fighter jet with a missile and was subsequently forced to land in Chinese territory. While diplomats from both countries worked to avert a major crisis, groups of hackers in both countries launched information warfare attacks that threatened to escalate it.

Espionage and Warfare

Intelligence agencies used computer networks to perform espionage long before the Internet existed. The best public account is to be found in Clifford Stoll's book, *The Cuckoo's Egg*. Stoll, an astrophysicist and system manager at the Laurence Berkley National Laboratory, discovered a 75-cent discrepancy in the accounting records on a computer. Investigating this minor discrepancy led to the discovery that the machine was being used as a staging post for attacks on U.S. military computers by German and Hungarian hackers who were selling the results to the KGB.

The use of computer networks to conduct espionage is not new, but the amount of information available to the Internet spy is unprecedented. Equally unprecedented is the ease with which information that at one time might have been regarded as highly sensitive can be obtained from nongovernment sources. Perhaps the most dramatic example of this is Google Earth, which allows anyone to view a satellite picture of virtually any part of the world. Satellite reconnaissance is no longer limited to governments.

Espionage is a national security concern but not necessarily a national security threat. What governments reveal about themselves is balanced by what they discover from others. A mutual exchange of information can help reduce mutual suspicion and the political instability that can create.

The possibility of cyberwarfare is of considerably greater concern. Paradoxically, governments might be drawn to cyberwarfare for precisely the reason that terrorists are likely to avoid it. By definition, the terrorist seeks to create fear and panic. Governments seek a least-risk means of achieving their political outcomes. Physical violence, even if performed by proxies, carries a high risk of retaliation. Since the end of the cold war, the number of states that actively sponsor terrorism has dropped. The number of states designated by the U.S. as "state sponsors of terrorism" has dropped from seven in 1979 to five in 2007.[11] If a similar list had existed in the 1970s, it would have numbered 15 or more.

Cyberwarfare might provide a new opportunity for belligerent states to engage in low-intensity conflict. As with the use of terrorist proxies, cyberwarfare provides a degree of plausible deniability.

Cyberwarfare is only an attractive mode of attack against an enemy that is sufficiently dependent on a high technology infrastructure to make its loss a serious concern. A country that is only able to provide power for a limited number of hours each day is not going to be brought to its knees by an Internet outage.

Until recently, the ephemeral nature of Internet vulnerabilities has made cyberwarfare impractical. It is not possible to stockpile weapons for a cyberattack as if they were tanks, planes, or bullets. A cyberweapon has an unknown and short shelf life. Maintaining a cyberwarfare capability would require constant research and development. One approach for the country looking to develop a cyberwarfare capability is, therefore, to acquiesce to if not actively encourage the growth of Internet crime rings so that their technical skills may be called upon should this be required. Evidence is beginning to emerge that might suggest that this is happening.[12]

Pedophile Rings

Phishing is real crime, and a lot of money is lost, but as a banker who used to be a policeman on a homicide squad pointed out to me once, "It is only stuff." The worst effects of the online world are what can happen to people, not their money.

The positive effects of the Internet vastly outweigh the bad. The Internet is bringing information on sanitation and health-care to slums around the world. It's giving the poor and the oppressed a voice in political systems from which they have been excluded. And the Internet has played a key role in the exposure of numerous abuses of children by pedophiles.

The threat of Internet pedophile rings was the first serious Internet crime that the mainstream media took seriously. The reports make it easy to believe that the Internet is filled with pedophile predators plotting to rape and murder children, a lawless frontier where law enforcement is impotent.

Fortunately, the truth is rather different; law enforcement was taking the problem of Internet pedophiles seriously before the first reports reached the mainstream media.

There will always be Internet sites offering pornographic material that offends the sensibilities of some government or other. Magazines sold openly on the shelves of newsstands in Germany would still result in a jail sentence if found in a UK home.

The material of concern for the purposes of this book is not what might merely offend but that which is universally prohib-ited, in particular explicit photographic or video depictions of prepubescent children in penetrative sex acts.

Internet pornography is a large, highly profitable, legal busi-ness. Child pornography is a threat to that business. The same is probably true albeit to a much lesser extent of the profession-al Internet criminal. Child pornography is a considerably greater risk than bank fraud; it is only going to be an attractive crime if it is considerably more profitable than the alternatives.

In 1995, the FBI began Operation Innocent Images, which tracked pedophile use of the Internet. FBI agents monitor online chat forums for criminal activities. Just as people who try to hire a hit man by responding to advertisements in the classified sec-tion of *Soldier of Fortune* magazine invariably end up talking to undercover law enforcement officers, pedophiles attempting to "groom" a victim in an online chat room are likely to receive a similar surprise.

In 1998 law enforcement agencies in 13 countries arrested 107 members of the Wonderland pedophile group. Police seized three quarters of a million images, many of which depicted sexual acts with minor children. Seven British members of the club received jail sentences of between 12 and 30 months, one received a 12-year sentence for rape, and another member committed suicide before the trial.

Even though the Wonderland club was extensive, its primary purpose was perversion rather than profit. Members of the club swapped images and videos. To join, a prospective member had to provide a large number of original images.

The breakup of the Wonderland gang and subsequent police operations demonstrate that the Internet does not allow pedophiles to operate without fear of prosecution. The members of Wonderland were caught despite attempting to use sophisticated encryption technology.

The use of technology cuts both ways; the most sophisticated Internet criminals can use technology to conceal their activities, but Internet technology also makes it easier to identify Internet criminals with ordinary skills or less. Even the most sophisticated Internet criminal only needs to make one mistake to get caught.

The Internet allows groups of all kinds to operate on a much larger scale than previously but does nothing to change the risks inherent in operating any criminal operation on a large scale. The more members that a criminal organization has, the greater the risk that one of the members will be caught with information that incriminates other members of the group.

The existence of the Wonderland club had been revealed by forensic examination of computers seized in an earlier 1996 investigation into a pedophile ring called The Orchid Club, which led to 19 defendants receiving sentences ranging from 12 months to 30 years.

Internet pedophiles remain a serious problem, but it is the only Internet crime problem that can be regarded as being under some measure of effective control.

The arrest and prosecution of Internet pedophiles demonstrates that Internet crime can be investigated and controlled. It *is* hard to get law enforcement in another country to investigate a case involving computer hacking, but pedophilia and bank fraud are a different matter.

Offline Safety

Online dating poses many risks, only some of which are criminal matters. The real safety concern is not what happens online. There are few places safer than the Internet; risks to life and limb occur only if the participants meet offline. Online chat rooms can result in emotional injuries, but there is no risk of physical harm unless online activities cross into the offline physical domain.

Despite widespread expressions of concern, safety appears as an afterthought in many popular books on Internet dating—a few chapters thrown in at the end. Heaven help the reader who starts dating before finishing the book!

The boundary between the online and offline world is an important safety control. Strictly speaking, the online world is not anonymous and never has been. An online **avatar** is a pseudonym, an *alternative* persona, a mask that is to be worn by its unique owner.

Maintaining the pseudonymity offered by online interactions allows participants to reduce the risk that the boundary between the online and the offline world will be broken without their permission. It also increases the risk of physical harm if those boundaries are breached.

The boundary between the online and offline worlds may sometimes be breached without permission. It takes some skill to hide effectively online. Occasionally, an involuntary breach leads to serious consequences. More often, the connection between the online and the offline world is made voluntarily. The point of online dating is to meet people after all.

Internet stalkers are a real risk for women in particular (and also for men). The risk of an unwanted pregnancy or contracting a sexually transmitted disease is considerably higher. A study of online dating by Dr. Paige M. Padgett at the University of Texas reports that "Seventy-seven percent of respondents who met an online partner did not use condoms for their first sexual encounter".[13] None of the online dating guides I read made mention of condoms or birth control either.

If you are a woman and you meet an Internet criminal in person, you may have worse to fear than crime. While researching this topic, I went to an airport bookstore and asked if she had any books on online dating safety. Immediately she handed me a book and said, "It's not the Internet, but you should warn women about the men who read this."

After reading the book, I agree. A how-to guide for lounge lizards,[14] the book advises men to peacock (that is, dress like a pimp), frequent places where lots of women congregate, and attempt to attract them through "demonstrations of high value" (that is, project a huge ego). The only counterintuitive part to the process is the idea that the man should demonstrate a high value relative to the woman by expressing a lack of interest in her and talking her down. Feminists will be disappointed to discover that the guy who insists that the woman buy her own drinks might well be a misogynist intent on establishing a high relative value rather than a champion of equality.

There is a curious mismatch between the shallowness of the pickup lines presented and the use of technical jargon. The mismatch is explained when it is realized that many of the terms used come from writers who are not generally regarded by mainstream psychology and whose theories are of the type that explain rather too much and predict rather too little.

Looking at the work a little closer, I noted some curious similarities between the self-styled "seduction community" and the activities of the online vandals who preceded the rise of the professional Internet criminal. Both groups display the same ego-centricity and obsessive use of jargon as a substitute for understanding, the same outlandish claims made for their success in applying their expertise. Finally, unpicking the wider social circle, I recognized some names of notorious (and some not so well known) Internet criminals.

In retrospect, it is obvious that someone specializing in "social engineering" would attempt to apply his skills for sexual advantage. As with all advice from such circles: *Caveat emptor*. If the author of a book openly boasts about his success in manipulating people, he is almost certainly attempting to manipulate his readers too.

Key Points

- Internet crime is a serious problem that causes real economic damage and major losses for the victims.

- The principle vectors for Internet crime are spam and zombie botnets.
  - Spam allows the Internet criminals to reach a large audience. The spam may be a direct solicitation for a criminal fraud or part of a larger scheme.
  - A zombie is a computer that has been taken over by a criminal. A botnet is a network of zombie computers controlled by a criminal.
    - Computer criminals use compromised computers to hide their tracks in the same way that bank robbers use stolen cars as getaway vehicles.
    - Turning a computer into a zombie allows the criminal to effectively steal the computer while the owner still pays for the electricity and network connection.
- Internet crimes are typically variations of traditional crimes—often confidence tricks.
  - Phishing is stealing credentials, usually credit card numbers or usernames and passwords for online bank accounts.
  - Carding is the process of turning stolen credentials into cash.
    - Package reshippers receive stolen goods and forward them on to the criminal gangs.
    - Money movers perform money laundering.
    - "Mules" are recruited into these schemes through online advertisements for work-at-home schemes.
  - Internet criminals also operate protection rackets.
    - If the victim refuses to pay, his site is targeted by a denial of service attack.
  - Advance fee frauds induce the mark to pay an upfront fee in the hope of realizing a large profit.
    - The letters that offer to share $20 million are advance fee frauds.
    - Other variations include lotteries that ask for an upfront fee and re-victimization fraud.
    - The victims of these scams are often seniors with large retirement savings.
  - Terrorists are unlikely to use the Internet for political direct action, but Internet crime may be an attractive means of raising money.

CHAPTER 2

Famous for Fifteen Minutes

It is often said that generals always prepare to fight the last war. A risk that is anticipated and planned for can usually be averted. It is the unplanned-for risks that overwhelm us.

The appearance of professional Internet criminals was predicted in fiction long before the Internet became a mass medium. During the early years of the Web, we spent a great deal of time and energy looking for ways to defeat the professional thief. The mischief maker, the prankster, and the juvenile delinquent were overlooked.

Then a group of hackers cracked the Web site of the CIA.[1]

The attack did not result in the loss of classified information, did not disrupt the work of the agency, and did not threaten the critical infrastructure. Nevertheless, the damage to the agency's reputation was considerable. In the 1960s and 1970s, a standard move for the plotters of a military coup was to take over the national television and radio stations. A group of teenage vandals had managed the cyberspace equivalent.

As the overlooked risk became the concern, the anticipated risk was forgotten. Companies building Web sites learned to think of Internet security in terms of protecting their brand from embarrassment. Users learned that they could use the Internet without concern for their own security because government regulations make financial institutions such as credit card companies responsible for risk.

Meanwhile, the Internet became an increasingly important part of the economy. When asked why he robbed banks, Willie Sutton replied, "That's where the money is." Today the Internet is where the money is—lots of it—and the Willie Suttons of the Internet have been busy finding out ways to direct some of that money into their own pockets.

Organized crime rings operating out of Eastern Europe, Russia,[2] Nigeria, and Boca Raton, Florida,[3] are using the Internet to steal hundreds of millions of dollars per year. Their methods include confidence tricks, consumer fraud, and extortion.

By the time the professional cybercriminal finally appeared on the scene, security experts had learned to avoid suggesting money as the motive for an attack. As far as the press, the public, and most customers were concerned, Internet security was almost entirely a problem of juvenile delinquency, and anyone who suggested otherwise was engaged in scare-mongering.

The only Internet security problem that could be acknowledged was teenage hackers whose amazing technical skills were matched by a complete lack of social skills. According to the carefully constructed media image, these hackers scoffed at the notion of monetary gain, being interested only in bragging rights. Their attacks were launched to gain an ephemeral fame, or as Andy Warhol might have put it, to be famous for 15 mouse clicks.

The term **hacker** is a somewhat controversial one in the industry, and some people still try to insist on the original definition, which is a prankster looking for some harmless fun. The term hacker was coined at MIT, where "hacks" have been a part of university culture since long before the first electronic computer arrived on campus.[4] Shortly before I arrived at MIT, a police cruiser appeared on top of the great dome above the main MIT entrance. On the centennial of the Wright brothers' first flight at Kittyhawk, a model of their biplane appeared in the same place. The opening of *Star Wars Episode One* was greeted by turning the dome into the head of the droid R2D2.

The hacker culture played a major part in the early development of the computer. Many of the most important developments in computer science began as "hacks," including *Space War*, the first computer game, and Internet e-mail.

During the 1980s, the term hacker began to be appropriated by another type of person whose idea of fun frequently involved actual malice. The MIT hacker culture acknowledged rules set by the university proctors and a set of self-imposed rules called the hacker ethic. The new hacker culture was an expression of teenage angst, angrily rejecting all forms of limitation and respecting the hacker ethic only when it suited them to do so.

The MIT hacker culture was concerned with creating what might now be called street theatre or performance art. It was this tradition that led to the World Wide Web Consortium (W3C) finding a natural home at MIT, because the Web is simply a work of performance art on an unusually extended scale. The new hacker culture was interested in expression of power, at first power over the machines but inevitably becoming power over their users.

In *The Hacker Crackdown*,[5] Bruce Sterling traces this new hacker culture to the **phone phreak** culture that surfaced on the West coast of the U.S. in the mid 1970s. The phone phreaks played pranks on the telephone system and occasionally managed to find ways to make a free phone call. Born of the era of flower power, protest, and the summer of love, the phone phreak culture has much more in common with the MIT culture than either had with the new hacker culture. In those days Ma Ball was *the* telephone company and fairly regarded as a part of the "system"—fair game for anything the phone phreaks might throw at it.

The hackers of the 1990s took their name from MIT, their language from the West coast phone phreaks, and their moral code from schoolyard bullies. Some were precocious in their technical skills, but few unusually so. The computer world has always been dominated by those who learned their craft at 12 and became masters before they left school. The fact that an idea is new does not mean that it must be difficult.

Many computing problems require little more than patience and eidetic memory and are thus a good match for the juvenile mind. We have all met 12-year-olds capable of prodigious feats of memory such as reciting the batting averages of every member of the Boston Red Sox or the results of every match ever played by Neasden United. Why should it be such a surprise that there are 12-year-olds who can recite a list of technological trivia?

As the Internet grew, it became a place where victims of schoolyard bullying could quickly aspire to become bullies themselves in an environment where their victims had no opportunity to retaliate. Hacking was quite easy when all you needed to do was to surf to a Web site, download some tools, and fire them up. Becoming known as an expert in this type of hacking did not require skill or expertise, only malice and good public relations work.

Social engineering is a type of confidence trick used to persuade the target to ignore his better judgment. Many of the new-style hackers were first-class social engineers, able to wheedle out pieces of information simply by pretending to be someone else. It should be no surprise, therefore, that so many journalists reported without question the claims made by these self-described con artists. Balanced reporting of hacker attacks had to wait until several years later when journalists became aware of the victim's side of the story.

The Internet was designed by a small circle of academics largely for their own personal use. Security, such as it was, followed what we would now call a **perimeter model**. To get access to the Internet, you had to first be granted access to one of the few computers connected to it, each of which cost as much as a house. Anyone caught misbehaving was liable to be banned from using the machines. Users of the primordial Internet were accountable for their behavior through peer pressure and responsibilities to their coresearchers. As a last resort, an issue could be referred to the university proctors.

As the Internet expanded beyond a small core of elite universities, accountability began to break down. The network had expanded to the point where a problem could no longer be traced to a source, and even if the individual responsible for an issue could be identified, addressing the matter would take much more than a telephone call to the department head.

Between 1993 and 1996, several factors converged to transform the Internet from a purely academic resource into a global mass medium. The most visible of these factors was the World Wide Web, which for the first time made the Internet accessible to users who were not prepared to navigate arcane and obscure user interfaces. Equally important, however, was the second factor: the transition from being a U.S. government–funded research project with a prohibition on commercial use to an open infrastructure where commercial use was encouraged.

A third factor was the commercial failure of interactive TV, a scheme whose rather too obvious premise was that turning the television screen into a 12-foot wide electronic billboard in the center of the living room and adding a buy-now button on the remote control would make a fortune for cable operators, particularly if it replaced the shopping mall. When the would-be hyperconsumers showed a complete lack of interest in this scheme, its backers suddenly found the need to find an alternative technology in which to funnel the vast sums earmarked for investment in interactive TV. Thus was the great dot-com boom begun.

The effect of these changes was that the Internet lost the accountability mechanisms that had limited malicious acts when it was a purely academic resource at the same time that the Web was becoming increasingly prominent in the mainstream media.

Web commerce was still in its infancy, there were few targets for the money-minded hacker, and, in any case, it was clear to almost everyone involved in the emerging Web that it would be much easier to make an honest fortune than a dishonest one.

Security specialists tend to worry most about the issues they are paid to worry about. In this period, the companies paying people to worry about Internet security tended to be companies involved in selling through the Internet, transferring money, and so on. Companies whose Web sites did not involve money often overlooked the fact that they had staked an even more valuable asset: their brand and reputation.

Defacing Web sites became something of a hacker sport, particularly when the hackers realized that a successful attack against a high-profile target could result in national publicity.

The defenses constructed by security specialists were like a shark barrier constructed by a town that finds nobody is visiting the beach because of the wasps. A hundred thousand **script kiddies** with no real skills using ready-made attack tools were causing so much mayhem that the activities of any professional criminals were lost in the noise. With attention focused on the wasps, the shark problem was forgotten.

It is often claimed that Internet security is an oxymoron, a contradiction in terms. In fact, the record shows that the industry has been effective at controlling security risks when it has put its mind to doing so. The problem has been that we have often been unsuccessful at persuading the industry to take risks seriously until after the criminal activity has become widespread.

No Professor Moriarty

Fictional cybercriminals are sophisticated types. They steal large sums of money from international banks that, in the Hollywood versions at least, appear to spend more on spiffy graphics than reliable security systems.

Cybercrime is a term that I dislike. The future has no prefix; telephone becomes phone, e-mail has only a tenuous grip on its hyphen, and will in time become simply "mail." More importantly, a word that bears the *cyber* prefix sounds like science fiction, not everyday life, which was, of course, William Gibson's intention when he coined the term to give his science fiction novels a sense of the future.

The term cybercrime has become a liability. It encourages an image of an elite criminal adversary with the cunning of Sherlock Holmes' nemesis Dr. Moriarty or James Bond's Ernst Stablo Blōfeld. James Bond has to single-handedly defeat a fresh megalomaniac bent on world domination in every film. This leads us to forget the fact that Ian Fleming, the creator of Bond, was a real-life spy and spymaster in a real war against Adolf Hitler, a real megalomaniac who had attempted to realize his goal of world domination by brute force rather than cunning.

Real Internet criminals usually prefer to avoid the sophisticated state-of-the-art security systems that protect the internal systems of the major banks. They attack the system at its weakest point, where security is almost entirely outside the control of the bank: the customers.

The methods of the professional criminal are chosen for effectiveness rather than subtlety. The methods may be clothed in numerous disguises, but in the end, the schemes they use are ages old, dating back long before the invention of the Internet, in the case of the 419 advance fee fraud, to the Middle Ages. Like a mountebank's shell game, the schemes appear complex if you spend your time watching the movements of the cups but simple if you know that the ball was never under the cups at all.

Sophisticated schemes usually require inside knowledge and are thus self-defeating because the number of suspects is comparatively small. Schemes that lack sophistication might stand less chance of success, but that does not matter to the Internet criminal who can program a computer to perform a million attacks for him simultaneously.

It is generally agreed that almost all spam is dishonest and a significant proportion is outright fraudulent. Peddling quack penis potions might only find a gullible customer one time in ten thousand, but that does not matter to the criminal if he can send a million spam advertisements and net a hundred new customers at negligible cost.

Real crime has always disappointed in its ordinariness in comparison to fiction. Sir Arthur Conan Doyle, the creator of Sherlock Holmes, frequently tried to explain this difference by beginning a story with the detective complaining that too few criminals provided a sufficient challenge for his deductive powers.

One big difference between the fictional and the real criminal is that it is usually detrimental to the plot if fictional criminals are caught as the result of an obvious mistake. Professor Moriarty would never make the mistake of traveling under his real name if he knew he was a wanted man, yet several of the 9/11 hijackers did exactly that.[6] Professor Moriarty must plan every criminal scheme with meticulous accuracy, leaving only one detail overlooked. Real criminals are usually lazy to begin with and often make careless mistakes under pressure.

Real detectives tend to rely on luck at least as much as the painstaking logical deductions of Holmes. But luck is usually directly proportional to the amount of effort put into following up leads. The criminal only needs to make one mistake to be caught. In 1999, a plot to blow up Los Angeles International airport was foiled by a chance inspection by a suspicious customs agent.[7] That this particular inspection led to the discovery of the plot was largely luck, but the inspection itself was the result of the customs and border patrols being put on high alert because an attack had been anticipated.

We need to make ourselves some luck.

The Internet Vandals Have Grown Up

One possible reason for the sudden rise in Internet crime is that the juvenile delinquents who made up the bulk of the new-style 1990s hackers have simply grown up and need to work for a living. The majority of crime in almost every country is committed by young males between 15 and 25 years of age. As juvenile delinquents grow up, most start working for a living and find that honest employment is more profitable than petty crime. Some take the opposite path and become professional criminals. This group tends to increase the number of crimes each commits to support their family and themselves.

There are no ideal policy options for dealing with juvenile crime. Judges and lawmakers know that prisons act as universities of crime. A juvenile delinquent who is sent to jail is more likely to return as a trained professional criminal than a reformed character. A juvenile delinquent who does not receive a custodial sentence is likely to reoffend anyway. Considerable effort and ingenuity has been expended in the search for finding a noncustodial punishment that serves as an effective deterrent to juvenile crime with little success.

As a result, courts have been unwilling to punish Internet crimes committed by juveniles with significant sentences. Even the recidivist computer criminal Kevin Mitnick received a sentence of less than four years for his second adult conviction in a decade-long crime spree that cost his victims millions of dollars.

Law enforcement usually follows the lead of the courts in detecting and prosecuting crime. Crimes that result in longer sentences tend to be given the highest priority. The widespread belief that Internet crime was almost exclusively online juvenile delinquency coupled with the difficulty of policing a crime with potentially global reach has led to Internet crime being assigned a low priority by law enforcement in almost every country.

Many of the juvenile delinquents behind the Web site defacements during the dot-com 1990s came of age after the bubble had burst. Economic prospects were gloomy, and the demand for computer skills in particular was a buyer's market with few buyers. Dreams of making millions through stock options evaporated and, for many, getting a job at all became a dream.

Emerging, Failed, and Kleptocratic States

Internet crime is frequently associated with states that are currently in the process of transformation from dictatorship to what in time may become either an open society or a different form of dictatorship. In the parts of the ex-USSR known as the

Global Balkans, this transformation is almost complete, and communist dictatorship has been replaced by autocratic dictatorship. Most of Eastern Europe has joined the European Union, and it is most likely that this will allow them to follow Spain and Greece in building enduring democratic institutions. In Russia and Western Africa, the outcome hangs in the balance.

Internet crime can be lucrative for some, but it's rarely so for the average foot soldier. A programmer in Russia offers to sell custom written viruses for between $50 and $100 apiece. Another offers to rent the use of a botnet for $25 an hour. Supply and demand drive income down to less than half the U.S. minimum wage. But what would be a pittance for a knowledge worker in an industrial economy is a living wage in many parts of the world.

In *Peter Pan*, the fairy Tinker Bell will die unless children believe in fairies. The rule of law can work in much the same way. When law enforcement is perceived to be weak, deterrence fails and crime rises.

In the Internet age, crime has become global. Policing international crime is inevitably more difficult than policing domestic crime. Local law enforcement often finds it difficult to understand why crime against foreigners should be made a law enforcement priority. This is a particular problem in kleptocratic states where the police and government are often in the pay of the criminals if not the actual perpetrators of the criminal schemes.

The drugs trade provides a dramatic demonstration of the consequences of failing to police transnational crime. The huge profits generated from the drugs trade can easily surpass the legitimate economy of a developing state. Inevitably, drug money finds its way into the political system. The drug cartels only need to corrupt a small number of officials to dramatically reduce the effectiveness of law enforcement. A vicious cycle is established as the violence and murder that accompanies the drugs trade drives away foreign investment and causes domestic capital to take flight. The legitimate economy shrinks further, leaving the country even more dependent on the drugs trade.[8]

The risk that Internet crime will create a similar cycle in the host states is high. Internet crime is a visible form of crime with the potential to cause major damage to the reputation of a host state.

Growth

In June 2004, Gartner issued a report[9] that estimated bank losses due to phishing fraud were $2.4 billion over the previous year. In September of the same year, the privacy advocacy group TRUSTE estimated that phishing scams had cost U.S. banks $500 million.[10]

At first sight, these reports appear to differ wildly in their assessment of the situation, but another report by the Anti-Phishing Working Group explains the difference. During the period covered by the reports, phishing attacks had been increasing at a rate of 50 percent *per month*.

The last time I saw a phenomenon grow as quickly as phishing was in 1992 when the World Wide Web grew from a core of 100 developers to millions of users in less than 12 months. When a phenomenon is growing that quickly, attempts to measure the absolute size of the problem are futile. It is more useful to ask what the limits to growth are and when they will be reached.

In the case of the Web, the number of users could not become larger than the number of users of the Internet, and the number of Internet users cannot become greater than the population of the planet. As the number of Web users grew, the number of Internet users who had not used the Web shrank, and the rate of growth slowed to the rate at which the Internet was growing. The result in each case is an S-shaped curve.

If nothing is done to control phishing fraud, we should expect the growth curve to look something like Figure 2-1.

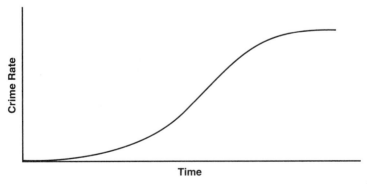

Figure 2-1   *Unchecked growth of Internet crime*

The unchecked growth of Internet crime is neither inevitable nor acceptable. If we are successful in providing effective security measures, the growth of phishing crime can be checked, and the Internet crime epidemic will crest and then decline.

Turning the Tide

If we are to win the fight to secure the Internet, we need to change our approach. We must understand security as a process of risk management rather than a binary state that we can either succeed or fail in achieving. We will never stop every scheme of every criminal, but it makes a big difference if the success rate for the criminal is 95 percent, 9.5 percent or 0.95 percent.

Even the best fire service cannot guarantee that your home will not burn to the ground. But this does not mean that a fire service is not a worthwhile investment.

From a commercial perspective, all transactions carry some degree of risk. What matters to the businesses is whether the risk is quantifiable and insurable at an acceptable cost.

As is the custom of our age, demands that the government address Internet crime are becoming more frequent. As is also our custom, these demands are countered by calls for self-regulation and voluntary compliance. Such ideological terms of debate are unhelpful; we need to know what action to take before deciding who should act.

Crime is a government issue. Without law and order, there is no government. Government must be part of the solution, but this does not mean that it is acceptable for businesses to leave the problem to government alone.

Policing crime is an expensive business. Police, courts, and prisons are all charges on the public purse that must be met by taxpayers. Internet crime is particularly expensive to investigate and prosecute; effective investigations require scarce and expensive expertise. It is more than reasonable for governments to object when insecure technologies result in costs to the public purse.

In the nineteenth century, the risk of fire was brought under control by organizing fire companies to put out fires and fire regulations that stopped fires from spreading. Fire regulations exist to protect the community interest and not just the individual from himself. My neighbors can be careless with matches and burn their own houses down if they please, but the fire regulations reduce the risk that I will be harmed by their negligence.

Government action may be necessary to align responsibility with the ability to act in a limited number of cases. It may be that the only way to protect the community interest is that ISPs are required to take certain security measures that benefit the community as a whole rather than providing a direct benefit to themselves. But before deciding that the government policy should either encourage or require any party to implement security measures, we must decide what security measures are needed and whether it is likely that they will be deployed of their own accord.

To combat Internet crime in all its forms, we must find the right arguments and the right strategy as well as the right technology. We can change the Internet infrastructure if we can make a case that is accepted by parties who can provide the necessary resources. We cannot simply develop a technology and demand its acceptance. Nor should we expect governments to subsidize a highly profitable and fast-growing industry with handouts or tax breaks for deploying security measures.

To unlock the necessary financial and technical resources in the private sector, we must make a business case for applying them. This means focusing on crimes where the cost/benefit of security controls is clearest: crimes where profit is the motive.

Focusing on professional Internet crime does not mean ignoring other serious Internet crimes such as terrorists, pedophiles, or the growing problem of harassment. The common denominator in all Internet crimes is the perception that the Internet is an accountability-free environment beyond the reach of law. As we build out accountability infrastructure to prevent professional Internet crimes, we are also acting against these other types of criminal behavior.

Key Points

- The Internet has changed since the 1990s, and so has Internet crime.
  - In the 1990s, there was little money to be made from Internet crime; most incidents were vandalism caused by juvenile delinquents.
  - The juvenile delinquents responsible for much of the Internet crime in the 1990s have grown up, and some have turned to hacking as a living.
- Professional Internet criminals treat their work as a business.
  - They choose their method for effect, not affect.
  - Computer crimes are usually online variations of long-established confidence tricks.
  - Internet crime is only lucrative for some. Most scams are only attractive to the perpetrators because they are living in countries with a depressed economy and lax law enforcement.
- Every country needs to take Internet crime seriously.
  - International investment will flee from any country that gains a reputation as a haven for Internet crime.
- Internet crime is growing rapidly, but this should not be considered inevitable.
  - If strong measures are taken to check Internet crime, the number of attacks will fall as rapidly as it has risen.

C H A P T E R   3

Learning from Mistakes

"We can't solve problems by using the same kind of thinking
we used when we created them."
—*Albert Einstein*

Mistakes are inevitable when a whole new form of engineering is being discovered. A greater challenge for the engineering architect is the cumulative legacy of decisions made for good reason in the past that severely constrain the present.

My native city, Chester, was founded by the first engineers—Roman soldiers. The name comes from the Latin *castra* meaning fort. Chester Castle has controlled traffic on the river Dee for more than two thousand years. Even though most of the historic remains are much more recent and few buildings in the city have more than four or five centuries of history, the layout of the city's streets is much older.

To understand the geography of Chester, we must understand the history, languages, and culture that shaped them. The racecourse called the Roodee takes its name from the Saxon *rood* meaning cross and *eye* meaning island. The isle of the cross is a small stone stump in the center of the racecourse, which in Saxon times was covered by water. The cross marks the spot where a wooden statue of the Virgin Mary was buried after having floated there from upriver in the village of Hawarden where it had been convicted of murder and sentenced to hang. Strange as this tale appears today, these actions made perfect sense in a culture removed a thousand years from our own.

Similar stories are found on every street in Chester. If you want to build within the city walls, you must take the history into account, or the excavation of your foundation is likely to be unexpectedly delayed by an unplanned archeological investigation. If you want to understand why the city has grown as it has, you must understand the many different cultures that have shaped its past.

Internet engineering is closer to the mode of development practiced by the architects of the great medieval cathedrals than that practiced by most modern engineers. The master masons depended on experience, judgment, and luck in equal measure. The craft advanced by learning from its failures. Many of the ancient cathedrals collapsed during construction, in some cases more than once. But the masons learned the reasons for the failure and built that knowledge into new designs.

Scientists have the luxury of being able to fashion and refashion their theories without regard for previous work. Science had no more use for models of the celestial spheres once Copernicus declared that the earth revolves around the sun. The speculative works of alchemists trying to transmute base metals into gold could be burned once Mendeleev discovered the periodic table. But engineers must constantly reconcile the past and the future.

The Internet has stood for a mere quarter century rather than two millennia, but even so the engineering architect must be acutely aware of the constraints that history places on decisions. We do not have the luxury of designing from scratch; we must contend with the world as it is and try to work within those constraints.

The Triumph of Slogans over Common Sense

In a perfect world, it would be possible to achieve perfect security at no cost. As we do not live in a perfect world, security is always imperfect and always comes at a price. **Security engineering** is the practice of managing risks, of balancing costs and benefits. It is a pragmatic discipline that rarely reduces to simple maxims and clearly defined rules. But this does not stop people from making the attempt.

What many security practitioners find difficult to understand is that it is rather easier to manage security in a high-risk environment where the balance between costs and benefits is clear than in a low-risk environment where the benefits are ambiguous.

The U.S. government spends several billion dollars each year attempting to subvert the communications networks of foreign governments. A security specialist can reasonably assume that foreign governments make similar efforts and that the design of security systems to protect communications infrastructures such as e-mail should reflect this level of threat.

Much of the security debate over the past two decades has been focused on the ultra-high-risk scenario where cost can be ignored. The result has been a series of security schemes that look good on paper but fail in the real world.

The World Is Waiting

Perhaps the biggest mistake we have made is to believe that the world is desperate for Internet security.

Although it is probably true that there is no bigger single *common* priority for Internet users, the same is not the case for *individual* users. Getting their work done always turns out to be the real (and only) priority.

Over the past 20 years, many security solutions have been proposed, but few have been widely used. No idea can stop a single criminal unless it is put into practice.

But even this is not enough unless the users are willing to use the tools provided. Almost every e-mail application in common use is capable of sending and receiving encrypted and authenticated mail messages—including Outlook, Outlook Express, Netscape Communicator, Lotus Notes, and most others. These features are not new; they have been standard for almost a decade now. Even so, few people know that these features exist, and they are rarely used even within the security community.

If the gods had not intervened with other plans, Prometheus would probably have found marketing fire to be an uphill task. Fire is, after all, a distinctly risky technology, a fact that would surely have led many to wait for the second release of the product; one that included some mechanism that made it self-extinguishing.

It is not enough to come up with a solution for Internet security; that is the easy part. The hard part is persuading people to put it into practice.

Security for Engineers

Why have we failed to persuade companies to implement solutions and users to use them? In many cases, the answer is that the security systems are designed by engineers for engineers, and in a style that is to user-friendly design what an iron maiden is to ergonomics.

In computer architecture class, the aspiring engineer is taught to think of a computer as an assembly of independently designed components. The connections between components are called **interfaces**. So the engineer-to-be learns about the memory interface, the disk interface, the screen interface, and so on. Interaction with the user is just one more connection: the user interface.

The designer of software to be sold to large corporations or used by engineers has been able to think this way. The person who signs the check never suffers the daily consequences.

The next time you are checking in for an airline flight at the counter rather than at a machine, take note of how much data the assistant needs to enter. With some airlines, the process takes almost no time at all even when a change is being made to the itinerary. With other airlines, it can literally take five minutes for the simplest request.

The designer of software sold to consumers has to be conscious of the fact that every decision he makes affects his customer personally. Satisfying the user is the entire purpose of the system. It is not enough to perform a task; *how the task is done* matters even more. Successful consumer-oriented software companies are increasingly talking about the **user experience**. It is not just the user interface component of the application that matters; everything that the user sees or might see—including the installation and configuration procedures, instruction manuals, help files, and even bugs and error reports—are part of the user experience.

My first paid work in the computer business was writing video games. One way to think of a video game is a computer program with a user experience so good that people will pay to use it.

Although it is easy to dismiss terms like *user experience* as mere marketing, using them provides a continuous reminder that intuitive command terms, clear documentation, and logical ordering are often at least as important to the user as what the program can do. Features that you do not know about might as well not exist. Features that you know exist but do not know how to use only result in frustration.

For some reason, security engineers in particular seem to have been incapable of producing genuinely user-friendly applications and have at times produced work that is positively user hostile. The hostile user experience would not matter much if the best were actually good. Unfortunately, the best has only been a qualified success.

And when some engineers did push to commit resources to designing systems that people could actually use, marketing would respond with catch-22: Engineering could have resources to build secure applications people would use as soon as there was evidence that people were using the existing unusable security features.

Most Web users know about the feature that allows their browser to use encryption when they go to an online bank or a Web merchant. The number who know that they are meant to look for the small padlock icon at the bottom of the browser window is much smaller. And even fewer know that you should click on the padlock icon to find out who issued the certificate, or indeed why knowing who issued the certificate would be important.

To make matters worse, the industry has failed to even agree on a common means of alerting the user to the use of security. Instead of a lock, Netscape Navigator used a key that was broken for normal browsing and became whole when the session was secure. And regardless of whether the icon is a key or a padlock, it is simply far too small to be noticeable.

Early on in the development of the Web, Dave Raggett proposed that the big icon in the top-right corner of the browser should be the place for the security icon, and that it should show the logo of the business the browser connects to. So when you visited your bank, you would see the logo of your bank there; when you visited Amazon or Dell, you would see its logo in the same place.

We lost this argument in 1995 and got the microscopic padlock icon instead (see Figure 3-1). Now that the problem of phishing has become a major concern, we must make sure that this battle is not lost a second time and that the next generation of browsers has a user experience designed for the ordinary user, not the expert.

Figure 3-1   *The padlock icon is inconspicuous*

Security Must Make Sense

The problem with engineer-oriented design is not just the user experience. Many systems are designed to meet security risks that are simply irrelevant to the users and fail to meet real risks.

A British Ministry of Defense maxim states, "Security must make sense." If people are going to take security seriously, they have to be told why it is important. Another Ministry maxim is, "Security is everyone's concern." It is no good if the only people who can use the security applications are a handful of technology specialists.

Respect for security procedures is sometimes found to be lacking in people responsible for handling the most critical state secrets. John Deutch, the disgraced director of the CIA, was found to have given a key to the closet where he kept top-secret documents to his cleaning lady, who not only lacked a security clearance but was not even a U.S. citizen.[1] Deutch had been issued a computer specially configured for handling classified information but had requested that it be removed because he found it too cumbersome. If a system is unacceptably complex for an MIT professor of science, it has a serious usability problem.

The rise of phishing crime illustrates the importance of the Ministry maxims. The original phishing attacks were possible because the criminals could send a message that appeared to anyone (but an alert expert) to come from a customer's bank. This would never have been possible if there was a practical way for a bank to send messages that clearly and conspicuously demonstrated that they were genuine. Over the years, many proposals have been made to secure e-mail communications, but every time the focus of these efforts has been encrypting personal messages or signing contracts. Proving messages authentic was an afterthought and, as with the confidentiality problem, only personal use was seriously considered.

The result has been programs with a user experience that can only be described as clueless. An e-mail program provided by one well-known ISP would *warn* users when they received an authenticated e-mail message, a user experience described to me by one of my customers in the banking industry as "scary." If the bank attempted to address the problem of phishing crime by signing its outgoing e-mail using that technology, the result would be a ruinously expensive avalanche of help desk calls.

Political Priorities

Like all communications infrastructures, the Internet is a political infrastructure, a fact that its designers were acutely aware of. It is not an accident that the Web and blogs have become a central part of the political process. For some of us, that was the original objective.

Security technology has political consequences. But security resists attempts to confine it with a political dogma. Security for engineers has led to security applications with a distinctly odd set of political priorities.

Perfect security is never achievable, and every security design requires a degree of trust in others. Trusting others is something that security engineers are exceptionally reluctant to do.

Government in particular has been considered with exceptional suspicion, and the design of many cryptographic systems is dominated by attempts to frustrate government control. This is not exclusively the fault of technologists. Modern computer security depends heavily on **cryptography**, a technology that a group of U.S. government agencies made a concerted effort to control during the 1990s. This attempt failed, and today there is a close and mutually beneficial relationship between commercial and government practitioners in cryptography.

Despite this, the legacy of the earlier antagonistic relationship still continues. The tools we have available today were shaped by the political priorities of that time and not our present-day needs to prevent Internet crime.

Government interest in the use of cryptography is understandable. The breaking of the Enigma codes by the British in World War II played a major part in the Allied forces victory.[2] Sir Winston Churchill's memoirs frequently record him making critical decisions on the basis of a "hunch" or a "premonition." These passages can now be understood as coded references to intelligence obtained by the code breakers, the men and women of Bletchley Park who Churchill called "the geese that laid the golden eggs and never cackled."

The Enigma decrypts were not the only major intelligence coup resulting from signals intelligence. Most successes of this type only become public long after the event. A recent exception that proves the rule is the news that the U.S. had been intercepting Iranian diplomatic communications until this capability was revealed to the Iranians by a highly placed traitor.

The past is an imperfect guide to future action. Controlling use of cryptography is a logical policy when cryptographic expertise is a scarce commodity and its use is limited to military applications. Controlling use of cryptography is a futile endeavor when the Internet creates a new set of security needs that can only be met by using cryptography at the same time that it makes world-class cryptographic expertise available to every part of the world.

An industrial country such as the United States with extensive telecommunications infrastructure will always be more vulnerable to a cyberwar attack than a country with no infrastructure. Cryptography is a vital tool for defending the country against cyberwarfare.

In 2000, a group of teenage Israeli hackers made the opening attack in what some have cited as the first cyberwar. Web sites supporting Hamas and Hezbollah were attacked in response to a series of suicide bombings. After an escalating series of retaliations by each side, the Israeli hackers discovered that they had run out of targets. Their opponents, on the other hand, had barely started and began to methodically work their way through every site in the Israel domain. The Israeli hackers were unable to respond; there was nothing left to attack. Instead, they began selling expensive consulting services to the victims of the cyberwarfare attacks that they had originally provoked.

In 1991, the delicate balance of interests between these two competing national security interests was upset. Phil Zimmermann, an independent programmer, released an e-mail encryption program called Pretty Good Privacy (PGP) that was intended to be as close to being unbreakable as possible. At first, the U.S. government ignored the release of PGP. Then, in 1993, Zimmermann was informed that he was the target of a U.S. Customs criminal investigation, an event that immediately made him an Internet *cause celebre*. Even though Zimmermann was never actually indicted and the case was dropped after three years, it was seen as an attempt to chill efforts to make strong encryption freely available.

The key escrow proposals made by the Clinton administration in 1993 were a classic example of a type of regulation that the civil service likes to spring on an incoming administration. The incoming appointees are assured that the proposals are modest, well prepared, and uncontroversial. Only after the administration members have committed do they discover the full implications.

Although there are several U.S. government agencies that have a stake in encryption policy, it was the FBI under director Louis Freeh that took the public lead in the campaign to establish government controls over the use of strong cryptography.

Freeh made the proverbial federal case out of both the Zimmermann investigation and the campaign for control of strong encryption. According to the Freeh plan, all use of strong encryption would be subject to a "mandatory escrow" scheme, which would enable the government to unscramble any encrypted communication. The somewhat-obvious flaw in Freeh's scheme was that there was no way to prevent criminals, terrorists, and foreign governments from obtaining access to programs already circulating on the Internet that did not observe the mandatory escrow requirement.

Freeh was a former prosecutor and conducted his campaign in the manner of a criminal prosecution. Every argument that could be made in favor of controls was thrown out regardless of credibility. Opponents were attacked as naïve, being unconcerned about the threat of terrorism, lacking understanding of the real world, a lunatic fringe who placed the country at risk and so on.

Within a short space of time, many security specialists felt personally threatened by Freeh's campaign. It was abundantly clear that Freeh should on no account be allowed to exercise any more power than he already did.

The proponents of control had a weak hand and played it poorly. After an administration has been persuaded to commit to an issue on the understanding that it will be uncontroversial, it is unlikely to be persuaded to expend its limited political capital on a drawn-out confrontation.

The dot-com boom quickly foreclosed the possibility of new legislation to control cryptography. No congressmen would vote for a bill threatening to bring the new economy to a halt.

The Clinton administration gradually distanced itself from its key escrow proposals and relaxed (but did not eliminate) export controls on cryptography in 1999.

After defeating the Romans at the battle of Asculum, King Pyrrhus is reputed to have said, "One more such victory and I am lost." It is now clear that the fight over strong cryptography rights was far more costly than either side knew at the time.

For over a decade, law enforcement and security specialists have generally regarded each other with suspicion rather than as natural allies. A decade that could have been spent developing tools to track and capture Internet criminals was wasted. Law enforcement is not a substitute for poor security technology, but a small investment in law enforcement can have a deterrent effect that greatly increases the effectiveness of security measures.

We now know that despite his public campaign for powers to gather more information, Freeh had failed to allocate resources to projects that would have allowed the FBI to analyze the information it already had. The Commission set up to investigate the 9/11 attack against the World Trade Center in New York and the Pentagon observed: "Finally, the FBI's information systems were woefully inadequate. The FBI lacked the ability to know what it knew; there was no effective mechanism for capturing or sharing its institutional knowledge." [3]

The cryptowars are over, but the security tools available today still bear their mark. The most visible consequence of the confrontation is the fact that large numbers of Internet users still use Web browsers that only support a deliberately weakened encryption scheme that an attacker can break in a matter of minutes.

A less visible and longer-lasting consequence is that many of the security systems we use today were designed when the primary concern of many people working in the security field was to defeat Freeh at all costs. As a result, it was difficult to get a standard approved for any cryptographic security system that did not meet a rather peculiar set of political requirements. The result was technology designed by geeks for geeks to protect themselves against dangers that only geeks were worried about.

Giving a copy of every encryption key to the U.S. government did not make much sense to most security specialists, particularly those who were not U.S. citizens. National intelligence agencies have been implicated in commercial espionage on many occasions. But keeping a spare copy of an encryption key for yourself makes perfect sense.

Imagine that all your work on your computer has been encrypted. If you lose the encryption key, you lose all your data, and there is absolutely no way of getting it back. Now imagine that you are a system manager and the computer belongs to a senior manager in your company. Do you want to be the person who is going to tell her that there is no way of getting her work back?

A system that allows the work to be recovered for the user also served the needs of law enforcement. Attempting to design systems to defeat government surveillance resulted in systems that did not meet real user requirements.

From an architectural point of view, a key recovery system to allow replacement of lost encryption keys stands alone. Only the holder of the encryption key is affected, so it is possible to add key recovery to almost any system that uses encryption. The same is not true when it comes to communication because every communication has at least two participants and, to be able to communicate successfully, they must speak the same language.

One of the ways in which security protocol designers attempted to frustrate government control of cryptography was by building resistance to these schemes into the Internet architecture—in particular, by insisting on the use of "end-to-end" security protocols that provided a cast-iron assurance that the communication could not be intercepted by a government-man-in-the-middle.

The End-to-End Principle

The central problem for the computer system architect and in particular a network architect is managing complexity. The mark of a good systems architect is to make the system as simple as possible but no simpler.

Each feature added to a software program increases the complexity of the system; every new code path represents a new opportunity to make a mistake. The simplest approach is usually the best, but leaving out functionality can also lead to unacceptable complexity.

An example of a system that is both too complicated and too simple was my coffee maker, Mr. Coffee. Like most modern kitchen appliances, Mr. Coffee had a built-in digital clock. If your morning commute does not allow the five minutes it takes to make fresh coffee, you can set the timer and have a pot of brewed coffee ready on your way out the door.

My morning commute consists of walking up the two flights of stairs from the kitchen to my office. As far as I am concerned, the clock is unnecessary. There are two clocks in the kitchen already; a third clock with a cheap quartz movement is just another thing that has to be reset if there is a power cut or the circuit trips. The designer of Mr. Coffee thought differently. He considered the clock so important that the machine would only make coffee if the time had been set. The unnecessary function became an unnecessary annoyance, and Mr. Coffee was replaced by a less argumentative machine.

From my point of view, the system was unnecessarily complex. But if I needed the alarm function, the problem is that the design was not quite sophisticated enough. A machine should not lose its settings during a momentary loss of power. Adding a two-cent capacitor to the clock circuit board would solve this problem. Leaving the capacitor out makes the machine simpler, but using it becomes more complex.

The problems solved with computers are complex. It is not always possible to avoid complexity in a design. The systems architect is left with the choice of where the complexity appears in a system and how it is managed. Building architects understand that they must put certain parts of heating, electricity, and plumbing systems in places that allow easy access for maintenance; systems architects face the same problem but with the key difference that the systems they design require more frequent changes.

The chief difference between the Internet and the telephone network is in the way that complexity is managed. In the telephone system, the communication starts and ends at a handset with four simple functions: The mouthpiece converts sounds to electrical signals, the earpiece does the reverse, the dial or keypad accepts dialing instructions from the user, and the ringer alerts the user to an incoming call.

All the complexity of the telephone system is in the network itself. In the original telephone system, a telephone "line" was exactly that—a wire connecting the subscriber to an exchange where an operator would set up a call by connecting two lines with a patch panel wire. Today, the wires have (mostly) been replaced by fiber-optic cables that can carry hundreds or thousands of calls at the same time. But the basic principle of operation has not changed. From the engineers' point of view, the electronic switches work the same way that the human operators once did: They create a logical circuit between the two subscribers that is maintained for the entire duration of the call.

The design of the Internet is like the telephone network inside out. The Internet network itself is designed to be as simple as possible, but no simpler. Complexity that could not be eliminated was located at the ends of the communication. An Internet "conversation" is broken up into a sequence of "packets" that make their way through the Internet independently.

Each packet of data is like a postcard: It contains an address and a short communication only slightly longer than the address. If you wanted to send a long message through the mail system using only postcards, you would first break up your message into pieces short enough to fit onto a card. Then you would add something like a sequence number to each card so that the recipient could reassemble them in the right order. If the mail system was not completely reliable and postcards were occasionally lost, you might also work out some scheme to allow the recipient to tell you which postcards were lost and which got through. The Internet works in the same way—complex operations such as telling the sender which packets to resend and reassembling the message in the original order are performed at the ends of the communication.

Figure 3-2 shows how a message might be sent through the Internet. The message is too big to be sent in one go, so the sender breaks it up into five packets. The first three packets sent take one path through the network, but the last two packets take a completely different path. When the packets are received at their final destination, they are out of order; packets 4 and 5 arrive before packets 2 and 3. The receiver has to reassemble them in the correct order.

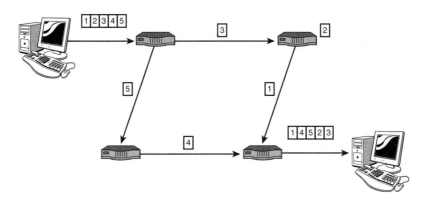

Figure 3-2 *Internet messages are sent as a sequence of "packets"*

Both the telephone system and the Internet are complex. The difference in their architectures lies in *where* the complexity is located. A packet-switched network such as the Internet is arguably much more complex taken as a whole than a circuit-switched network like the telephone network, but most of that complexity is concentrated at the edges of the network rather than in the network core.

This idea of a simple network core with the complexity at the endpoints is known as the **end-to-end principle.**[4]

This architecture has allowed the Internet to adapt to new uses far more quickly than the telephone network could. The telephone network is a monumental engineering feat, but every aspect of its design has been optimized for the single purpose of communicating the human voice. Every part of the network must be rethought, re-engineered, and replaced before the network can do anything new.

The Internet is designed to be a jack of all trades. The killer applications of the Internet—e-mail and the Web—did not exist when the architecture was designed.

Adapting the telephone system to support exchange of text, video, or even music as a core function would require a major engineering effort because every switch in the network would need to be changed. These technologies were added to the Internet without compromise to the applications and without changing the network infrastructure. As far as the Internet is concerned, the switches just move packets of data. Working out what those packets mean is the job of the endpoints.

The end-to-end principle is one of the reasons that the Internet has been able to grow to a billion users. But, in the process, the Internet has developed in ways that change the original premises on which the end-to-end principle is based. The original argument that led to the end-to-end principle was that a designer should try to locate complexity in the parts of the network that are most easily changed. When the original end-to-end argument was made in the 1980s, that place was the communication endpoints. Today there are a billion users of the Internet, and a billion or so machines at the endpoints. Making changes to the Internet infrastructure is still possible, but changes that require a billion users to update their machines are going to be slow.

The problem of managing complexity is still as important as ever, but the end-to-end architecture is not always the best, most appropriate means of achieving that end. If we want to deploy a security solution in a network with a hundred machines, we want to touch as few machines as possible to do so.

The telephone networks were designed with the complexity in the middle because they were from the start designed to insulate the user from complexity and the need to constantly upgrade and maintain his system. To meet the needs of today's Internet, we must arrive at a synthesis of the two approaches so that we insulate both the network core and the end user from the demands of constant change.

Powerful ideas can have a life of their own and frequently come to be applied in situations far removed from the context and intentions of the original authors. The end-to-end argument has been one of those most unfortunate of ideas, an argument that has been turned into an all-purpose absolute truth.

When I was younger, there were people who stood on street corners to loudly protest to anyone who would listen that the answer to every problem of an advanced industrial society in the closing years of the twentieth century had been anticipated by the carder's favorite philosopher, Karl Marx. This despite the fact that Marx had died a century earlier, before the invention of the internal combustion engine, powered flight, assembly line manufacture, the computer, and universal suffrage. Was it seeing this type of absolutism in his followers that prompted Marx to write to his friend Engels, "All I know is I am not a Marxist"?

The **end-to-end complexity** principle has roots in the earlier **end-to-end security** principle. According to the end-to-end security principle, cryptography should be applied to a message at its point of origin and removed only at its ultimate destination. Any deviation from this principle is to be considered unacceptably insecure.

The theory is fine, but in practice there is not one Internet security protocol based on the pure end-to-end principle that is widely used. The end-to-end e-mail security protocol S/MIME is as widely deployed as a designer could reasonably hope, but few Internet users are aware that it exists, let alone actually use it.

The generally acknowledged reasons for the lack of deployment of S/MIME are the difficulty of enrolling every e-mail client for the necessary digital certificate (to be addressed in Chapters 11, "Establishing Trust," and 13, "Secure Messaging") and the poor quality of the user applications. These objections are certainly justified, but these are problems that we could fix with little effort. We have had the technical means to do so for more than five years.

In the case of a personal e-mail sent from one individual to another, the end-to-end principle offers a clear security advantage because only the sender and the receiver need to trust each other. We can prevent network administrators at either end of the communication from reading or modifying the contents of a message. But this circumstance represents only one of the many situations in which e-mail is used. If e-mail is sent on behalf of a company rather than an individual, it is the company that needs to take responsibility for its security, not the individual user. If an encrypted e-mail is received, it is the IT administrator who has responsibility for making sure it does not contain a virus, not the individual end user.

Attempting to reconcile end-to-end security with centralized enterprise-wide management capabilities inevitably leads to confusion and unnecessary complexity, the very thing that the end-to-end complexity argument tells us to avoid.

Ironically, the end-to-end security principle has encouraged a mode of thinking where the real endpoints of the security problem are ignored. *The endpoint of the conversation is the user, not a machine.* The major security oversight in the design of the Internet is the last two feet between the user's eyeball and the screen.

End-to-end security is certainly the right approach in some situations, but insisting that security must be end-to-end or nothing has left us with nothing. We need to take a more flexible approach in which end-to-end is one of a range of security options.

Security through Obscurity

One of the hazards of writing about crime is that the information may be useful to the criminals. In the Internet age, this concern has been rendered obsolete: The criminals share information through a network of underground Web sites, chat rooms, and blogs.

The issue of disclosure has always been contentious for security specialists. When the first security standards were proposed, there was an extended debate over whether this was a contradiction in terms: The design process would require sharing of information that might compromise the system.

Secret knowledge has a habit of becoming public. A system that relied on the obscurity of its design architecture alone for security was likely to fail anyway. Publication of the design might help the attacker discover a flaw, but this risk is generally considered an acceptable price for widespread expert review.

Today, it is generally agreed that the benefits of having a standard outweigh the risks of giving the attacker more information to work with. Modern cryptography made it possible to design systems that are secure even if the attacker knows every detail of their design. The only knowledge that must be kept secret is the cryptographic key(s).

Over time, "security through obscurity" has become a byword for bad security. This is certainly true if obscurity is your only strategy; at the tactical level, however, obscurity might well be the best choice available.

The security through obscurity argument is frequently raised in the context of the current industry schism between proprietary and open source code. The open source advocates identify closed proprietary code with "obscurity," presenting the open source alternative as the ideal.

Security resists serving political dogma. Regardless of what position you take on the political issue, this argument is at best misleading. Publication will not improve the security of a system unless it leads to expert review *and* the weaknesses uncovered as a result are fixed. *Some* open source projects have exceptionally good security processes with no code being accepted into the distribution without a thorough review by a team of handpicked security experts. *Many* open source projects have no quality control processes of any kind.

Security through obscurity of *design* is almost always avoidable; security through obscurity of *knowledge* is undesirable but must be carefully weighed against other security risks. The design of HTTP, the core protocol of the World Wide Web, provides an example of misapplication of the security through obscurity doctrine, causing the design to protect against the wrong threat.

As the Web began the transition from a pure publication medium to an interactive medium, the need for a password-based security mechanism quickly became apparent. Public key cryptography would have been the preferred form of authentication, but use in the U.S. was encumbered by patents. This created a dilemma for me as the designer: Unless public key cryptography is used, the system must either send unencrypted password data over the network or store unencrypted password data on the server where the password is checked.

From my point of view, the correct choice was obvious. Sending data over the network in the clear was a serious risk that was already being exploited by hackers. The Ethernet protocol supporting the local network at CERN and most academic sites allows any machine to see all the traffic on that network segment. Protecting the password data stored in the clear on the Web server was a much easier task; we could use the existing operating system security mechanisms to do this. Working with a number of other security specialists, I wrote a proposal that became HTTP "Digest" authentication. This uses cryptography to prevent passwords being read from the network and minimizes the consequences of the password database on the server being compromised.

The alternative to the Digest mechanism was a simpler scheme called Basic, which does not encrypt the password on the network (see Figure 3-3). One justification for this design decision was that all the other Internet protocols did the same thing, which essentially amounted to saying that when designing new protocols we should learn nothing from their predecessors. The main reason that Basic was preferred was that it allowed the use of existing password files where the passwords were stored in one way encrypted form so that they could be used to verify a password but the password could not be read from the file.

HTTP Basic Authentication
Client request header (username "Aladdin", password "open sesame"):

```
GET /private/index.html HTTP/1.0
Host: localhost
Authorization: Basic QWxhZGRpbjpvcGVuIHNlc2FtZQ==
```

Base64 ("Aladdin:open sesame") = QWxhZGRpbjpvcGVuIHNlc2FtZQ==
Base64 is not an encryption scheme; there is no secret key. If you enter the string QWxhZGRpbjpvcGVuIHNlc2FtZQ== into any Base64 decoder (you can find one on the Web using Google), the username and password will be returned.

Figure 3-3 *HTTP Basic authentication*

I lost the argument then. Relying on the operating system to control access to the password file of a Web server was decried as relying on "obscurity." The specter of security through obscurity trumped consideration of the actual risks. Instead of addressing the vulnerability that was known and unavoidable, we instead accepted a design to address a theoretical problem that could be controlled in other ways. Basic authentication became part of the core HTTP protocol, and Digest authentication was relegated to an optional "extension."

The security through obscurity argument is misapplied with monotonous regularity. Years before the dispute over Digest authentication, a similar dispute took place on the question of whether a password file should be encrypted and protected from being read or only encrypted. Computers had just become fast enough to make it feasible to break passwords by a "dictionary attack." On the VMS operating system, the password file could only be read by an administrator, so only an administrator (who could do anything he wanted in any case) could attempt a dictionary attack. At the time, the rival UNIX system made it a point of honor that the actual password file was readable by any user.

Eventually, "shadow passwords" became a standard UNIX feature, but this could have happened much sooner if not for the chorus arguing that relying on the operating system to enforce security controls rather than a cryptographic scheme known to be weak was "security through obscurity."

Flawed Analogy

Analogy and metaphor are powerful modes of argument. Early computers were difficult to use until Xerox Parc introduced the "desktop" metaphor later adopted by the Apple Lisa and Mac. Most people find it easier to understand new ideas through analogy to familiar concepts than from first principles.

The problem with arguments from analogy is that the human mind can be rather too busy constructing analogies and end up seeing parallels where none exist. People end up being carried up to the top of pyramids to have their hearts cut out.

We just saw how an argument for a defective password mechanism was made by claiming that it was "as good as" another system that was widely used, despite the fact that the scheme was known to be defective.

Before making an argument by analogy to another system, it is critically important to understand both the design being proposed and the system it is being compared to. Security is a property of systems, not technologies. The fact that a particular technology is used in a system that is known to be secure tells us nothing about whether the technology will provide security in another context unless we know what other measures are involved.

Why Four Digits Are Not Enough

Take Automatic Teller Machines (ATMs), for example. Early on when Web-based financial services began to emerge, some online stock brokers used the customer's account number and a four-digit PIN number to authenticate them. After all, four-digit PIN numbers are secure enough for ATMs; they should be secure enough for brokerage accounts, right?

Unfortunately, the argument does not hold. The average balance of a brokerage account is many times that of the average bank account, withdrawals from ATMs are usually limited to a few hundred dollars a day, and a Web browser running on a personal computer is a considerably less controlled security environment than an ATM. Four-digit PIN numbers are arguably sufficient in the context of controlling withdrawal of limited quantities of cash from an ATM in a controlled environment; they are not sufficient in the context of a brokerage transaction mediated by a Web browser in the home.

Wired Equivalent Privacy

One of the biggest security design fiascos in recent years advertises its flawed analogy in its name—Wired Equivalent Privacy (WEP).

WEP was developed to provide security for a low-cost, short-range, high-speed wireless networking technology known as IEEE 802.11b. This title proved somewhat uninspiring to the marketing community, who decided on the name "WiFi" instead. WiFi has been a conspicuous success, and most new laptops now come with support for at least one 802.11 variant; the original b specification has been joined by a, g, and n flavors offering higher speeds.

802.11b began to appear in the early 1990s but only became a mass market phenomena after Apple began shipping 802.11b technology in its laptops under the brand "AirPort." The security community at large started to take notice of the technology as wireless networks began to appear around most technology hubs—in particular, the Stanford University and Microsoft campuses. The technology was cheap, and many wireless network access points were neither authorized nor secure.

As security specialists at Stanford and Microsoft started to examine the WEP protocol, problem after problem began to emerge. Internet discussion has tended to focus on the cryptographic flaws that allow an attacker armed with the right tools to quickly discover the encryption key or to bypass the cryptography altogether. These have tended to obscure the fact that even if it had worked as intended, the scheme did not provide protection from the real security risks of wireless networking.

Like many nonspecialists, the designers had assumed that the main security concern was confidentiality. (Security specialists use the term **privacy** to refer to a set of requirements that is even stronger.) The assumption was that WEP confidentiality should be equivalent to Ethernet, which is to say not very good at all. Anyone with access to Ethernet can read every piece of data that is sent over the wire. The WEP designers decided to replace the need for physical access to the network with the need to know the encryption key for the network. In effect, there is a single "password," *which is the same for every user of the network.* Also, anyone with access to the network can read any traffic he chooses.

Think about this for a moment. Imagine that you are managing a network for a university with several thousand students, and they are all going to be issued the same "secret" password. If every student needs to know the password to gain access to the network, it is not going to be long before it is "shared" with friends who live locally, students from previous years, and so on. The password will soon end up on the Internet.

Businesses face similar issues that are compounded by the fact that they are rather more likely to be dealing with sensitive information. What do you do when an employee is terminated? Changing the password on an office network is going to take a lot of time with a hundred people using it. If the password is not changed, you may end up with a disgruntled ex-employee surfing the office network from the car park.

The important difference between a wired and wireless network is not the loss of privacy; it's the ease of access. Connecting to a wired network requires physical presence. This in turn means that a perpetrator faces a significant chance of being caught. Connection to a wireless network can be made at a distance; a serious attacker working from a car or van can use a large directional antenna to pick up signals from half a mile away or more with ease.

The analogy to Ethernet security was flawed because businesses use Ethernet in the context of physical security measures that control physical access to the network. Allowing wireless access rendered the security guard at the front desk ineffective without providing a replacement control.

Fortunately, most of the problems of the original WEP security scheme have been fixed. The cryptography flaws and the administration flaws have been fixed in a new protocol called IEEE 802.11i (also known as WPA and WPA2). Even so, the changes miss the real problems with the protocol.

The real problem with WEP was that it failed the usability test: Most people didn't use it. Setting up the system is just too hard for the average home user.

Enabling encryption on my small home network of just six computers and two printers has at times been close to exceeding my tolerance of incalcitrant technology. I can only wonder how the user who does not have 25 years' computing experience would react to being required to type an exact sequence of 28 hexadecimal digits. In Windows XP, you have to enter the secret *twice*, and you can't see what you're typing.

For many users, any security system that requires them to think is too complex. The problem is that the designers didn't even think that home users might need security.

Do home users need better security to protect their networks? Their communications with their bank will be secured separately after all. Unfortunately, the answer is yes. People need security on their home wireless networks for their own protection and to protect the rest of the network.

Let us consider personal protection first. Most users store sensitive data on their machine without being aware of it. If you used your computer to prepare your taxes, the chances are that the data files have your bank and brokerage account details entered. The same applies to financial management software such as Money or Quicken. Even if the attacker finds no compromising data *stored* on the machine, he might plant spyware to look for some.

Alternatively, the attacker might not be interested in victimizing the owner of the access point; he might plan to victimize the rest of the world instead. An open wireless access point provides an attacker with the digital equivalent of a stolen getaway vehicle. He might send spam, launch a virus or phishing scheme, or merely use your machine as the control point for a botnet. His motive might not even be theft of any kind; he might just want to trade some pedophile pornography and prefer that the police end up knocking on your door rather than his own. In 2003, the Toronto police arrested a man driving a car naked from the waist down with an open laptop by his side. He was later charged with possession, distribution, and creation of child pornography, as well as theft of telecommunications.[5]

Home users need security every bit as badly as enterprise users; they are even willing to pay for it at a reasonable price. They are not prepared to pay several thousand dollars extra for a $50 wireless access point for features to benefit other network users. They are certainly not prepared to read a manual under any circumstance. The challenge that must be met is providing home users with simple, effective, and transparent security at a cost that is reasonable to them.

False Reduction

Engineers create, whereas scientists and mathematicians merely discover.

Engineering is a complex art that requires skill and imagination. At its highest levels, it also requires a considerable degree of self-confidence. It takes nerve to design a dam, a skyscraper, or an airplane or to commit a billion or so dollars to some enterprise knowing that a failure could be catastrophic.

The real point of a university engineering degree is not so much to teach skills as to teach students how to solve large problems by breaking them down into smaller ones. My computer has a display, a motherboard, a case, and a hard disk drive. The hard disk drive has a stack of magnetic platters, a read/write head, a motor, and a logic board. The key skill of engineering architecture is identifying a way to break down the system into a set of smaller problems that can be solved independently.

Security breaks those rules because security is always a property of a system. When we break down a system into pieces, the attacker looks for the cracks in between. We have to unlearn those rules and think in terms of systems again.

Is No Security Better Than Bad Security?

A common concern in the security community is that a security scheme that does not work might make matters even worse. People might rely on the bad security scheme as if it really was secure and end up considerably more exposed than if they had known that they were vulnerable.

Numerous anecdotes support this concern.

The U.S. atomic spy Julius Rosenberg and his wife Ethel were discovered and sentenced to death as a result of the KGB botching the use of a cipher called a one-time pad. If used correctly, a one-time pad provides an unbreakable means of encryption, but when misused, the cipher becomes easy to break. The Rosenbergs' false confidence in Soviet security led to them being executed. Mary Queen of Scotts was likewise executed in an earlier time after unwisely trusting the security of a cipher she was using to plot treason.

Clearly, it is a bad idea to rely on a weak security system when doing something that you would otherwise consider unsafe. But relying on a weak security system is still better than no security at all when you are going to do something anyway.

Getting a protocol right is important, but so is delivering the product on time. I have worked on the Web for 15 years now—long enough to know firsthand that the concept of "Internet time" being faster than normal is somewhat silly. Developing and deploying technology takes time; ideas take years, not months, to reach maturity. But there is a kernel of truth to the silly "Internet time" myth. For an idea to be successful, it must emerge at exactly the right time. Too early, and the market does not yet see the need; too late, and that need will have been met in other ways.

The Internet can wait six months or even a year to get a protocol right. But in the case of two key Internet security protocols—DNS Security and IP Security—the designers were still unfinished after more than a decade.

The demand for perfection can prevent protocols from being used even after they are widely deployed. The e-mail encryption standard S/MIME is implemented by practically every widely used e-mail client. Few people bother to use it. The end-to-end architecture of S/MIME requires that each e-mail program be enrolled for a digital certificate before encrypted messages can be received. This has only proved to be an acceptable burden in environments where most of the mail being sent and received must be secured. As a result, S/MIME has become an internal e-mail security infrastructure and not the Internet e-mail security infrastructure it was intended to be.

The results of the demand for perfection of a certain type should be compared to the clear success of SSL and WEP security protocols. Even though the initial implementation of these protocols was deeply flawed, these errors were quickly corrected. Even though the cryptography in WEP was badly botched, its successors are widely deployed and used. Security is not all or nothing; if a protocol is deployed, we at least get a second chance. If we never bring ourselves to decide a protocol is ready to try in the real world, we never get the chance to learn.

Far from delaying deployment of strong cryptographic protocols, the earlier weak systems paved the way for the strong. System administrators were used to the fact that these applications required security configuration. When it was discovered that the security protocols were flawed, the vendors were required to provide an immediate correction.

The conclusion I draw from this experience is that, in practice, a flawed but deployed and implemented protocol is much more valuable than one that is theoretically perfect but still pending final status. Mistakes do matter: They reduce sales and cost time and money to correct. But we cannot allow fear of making a mistake to be an excuse for inaction.

If we want to deserve the title security engineer, we have to be willing to take the risk of putting our designs to the only test that matters: deployment. Although we approach our task with far less proven practice to rely on than other forms of engineering, we can hardly claim that we face consequences more catastrophic than engineers designing airplanes or bridges or dams or large buildings.

Bad security might lead to a false sense of security, but so can no security at all. Over the past ten years, consumers have increasingly relied on the Internet infrastructure and made little distinction between those parts secured by cryptography and those that are insecure. Nor is there any reason to believe that consumer habits are likely to change through education. Security is a means of controlling risk and, in most cases, consumers have been effective in controlling their risk exposure by transferring it to other parties.

Taken literally, the slogan leads to paralysis. We need a more precise wording. A system must never deliver less security than the users expect.

Familiarity Leads to Complacency

Having described some of the common security misperceptions inside the field, it is worth pointing out that there are also plenty of false assumptions outside the field. In particular, it is easy to underestimate the risks of the familiar and overestimate the risks of the alternative. Often people are stuck in a less secure situation or spending large sums of money for illusory security benefits because they do not fully consider the real risks they are taking.

I still meet corporate "security" officers who believe that their business is far too sensitive to risk exposure on the Internet. That's fair enough, but they have a corporate network. How does that work? Do they have their own private network of telephone wires for their exclusive use?

The answer is that companies with a "private" network lease "lines" from the telephone companies. But a "leased line" is not a physical wire or fiber; it is the ability to send a certain amount of data over a network shared by all the other customers of the telephone network. The feeling of security that comes from "knowing" the path the data travels to reach its destination is entirely illusory.

Take the fax in my office, for example. It appears to be simply an ordinary fax machine plugged into a telephone line, but it also works as a printer and plugs into my office network. The machine can be configured to forward incoming faxes by e-mail.

So a fax comes in over the telephone network but goes back out over the Internet. If you look closely at the fax, you will see that the telephone cable actually leads to a Voice over IP interface box, which also plugs into the office network, which in turn connects to a cable modem on the floor below via a wireless network bridge.

So when someone thinks he is sending me a fax using the "telephone system," the data is actually reaching my house via the Internet. It travels from the second floor to the third over a wireless network and is only converted back into telephone signals a few feet away from the fax machine. The fax machine then converts the data into an e-mail, which it sends to a mail server on the other side of the continent, from which I will retrieve it from any part of the world over the Internet.

The only reason that I have a fax machine in the first place is that there are people who refuse to send me important documents over the Internet *because it is insecure*. I could tell them that by the time I read their fax, it will have passed over the Internet at least twice, but I am diplomatic.

The systems that manage the telephone network have their own set of security problems. The chief concern of its architects was keeping the system going regardless of physical damage and equipment failures. It's better to risk a rogue employee of *the* telephone company illegally rerouting a circuit than the system going down because it did not allow someone to do his job. In the countries where *the* telephone company became *many*, the process did not allow for a rethinking of telephone network security. The result is that, in many countries, the telephone system is even more vulnerable than the Internet.

Another aspect of the same problem is the common assumption that the effects of the Internet are limited to the Internet itself. Just ask any bartender who has been presented with a fake driving license created using a template from the Internet. The Internet and Web allow people to collaborate and exchange information on an unprecedented scale, and those capabilities are available for bad use as well as good.

Failing to Recognize Success

Finally, the security field has been unable or unwilling to recognize the successes that have been achieved. In a recent meeting, a participant complained that the problem of building a global public key infrastructure was likely to remain unsolved in ten years' time. I took objection to this claim because VeriSign has been operating such an infrastructure for more than a decade, with over more than 910,000 Web site certificates currently active.

What the speaker really meant was that the infrastructure that had come into existence was rather different from the one that he had anticipated. It was not a ubiquitous infrastructure that authenticated every Internet user without charge. Instead, the infrastructure that developed was a commercial infrastructure allowing particular types of Internet use to be secured against certain specific risks in return for a fee. After all, if an asset is not considered worth paying something to protect, it cannot be considered much of an asset.

When I was at MIT, I spent some time in the Artificial Intelligence laboratory. AI has suffered from a similar failure to recognize success. Although it is true that nobody has built a machine capable of emulating human intelligence in the manner of Arthur C. Clarke's HAL, every person living in the developed world interacts with artificial intelligence technology and the products of that technology every day. The car I drive was largely built by computer-controlled robots, every time I use my credit card a fraud detection system looks for suspicious transactions, and I do the bulk of my research online using automated Web search engines. AI exists, but in a form that is very different from the original goal; instead of building machines capable of thinking *instead* of humans, we built machines that help humans think *better*. Less admirably perhaps, voice recognition techniques have made ubiquitous, automated telephone answering systems that are anything but "intelligent."

Nobody can provide perfect security. Even if every military, terrorist, and criminal threat was eliminated and world peace established, you would still face the risk of being run over by a car, struck by lightning, or hit by a meteor. But the lack of perfect security does not mean that there are no opportunities to achieve significant reductions in risk at an acceptable cost.

Key Points

- We must reject slogans and return to the thinking behind them.
  - We need to design for real-world risks and real-world users.
  - Security is risk control, not risk elimination.
  - Security must be automatic and transparent.
- We must understand that although we say we want security, we only want security on our own terms.
  - Security must be designed for real people, not the designers.
  - Security must make sense to the people expected to use it.
  - Security protocols must serve needs, not ideology.
- Bad security is not necessarily worse than no security.
  - A system that provides less security than its users expect will encourage them to rely on it in cases where they should not.
  - We should not be so afraid of a security failure that we provide no security at all. The market causes bad systems to be improved.
- We should treat analogies with caution.
  - An analogy can provide a powerful means of communicating a security argument, but it is not a substitute for a thorough security analysis.
  - Experience can inform risk, but it can also mislead.
- We must recognize that even though a system might not meet our expectations, it might still be successful in its own terms.

Making Change Happen

As the opposition's favorite philosopher put it, "The philosophers have only interpreted the world in various ways; the point, however, is to change it."[1]

Changing the world is hard; if it was easy, the world would change rather too often. It is not enough to come up with an idea to secure the Internet. The idea is the easy part. For an idea to count, you must persuade others to act.

As the Internet has grown, so has the number of people who must be persuaded to act in order to change. Putting even the simplest new idea into practice has become a major undertaking. In the early days of the Web, a good idea could be realized in a few days. Today it requires a tremendous effort to achieve even small changes within a few years.

That Dizzy Dot.Com Growth

Most engineers prefer engineering to marketing or politics, and persuading them that either is important is a hard task at the best of times. In the Internet world, the task is much harder because many of us experienced a period when it appeared that the Internet and the Web simply took off of their own accord.

For people who started using it in 1995, the growth of the Web was always out of control of any individual or organization. A critical mass of users had been reached and a network effect had taken hold: Each additional user increased the value of being on the Web, and every satisfied user became a new salesperson for the Web.

Let's take another look at the growth of the Web. The growth of the Web as a proportion of Internet users is believed to have followed the familiar *S* curve shown in Figure 4-1. At the start of

1993, the number of Web users was negligible; by the middle of 1994, practically every user of the Internet had used the Web.

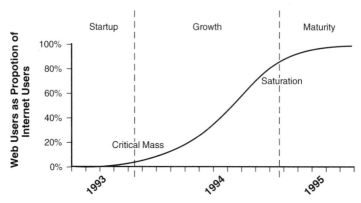

Figure 4-1   *Estimated growth of the Web as a proportion of Internet users*

In practice, the growth was rather too fast to be able to measure reliably—the only data points that are known with certainty being the beginning and the end. At one point during the early growth of the Web, a survey of Internet use came out that showed the Web growing at a rate of 150 percent each month. Much was made of the explosive rate of growth which, if sustained, would mean that every sentient being in our galaxy would by now be a user. When growth is so fast, the only questions that are really interesting are where the limit will be reached and how long it will take to reach it. This did not stop academics from producing papers quibbling over whether the techniques used by this survey or that might overstate the number of Internet users by 20 percent or so. The growth of the Internet within the industrial world followed the same S-shaped curve, and the same shape is currently being repeated on a global scale.

I divide the S-growth curve into three parts: startup, growth, and maturity. The part that attracts media attention is the growth phase. This is the point at which breathless stories can be written about the changes being wrought, and so on. The questions for business are the size of the market at maturity and when maturity will be reached. But for the designer trying to change the world, the really important part of the curve is the startup phase, before critical mass has been achieved, before growth has become self-sustaining.

It has become fashionable of late for commercial ventures to promote the *network effect* that comes from using their product. As Bob Metcalf, the inventor of Ethernet, observed, the value of a computer network is proportional to its size. A network with only one fax machine is useless; it has nothing to talk to. A network with two fax machines has a limited value. A network with a hundred machines is considerably more useful, and when almost every business has one, the fax machine becomes a vital tool.

The downside to the **network effect** (or to use the fashionable buzzword **viral marketing**) is that however beneficial it might be during the growth phase, it is known as the chicken and egg problem during startup.

The growth of the Web became self-sustaining at some point in 1993. But getting to that point took a lot of time and effort. In particular, the Web had been designed to allow rapid growth. If you had Internet access, all you needed to use the Web was to download a free program. Publishing on the Web required only a little more effort. The Web was free, which encouraged students to download the programs to try them out. The free trial effect was essential because the value of the Web is something that only really becomes apparent to most people when they either see it demonstrated, or better, use it themselves.

As we saw earlier, Internet crime currently follows an S-shaped curve. If nothing is done, a limit will eventually be reached, but the Internet would probably not be worth using by then.

Already there are some indications that the rate of growth in the number of attacks might be declining and we might be reaching the upper curve. Unfortunately, one likely explanation for this phenomenon is that the professional Internet criminals are becoming more adept at focusing on the most profitable targets.

Fortunately, there is no law of nature that growth must follow an S-curve. The growth of the network hypertext programs that once competed with the Web did not follow that curve. These began growing at more or less the same rate, but the Web began to pull away after a short time. At this point, the network effect began to work against the competing systems as users defected to the larger network.

A hypothetical example of this mode of growth is the bell-shaped curve seen in Figure 4-2.

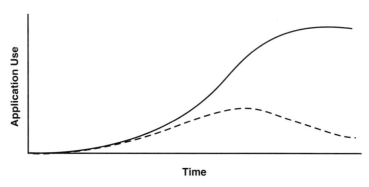

Figure 4-2   *Growth and decline*

The bell-shaped curve of growth and decline is the course that we want to cause Internet crime to follow. To do that, we must introduce security controls that defeat the Internet criminals.

Sometimes it is possible to suggest a security mechanism that, like the Web, is easy to deploy because it provides an immediate benefit to the party who deploys it. Spam filters are an example of this type of security measure; subscribing to a good spam-filtering service immediately reduces the amount of spam annoyance. The effectiveness of my spam filter does not depend on anyone else using one. I call measures of this type **tactical**; they provide immediate value to the party who deploys them even though they do not necessarily address the root cause of the problem.

Tactical measures are generally preferred by vendors of security products because it is easy to explain the benefit to the customer. The market tends to be efficient in identifying and deploying tactical security measures.

Deployment of security controls where the benefits and the cost of deployment are not so neatly aligned is much harder. This is frequently the case with the measures I call **strategic**— controls that are designed to make the Internet infrastructure less criminal friendly.

The primary engines for Internet crime are spam and botnets. Nobody wants to be pestered by spam or have his machine recruited into a botnet, and plenty of tactical measures have been developed to help people prevent their machines from being the ones affected by the attackers. The problem with tactical measures is that they tend to work a bit like car alarms, which have a marked effect on which particular cars the thieves attempt to steal. All things being equal, thieves will try to steal the car without an alarm. Car alarms can even deter the opportunist or the joy rider, but they do little to affect the number of cars being stolen by professional thieves.

Considerable effort has gone into tactical measures to prevent machines from being compromised in the first place. Less effort has gone into preventing a compromised machine from being used by the criminals even though, as we shall see later, this is an easier technical problem. The business model for tactical measures is compelling regardless of who deploys them; the business model for strategic measures is only compelling if they are likely to achieve critical mass.

Finding the Killer Application

The key to driving infrastructure deployment is to find a compelling benefit that does not depend on the network already being established. In the computer world, an application that realizes this type of benefit is known as a **killer application**.

A killer application gets a technology to the point where there is a critical mass of infrastructure to support. After that infrastructure is in place, new applications often supplant it.

The killer application for the microcomputer, the forerunner of the modern PC, was the VisiCalc spreadsheet program. In the early 1980s, typing was strictly for secretaries. A manager would no more think about buying a word processor for his own use than he would a mop and broom. But a *spreadsheet* was a *management* tool.

Although e-mail was the killer application for computer networking, it was the World Wide Web that became the killer application for the Internet in its competition with rival networks.

Before the Web, many computer networks were running many different network protocols. The Internet was popular in the U.S., but most UK universities used a network called JANET. The machines I used at Oxford were connected to both JANET and a private network for international research labs working in high-energy physics and astronomy called HEPNET.

Most of the networks were connected to each other through machines called **gateways** so that it was not necessary to be on the same network as someone to send that person an e-mail. Being on the same network made it easier, of course, but usability was not a priority on HEPNET, a network exclusively for the use of researchers who either had a degree in nuclear physics already or were studying for one.

If e-mail had been the only important application of computer networking, the convergence of the network protocols would have taken considerably longer, if it had been completed at all. The arrival of the Web meant that the network you connected to did make a difference. Even though the early Web software could connect to other computer networks, the Internet was by far the largest and offered the most information. You could receive e-mail on HEPNET, but you couldn't access Internet Web sites.

The Web itself required a killer application to get started. When the Web first started, the only information that was available on the Web described the Web protocols. The amount of information available grew slowly in the first three years, so slowly in fact that in 1992 I surfed the entire Web in one evening.

Tim Berners-Lee, the inventor of the Web, realized that providing content was the key to making the Web useful and that a lot of information would be required to "prime the pump." The breakthrough information source was of all things the CERN telephone directory. This was available in two forms—as a printed directory and as an online service—but only on one machine out of the thousands of computer systems that were in use at CERN, a machine running an antiquated operating system deservedly notorious as being a pig to use.

After the CERN phone book was made available on the Web, researchers at CERN discovered that the Web was the quickest way to look up a phone number. As physicists turned to the Web to access the phone book, a critical mass of infrastructure was established to support other uses.

Why Standards Matter

The Internet has almost a billion users. If the Internet is still going to be useful as a global communication medium, most of those users are going to have to use programs that can talk to each other.

Imagine how hard it would be to use electrical appliances if every socket in your house was a different shape and required a different plug. Standard plugs and sockets make taking a lamp from one room to another easy. Try to take it abroad, however, and you need either a plug that meets the local standard or possibly a voltage adapter.

Standardization has not yet reached the other end of the power cord. Each time I travel, I take between five and fifteen electronic devices with me—at a minimum my cell phone, headset, computer, music player, and wireless hub. Each of these devices requires its own "power supply." Each power supply does almost the same thing, converting AC power at various mains voltages and frequencies into 9 to 12 volts DC. If the various gadget manufacturers would only agree on a standard, I could take one adapter to recharge the whole lot, and there would be room in my travel bag for some new gadgets.

Several manufacturers have tried to address this problem with "universal" power adapters, which offer a range of interchangeable tips to power the assorted devices. Unfortunately, these are a poor substitute for a standard. Most of the adapters will only recharge one device at a time, and each new device usually requires a new tip that is only available from the manufacturer. The miniature USB connector looks likely to emerge as the standard for charging mobile phones and accessories, but progress has been slow, and the specification only supports low power devices.

Design is largely a matter of reducing complexity. Standards reduce complexity by reducing the number of decisions the designer needs to take. In most cases, this is a net benefit even if the design chosen for the standard is not the best from a technical point of view.

U.S. readers will be familiar with a style of light bulb with an Edison screw on the end. European readers are more likely to be familiar with the Swan bayonet fitting, where the end of the light bulb is flat and has two prongs at the end (see Figure 4-3).

Figure 4-3   *Swan bayonet and Edison screw bulbs*

Like most major inventions, the light bulb had more than one inventor. Although Edison is usually credited with its invention in the U.S., he worked with Joseph Swan, a British inventor who applied for his patent a year earlier.

Edison developed his screw thread design while testing a large number of different filaments to see which gave the most light and were most durable. After painstakingly soldering the first trial bulbs into the test rig, Edison had the idea of mounting each test bulb onto a one-inch screw thread allowing them to be easily inserted and removed.

The Swan bayonet fixture was the invention of Alfred Swan, Joseph's brother. A prolific inventor in his own right, Alfred worked patiently and methodically on improvements to his brother's invention—in particular, the design of the light bulb base. His numerous contributions included the invention of Vitrite, a glass-like insulator used for making the bulb base.

By 1895, the number of bulb bases had proliferated, and 14 different variations were in use. Interchanging bulbs required the use of adapters and could be dangerous, possibly causing a fire. An editorial in *The Electrical Engineer* pled the case for standardization,[2] leading to a debate on the merits of the various designs. Even at the time, it was clear that the Edison screw was flawed. Edison screw bulbs have a tendency to work themselves loose over time, and over-tightening can cause them to break. But in the U.S., at least, the Edison screw won, because it was in widespread use, and making a choice was much more important than making the absolutely best choice.

Marry in Haste, Repent at Leisure

One of the many reasons that setting standards is hard is that the consequences of badly chosen standards are all around us. I am typing at a QWERTY keyboard that was originally designed to prevent typists from typing too fast, causing the machine to jam. The QWERTY arrangement is designed to avoid placing keys close together that are often typed in succession (for example, *th*). Even though the mechanical issue that led to the problem of jamming was solved decisively within a few years of the invention of QWERTY, we are still stuck with it today. When a mistake is made, the effects can last for decades or even centuries.

The lightning-fast development pace in the early days of the Web led to plenty of mistakes that we have since had cause to regret. Soon after I first saw the Web, I decided it would be nice if there was a way to follow links in the reverse direction, being able to follow the links that point *to* a page as well as the ones leading from it. This lead to the idea of the "Referer" field, which specifies the URL of the page containing the link the user followed when making the request.

Unfortunately, I typed the field name with one *r* fewer than some feel it deserves. The shorter spelling has saved vast quantities of network bandwidth. Perhaps there is somewhere the driver of a mechanical digger who might have found several days' extra employment laying fiber for Internet distribution had I chosen to use the conventional spelling. My choice of spelling has also resulted in endless complaints, some of which include a demand to "correct" it. This would require updates to every Web browser and Web server on the planet. With a billion users and a cost of $50 per user, I believe it is rather more likely that the editors of the *Oxford English Dictionary* will come around to accept my spelling first.

Although these mistakes were harmless, others resulted in long-term difficulties. The original mechanism for embedding images in Web pages uses pixels as a unit of measure. A **pixel** is the smallest dot that can be shown on the computer monitor. A typical computer monitor has a resolution of between 75 and 100 dots per inch. Using pixels as a unit of measure made some sense when practically every computer display was roughly the same size and resolution. If you have a high-resolution display that packs twice the usual number of dots into a given space, then all your pictures will shrink to half the size intended. This problem could have been avoided if a bit more time had been available to refine the original design before it became set in stone.

Some people find the idea that the free market might make the "wrong" choice to be unacceptable.[3] But there is no law of economics that dictates that free markets must or should choose the *technically* superior solution. The dominance of QWERTY demonstrates only that nobody has proposed an alternative that is compelling enough to switch.

Ownership and Control

Early on in the dot-com boom, many people had the idea that if they could just arrange for a "few cents" of every dollar that flowed through the Internet to stick to their fingers, they would become phenomenally rich. Very few of these ideas ever came to anything, not least because the "few cents" that these entrepreneurs felt was their due was often the entire gross margin of the businesses they were attempting to prey upon.

The Internet is a fiercely competitive market where most startups fail having produced nothing but rivers of red ink. There are no easy profits to be made from providing Internet technology. Every penny of revenue earned is a cost that another will resent.

One of the reasons that the dispute over the standard for the light bulb socket took so long to resolve was that it was also a dispute over property. Alfred Swan's designs did have real advantages over the Edison screw, but these came at a cost because Swan owned patents on both the design and the materials used to build it. By the time that the need for a standard had become evident, the original Edison patents had expired and could be adopted by rival manufacturers without fee.

Agreements over standards inevitably involve economic interests. A patent might soar in value if the technology claimed is essential to implement a standard or become worthless if another technology is chosen.

Patents are not the only potential cause of dispute. Arcane details of a standard might favor one company over its competitors. A large complex standard might favor a company with significant engineering resources over rivals whose resources are severely constrained. A vendor who has already developed a product is likely to push for a standard that closely matches his existing product, whereas a new entrant to the market is likely to prefer a completely fresh approach.

Sometimes a faction might not believe it is in its interests for an agreement to be reached at all. The point of a standard is, after all, to turn an idea into a commodity. This is good for the customer but bad for the established company whose main product is about to be commoditized.

Adam Smith observed that when people of the same trade meet together, the result is usually a conspiracy against the public. Smith's particular concern was monopolies, which he demonstrated were detrimental to the public good. A **standard** is a type of monopoly and does not always represent the best interests of the public.

The DVD specification has built-in restrictions to prevent a disk sold in the U.S. from playing on an unmodified DVD player sold in Europe. The purported justification for this restriction is that it allows the major studios to avoid the release of a DVD in the U.S., drawing customers away from a coinciding European theatrical release. Critics note that the scheme also allowed the studios to maintain differential pricing, charging European consumers up to twice the U.S. price for the same material.

A standards process is potentially a highly political affair. Fortunately, the more astute participants usually understand that the reason they are there in the first place is to achieve something together that they cannot achieve alone, and that if they insist on demands that the other participants feel are unreasonable, the result might be that the other parties reach agreement without them.

It is rare for an Internet standard to require the use of a patented technology unless the patent holder agrees to issue a license to use the technology for the purpose of implementing the standard without charge. It makes little sense for 20 or more major companies to send some of their most expert and highly paid engineers to a forum to create a common standard if one party is going to be paid for his efforts and the rest are not. The advantage provided by a patented technology must be very significant to outweigh the cost of the patent license.

In retrospect, one of the mistakes we made in the design of the Web was not introducing a default audio format into the early browsers. This was largely due to the fact that only a few of the engineering workstations that were in use at the time could make sounds. The lack of a default audio format led to a continuous tug of war between rival proprietary audio compression schemes fighting it out to become king of the hill. Even if the default audio format had been the uncompressed stream of samples used in CD players, the fact that every browser supported a common standard would have confined this dispute to a squabble over the optimal means of realizing a capability that the users already had rather than a competition to control the standard for providing that capability. Instead of expecting to receive a patent royalty rate proportional to the size of the market for online audio content (i.e. billions of dollars) the patent holders could only expect to receive royalties proportional to the savings in cost of bandwidth that their invention allowed (i.e. millions).

Another decision that later turned out to have been a mistake was the decision to use what was then known as the **CompuServe GIF format**. This was a simple compression scheme that had originally been developed by one of the pre-Internet dialup networking services that later became part of AOL. Even at the time, the GIF format was beginning to show its age, but it was widely used, and CompuServe made no proprietary claims to the scheme. Then, in December of 1994, after the GIF algorithm had become firmly entrenched as a Web standard, the Unisys Corporation issued a statement claiming that GIF infringed a patent it held and began demanding substantial royalties from every program that used the technology.

One of the peculiarities of the U.S. patent system at the time the GIF patent was filed was that patent applications were not published until after the patent was granted. If the GIF designers had known that a patent had been applied for, they could easily have chosen a slightly different technique.

Standards Organizations

A standard can come into being in two ways. The first path is the accidental **de facto standard** that emerged because a well-known design that met a particular need was copied. The power socket in cars that began life as the place one would plug in a cigarette lighter is an example of this type of standard. Nobody sat down with a plan to design a standard power socket for plugging accessories into a car. It just happened that most cars had cigarette lighters with electrical contacts in the same place.

The second path is to take the proposal to an organization that has established a formal standards process. These are known as **de jure standards.**

The best layperson's guide to formal standards processes is Kafka's *The Trial*[4] where we are told, "All the ways are guarded, even this one."

There are many ways to establish a standard, but all are guarded. It is often said that one of the nice things about standards is that there are so many to choose from. Today there are three major Internet standards organizations: the IETF, the World Wide Web Consortium (W3C), and Oasis. In addition, ANSI, the IEEE, ITU, and an alphabet soup of smaller, more narrowly focused organizations write or endorse standards.

The proliferation of standards bodies is partly a result of the fact that there is too much work for one body to manage, but there are also social, political, and cultural pressures that lead to fragmentation. Some standards organizations are more professional and effective than others, but all of them might be described by Winston Churchill's definition of democracy: "the worst possible system of government, apart from all the alternatives." All standards processes take longer than it appears should be necessary, all involve protracted circular arguments over technical details that are probably unnecessary, and none arrives at a perfect result.

One of the many problems with a standards process is that any activity that requires a large number of people (more than five) to come to agreement inevitably involves a great deal of argument and politics. The process becomes even more difficult when there are 20 to 50 participants who live in different parts of the world and most of the business must be conducted through mailing lists or telephone conferences.

There is, however, an even more fundamental problem with standards processes, which is that there is a big difference between what they *can* achieve and what many people who attend them believe that they *should* achieve or *might* achieve.

A standard that is widely adopted can quickly achieve the status of a kind of law. If you want to sell light bulbs, they have to fit the sockets in the lights. If you want to sell lights, then the sockets have to match the available light bulbs supply. There is, however, no law that approval of a standard will cause it to become widely adopted.

One of the side effects of the explosive growth of the Web was that the need for a formal standard became apparent at an early stage when the number of users was measured in hundreds of thousands rather than tens of millions. I can see now that this accident of history misled me into seeing the primary role of standards processes as a means of initiating change rather than a means of sustaining the momentum of change that is already taking place.

Returning to our S curve for a moment, a standard can enable an application to grow faster and for longer in the growth phase, allowing a higher degree of deployment to be achieved at maturity, but a standard does little to help if you get to the growth phase when you are still stuck at startup.

Less important than the actual standards document are the stakeholders who support it. The real value of a formal standards process is that it provides a means of assembling a broad coalition of supporters who can help it to succeed.

Inclusiveness

In the span of five years, the Internet metamorphosized from an academic experiment connecting a handful of universities into a global medium for communication and commerce. It would be surprising if the institutions that define Internet standards had kept pace with the political implications of this change.

The number of stakeholders affected by any change is now very large, and some feel that they are being excluded from the decision-making process, often with justification.

For many years, a point of contention was the length of time it took to change the domain name system to allow Arabic, Chinese, Korean, and other non-European Internet users to register domain names in their own character set. It was rather hard to believe that this was being given a high priority when the standards documents themselves had to be prepared exclusively in English and using a format that only allows for the 26-letter Roman alphabet.

The official justification for this state of affairs is again inclusiveness, but in the technical rather than the cultural sense. If the standards required state-of-the-art technology to read them, they could only be read by people with access to that technology, and if the technology were to change in the future, the documents might become unreadable. The surest way to ensure technical inclusiveness is to stick to the capabilities of 1960s-era teletype printers (even if the documents only print reliably if you happen to be using a size of paper only used in North America, cannot include readable diagrams, and are difficult to read).

Lack of readability is a particular problem in a document that in theory has been carefully written to avoid confusion and ambiguity. The purpose of modern typography is not just aesthetics; it is to make documents easier to read.

The refusal to adopt a more modern document structure has nothing to do with any shortcomings in the alternatives. The W3C has used HTML as the format for its standards documents for more than a decade without difficulty. The real problem is that engineers working on advanced computer technology are often the most resistant to technical change that might devalue their experience. There is a trade guild aspect to the process.

Computers have always attracted a priesthood believing that their secrets should be reserved for the initiated. People who define their sense of self-importance through the accumulation of arcane knowledge can feel threatened by attempts to render their knowledge obsolete. The idea of making a computer easy for the common man to use is considered a threat.

The trade guild aspect is particularly worrying when you consider that the one interest that is never directly represented at the table are the ordinary users who just want to get their work done, pay their bills, find interesting information, chat, and so on—in short, the people who want to use the computer as a tool rather than an end in itself.

Consistency

Someone once wrote about foolish consistency being the hobgoblin of tiny minds. When it comes to computing systems, consistency counts for a lot.

Consistency is not the same as standardization. For a light bulb to be useful, it must comply with the standard for light bulbs, or it will not fit in the socket. But light bulbs come in different sizes and shapes, so there is more than one standard for light bulbs even though in practice the standards are similar. The standardization board could have chosen one design for the large base and an entirely different design for the smaller size, or it could in a fit of perversity have decided that a large base bulb would screw in clockwise but the small base bulb would have a reverse thread screwed in counterclockwise. From a purely mechanical and electrical point of view, the reverse-threaded bulb would work just as well, but from a usability point of view, the choice would be a disaster.

Consistency matters because machines are used by people, and it takes time and effort for people to learn. Designs that are inconsistent tend to cause people to make mistakes.

Consistency does not come for free, however; it is not even easily defined. Inconsistent design becomes obvious, but consistency is subjective. Making a design consistent takes a considerable amount of time, effort, and skill.

Achieving consistency across a set of related standards is harder still, particularly in the case of a design in a rapidly moving technical field such as computer science. The basic e-mail protocols were defined 25 years ago, the basic protocol of the Web 15 years ago. A great deal was learned about computer network protocol design in the intervening years, and that is reflected in the different design choices made. Experts would probably agree that some of these design choices are at least in part the reason for the success of the Web, whereas others are simply design inconsistencies that provide no real value. But it is doubtful that there would be much agreement as to which choices fall into either category.

The anthropologist Robin Dunbar argued that 150 is a particular number where the size of human groups is concerned.[5] When the group size begins to exceed this number, social relationships start to break down, and the group naturally begins to separate into factions. The size of IETF meetings peaked during the dot-com boom in 2000 at 2810 attendees. Attendance since 2004 has averaged less than half that number but is even so almost 10 times the limit suggested by Dunbar.

The number of individuals participating in the W3C and OASIS working groups is probably comparable although somewhat more difficult to measure because the working groups tend to hold their face-to-face meetings independently.

If consistency is to be achieved, there must be coordination between the different working groups, yet the organizations have already grown beyond the size where direct social interactions scale. The result is that organizations such as the IETF, which have made a concerted attempt to impose a particular concept of consistency on standards, end up with a process that has become unacceptably slow.

Dependency

Standards organization politics is further complicated by the fact that people are not only concerned by what you *intend* to do; what you *might* do often worries them even more. And because a lot of people are uncomfortable raising issues that might appear to be accusations, a simple problem can often get bogged down under a barrage of unrelated issues that are really substitutes for their real concern.

One of these problems started to affect the W3C a few years after I left. Sir Tim Berners-Lee, the inventor of the Web and director of the Consortium, has spent a lot of time in recent years on his personal research interest, the Semantic Web. When I joined VeriSign and started working in W3C working groups as a company representative rather than a member of W3C staff, I started to hear complaints about the amount of time and effort the W3C was spending on this work.

I did not understand the complaints at the time because if anyone has earned the right to spend some time doing blue sky research with money from companies who have made a fortune from the Web, then Tim has. If you attend a concert by a virtuoso, you should understand that part of the price for the Mozart and Vivaldi is listening to the Messiaen. The actual sums spent on the work were not large and were in any case mostly funded from government research grants.

It was only several years later that I realized what the real concern behind the complaints. I found myself in a position where a proposal I was supporting as a way to help control spam was being held hostage by a group with a rather different agenda. The complaints about the semantic Web were not really about staffing or resources; the real concern was *dependency*.

The U.S. Congress suffers from a similar institutional pathology that illustrates the problem rather well: The more popular and urgent a bill is, the less chance it has of becoming law. A bill that is considered "must pass" becomes a magnet for opportunist measures that would have no chance of passing by themselves. The result is known as a "Christmas tree" and as often as not collapses under the weight of the unwanted decorations.

The standards world equivalent is dependency. All standards build on previous work. The protocols for the World Wide Web are built in the manner of a multistory building. The Internet Protocol (IP) forms the foundation, and on top of this is built another layer of protocols called TCP and UDP. HTTP is built on top of TCP and a protocol called DNS, which in turn is built on UDP and TCP. Building on existing work in this way is a good thing.

The problem comes when someone tries to make others do his work of securing deployment by forcing others to make their plans rely on it.

The real concern of the Semantic Web opponents was that they were concerned that all future work by the Consortium might be required to build on the Semantic Web framework. After it was understood that the Semantic Web would be required to stand or fall on its own merits, the opposition disappeared.

The problem of dependency works both ways. Relying on another group to succeed in deploying its work is an obvious hazard. What is less obvious is that allowing others to rely on your work before it is ready is also a mistake. A killer application can quickly become a killed application, which is no use to anyone.

This problem arose in the design of DKIM, a technology designed to help in the fight against spam and phishing discussed in Chapter 13, "Secure Messaging." The design of DKIM uses the Domain Name System (DNS), which changes user-friendly Internet names such as www.example.com into IP addresses, the Internet equivalent of telephone numbers, which are used to direct packets of data. The question for the designers was whether DKIM should work with the DNS infrastructure as currently deployed or whether it should use proposed changes to the DNS infrastructure.

In smaller companies and ISPs, the same network administrator is often responsible for both the DNS server and the e-mail server. These are often separate duties in large organizations, and one or both services might be outsourced. This constraint means that the cost of upgrading the two independent systems is at least twice as high as the cost of modifying one.

If we assume that the cost of deployment of the two systems is equal, but that the incentive to deploy the e-mail change is twice the incentive to deploy the DNS change, and the two changes take place independently, a simulation results in the growth curve of Figure 4-4.

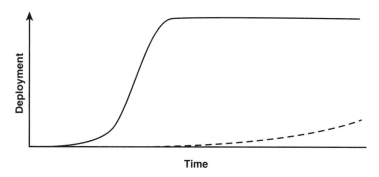

Figure 4-4 *Deployment of e-mail server and DNS server*

If we now assume that the deployment of the e-mail server is dependent on the prior deployment of the DNS server, the deployment of the DNS system is accelerated somewhat, but the deployment of the e-mail server application is practically stalled (see Figure 4-5).

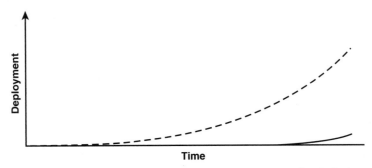

Figure 4-5   *Deployment of e-mail server and DNS system, when linked*

A more effective strategy is to engineer a situation where deployment of the killer application is not dependent on the infrastructure deployment, but there is an additional advantage realized through the infrastructure deployment.

If the deployment of the e-mail server is allowed to go ahead at its own pace and is not made dependent on the DNS server upgrade, but deployment of the e-mail application provides an additional advantage for the DNS deployment, the result is the curve of Figure 4-6. The deployment of the e-mail server is not affected, but the DNS server deployment goes ahead much faster than in any of the previous scenarios.

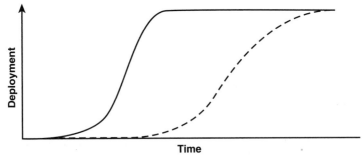

Figure 4-6   *Deployment of e-mail server and DNS system, with incentive*

DKIM has been carefully designed so that deployment of upgrades infrastructure, in particular the DNSSEC security protocol described in Chapter 16, "Secure Networks," is strongly encouraged but not a requirement for deployment of DKIM.

Advocacy

Regardless of the standards strategy, the case for deployment must be made to the wider Internet community beyond the small group that developed the proposal. Unless a proposal addresses a universally acknowledged pain point such as spam, a compelling need must be demonstrated. In every case, the advocates for the proposal must provide a convincing argument for how it will address the problem and why it is better than any alternatives on offer, including the always-present alternative of carrying on as before.

In recent years, there has been a trend toward the creation of advocacy groups that push for the deployment of technology developed in another forum. Sometimes the advocacy group is focused on a particular specification, but in other cases the group is focused on a specific industry or a particular problem and proposes a range of technologies that it believes address that need.

The main tools of technology advocates are public speaking at conferences, industry association meetings, and interviews with the media. Occasionally, they might find time to write a book such as the one you are now reading.

The effect is cumulative. The first time an idea is aired, it is usually met with indifference or outright hostility. Hostility is a good sign because it at least shows that someone is listening. To convince people that the benefits of the proposal outweigh the cost or other disadvantages, they have to hear the same message repeated from many different sources.

The Four Horsemen of Internet Change

In 1798, Thomas Malthus predicted[6] that if humans did not limit population growth of their own accord, this would be achieved by "the ravages of war, pestilence, famine, or the convulsions of nature." The four forces that Malthus predicted would compel change are traditionally identified with the four horsemen of the apocalypse in *Revelation* 6:1-8.

The forces that compel change in the commercial world are less spectacular than the biblical riders of the apocalypse, but they are equally effective: customers, liability, audit, and regulation.

Customers

Vendors who intend to survive listen to their customers. Most medium to large companies have extensive mechanisms for soliciting input from their customers. But the most effective means by which customers communicate with their vendors is by soliciting tenders for the acquisition of new technology through a Request For Proposals (RFP) process. A feature that appears infrequently in RFPs is unlikely to make it into a product roadmap unless the software vendor is convinced it offers significant advantages. A feature that appears frequently in RFPs is almost certain to make it into the product roadmap regardless of whether the software vendor thinks it has value.

This provides a powerful opportunity to effect change by appealing directly to the authors of RFPs. The task of writing RFPs is often outsourced to a consulting company that advises on the procurement process. This means that a single presentation at the right trade show can result in a question about support for a standard being added to a large number of RFP check lists.

Liability

Opinions differ as to who should be held liable for losses due to Internet crime. At some point, those differences will be argued extensively and expensively in a variety of law courts.

In the medium term, the question of who is liable will inevitably be settled in favor of the consumer. The experience of the credit card companies is instructive. After fighting government regulations to make them liable for fraud losses tooth and nail, the card issuers discovered that it was the most important benefit of their product.

Liability is an unpredictable cost that businesses typically attempt to make predictable by means of insurance. The insurer is in turn anxious to keep losses to a minimum by either requiring customers to take appropriate security measures or discounting insurance rates for those who do.

Audit

One of the major factors that is driving deployment of corporate computer security measures today is audit requirements.

One of the largely unforeseen side effects of the U.S. Sarbanes-Oxley act is that for a company to be confident that its accounting information is accurate, it must be confident that the computer systems used to prepare and analyze that data are secure.

Security audits are also being required by large numbers of companies that process data covered by the European Union privacy directive.

Audits of information systems frequently result in a "domino effect" in which an audit of one system leads to a requirement to audit the systems that feed it, which in turn lead to a requirement to audit the systems that feed them. The "Y2K fever" over the millennium bug was largely driven by companies requesting their suppliers to provide a satisfactory Y2K audit, which required the suppliers to request a Y2K audit from their suppliers in turn.

Regulation

Internet crime, like every other form of crime, is a government concern. Government action is inevitable if Internet crime cannot be controlled by any other means.

There is a marked difference in the approach to regulation in Europe and the U.S. The U.S. approach is generally to resist legislation on principle until the last minute, thus ensuring that the legislation can only be passed when the pressure has become irresistible and the ability to mitigate undesirable effects has been lost. European governments tend to be much more open to legislate at an early stage, particularly when the government in question has absolutely no intention of enforcing the measures passed.

Regulation is, unfortunately, a blunt instrument, particularly in a field that moves as fast as technology. The information available to government policy makers is unfortunately no better than the information available to any other party. As a result, technology regulation occasionally appears inspired, but more usually it ends up backing the wrong technology.

Germany was widely praised for promoting the deployment of digital ISDN telephone technology in the late 1980s. This policy has looked less visionary in the decades since and is now seen as having delayed the adoption of high-speed Internet access via ADSL.

Regulation is a blunt instrument, but one that becomes inevitable if the other forces fail to result in a satisfactory rate of change.

Key Points

- Proposing change is not enough. Advocacy and strategy are required if others are going to act on the proposal.
  - It is particularly important to unlearn the lessons of the "dot-com bubble." Many of the factors that made change happen during that period no longer apply.
- Proposals might be tactical or strategic according to how the benefits affect the party deploying the solution.
  - A tactical proposal can be deployed unilaterally and provides an immediate benefit to the party who deploys it.
    - Tactical proposals do not require a critical mass to provide value and can be deployed quickly.
    - Tactical proposals are more marketable, but it is not always possible to provide a tactical solution.
  - A strategic proposal changes the Internet infrastructure, usually requiring changes to made that do not provide an immediate benefit to the party deploying them.
    - For a strategic proposal to be worthwhile, adopting it must provide a significant benefit.
    - The key to driving deployment of the infrastructure required to support a strategic solution is to find a killer application.
      - A killer application is simply a pump-primer; it need not be a major use of the infrastructure after it is deployed.
- Standards are important accelerators for adoption but do not drive adoption in themselves.
  - Incompatibility leads to expense.
  - After they are established, standards are hard to change.

- Standards raise complicated questions of ownership and control.
  - The existence of a standard can transform a worthless patent claim into an essential and valuable one.
  - Most participants in a standards process will attempt to prevent any patent claim becoming essential in this way.
- Standards organizations play a major role in setting standards.
  - The purpose of a standards organization is to generate the constituency needed for deployment.
  - If you are trying to do design in a committee, you are making a mistake.
  - Standards organizations have their own agendas, which might include inclusiveness and consistency.
    - These are generally desirable outcomes but might be interpreted in counterproductive fashion.
  - If the price of getting a standard ratified is dependency, it is almost certainly better to walk out of the room without ratification.
    - Dependency kills deployment.
- Commercial entities are driven by the four horsemen: customer requirements, liability, audit, and regulation.

Design for Deployment

Changing the Internet is hard but not impossible. To change the Internet, it is necessary to consider the deployment strategy as a principal design consideration. A civil engineer does not just design a bridge; he provides a plan for constructing it. An electronic engineer does not just design a gadget; he provides a plan for manufacturing and testing it as well. Constructing the bridge and manufacturing and testing the gadget are central considerations in the original design. If Internet engineering is to advance, the deployment plan must be a central part of our design.

I call this approach **design for deployment**.

Objectives	Identify the characteristics of the infrastructure you want to establish.
Architecture	Consider the possible architectures that realize that infrastructure.
	Rank according to the feasibility of deployment.
Strategy	Identify potential killer applications that might drive deployment.
	Rank according to the value delivered to early adopters.
Design	Select the architecture that appears to have the best chance of success.
	Complete the detailed design.
Evangelize	Convince others to act.

These stages are the infrastructure equivalent of a marketing plan.

The process is recursive: A large infrastructure change must be broken down into manageable pieces and the principles of design for deployment applied to each constituent piece.

In the remainder of this chapter, we will look at the master deployment plan for the Accountable Web. Then in later chapters, we will look at proposals designed to address specific threats such as spam, phishing, botnets, and so on. By itself, each proposal is comparatively modest, but the cumulative effect is significant for both users and criminals.

Objectives

Our objective is to have it all; we want to make the Internet a safer place without giving anything up. We don't want to give up the ability to send e-mail to anyone we please. We don't want to give up the ability to read any public Web site we might choose. We don't want to give up the ability to create new identities.

As we saw in Chapter 1, "Motive," **pseudonymity**, the ability to separate the online and the offline world, is an essential safety control in situations such as online dating. Pseudonymity provides real security value, *provided that* all parties involved are aware that they are dealing with an online identity and that they should not expect hold them accountable offline. **Impersonation**, the ability to steal the identity and reputation of another, provides nothing positive. You can be any made-up identity you like on the Internet, but only you can be you and only I can be me.

This means that we can't expect to achieve what we want using only the traditional computer security paradigm of access control where we build a wall around the assets we want to protect and guard them closely. Instead, we must look to combine the access control approach with the accountability approach.

We have already seen how the problems of spam and telephone fraud are caused by the lack of accountability. An accountability gap is the common feature in every one of the forms of Internet abuse we consider in this book.

To establish accountability controls, we need three components: authentication, accreditation, and consequences.

- **Authentication**—To hold people accountable for their actions, we need the ability to make an exclusive claim on a particular identity. This identity might or might not correspond to a real-world identity. We do not need to know a real-world identity to stop offensive blog comments. If, on the other hand, someone wants to run an online shop or bank, his real-world identity and reputation matters a great deal. We cannot allow any party to fraudulently pass himself off as a trusted real-world identity.

- **Accreditation**—Having authenticated a claim to an unambiguous Internet identity, we can use statements other parties make concerning the party with that identity. For example, we are more likely to accept e-mail from an authenticated sender if a trusted third party states that it is a legitimate business and has not been observed sending spam.

- **Consequences**—For accountability to work, there must be consequences for abuse. These consequences can range from the loss of communication privileges (for example, refuse to accept e-mail from a known spammer) to civil and in some cases criminal penalties.

The accountability approach complements and extends rather than replaces traditional access control.

In traditional access control, we authenticate the person making a request; then we ask, "Is he permitted?" In an accountability scheme, we authenticate the person making the request and ask, "Can he be held accountable?"

Architecture

As we have seen, the "end-to-end" principle is one of the core design principles of the Internet. Complexity must be kept out of the Internet core at all costs. Deployment of changes to the core of the Internet is an exceedingly slow process indeed.

The need to keep complexity out of the Internet core reflects another Internet architectural principle: the distinction between a network and an internetwork. A **network** is an organizational unit under unified administrative control. An **internetwork** is a network of autonomous networks. By definition, an internetwork does not have a unified administrative control.

A computer network that serves a house, a small business, a university, or even a research network serving an entire country typically has a single authority responsible for administration and planning. When two independent networks are linked, something different emerges: The machines in one network can talk to machines in the other, but there are now two authorities responsible for administering the combined network.

The distinction between a network and an internetwork is critical when we are attempting to make changes. There is no central governance authority that can make the decision to act. Instead, it is necessary to persuade each of the autonomous member networks to act independently.

The lack of central governance in the Internet creates tension at the diplomatic level as certain governments appear to believe that there must be a control apparatus somewhere if only they can find out where it is.

The Internet emerged as the dominant internetwork precisely because it was designed as an internetwork rather than a network. Joining HEPNET required a major effort on the part of a university department. Machines would have to run particular software and be administered in particular ways. The Internet recognized the member networks as autonomous entities with the right to administer their own internal networks as they saw fit. The only rules in the Internet were that all networks had to support the Domain Name System (DNS) and that all communication between the networks would use the Internet Protocol (IP).

The lower entry cost of joining the Internet made it the natural choice for a computer network seeking limited internetworking capabilities. Over time, the ability of the Internet to glue together unlike networks at low cost made it the eventual winner of the networking standards wars. America Online (AOL) began in 1983 as a bulletin board for Macintosh computer systems but did not connect to the Internet until a decade later. When AOL did finally join the Internet, it did so slowly and gracefully, first giving its subscribers the ability to exchange e-mail with Internet users and then adding features such as Web browsing. Conversion of AOL's internal network to IP took many years more, and even today AOL still supports some older editions of the AOL client software that are not IP based.

The Internet provides the technical infrastructure that allows machines on different networks to communicate with each other. It does not establish the necessary accountability controls between the networks. Our objective is to establish those controls.

Understanding the internetwork as a network of networks provides us with three places where we might attempt to deploy changes to the Internet infrastructure: within the machine that provides the backbone of the Internet connecting networks to networks, at the communication endpoints where conversations begin and end, and at the interfaces between the constituent networks and the network of networks. These three locations are known as the core, end, and edge respectively (see Figure 5-1):

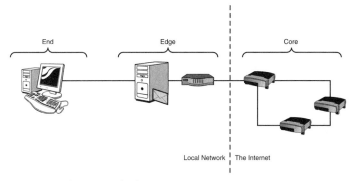

Figure 5-1   *End, core, and edge*

- **The core**—Keeping complexity out of the Internet core is one of the foundational principles of the Internet. Making changes to the Internet core is a slow and difficult process. The routers that serve the Internet backbone are switches designed to move data at exceptionally high speeds. They are not designed to perform other tasks.

  In practice, this means that the only type of infrastructure change that is feasible at the Internet core is one designed to protect the core infrastructure.

- **The end**—The Internet has more than a billion users and a billion machines. Infrastructure changes that require updates to the endpoints are possible but take many years to take effect. Getting a feature implemented in a popular application takes a minimum of three years, and it will be at least another three years before a majority of users are using it.

- **The edge**—The Internet is a network of networks. At the edge of each network are machines that connect one network to another. When the Internet began, these machines were simple switches. Today the edge is patrolled by mail servers, firewalls, spam filters, VPN boxes, wireless routers, and proxies—machines that are managed by specialist administrators and serve functions that are largely transparent to the average Internet user. It still takes a great deal of persuasion to get a professional technical specialist to change the configuration of a machine under his control, but if the right argument is made, critical mass can be established much more quickly than at the end or the core. Deployment at the edge servers managed by the largest ISPs can cause a protocol change to be deployed extremely rapidly.

The most deployable architecture is to put new functionality at the edge where the network connects to the internetwork.

Deploying complexity at the edge rather than the end is not really a major departure from the end-to-end principle. When the Internet started, computers were bought one machine at a time. When you only have one computer connected to the Internet, the distinction between the end and the edge disappears.

Naturally, there are some cases where it is impossible to meet our goals through edge deployment alone. Earlier we identified usability as a key defect in existing Internet security schemes. We cannot rectify a defective user experience unless our solution touches the application that the user interacts with.

To address usability issues, our changes must affect the communication endpoints by necessity. But even though we must make *some* changes here, we are not required to make *all* our changes at the endpoint. We can begin by deploying complementary infrastructure at the edge where deployment can take place more quickly and only move to the end when sufficient edge infrastructure has been established to create critical mass.

This edge-then-end strategy has continuing advantages after the original deployment is achieved. By placing the complexity at the edge rather than the endpoint, we provide ourselves with the flexibility to address future challenges as the changes made to a few key points can now effect every one of the updated endpoints without the need for an additional update.

Strategy

Strategy is the process of identifying other people's interests that are consistent with the outcomes you want to effect. No one individual or even one corporation can change a global infrastructure with a billion users by acting alone. Attempts to do so have invariably been humbling.

The rapid expansion of the Web was not an accident; the Web was designed for deployment from the start. In particular, the technology choices for the Web platforms were governed by political expediency and not technical superiority alone. SGML was not chosen as the basis for HTML because it was the best document markup language that could be developed; it was not even the best system available at the time. But SGML brought the support of the publishing industry, which had already committed to using SGML.

The key in developing a strategy is to identify areas where the interests are essential and those where compromise can be made. Compromise that makes it easier to reach critical mass is beneficial. The temptation that has to be resisted is compromise for the sake of compromise, dependencies that make it harder to reach critical mass and the self-sustaining growth phase.

When developing strategy, I consider the two principles that drive technological change: pain and opportunity.

Change in the security field tends to be driven by pain. In particular, it is pain that can be attributed to a specific narrowly defined cause—a pain point.

Every few months, I compile a list of the current pain points that I see as the top issues for Internet security. For the past five years, spam and Internet crime have been at the top of the list. Other important pain points are compliance with audit and regulatory requirements (those four horsemen again) and the rising cost and complexity of administering networks in both the home and the enterprise.

An emerging pain point is an effect given the unlovely term **deperimeterization**, which we will return to in Chapter 16, "Secure Networks." Deperimeterization has attracted a lot of attention in Europe, but less in the U.S. Perimeter security is the dominant paradigm of network security today even as it is being undermined in many different ways, by laptops that move in and out of the company every night, flash memory, connections to partner networks, and wireless networking.

Deperimeterization is an important pain point for the enterprise security world because it requires us to rethink our entire approach to networking and not just the security aspect of it. It is a pain point we must be aware of when proposing solutions to Internet crime, because it is the one that is likely to drive the development of most security challenges targeted at the enterprise over the next five to ten years.

Although the principal driver for Internet security deployment is pain (that is, the need to develop controls for existing risks that are already being felt), opportunity also plays a role.

The Internet has been a mass medium for a decade. In 1995, the principal means of access was dialup. Today, most home users connect through high-speed broadband capable of delivering video on demand. But even though the potential for delivering high-quality video content to consumers via the Internet is clear, this opportunity cannot be realized without both a security infrastructure and an economic model that allows the studio to recoup the cost of films totaling $100 million or more to make.

Another important area of opportunity is personal expression. People want to use the Internet to express their own thoughts and ideas through blogs and personal networking sites such as MySpace and LinkedIn. These sites are important and valuable to the users, but the boundaries imposed by the lack of an effective security infrastructure are becoming apparent.

A third area of opportunity is the machine-machine Web. The first generation of the Web provided a natural means for a human to obtain information from a machine. Although humans are the ultimate consumers of information (at least until strong AI is developed), it is not necessarily desirable for a human to mediate every link in a chain.

Today I would arrange a business trip by interacting with a series of Web sites to register for a conference; book a flight, car, and hotel; create driving instructions from the airport to the hotel and from the hotel to the conference venue; and so on. In each case, I am the mediator in the process; I have to take information delivered by one Web site and enter it into another. A much better way to solve this problem is to have a program that can take the information provided by one site and feed it into another. Such programs are becoming known as **mashups**.

One way I could do this is by writing a program that takes information from each site as if it were a person, taking the HTML markup designed to render the information to the human viewer and extracting the information I need. This process is known as **screen scraping**. One of the earliest jobs I got in a large company was writing a program that screen scraped information from the corporate mainframe and wrote it out to a spreadsheet. A much better way to achieve the same result would, of course, have been for the programmer maintaining the mainframe to produce a report in the machine-friendly format required directly from the database, but that is not how things were done then.

Today we know better: Making the information available to the user in the most usable form makes the information, and thus the service provided most valuable to them. Web Services and the Semantic Web are two technologies that make providing and using machine-machine interfaces easier.

Design

For me, design is the fun part of the process. Designing an Internet infrastructure is like solving a huge multidimensional crossword puzzle. Design can be frustrating, but there is nothing like the feeling you get when you can find a solution to a puzzle with a large number of constraints.

Design for deployment does not require a major change in the design process; it's just one more set of constraints: Who are going to be the first people to deploy this infrastructure? What benefit will they hope to realize? What is the best architecture to achieve critical mass? How can we use the infrastructure established by early adopters to meet our original goals? How do we avoid a situation where we arrive at a technological cul-de-sac? What type(s) of network effect do we hope for?

Design is a process of making choices; in some cases the choice made makes a difference. In most cases, the decision to make a choice is much more important than the actual choice made.

The choice of spelling for the HTTP Referer field mentioned in Chapter 4, "Making Change Happen," is an example of this kind of choice. The protocol requires each piece of information describing a request to have a label. The label will never be seen by users in normal operation, so the specific choice of label does not matter provided that all the Web servers and all the Web browsers agree to use the same label for the same purpose. From this point of view, the labels "Shrubbery," "Fred," or even "Referrer" would have worked just as well. Choosing a label that clearly indicates its function has the advantage of making problems rather easier to diagnose and solve, but this is not an essential criterion.

Reducing the complexity of a design to the minimum is certainly desirable, but it is far more important to avoid reducing the complexity further than the minimum. Many systems that have grown incomprehensibly complex got that way due to an initial design that neglected important needs and failed to provide an effective extension mechanism to allow them to be added at a later date.

As we have seen in the design of the Internet, more important than the amount of complexity is where the design locates it. A design that attempts to locate complexity within the fabric of the Internet core is almost certainly doomed to failure. A solution that can be deployed at the edge is likely to be deployed more quickly than one that requires changes to be made at the endpoint, but only if the deployment strategy can identify a sufficiently powerful incentive for the maintainers of that infrastructure.

Evangelize

The mere fact that a design will help the intended early adopters is not enough for them to deploy it. The intended early adopters must know about the design before they can even consider it and, having heard about it, they need to be persuaded that deploying this particular change is more important to them than all the other competing calls on their time.

I spend a lot of time talking to customers, to providers of programs intended to implement the infrastructure. In addition to this book, I write papers, post on my corporate and personal blogs, speak at conferences, and give frequent press interviews.

The other thing I spend a lot of time on is working in standards organizations. A communications infrastructure is only possible if all the machines in the network understand the same way of talking to each other.

The common understanding of the standards process is that it exists for the purpose of creating a design. I think this view is mistaken. To arrive at the best possible design, the best approach is usually to find no more than five experts and put them in a room together to work.

Design is possible in a group of 10 or even 15 people, but it's no more productive. If anything, progress tends to be slower. A group of this size is best for gathering data rather than analyzing it. As Fred Brooks observed in *The Mythical Man-Month,*[1] "Oversimplifying outrageously, we state Brooks' Law, 'Adding manpower to a late software project makes it later.'"

It does not take a hundred people to design an infrastructure, but it takes at least that number to get it deployed. If you are lucky, you will emerge from the standards process with a design that is slightly better than the design you started with. The real figure of merit for a standards process is the number of supporters you can collect on the way.

Key Points

- The Internet has a billion users; changing the Internet is a major challenge.
  - Architects must design for deployment.
- Our objective is to introduce accountability to the Internet without giving anything up.
- Architectures where the change is made at the network edge are likely to deploy faster than at the end or core.
- A design must establish an early-adopter community capable of establishing critical mass.
  - The process is driven by pain and opportunity.
- Evangelism is essential for people to act.

Spam Whack-a-Mole

"Expect the unexpected."
—Douglas Adams,
The Hitchhiker's Guide to the Galaxy

S pam is the swamp in which almost every Internet crime festers. If we want to stop the growth of Internet crime, we must drain the swamp.

The spam crisis illustrates the consequence of letting trivial problems grow unchecked. In the space of about 18 months, the problem of spam grew from a minor nuisance to the biggest and most serious security problem on the Internet.

Spam is not merely a nuisance; it is a conduit for crime. A study by the Federal Trade Commission in 2003 reported that 66 percent of spam messages sent contained a statement that was false.[1] This number represents the proportion of messages that can be proved beyond a doubt to be illegal. Other studies suggest that a much larger proportion of spam sent is outright criminal—at least 80 percent and possibly as much as 95 percent.

It is not surprising that so much spam is criminal. Few legitimate businesses would want to use a marketing scheme so disreputable that it is guaranteed to create at least 20 enemies for every sale. Spam is subject to a peculiar variation of Gresham's law that bad money drives out the good. The bad spam—the spam that is merely an annoyance—has been driven out by the worst. It is no exaggeration to say that spam has become the primary form of Internet crime.

The Green Card Spam

Spam began with a dishonest message offering to fill out applications for the U.S. green card immigration lottery posted to every newsgroup in the Usenet news system on April 12, 1994 by husband and wife law firm Canter and Siegal. Within a few years, spam had rendered large parts of Usenet unusable, as discussions were drowned in a sea of indiscriminate advertisements.

Few people can have realized the commercial potential of the Internet as early as Laurence Canter and Martha Siegal, tried as hard to make a fortune and failed as utterly. There had been commercial messages on the Internet before the green card spam, but previous experiments had been short lived and had usually ended in an abject apology. Martha Siegal was unrepentant, considering herself to be a farsighted e-commerce visionary, the first to realize the true importance of the Internet. Martha dismissed her critics as unimportant nobodies too stupid to realize that the Internet would shortly be the property of people like herself.

Canter and Siegal did not "Make a Fortune on the Information Superhighway" as the title of Martha's book proclaimed. Instead, both the book and business flopped, and Canter quickly lost his license to practice law as his past was uncovered by Internet sleuths. This might have been superfluous because Canter was already facing disciplinary charges involving misuse of client funds and failure to pay employees.

The green card spam was typical of what was to come, offering a service that was both useless and dishonest. Canter and Siegal were offering to fill in forms that required no legal expertise for $75 a time. Having a lawyer fill out the form would not affect the chance of winning.

Canter and Siegal soon had many imitators, many of whom shared Martha Siegal's fondness for self-promotion. Stanford Wallace moved into spam after Congress made his junk fax business illegal. Styling himself "Spamford," Wallace quickly became the first spam king. Canter and Siegal's business had quickly crumbled after being disconnected by their Internet service provider (ISP). To their surprise, Canter and Siegal found that ISPs turned out to be unintimidated by threats of legal action: they were not the first lawyers to have discovered the Internet, after all. Wallace realized that keeping access to the Internet open was going to be the key to staying in business for any length of time.

Wallace was probably the first spammer to sign what soon became known as a **pink contract** with an ISP. Unlike a normal ISP contract that gives the ISP the right to terminate the account for abuse, a pink contract acknowledged that Wallace intended to send large volumes of unsolicited e-mails containing advertisements and that the ISP waived its right to terminate the contract for doing so. The name *pink contract* was coined after the improbably violent shade of pink of Hormel's canned "ham product" SPAM.

Blacklists: Shutting Spammers Down

As the tide of spam rose, antispam activists tried to shut the spammers out of the Internet. This is a bit like playing the fairground game whack-a-mole. Each time the plastic mole sticks his head up out of a hole, you try to bash it on the head with a hammer. Hitting a mole provides a temporary feeling of satisfaction, but only until the next mole sticks his head up.

At first, complaints were directed at the ISP hosting the spammer, a strategy that experienced mixed results. Some ISPs dumped the spammers as soon as they could. Others saw an opportunity to serve a new market willing to pay premium rates for pink contracts. These ISPs were immune to complaints because all their customers were spammers. Some spammers took their operations offshore. Complaints slowed them down, but the spam continued.

As the spam tide rose further, blacklists of spammer IP addresses started to circulate among system administrators. As the number of spammers increased, maintaining these blacklists became a major undertaking.

Blacklists hit the mainstream when Paul Vixie established the MAPS (SPAM spelled backward) blacklist. Unlike previous blacklist schemes that had circulated as text files, Vixie used the DNS system to publish his blacklist. This meant that everyone had immediate access to the latest copy of the MAPS list. Using MAPS, any mail server could check whether a computer trying to connect to send mail was using an IP address listed as belonging to a spammer.

MAPS soon established a significant following. As the popularity of MAPS continued to grow, Vixie started to promote a policy he called **collateral damage**. If an ISP refused to terminate access to a spammer, MAPS would list all the IP addresses assigned to an ISP. This meant that mail from the other customers of the ISP would be blocked. The idea was that these customers would put pressure on their ISP to terminate the contract of the spammer so that their own mail would get through.

Collateral damage was a step too far. As Vixie himself admitted, he was attempting to force ISPs to terminate service to customers he disapproved of. Vixie had appointed himself as the unilateral arbiter of acceptable Internet e-mail use. Those listed on MAPS frequently disagreed with Vixie. Lawsuits followed.

Like many companies formed during the dot-com boom, MAPS had been established on a business model that was new and a legal theory that was untested. In statements to the media, Vixie appeared to believe that the first amendment to the U.S. constitution provided MAPS with a cast iron defense against any legal challenge that might be brought against it. When the lawsuits began to fly, MAPS discovered that a constitutional right intended to protect freedom of speech is not the best argument for a company making its living from what is an objective point of view—censorship.

Censorship is, of course, an ugly word. The blacklist's managers did not see themselves as censors. Like many people who consider what they are doing to be righteous, they thought that the rest of the world would understand the purity of their motives and not question their deeds.

This might be why MAPS appeared to be completely unprepared for the flurry of lawsuits that resulted when others disputed their claim to be the ultimate arbiter of acceptable e-mail practice.

Real problems did occur. Some people would subscribe to the mailing lists of political groups they were opposed to in order to report them as spam and get them blacklisted.

Even blacklists that attempt to apply methods that are purely objective can be gamed. Some blacklists identify spam sources by monitoring **honeypot** e-mail addresses that have never been used by a real user and should never receive legitimate e-mail. This is a good test unless the honeypot address becomes known by an attacker, at which point it becomes a way to add any e-mail sender the attacker wants to block to the blacklist. Some attacks of this type have a commercial motive. In one case, a competitor caused a rival jewelry store to be blacklisted by subscribing a known blacklist to the rival's newsletter.

MAPS was hopelessly undercapitalized for a business that would inevitably be lawsuit intensive. At one point, AOL, Microsoft Hotmail, and most of the leading ISPs in the U.S. used MAPS to block spam. A business listed as a spammer on the MAPS blacklist was effectively cut off from a large part of the Internet. MAPS won some early legal victories in some preliminary decisions, but court cases soon fell into a regular pattern. After initial bluster, a confidential settlement would be reached, and both sides would declare victory. MAPS would claim the plaintiff had agreed not to spam, and the plaintiff would state that MAPS had unblocked him.

Some observers started to believe that any spammer inconvenienced by MAPS could quickly become removed from the blacklist by threatening a lawsuit. Attention was also drawn to the substantial fees that MAPS was charging ISPs for its services.

Suddenly MAPS faced criticism from the user community as well as people who claimed they had been unfairly blacklisted. Competing blacklists started to sprout like mushrooms. At one point, there were more than a thousand blacklists operating in various degrees with accuracy varying from good to appalling.

The number of blacklists that gained a significant constituency is unknown. After a litigant listed the customers of MAPS in a lawsuit claiming antitrust violations in addition to MAPS itself, few ISPs will state which blacklists they use.

Each new blacklist was being marketed as tougher on spammers than the last. The criteria applied became ever more arbitrary. The number of IP addresses blocked and the aggressiveness with which "collateral damage" was caused became selling points. Adding entries to the blacklist generally took priority over resolving disputes over the accuracy of existing listings. Often there was no dispute resolution process.

Most blacklists were inaccurate because of mere negligence, but many became completely obsolete as the operator became bored with the game but continued to publish the out-of-date information. In occasional cases, this was due to actual malice. When one blacklist maintainer was told by his ISP that his Internet connection would be cut off if he didn't pay his bills, he retaliated by blacklisting the ISP as a spammer. Many blacklist operators believed that they were answerable to no one.

Perversely, the lawsuits that should have held the blacklists accountable had the opposite effect. Each round of litigation resulted in a search for ways to put themselves even further beyond the law.

The nadir of this process was Spam Prevention Early Warning System (SPEWS), an underground blacklist with a Web site that regularly moved from country to country but always far from the jurisdiction of the U.S. courts. Membership of the cabal that operated SPEWS was secret, and the only way to complain was to post a message in a Usenet discussion group. All decisions were final with no appeal.

SPEWS was both "judgment proof" and impossible to trust. It is not beyond possibility that the list was from start to finish a front run by a spammer whose real purpose was to block messages from his competitors.

Blacklists are an unsatisfactory solution for many reasons. They are blunt instruments that affect the innocent as well as the guilty, in many cases by design. They act as a law unto themselves seeking to force ISPs to comply with their demands, however arbitrary. I have met many network managers, including several who work for major ISPs, who loathe blacklist vigilantes more than the spammers.

The blacklists failed because they tried to hold others accountable but refused to be held accountable themselves. All refused to accept liability for an incorrect or downright malicious listing regardless of fault.

Filters: An Effective Palliative, Not a Cure

The most effective method of keeping spam out of your e-mail Inbox is to use a spam filter. A spam filter looks for features in an e-mail message that mean it is likely to be spam. Like taking aspirin for a cold, filtering provides a necessary palliative but unfortunately not a cure. Without spam filtering, e-mail would now be useless to me. I receive 3,000 messages a day, 85 percent of which are spam. The problem with spam filtering as crime prevention is that it only stops spam affecting me personally; it does not put the spammers out of business if their fraudulent offers still reach enough people without a spam filter.

Blacklists are one source of information that some filters use, but only the most basic spam filters now rely on blacklist data alone, and many do not use externally maintained blacklists at all.

Early spam filters looked for words and phrases that were commonly used in spam but rarely appeared in legitimate e-mail. An e-mail message that contains the word *Viagra* is almost certainly spam, but it might be a genuine discussion of a medical condition for which Viagra is a treatment.

Other spam filters look at the way in which the messages are sent. Most spammers are outright criminals and do not want to be identified as the source of their messages. The tactics that the spammers use to conceal the origin of their messages often leave distinctive marks.

All filters fail part of the time. Spam that should have been squelched is delivered to the user. Wanted messages that should have been retained are marked as spam. Filters are usually written with a bias in favor of accepting suspect mail because seeing some spam is a nuisance, but losing important mail can be a catastrophe. If you get as much spam as I do, there is simply no time to second guess the filter and spend time checking the junk mail folder to see if an important message found its way in there by mistake.

Unless they have some means of being kept up-to-date with the latest spammer tricks, spam filters that are widely used will lose their effectiveness over time. Spammers have the greatest incentive to develop countermeasures against the filters that are most widely used.

Simply looking for *Viagra* does not work very well as a spam filter any more. Spammers have discovered that more of their messages get through if they use the spelling Vlagra or V1agra.

It is, of course, a minor matter to update the spam filter to the new spelling, but as soon as this is done, the spammer will have a new trick. The filter writers have to keep working to stay ahead of the spammers because the last player to move always holds the advantage. I don't like that type of game. I don't want the odds to be even; I want them to be tipped heavily in my favor. I want to make the bad guys have to work so much harder than the good guys that they start to think that they should look for another game to play.

An indication that a message is likely to be spam is known as a **feature**. A feature might be a word that often appears in spam, like *Viagra,* or the fact that the message comes from a blacklisted IP address. Some of the most useful features are telltale traces that are usually left by the spammer's attempts to cover his tracks. An e-mail that contains the word *Viagra* is quite likely to be spam; an e-mail that contains the spelling *V1agra* is almost certain to be spam.

The best spam filters use large numbers of features, scoring each according to how likely a message with that type of feature is likely to be spam. Microsoft measures the effectiveness of more than 4,000 spam features on several million messages each day and uses the results to decide what features to use to filter the billions of e-mails Hotmail receives each day.[2]

Filtering works, but the effort required to make it work is huge. Imagine a room the size of a football field filled with row upon row of computers. That is what the data center of one of the largest ISPs looks like. The vast majority of that computing power is not handling the mail people want; it is handling the spam people do not want. Spam accounts for the majority of the messages received, and analyzing messages to identify probable spam content is the most processor-intensive step in the message-handling process. Each of those machines costs real money to buy, power, and maintain.

Sue and Jail Them

A spam control technique that has been used with a considerable degree of success is to track down the spammers and sue them for damages. In a recent case, a judge awarded a default judgment of more than a billion dollars against a spammer. Awards of more than a million dollars have become routine.

The recent CANSPAM legislation passed in the U.S. provides another useful tool. CANSPAM requires senders of unsolicited e-mail to provide an opt-out mechanism, valid subject line, routing information, and legitimate physical address. Adult material must be labeled.

Although some have criticized CANSPAM as being too permissive, it has been successful in criminalizing the behavior of the most prolific spammers. Law enforcement resources are limited and criminal prosecution must be targeted at the worst and most extreme offenders. The CANSPAM act is a tool for prosecutors; it is not intended to define best practices for e-mail use.

Technology people tend to be at best skeptical about the idea of suing or prosecuting spammers. Using the law looks like moving a haystack one wisp of straw at a time while someone else is using a pitchfork to add new straw to the pile. This is a pity because so far lawsuits and criminal prosecutions are the only methods that have put spammers out of business for good. It has also effectively persuaded the media to stop encouraging others to get a pitchfork and add to the pile.

Early newspaper stories about spam frequently described it as a foolproof get-rich-quick scheme. The bulk of the story would consist of an interview with a spammer and focus on his incredible financial success with at best a couple of comments from an antispam zealot tacked on to the end to give the appearance of balance.[3] The spammers had an interest in inflating their success; it helped them to convince new customers that their spamming services were an inexpensive and highly effective form of advertising.

The lawsuits and prosecutions have effectively ended this type of reporting. The spammers are considerably less keen to give interviews for a start; also, stories in the press are likely to attract unwanted attention from lawyers. Any story that does appear is likely to mention the lawsuits and drive off potential customers.

The threat of lawsuits and prosecutions has also changed the nature of the spammer's business. At one time, a person trying to become a spammer could concentrate on sending spam for other businesses. Legitimate companies do not want to use an advertising method that might land them with a lawsuit regardless of how profitable or effective it might appear, so this route is effectively closed to entrants without criminal contacts.

The main drawback to using prosecutions is scale. Courts and lawyers are an expensive remedy, and prisons are even more so. If the law is going to be an effective deterrent, it must become a more credible deterrent, which means that the difficulty and cost of bringing a case must be significantly reduced. The main challenge in bringing a case against a spammer is finding out who the spammer is. The law provides a range of tools that can help uncover the true identity of a spammer, but they are expensive and cumbersome to use.

The Longitude of the Internet Age

In 1707, Admiral Sir Clowdisley Shovell ran his fleet of four ships aground off the Scilly Isles. Almost 2,000 men died in the disaster. The admiral himself was one of the only two men washed to shore, where a fisherwoman murdered him for his ring. The disaster led to the Longitude Act of 1714, which established a prize for finding a method of determining longitude, the pursuit of which quickly became synonymous with lunacy.[4]

My favorite crackpot longitude scheme is the "powder of sympathy," which it was claimed would cause a patient to heal when sprinkled on an article belonging to them, such as a bandage. The sympathetic magic was alleged to work instantaneously and at any distance, but not painlessly. In fact, the patients were alleged to jump with pain when the powder was applied to the sympathetic article.

A supply of sympathetic power provides a means of obtaining the longitude: A wounded dog is taken aboard the ship, and the bandage is kept in the harbor. Each day at noon precisely, the powder of sympathy would be applied to the bandage, causing its sympathetic partner to howl in agony and thereby tell the ship's company the time of noon at the meridian.

The search for a solution to spam has become the longitude problem of the Internet. Like the longitude problem, the problem of spam is easily explained and understood; understanding the environment in which the problem must be solved is the hard part.

Galileo had discovered a precise means of measuring longitude using the moons of Jupiter more than a hundred years before Sir Clowdisley sailed. The problem was that it depended on precise astronomical observations that would be impossible to make on board a ship, even in the calmest of seas.

For a solution to the spam problem to be acceptable, it must have the minimum possible impact on the legitimate uses of e-mail. Solutions that attempt to deter spammers by introducing a charge for every e-mail sent completely fail in this regard because a charge that was large enough to deter spammers would completely change the economics of sending e-mail.

Another reason the "penny post" approach to spam control fails is that it presupposes the existence of an international payments infrastructure capable of transferring very small amounts of money. This solution is like suggesting inventing radio as a solution to the longitude problem without providing any further insight into solving the problem of actually inventing radio.

The idea of making it uneconomic to send spam is a sound one. But there is no need to charge the legitimate e-mail user fees in order to deter the illegitimate user. The way to deter spammers is to make *spammers* pay.

Another common problem in bad antispam schemes is that they actually create more spam than they eliminate. Of course, nobody is going to use an antispam scheme if it increases the amount of spam he receives. But lots of people use antispam schemes that send spam to other people.

The main scheme of this type is called **challenge-response**. The idea is that when you send someone an e-mail, his robot replies with a message that says, "Did you really mean to send this message?" The mail will only be delivered to the user if you send an e-mail confirming that you did really send it. The marginally less objectionable schemes of this type will only challenge someone the first time you try to send him a message. Others will send a challenge every time.

Most schemes only require a response to the e-mail. Others require you to solve a puzzle intended to distinguish a human from a machine, such as reading a word that has been distorted in a way that makes it difficult to read using standard machine-reading methods (see Figure 6-1).

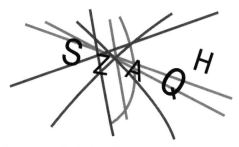

Figure 6-1 *Turing test to check that the user is a human*

Whether these schemes actually work as intended is a matter of current debate. Are the problems genuinely hard for machines to solve, or is it just that nobody has had an incentive to make an attempt? The seminal CMU paper that introduced the idea of using Turing tests in this way (and the unlovely acronym CAPTCHA) is subtitled "How Lazy Cryptographers Do AI."[5]

The schemes are also vulnerable to a man-in-the-middle attack. When the user answers a puzzle presented at one site, he might in fact be answering a puzzle set at another site. Alternatively, an attacker can simply pay people living in low-wage countries to spend their days solving the puzzles.

The basic challenge-response scheme has been reinvented several times. The earliest invention I am aware of is by John Mallery at MIT for the Open Meeting project, an online forum that the AI lab ran as a part of Vice President Al Gore's Reinventing Government initiative.[6]

Some uses of challenge-response are justified. The messages sent to the Open Meeting would be forwarded to thousands of people; it was important to make sure that the comments really did come from the people they appeared to. There are many other uses that are generally considered legitimate.

Most e-mail lists now use challenge-response to verify subscribers before adding them to the list. This went from being rare to being a near-universal practice in a matter of a few days after someone decided it would be fun to subscribe the White House to a few thousand e-mail lists. To increase the effect, they caused some of the mailing lists to be subscribed to each other in such a way that a single e-mail sent to one mailing list would fan out to a thousand other lists, which would forward it on to the White House. Fortunately, the White House had already experienced a large number of e-mail attacks and was ready for this sort of thing. The mailing lists used to mount the attack were less prepared.

Challenge-response is a useful technique that is widely used on the Internet. It is also a pain in the neck. Every site on the Internet seems to want me to fill out a subscription form. Then they want to check my e-mail address so they can send me spam later on. Like many other frequent Internet users, I have an e-mail account I use just for this.

Using challenge-response to filter your personal e-mail is a spam-shifter, not a spam solution. You get less spam, but I get spammed by your challenges.

One thing I find objectionable about these schemes is the implicit assertion that their user is somehow especially important and that special permission is necessary before speaking to him. What I find really infuriating though is the way they will proclaim that they have never had anyone complain. Of course, there are no complaints when the people who find these schemes objectionable can't talk to you without using them!

I recently got a message from a student asking me for some information on a protocol I had designed. Although I rarely have time to respond to these requests, I took ten minutes or so to write a reply even though the point was addressed in the specification, which was easy enough to find. In return, I received a challenge from the student's mail service asking me to prove I was not a spam sender.

A question that I have never had a satisfactory answer to from proponents of these schemes is what happens when two people using this type of scheme try to talk to each other? Alice sends an e-mail to Bob, whose e-mail program sends back a challenge to Alice. With most challenge-response systems, this is the point at which Alice then sends back a challenge to Bob and the challenges just ping-pong back and forth between the systems. Sometimes the schemes try to be clever and always allow a challenge through, but how can they tell the difference between a challenge and spam? If challenges are allowed through, then a spammer can send spam disguised as a challenge.

Challenge-response is a good example of an antispam measure that faces the car burglar alarm problem: It works only for as long as the number of people using it is small. After large numbers of people start using the scheme, spam senders have an incentive to do the trivial amount of work necessary to bypass it.

This example shows the importance of measuring the success of spam control mechanisms correctly. Proponents of challenge response schemes often claim that they have a **zero false positive rate**—that is there is no risk that a legitimate message will be misclassified as spam. By my way of thinking, however, the false positive rate is actually 100 percent because every message is considered spam and quarantined until proven legitimate.

What really matters is the amount of e-mail that will end up lost. Even if every recipient of a challenge was willing to respond to it (I never do), a high error rate is still inevitable. Many people will send out an e-mail and then shut down their computer. By the time they return, they will have forgotten that they had sent the message.

The challenge-response schemes are an attempt to reduce spam by checking that the purported sender of the e-mail is the real sender—that is, they are a form of authentication. The principle is sound, but the mechanism used is too disruptive. Every e-mail user is required to personally authenticate himself to every new correspondent.

The Worst of the Worst

The worst spam reduction idea of all is to fight fire with fire and attempt to hack into or otherwise disable the machines sending the spam. The idea of vigilante justice is always tempting in theory, particularly when it appears that law enforcement is ineffective. In practice, vigilantes create more problems than they solve; mob rule inevitably leads to attacks against the innocent as well as the guilty. The blacklists lost credibility by targeting the innocent as well as the guilty. There is no reason to believe that vigilantes would be any better.

The interdependent nature of much of the Internet infrastructure means that vigilante attacks will inevitably affect innocent parties even if they only intend to target the guilty. If a vigilante attempts to disable one customer of an ISP, the effects will inevitably be felt by every other customer.

People who are caught often attempt to claim that they are really misunderstood vigilantes attempting to protect the public interest. If vigilante actions are legitimized, there is no hope of ever establishing the rule of law on the Internet.

A screensaver promoted by a search engine company demonstrates how a scheme of this type can go wrong. The screensaver was designed to perform a denial-of-service attack against alleged spammer sites. The machine used to direct the attacks was quickly compromised and used to attack a series of entirely innocent machines until a cabal of network administrators effectively disconnected the controller from the Internet.

Out of the Ashes

So far, the history of spam control has been somewhat depressing. The e-mail system continues to function, but only at great cost and effort. The good guys are at best one step ahead of the spammers.

We can learn many lessons from this history, but I believe two particular lessons to be critical. First, a party that attempts to hold others accountable must accept accountability itself. Second, we cannot win if we allow the spammers to set the rules of the game. We will apply these lessons in Chapter 7 where we consider the problem of e-mail spam, and again in Chapters 13 through 15, when we consider the larger problem of establishing abuse-resistant communication systems.

Key Points

- Many proposals have been made to stop spam.
  - It is easy to propose a mechanism that stops spam on a small scale, but these rarely work at Internet scale.
  - Schemes that require major changes to the way in which e-mail is used are unacceptable.

- Blacklists are lists of IP addresses of known or alleged spammers.
  - Maintaining an accurate blacklist requires a considerable effort.
  - Complaints about spam may be malicious.
  - Blacklists demand accountability from others but refuse to be held accountable themselves.
- Per message charges
  - Would have a major impact on the way e-mail is used.
    - A charge that is large enough to deter spammers would deter many current uses, especially mailing list hosting.
  - Might legitimize sending practices considered to be spam.
  - Depend on the creation of a low-cost "micro-payments" infrastructure that nobody has succeeded in building.
- Challenge response schemes
  - Provide a lightweight authentication mechanism.
  - Are generally considered reasonable when used to prevent abuse of mailing lists.
  - Are highly objectionable when used as a personal spam control scheme. They are a spam displacement tool.
- Retaliation schemes in which the spammer is counter attacked frequently end up attacking innocent parties.

CHAPTER 7

Stopping Spam

We have to stop letting the spammers choose the game. Whack-a-mole is not much fun when the mole has a million holes to choose from and you only get one hammer.

Chess is a better game. The key to winning chess is to predict and pre-empt your opponent's moves. At this point, we are still in the opening phase of the game against the spammers, so some of our moves will appear to be of limited value. The object is to control the board at the *end* of the game.

For the time being, spammers get to choose the game, but we get to change the rules; more hammers and less holes means less spam.

Every form of Internet communication is affected by spam: e-mail, blog comments, network news, wikis, voice, and instant messaging.

In this chapter, we will focus on e-mail spam because it is the hardest problem. The e-mail infrastructure is the oldest and largest medium affected by spam. In later chapters, we will return to the problem and look at emerging identity infrastructure that will allow us to extend our approach to other media. After we know how to stop e-mail spam, we can apply the same principals to stop the other forms of spam as well.

As the proportion of spam in my Inbox climbed from 1 percent to 5 percent, 10 percent, and 20 percent, it became clear that soon the spam would outnumber the legitimate mail. We were looking at the problem the wrong way around: We should focus on the messages we want and ignore the rest.

At the same time, David Berlind, a reporter at ZDNET, started writing about the problem of legitimate e-mails getting blocked as the dark side of the blacklists emerged.

Berlind organized a series of war councils in the ZDNET offices bringing together people working on the problem of spam. A new approach began to emerge: Allow legitimate senders to prove that they are legitimate.

This led to looking at the spam problem as a computer security problem. In computer security terminology, we have an access control problem: Who do I want to accept mail from?

The access control problem is divided into two parts: authentication and authorization. If we have a request from a party calling itself "Alice," to access a document we first check to see if "Alice" is the real Alice (the authentication step). Then we check to see if Alice is allowed to access that document (the authorization step).

This approach was promising, but the spam problem did not fit neatly into the conventional definition of access control. Something was missing.

Accountability

In December 2003, I attended an Aspen Institute roundtable on Internet security issues including spam. Hans Peter Bromondo convinced us that we should look at these problems in terms of accountability. This led to the idea of **The Accountable Net**, which was that the key to stopping Internet vandals and spam is to restore accountability to the Internet.

The scheme we had developed did not fit the conventional access control model because there was no way to list in advance the *name* of every person who we might want to accept mail from. We needed a scheme that allowed us to describe the *type* of person who could send us mail: Who would accept responsibility for a message, and could this person be held accountable?

The early Internet did not have cryptographic security, but it did have accountability. Every user knew that his access to this unique resource depended on his good behavior. As the Internet grew, the accountability mechanisms were stretched beyond their breaking point. The spam blacklists attempted to create a new form of accountability mechanism but ultimately failed because they were trying to impose accountability on others but were not prepared to accept accountability themselves.

The introduction of new technology often creates what appear at first to be intractable problems. The motor car led to a road safety problem of epidemic proportions. Speed limits of 14 mph did little to control traffic when there was no way to know the driver and no way for the police officer to catch up with him unless he could borrow a private car!

Road safety remains a problem, but a measure of control has been achieved through accountability. The French police invented the license plate in 1893, and within a decade, plates were required in most industrialized countries. Driving licenses appeared soon after.

Accountability on the highway has three important elements: identification, accreditation, and consequences. The license plate on the car identifies the vehicle with a reasonable degree of reliability. The car itself is required to undergo regular inspection, and the driver must pass a test before a driving license is issued. Failure to obey the traffic laws might result in consequences that include fines, suspension of driving privileges, and imprisonment.

Neither the car license plate nor the driving license is proof against forgery. Obtaining a fake license plate takes remarkably little effort in the UK, where some shops will make one on the spot without bothering to check documentation. Even in the U.S., where license plates are traditionally made by convicts in state prisons, a license plate can be stolen off a car parked on the street with nothing more than a screwdriver. But these apparently "obvious" security problems are in practice difficult to exploit for any length of time.

The driver of a car with a legitimate license plate knows that any traffic offenses can be traced back to the authorized owner and consequences will follow. If the car carries a false license plate, this is also noticeable and will result in even more serious consequences.

Accountability does not make every person out on the road a good driver, nor does it ensure that people always drive safely, but it does ensure that drivers are always aware that they can be held accountable for bad driving and has reduced the number of road traffic accidents that would otherwise occur.

The number of potential spammers is fortunately much fewer than the number of potential bad drivers.

Who to Hold Accountable

To make accountability work, we need to determine who to hold accountable. The Internet has a billion users; we cannot build a system that can hold each user personally responsible. We don't even know who those users are.

The traditional accountability mechanism of the Internet worked in two stages. The Internet is a network of networks that communicate with each other. The networks hold each other accountable for abuses that affect other networks. The individual networks choose for themselves how to control abuse within their network.

In the original Internet, the term **network** was more or less synonymous with **university** and referred to a distinct set of IP and DNS addresses. The MIT network was identified by DNS names that ended in .mit.edu and had IP addresses that started with the number 18.

Over time, the idea of a "network" within the Internet became much more complex. Corporations—mostly computer companies—started to join the Internet. Some companies went into the business of providing Internet access, and the term **ISP** (**Internet service provider**) was born.

The structure of the modern Internet looks something like a tree with many branches. The term *network* can be applied to the trunk, to a large branch, to smaller branches, and so on right down to the individual twigs (see Figure 7-1).

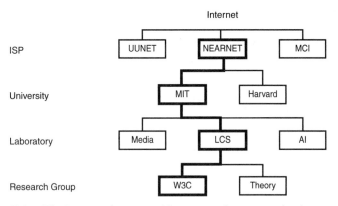

Figure 7-1   *The Internet decomposed into networks at many levels*

The mapping from an IP address to the concept of a "network" is already too complex to make it a practical unit of accountability and will become even more complex over time. The current Internet protocol, IPv4, only allows for 4 billion unique Internet addresses; with a billion Internet users, we are already running out. Deployment of the next-generation Internet protocol, IPv6, described in Chapter 16, "Secure Networks," is a big enough challenge without creating new dependencies on particular IP address assignments.

The natural unit of accountability in the Internet is the DNS name. Remembering a number such as 18.7.22.69 is much harder for people than remembering the name web.mit.edu.

Using names in place of numbers has an operational advantage: It allows management of the network to be separated from management of network applications. I don't want to have to change my e-mail or Web site address just because I have changed my network provider.

If we know with certainty that an e-mail comes from aol.com and that aol.com implements effective measures that prevent its users from sending out vast quantities of spam, we can predict with a high degree of confidence that the e-mail is legitimate. We cannot expect the prediction to be perfect, however; AOL has tens of millions of users, some of whom will end up behaving in an antisocial manner. But we can expect AOL to maintain a reasonable level of order, weeding out the worst troublemakers and making sure that nobody is sending out thousands of e-mails an hour. If AOL fails to meet this expectation, then e-mail receivers will be less willing to accept e-mail that comes from aol.com.

Like the car license plate scheme, the accountability system has three parts: authentication, accreditation, and consequences:

- **Authentication**—The receiver makes sure that the e-mail coming from aol.com is endorsed by the owner of the aol.com domain.
- **Accreditation**—The receiver determines the likelihood that aol.com would be a source of spam.
- **Consequences**—Should aol.com fail to meet our expectation of being spam free, this should have consequences.

Today there are upward of 100 million domain names. Although many names are inactive and many others are duplicates, these still represent upward of 10 million separate domain names used to send e-mail. It is far too many to expect to hold all of them accountable.

Fortunately, we don't need to. All we need is to know that there is some party that will accept responsibility for the e-mail. That might be the sender listed in the From address, or it might be the ISP responsible for the mail server through which the message was sent. We can be reasonably sure that a message is not likely to be spam provided that there is *some* party willing to be held accountable for it.

Authentication

A system must not provide less security than users expect. The e-mail system fails this test: It is easy to send an e-mail that impersonates anyone the sender chooses.

This vulnerability is not only exploited for criminal gain against banks. Adelyn Lee, a senior executive at Oracle Corporation, was at one time the girlfriend of CEO Larry Ellison. Some time after the relationship between Lee and Ellison ended, Lee was fired, and a messy wrongful termination lawsuit followed that was settled for $100,000. The principal piece of evidence used by Lee to support her case was an incriminating e-mail that purported to have been sent by Ellison to the head of HR. The message was subsequently proved to be fake. Oracle recovered the money, and Lee was sentenced to jail for a year.

The conventional metaphor used to explain the e-mail security problem is to say that sending e-mail is like sending a message on a postcard—anyone can read it. This is a valid point; e-mail messages are not encrypted by default and can be read by operators of the Internet infrastructure that the message passes through. The lack of confidentiality in the e-mail transport system certainly represents a risk, but not the most serious one. The reader can usually tell if a postcard is genuine by looking at the handwriting and signature. Internet messages are more like a telegram than a postcard.

The lack of integrity or the authenticity protections creates much greater opportunities for criminal mischief. Anyone can impersonate anyone he pleases: a friend, his boss, a bank, or the president of the United States of America. This did not matter much in the days before banks and presidents were considered likely to send information by e-mail. Today it is a major security weakness.

This capability was fun for amusing pranks in the early 1990s when the Internet was a research tool. It is rather less amusing now that the Internet is the principal engine of world commerce.

The lack of an authentication infrastructure for e-mail is a serious security issue, but not one that we need to solve definitively to tackle the problem of spam. Spam is (mostly) a problem of volume, and we can be satisfied with a mechanism that makes it difficult to send forged e-mails in volume. We will return to the bigger problem later on.

For the purpose of spam control, we do not even need to be able to establish the original sender of the e-mail. All we need to do is to determine that there is at least one trustworthy party willing to accept responsibility for it, who can assure the recipient that the message is not likely to be spam.

We have already seen that the Internet uses two different types of addresses. **Domain names** are the part that comes after the @ symbol in an e-mail address. A domain name is designed for people to use and consists of a sequence of letters and numbers separated by dots. An **IP address** consists of a 32-bit number that is conventionally written as a sequence of numbers separated by dots (see Figure 7-2).

hallam@example.com	E-mail Address
example.com	Domain name
10.2.1.2	Internet address

Figure 7-2 *E-mail addresses, IP addresses, and domain names*

Domain names are like a layer of icing on a cake: Although the icing is what you see when you look at the cake, the inside of the cake consists of sponge, and the icing is only on the outside. The domain names are only designed for human consumption and are only used at the very ends of an Internet conversation as a convenient substitute for the Internet address. The routers and fiber-optic cables that provide the Internet backbone only see the IP address.

The Internet provides a directory system called the DNS that maps a human-readable domain name onto a machine-readable IP address. The DNS system was originally designed to work in one direction—from names to addresses. When the e-mail server at AOL tries to send e-mail to example.com, it uses the DNS to convert the domain name into a list of IP addresses of e-mail servers at example.com and chooses one of them to connect to.

Sender-ID/SPF is a lightweight authentication scheme with broad industry support that provides a complimentary process for the e-mail server receiving the message so that it can obtain a list of the official outgoing e-mail servers for aol.com (see Figure 7-3).

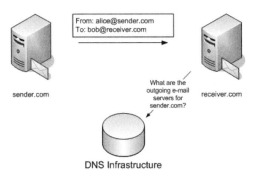

Figure 7-3   *Reverse mail server lookup*

Although the idea is simple in practice and implementing it for a small business such as scones-with-devon-cream.co.uk takes only a few minutes, tracking IP address assignments is a major undertaking in large networks such as AOL, where the infrastructure is always changing. It is like the difference between building a garden wall and building the Great Wall of China: The principles of construction might be the same, but the scale means that issues that are not even noticeable on a small scale become major undertakings.

One layer of complexity is added by the fact that AOL provides e-mail service for more than just the aol.com domain. In addition to networks such as CompuServe that have been acquired by AOL, there are other individuals and companies who use the AOL infrastructure but use their own domain name.

Yet more layers of complexity are created by the two decades of infrastructure deployed when nobody checked the IP address that an e-mail was coming from. It is quite common for an e-mail with a From address indicating that it comes from MIT (mit.edu) to be sent through a Comcast e-mail server. Comcast is the main cable operator in the towns within commuting distance of MIT. In the days when nobody was bothering to check the origin of an e-mail, it made more sense for someone working from home to direct outgoing e-mail through Comcast's e-mail servers rather than MIT. In many cases, the cable company does not even allow a direct connection to any other mail server because abuse of this type of connection was once a favorite method of the spammers.

These complications mean that the term "sent by" could refer to two domain names: the domain name of the e-mail address of the alleged sender and the host address of the e-mail server. Which address should we authenticate? Should we authenticate the e-mail server address or the address that appears in the Sender line of the e-mail message? But wait, there are more complications that have to be considered before we make a choice.

E-mail has been in use for a quarter century. It has become a major infrastructure for social, entertainment, and commercial purposes. As a result, there is no longer a single "typical" e-mail user. Businesses will often hire a specialist e-mail sender to send out large quantities of e-mail such as newsletters, invoices, statements, and hundreds of other items that previously would have involved chopping down trees. Most Internet users are familiar with **mailing lists**, where a message sent to the list is forwarded to people who have subscribed to the list. Yet another curlicue is the need to support alumni e-mail forwarding services. Many people would like to have an e-mail address that they can use and will remain the same for their whole life no matter how many times they change their job or ISP. Universities—particularly in the U.S.—like to keep in contact with their alumni for fund-raising and other purposes. Providing a life-long e-mail address is a low cost for an institution to keep in contact with its alumni.

The complexity and diversity of the e-mail infrastructure means that there are many e-mail addresses, IP addresses, and domain names that can be associated with a message as it flows through the Internet. Figure 7-4 shows some of the possibilities.

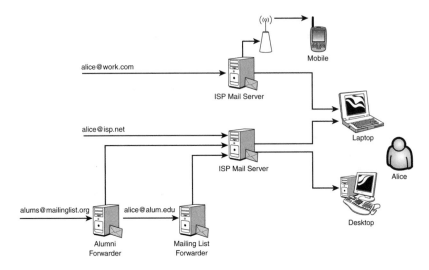

Figure 7-4   *Diversity of e-mail infrastructure*

Each choice of address has advantages and disadvantages. If we attempt to authenticate the sender address of the e-mail, we cannot rely on the IP address of the e-mail server sending it as evidence that the e-mail is forged because the message might have passed through an e-mail forwarder. If we attempt to authenticate the address of the mail server, we meet another set of problems, and it will still be possible for people to send forged e-mail.

Technical discussions over the correct choice of e-mail address to authenticate have consumed encyclopedic volumes of network chatter. Like the question of what color to paint a house, it is a problem where there is no perfect answer and anyone can have an opinion. Fortunately, we do not need to make a choice; *all we need to accept that an e-mail message is not likely to be spam is one trustworthy address that accepts responsibility for the message.*

We need to keep reminding ourselves that all we are trying to do is to establish an accountability mechanism to control spam. We will deal with the forgery problem later.

If an e-mail can be demonstrated to have passed through an official e-mail server for aol.com with a reasonable degree of certainty and AOL Inc. is willing to be held accountable for ensuring that the probability that the e-mail is spam is acceptably low, our task with respect to the spam problem is complete. The authenticated and accredited mail can be allowed to bypass the normal spam-filtering systems, avoiding the risk that the message might end up in a spam folder by mistake and saving time, money, and electricity (see Figure 7-5).

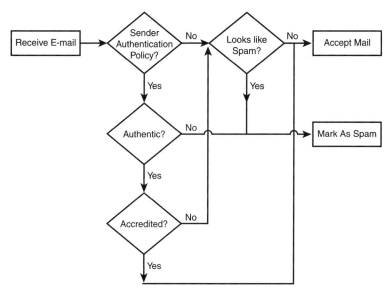

Figure 7-5 *Spam processing with authentication*

For a large ISP, the issue is more than customer satisfaction; the savings in electricity alone can be significant. A fully loaded rack of computing equipment containing a hundred or so processors consumes a large amount of electricity and puts out a phenomenal quantity of heat that requires even more electricity to move. It is depressing to visit the data processing center of a large ISP, see a room the size of a football field filled with machines drawing enough electricity to power a city, and be told that 90 percent of that infrastructure is only there to deal with spam.

A simple means of authenticating outgoing e-mail is to publish a list of official outgoing e-mail servers for each domain in the DNS. The receiving server can then check to see if a message comes from an official source (see Figure 7-6).

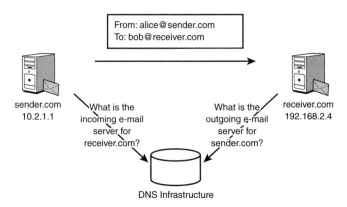

Figure 7-6   E-mail authentication by DNS IP address lookup

Like many ideas in the field, the idea of publishing the mail sender IP address in the DNS has been invented and reinvented a few times. The first known proposal was made in 1997 by Jim Miller. Paul Vixie wrote a formal proposal in 2002, but the spam problem had yet to attract general attention, and the proposal was premature. The idea was resurrected a few years later by Hadmut Danish, but he was unable to build a community of support for the idea. Around the same time, a group of researchers at Microsoft pursued the same idea in a slightly different form under the name Caller-Id for e-mail.

The idea only began to gain critical mass when Meng Weng Wong took ideas from a number of existing proposals to create a scheme he called SPF and succeeded in convincing a group of developers to build systems to make the idea practical. As this grassroots movement was attempting to change the Internet from the ground up, Microsoft promoted its scheme in top-down fashion through an alliance of leading ISPs.

For a while, it appeared that there might be two incompatible standards for authenticating e-mail senders against a list of e-mail server IP addresses distributed through the DNS. After an interesting standards process, we ended up with two documents that describe what is essentially the same scheme in every detail that matters.

The merger of the two documents was ultimately stalled by an obscure legal issue concerning the precise terms on which Microsoft offered to license the patents it had applied for that if issued would apply to its version of the scheme.

Applying for defensive patents is now routine procedure. Junk patents have become a serious problem in the U.S., where the USPTO measures its success by the number of patents it issues regardless of quality rather than the number of bad patent applications it rejects. The USPTO allows exceptionally broad patents and applies a trivial standard for novelty. The cost of litigating patent cases in the U.S. is obscene, as are the damages that have been awarded for numerous patents that should never have been issued. Defending a patent case can easily cost $5 million.

Microsoft offered to license its patent without payment of royalties, but in the wake of a recent court case, it made a subtle change in the traditional terms for providing a royalty-free license to use a patent. This change was then found to be incompatible with the terms under which the open source software community was used to working. A protracted argument among the lawyers ensued, with neither side prepared to give an inch.

After attempts to draft a set of mutually acceptable license terms failed, people started to think about what they really needed rather than what they had been asking for. What software providers wanted was to use the technology without the risk of being sued for patent infringement. What Microsoft wanted was to allow free use of the technology by anyone who did not make a royalty claim against Microsoft for some other patent that the specification might be found to infringe. Both objectives could be achieved without the need for anyone to obtain a license.

Instead of requiring users of the technology to obtain a patent license, Microsoft made an irrevocable promise to grant a royalty-free license to any party on request. These "Open Promise" terms met the needs of the open source community[1] but came too late to stop the production of two rival documents.

Two documents would normally spell disaster, opening up the type of destructive competition that set Betamax against rival video recorder format VHS or the equally pointless competition between high-definition DVD formats Blu-Ray and HD-DVD. In the case of Sender-ID and SPF, however, the differences between the specifications can and should be ignored unless you are designing a spam filtering engine.

Accreditation

Strong authentication tells us with great certainty that a message was definitely sent by the legitimate owner of a domain name that can be bought for ten dollars. If all we have is authentication, the spammers can easily comply; all they need to do is to buy a few thousand domain names. Meeting this need is the function of an accreditation infrastructure such as the Certification Authorities described in Chapter 11, "Establishing Trust."

What we need to control spam is to predict the likelihood that authenticated messages sent from a particular domain name are spam. If the system cannot answer this question with a sufficient degree of confidence, the message might be processed using a spam filter.

An effective way to determine that an e-mail sender is not a spammer is to look at the address book of the recipient. If Alice has sent e-mail to Bob, it is unlikely that she will consider messages that Bob sends to Alice to be spam. If we are sure that the e-mail is really from the purported sender, we can go further and infer that if bob@example.com is not a spammer, we can predict with some confidence that carol@example.com is not a spammer either.

The point of the Internet is to facilitate communication. We are not realizing the full potential of the Internet if we create a world where the only people we talk to are the people we have talked to in the past.

We need a mechanism that makes it possible for any e-mail receiver to receive an accurate assessment of a previously unknown sender's propensity to send spam. Because the recipient does not know this information by definition and the sender cannot be trusted to report his reputation honestly, this information must be provided by a third party known as an **accreditation authority**.

A **reputation authority** is an accreditation authority that reports on the past behavior of an e-mail sender. If someone has been well behaved in the past, it is more likely that he will be well behaved in the future.

Reputation authorities are a necessary part of an accreditation infrastructure, but they are not sufficient by themselves. The past is not always indicative of future performance, and there is not always a past to report on in any case. New businesses are started every day. Relying on reputation alone puts new businesses in a catch-22 situation; to get people to accept their mail, they must establish a reputation, and they must establish a reputation before people will accept their mail.

Validation authorities report on whether the e-mail sender can be held accountable. Specifically, they examine and verify the articles of incorporation of a business and issue a positive report if these are acceptable.

Opinions on the precise definition of spam vary, but accountability is an exceptionally powerful discriminator. The vast majority of spam sent today is unambiguously criminal in intent. If an e-mail sender can prove that he is a legitimate business and provide a verifiable address where legal process can be served, the chance that he is a spammer is small.

There is already an Internet infrastructure established to distinguish legitimate businesses from criminals: the Certificate Authorities that issue the SSL certificates used to secure Internet commerce. We will return to discuss Certificate Authorities in depth in Chapter 11. It is, of course, possible that other companies and other products might emerge to meet this need. For now, however, the important point is that at least one group of businesses is capable of supporting the necessary infrastructure and has established a competitive market and a business proposition that is attractive to customers.

An early pioneer in the accreditation of e-mail senders is the Bonded Sender program started by IronPort, a spam filtering company. Bonded Sender is designed for specialist bulk e-mail senders who send out e-mail on behalf of hundreds of customers. The program is effective and works well for this specialist market, but its costs are substantially higher than the cost of an SSL certificate.

The main problem in starting a mass market for accreditation services is how to reach critical mass. There is little incentive for anyone to buy the services until there are e-mail receivers who take notice of them and little incentive for e-mail receivers to take notice of accreditation data until there is enough to be worth taking notice of.

My first attempt to establish a critical mass was to give away a large corpus of accreditation data that had already been collected. In 2004, VeriSign began making a specially encrypted list of the domain names of its SSL customers available to large ISPs and to vendors of spam-filtering products at no charge. The Verified Domains List (VDL) is created from a database of more than 440,000 active certificates that VeriSign has issued and whose holders have already had their credentials authenticated.

Providing accreditation information at no charge provides a short-term solution to the problem of establishing the critical mass necessary for the accreditation market to grow of its own accord. In the short term, such costs can be absorbed as simply a contribution to the common fight against Internet crime, but this cannot serve the long-term needs of the e-mail users, senders, and receivers, which dictate that all parties, including the accreditation authorities, be held accountable for their actions. No enterprise is going to be held as accountable for a service it provides for the common good as for a product it considers part of its core mission.

If the accreditation market is to be viable in the long term, it must be a profitable one for all concerned. The Internet is now a serious, professional means of communication that demands an equally serious and professionally operated infrastructure. The VDL is not cost free; the domain name holders have paid for a Digital Certificate to be issued to allow them to use SSL; inclusion in the VDL potentially represents a valuable brand differentiator for the VeriSign SSL certificate services. But a brand differentiator cannot hold the attention of a marketing department with the same effect as a revenue source.

For the market to be viable in the long term, we must either persuade people to pay for what they have become used to receiving as a free service or persuade them to buy the service as part of a larger package of e-mail security solutions. The second is the more attractive approach for all concerned. In the coming chapters, we will see how technologies such as Secure Internet Letterhead and strong encryption provide the confidentiality and authentication infrastructure necessary to make e-mail secure.

Consequences

A popular series of technical computing guides has a line drawing of an animal on the cover of each book. A parody T-shirt often spotted at geek gatherings shows the cover of a book in the same style titled *Tracing Spammers* with a drawing of a guillotine.

If accountability is going to be effective, bad behavior must result in consequences. Although you might imagine any number of suitably condign or unusual punishments for spammers, we are in practice limited to more pedestrian measures such as forfeiting a bond, having other companies refuse to accept your e-mail, or in the worst cases, civil lawsuits and criminal prosecutions.

For most legitimate businesses, the most effective consequence is finding that other companies refuse to accept your mail. A marketing department at a medium-sized company might well consider forfeiting a hundred thousand dollar bond as simply a cost of doing business. If the e-mail system stops working, the impact will be felt in the executive suite within a few hours or days and be considered much more seriously.

Critical Mass and the Tipping Point

Earlier I argued that the ideas are the easy part and deployment is where the real problems are found. How then is the spam reduction strategy to be implemented?

Most people proposing an infrastructure-based approach to stopping spam have started from the observation that a small number of ISPs are responsible for the vast bulk of e-mail that is sent and received. The large ISPs and Web mail providers represent at least half of all the e-mail sent and received in all the major Internet markets.

As a result, considerable attention was focused on the anti-spam group originally known as AMEY after its four founding members AOL, Microsoft, EarthLink, and Yahoo. The group later expanded to become the Anti-Spam Technical Alliance with the inclusion of other leading ISPs including BT and Comcast. One of the original objectives of the group was to promote the deployment of technology to make it easier for the sender of an e-mail to convince a receiver that it was genuine. All the major ISPs have been forced to spend a lot of time and effort maintaining whitelists of e-mail senders known to be legitimate. Automating that process represents an opportunity for substantial cost savings by itself.

The problem with the top-down approach is that it is like trying to look for the North West Passage in a supertanker. It might well be that a supertanker is the ideal craft for exploiting the route after it is found. For exploratory purposes, however, something that is somewhat smaller and lighter might be more convenient.

At the time of this writing, the authentication component of the accountability strategy had already gained a critical mass of implementations and deployment. More than eight million domains have published SPF/Sender-ID framework records. More significantly perhaps, the major spam filter providers have either begun using SPF data in their systems or have plans to do so. Microsoft recently announced that it would begin rejecting mail from certain sources that is not authenticated by SPF/Sender-ID. The accountability part of the strategy is less advanced, but an increasing number of antispam vendors are using the VDL and other accreditation services.

We are hopefully past the first part of the S curve where we must still perform the slow process of building critical mass. The part of the curve where the network effects cause deployment to drive itself of its own accord is at the very least in sight.

Eventually a tipping point will be reached. The vast majority of legitimate e-mail will be both authenticated and accredited. Almost all the e-mail that is not authenticated and accredited will be spam. As the remaining spammers attempt to make up for the attrition due to filtering by increasing the volume of mail they send, e-mail filters will treat unauthenticated and unaccredited e-mail with ever-increasing suspicion. At some point, some of the largest ISPs will simply turn off their football field–sized rooms of computers and shut down the spam filters entirely. E-mail that is not authenticated will at best end up in the junk folder.

This situation might appear to be bad for spam-filtering companies; if the spam crisis ends, so will the willingness of customers to pay for costly spam-filtering systems. Fortunately for these vendors, spam filtering represents only the starting point for e-mail security. If e-mail is to be made secure, the mail systems must ensure the confidentiality, integrity, and authenticity of every message that is sent. After the security problem is solved, the relevance problem must be addressed. More than 85 percent of the e-mail messages I receive each day are spam. That still leaves me with the job of managing the remaining 500 messages.

By the time the spammers are finally put out of business, the businesses once known as spam filter providers will be called e-mail security services and provide much more than spam control.

Deploying SenderID/SPF

If you are responsible for an IT system that sends e-mail, you should consider deploying SenderID/SPF.

1. **Resources**—Read the technical documentation on SenderID/SPF. You can find links to the latest versions of the specifications and the latest installation guides in the "deployment" section of http:// dotcrimemanifesto.com/.

2. **Identify your outgoing mail servers**—Identify each of the mail servers you use to send outgoing mail and write out a list of their IP addresses. This task should be straightforward for most mail administrators but might take a considerable amount of time if you have a large or complicated IT infrastructure. While you are doing this, you might want to take a note of the mail server software you are using, because you might need it later.

3. **Create your records**—Microsoft provides a free and easy-to-use Web tool that generates SenderID/SPF records for you automatically. Alternatively, if you like to be sure you understand what is going on, you can read the specifications and code the records yourself.

4. **Publish your records**—To publish your records, you need to be able to insert a TXT record into your DNS zone file. Consult your DNS administrator. If he doesn't know what a TXT record is, you need a new DNS administrator.

5. **Test**—Several Web sites provide testing services. The service provided by the E-Mail Service Provider Coalition tests for both SenderID/SPF and the DKIM scheme are described in Chapter 13, "Secure Messaging." See http://senderid.espcoalition.org/.

Step 2 might take some time if you have a large organization or a complex IT infrastructure. If deployment of SenderID/SPF is going to take you more than a few hours, you will definitely want to read about the Domain Keys Identified Mail (DKIM) e-mail authentication scheme described in Chapter 13 before you start.

You should also consider using SenderID/SPF if you own a DNS domain name and you don't intend to use it to send any mail whatsoever. You might have registered the name for a project that you have not started yet, or you might have registered the name to deter cybersquatters. Don't let a spammer use it! In this case, you will have zero outgoing mail servers, and deployment should take no more than a few minutes.

Key Points

Spam is the result of the e-mail system lacking accountability. To solve the spam problem, we must restore accountability with a strategy that combines authentication, accreditation, and consequences:

- **Authentication**—The receiver verifies that the party purportedly responsible for the message does in fact accept responsibility for it.
- **Accreditation**—The receiver determines the likelihood that the responsible party would be a source of spam.
- **Consequences**—Should the responsible party fail to meet expectations, there must be consequences.

SenderID/SPF:

- Provides a lightweight mechanism that allows the last mail server through which a message passed to claim responsibility for it
- Has a strong base of industry support
- Is adequate for spam control but does not attempt to prevent e-mail forgery

CHAPTER 8

Stopping Phishing

S topping spam is an important objective in its own right, but stopping or even eliminating spam will not by itself stop phishing.

Impersonation spam is only a tactic. Phishing gangs also create fake merchant Web sites, sometimes using a domain name that is a common mistyping of a well-known online merchant. Some use a virus to install spyware; others run Internet cafés with hardware key-loggers built into their machines. It is important to focus on the crime and not just ephemeral tactics. The tactics change, but the basic principle remains the same: Trick the user into revealing his access information, and then use it for financial gain.

Stealing credit card numbers is only one part of a complex criminal ecology. The criminals don't want the card numbers; they want the money. Stolen card numbers are sold wholesale to specialists in turning card numbers to cash, known as **carding rings**. The carding rings can use the stolen card numbers to buy fencible goods online or create actual forged credit cards and sell them to petty criminals who use them in stores (see Figure 8-1).

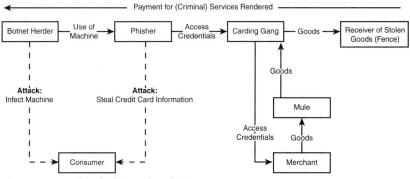

Figure 8-1 *The phishing value chain*

Direct losses due to phishing are significant, estimated to be in the region of $1 billion for 2006.[1] Indirect losses are larger still. The primary product of the banking industry is trust. Each phishing attack reduces trust in online banking. The biggest fear of the major banks is that their customers will stop banking *online* and go back to banking *in lines* at their local branch. This would mean a return to pre-Internet costs and service levels after customers have grown used to the convenience of 24-hour home banking.

Although the direct losses are large, the amounts made by the criminals are likely to be more modest. Fraud tends to have high overheads; a perpetrator might pocket only $5 of each $100 that is lost by the victim. Money laundering schemes tend to involve large commissions paid at each step in the process. Stolen goods are sold at a fraction of their purchase price to ensure a fast turnover. Large losses do not necessarily mean large profits for the gangs.

The Phishing Cycle

A typical phishing attack follows the basic plan shown in Figure 8-2. The perpetrator first sets up a network of anonymous hosts to insulate herself from her criminal communications ❶. Next, a capture site ❷ is established to collect the personal data from the target. The perpetrator then advertises the capture site to the targets ❸ by sending spam through an anonymous host. If the perpetrator is successful, the target reveals his information to the capture site ❹, which forwards it to the perpetrator ❺, ❻.

There are many variations on the basic theme, but three common elements are always required. Think of them as the three Cs.

- **Contact**—The perpetrator must initiate contact with the victim.
- **Capture**—The perpetrator must collect the stolen credentials.
- **Concealment**—The perpetrator must avoid being identified.

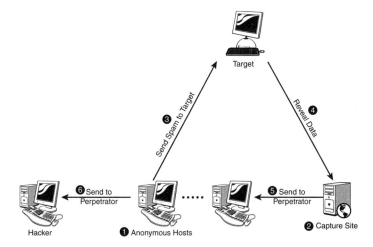

Figure 8-2 *The phishing cycle*

E-mail is likely to remain the favorite method of contact until antispam measures are sufficiently widespread. E-mail allows the criminal to initiate the contact and thus control the timing of the attack. Spyware installed on the user's machine allows a surreptitious approach but depends on the victim actually visiting his online banking account before the capture network is shut down.

Attacks by telephone are the current emerging trend. Internet telephony, otherwise known as **Voice Over IP (VOIP)**, allows an attacker to make many calls at essentially no cost. Currently, the attack is at the gray-market" stage in the U.S., with allegedly legitimate companies routinely making tens of thousands of calls every day in flagrant disregard of the U.S. Do Not Call list and the prohibition on making commercial calls to mobile telephone numbers.

In the e-mail phishing attack, the capture site is a Web site that mimics the look and feel of the bank or other brand that is being impersonated. In a spyware attack, the success of the attack depends on the capture mechanism being active long enough to capture a sufficiently large number of card numbers.

Most customers now understand that they should ignore e-mail requests for personal details. Fewer customers are on their guard during a telephone call. Many banks use automatic attendant systems that require the customer to enter his credit card

number via the telephone keypad, effectively training their customers to respond to this attack.

Credentials of Any Kind

Criminals can turn more than credit card numbers into profit.

- **Bank or Brokerage Account**—The most blatant phishing
  scams ask for account access information for a bank or
  brokerage account. These scams are usually easy to spot
  because the banks already know their customer's usernames and passwords and there is no reason that they
  would ever send an e-mail asking their customer to enter it.

- **Credit Card Number**—Phishing scams targeting credit
  card numbers can be much harder to spot. Any merchant
  selling his product through spam might be running a
  phishing scam. Many of the spammers behind the penis
  potions and other dubious products sold through spam
  have criminal convictions. One well-known spam kingpin
  has convictions for cocaine trafficking and money laundering. Other spammers openly sell pirated software. Would
  you trust a spammer not to sell your credit card number
  to a carding ring?

- **Identity Profile**—An identity profile of a phishing target
  allows the phishing ring to apply for credit in their name.
  The phishing gang looks for information such as the target's name, address, date of birth, and social security number. Partial information from one source can be supple-
  mented with information from other sources.

- **Auction Site Account**—Phishing gangs will impersonate
  any trusted brand that can be used to convince someone
  to part with his money. Getting access to an online auction account with a high reputation rating allows the
  phishing gang to place fraudulent auctions.

Some phishing gangs are scavengers, taking any information
they can and selling it where they can.

Variations on the Theme

Some phishing attacks try to bully the customer by telling him
that there is a security problem with his account, which he must
fix urgently or lose access to his account. Figure 8-3 shows a

subtler variation on the usual theme; it is designed to counter antiphishing measures in three different ways:

- Instead of asking for personal details directly, it announces a new security measure and invites the user to ask for more details.
- The message contains a long URL that appears to be an attempt to exploit a buffer overrun bug in a popular Web browser and gain control of the target's machine.
- If the buffer overrun exploit fails, the recipient is directed to the phishing capture site, but only the first time the link in each e-mail is followed. An ISP following up on an abuse report will see what appears to be a legitimate site.

From: XxxxxSupport [mailto:support-auto75@xxxx.com]
Sent: Friday, October 17, 2007
To: XXXX, XXXX
Subject: Debit Card

Dear customer,
We want to inform that Xxxxx is switching to new
transactions security standards.
Xxxxx ATM services utilize advanced security technology to
protect your personal financial information.
This security update will be effective immediately.

Follow this reference please.
We offer you a new convenient and safe high-quality level of
service to handle your ATM card.
We thank you for cooperation.

Xxxxx customer department.

Figure 8-3   *A subtler approach*

Intervention

An individual phishing attack has three main phases (see Figure 8-4). First, there is the **preparation** phase during which the perpetrator sets up his capture sites, registers cousin domain names, and so on. After the attack starts, it will run undetected for some time until **discovery**. The responder will then attempt to contact the ISP(s) hosting the site(s) for a **takedown**.

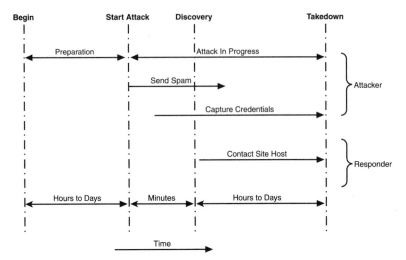

Figure 8-4   *A phishing timeline*

When the phishing epidemic started, most attacks were discovered quickly, almost always within an hour, but often sooner. Shutting down the capture sites took much longer, often days or even weeks. As a result, most early antiphishing measures were concentrated on shortening the time between discovery and takedown.

The perpetrator's profits depend on keeping as many capture sites up for as long as possible. So, even though takedown is the last step in the process, it is easiest to understand the tactics used by the phishing gangs in the preparation phase if takedown is considered first.

Takedown

Most modern businesses consider their brand to be one of if not their *most* important asset. Attacking a well-known brand is a sure way to gain the immediate and focused attention of the owner.

Banks targeted by phishing attacks respond aggressively, calling the ISPs hosting the phishing capture site to demand its removal. When the phishing phenomena first appeared, the phishing gangs would attempt to overwhelm the bank security staff by saturating them with increasing numbers of capture sites and increasing volumes of phishing spam in the hope that the bank might give up.

To meet this challenge, most banks have adopted the tactics

of the phishing gangs, outsourcing the task of contacting ISPs to request and if necessary require a capture site to be brought down. A specialist business with a 24-hour security staff on call is more likely to know the right person to contact and how to reach them.

The cat and mouse game continues, 24 hours a day, seven days a week, and in every corner of the globe. We have found capture sites on machines in homes, schools, government offices, and in one case a fish market. The phishing gangs try to locate their capture sites in places that are as hard to contact as possible, choosing time zones where the business day ended long ago and countries where they hope the language barrier will impede the response most. A U.S. bank might face an attack at 5 p.m. Pacific time from capture sites situated in Riga, where the local time is 3 a.m.

The takedown service provides a tactical advantage but not a strategic solution. Like fitting a burglar alarm to a car, a phishing takedown service does not persuade the criminal to give up stealing, but it does encourage him to pick another target. My customer's immediate needs are met, but the crime continues.

When every new car was fitted with a burglar alarm, the determined criminals learned how to steal cars with alarms. Deployment of tactical measures must be used wisely. If we don't use the time they buy to deploy a strategic solution, we will eventually run out of tactical options.

Discovery

As the time interval between discovery and takedown is closed, it becomes increasingly important to discover phishing attacks quickly.

Phishing gangs prefer to impersonate the real domain of their target in their phishing e-mails. A consumer targeted by a phishing attack is much less likely to respond to a letter from security@a39eu2.biz than security@bizybank.com.

Spam lists inevitably contain large numbers of obsolete or nonexistent e-mail addresses. Whenever a million spam messages are sent out, a significant number will bounce back to the purported sender. In theory, the message should be bounced to a specific address defined in the e-mail standard. In practice, however, there are plenty of misconfigured and misprogrammed e-mail systems that will bounce the message to the e-mail server at bizybank.com. This provides an early warning system for the response teams.

The backwash effect of bounced mail depends on the phishing attack attempting to impersonate the real domain name of the bank; the phishing gangs are already avoiding this, and new discovery techniques will be needed.

Many hosted Web mail systems have a feature that allows users to report phishing. At present, this data is mostly used internally by the hosted Web mail service, but the data could in principle be reported to the banks themselves and their antiphishing services.

Preparation

As methods for takedown and discovery are improved, it becomes interesting to look at prospects for detecting phishing attacks before they are started. Unfortunately, the effectiveness of these techniques typically depends on the phishing gangs not knowing that they are being used, so I can't describe them here.

A preparation step that can be discussed is detecting registration of "lookalike" or "cousin" domain names such as bizybank-security.com or B1ZYBANK.COM instead of bizybank.com.

Most major brands already use services that pre-empt registration of cousin domains by aggressively registering international variations—likely typographic mistakes and names like theirbank-security.com. Unfortunately, the number of variations is usually large, and the cost of maintaining a large portfolio of registrations soon mounts up. There are approximately two hundred top-level domains, and registering all the variations of just one name in every domain can easily cost $100,000. Brands have to be selective in the domains they choose to register.

Digital Brand Management Services were set up in response to the problems of domain name squatting and trademark violation. Phishing is also a trademark violation, of course; the difference is that the reaction must take place in hours, not days. Providing the necessary faster response is a bit like a weekly news magazine trying to turn into a 24-hour cable news channel. The journalists are still doing the same job of reporting news, but to a much more demanding schedule.

Many brand management services are currently transforming their businesses to provide the necessary faster discovery. The problem with this approach is developing a "fast-track" procedure for challenging a fraudulent domain name registration.

The ICANN Uniform Dispute Resolution Policy (UDRP) was adopted in 1999 to respond to a very different set of problems. Domain name squatters would register names of well-known companies to charge the trademark owners exorbitant sums to get them back. Other companies attempted to obtain domain names they had no legitimate claim to but would like to have by threatening an expensive lawsuit.

The timescales built into the UDRP are designed to support a deliberative, judicial proceeding. At the start of the process, the respondent is allowed 20 days to respond. By the time the UDRP has begun, the phishing attack is long since over.

From time to time, proposals are made to change the UDRP to make it more responsive to phishing attacks. But streamlined procedures designed to optimize response to phishing attacks create their own problems by upsetting the delicate balance of interests that the UDRP is designed to protect. Domain names are too important to accept a process that allows them to be cancelled with no time for thought or objection. Companies cannot build a business on a domain name that might be suddenly suspended without notice or appeal.

The best hope for streamlining the dispute resolution process without upsetting the balance of interests is to concentrate on the period immediately following registration. It is unlikely that a company will have built a substantial business around a domain name that has been registered less than a week.

Concentrating on the initial registration period has benefits for the domain name registrars as well as the brands attacked by the phishing gangs. One of the biggest problems the registrars face is **chargebacks**—credit card charges that are challenged by the card owner. It is not unusual for up to 30 percent of registration attempts to be backed by a stolen credit card. The registrar is fined for every chargeback, and if the chargeback rate is too high, his merchant account may be cancelled. What the brand name owners and the registrars really need is a better mechanism for trapping the fraudulent registration attempts by flagging domain names that are likely to be fraudulent.

Intelligence

People often propose "user education" as a solution to the phishing problem. This creates a new problem—agreeing on what is meant by user education.

What I consider to be user education is warning people about the scams and the tricks used by the criminals. Others mean telling the customers that they are the ones at fault.

The light bulb and car existed as curiosities for the rich in the nineteenth century. The great engineering achievements of the twentieth century were the ability to turn on a light without having to understand how that generator worked and the ability to drive a car without having to understand more about its internal operation than the need to insert fuel, oil, water, and air in the appropriate receptacles from time to time. We have to vastly improve the quality of the security interface in the Web browsers before we start thinking about blaming the users. And even then we have to keep in mind the fact that there will always be a significant number of Web users whose ability to protect themselves is limited.

Some phishing attacks do not leave telltale signs unless you know exactly how to look for them. I usually know instantly that a message is a scam because I don't have an account with the bank in question, but it can take five or ten minutes to work out the tricks being used, and I know what I am looking for.

Local Intelligence

We could teach users how to recognize the tricks used by the phishing gangs, but teaching the computer to look for them is a much simpler and more effective approach. For example, a common phishing tactic is to use a disguised hypertext link. The text of the e-mail might suggest checking your account status at www.bizybank.com/, but under the covers, the e-mail actually links to www.phishing-incorporated.crime/.

The problem with building intelligence into the browser is that the phishing gangs tend to be able to switch to new techniques faster than people update their Web browser. In 1995, a Web browser update was released practically every month; today I use a Web browser that is just having its first major update in four years. Even though a new rivalry appears to be emerging between Web browser providers, it is unlikely to return to the frenetic pace of the late 1990s. The new browser competition is focusing on stability, robustness, and security, an approach that we want to encourage rather than the endless accretion of new features.

As the introduction of new browser platforms slackened, companies such as Google and Yahoo have offered "toolbars" that add features such as an improved search capability. Some of these toolbars offer antispyware and antiphishing features. A toolbar need not even be visible to the user to be providing an effective protection against common phishing attacks.

The toolbar approach allows antiphishing protection to be deployed without waiting for the next major browser release, but the release schedule is still too slow to defeat the most persistent phishing gangs. The problem is similar to that of stopping spam. Local rules can be used very effectively to stop a large proportion of attacks, but only until the attackers develop countermeasures. To provide a robust solution, it is necessary to combine local rules with an external information source providing up-to-date intelligence.

The combination of local rules and external intelligence is very powerful. Reliance on external intelligence alone requires a major commitment of resources to provide information in a reliable and trustworthy manner. Reliance on local rules alone is vulnerable to countermeasures. Support for both provides the power of external intelligence with only limited additional cost. The attacker has much less incentive to develop countermeasures to defeat the local rules because he knows that the external intelligence is capable of keeping up with his countermeasure.

External Intelligence

External intelligence is a good thing, but how is it to be found? One source of information for such a service would be the antiphishing takedown services.

One of the big problems with the takedown service approach is that it depends on reaching one of a small number of individuals responsible for the server causing a problem. This is usually fast but sometimes very slow. If it is impossible to reach a responsible person, the takedown service has to walk up the chain of responsibility, calling the ISP that provides its Internet service, the backbone carrier through which it connects and local law enforcement. If all else fails, there are other measures that can be taken, but they cannot be applied on a large scale.

Rather than rely on reaching a small number of individuals, a better approach would be some sort of service that delivers information that can be used to block active phishing sites to a Web browser: a network gateway appliance or e-mail filtering service. The information service would be similar to the old-style spam blacklists but considerably narrower in scope. Such a service would allow for a "virtual takedown" of phishing and spyware sites before the responsible ISP could be contacted.

The Carding Cycle

Stealing credentials is only one-half of the phishing crime. To make a profit, the criminal must turn his stolen credentials into money without being caught. This is by far the most difficult and complex part of the criminal value chain, because the only way for the criminal to profit from his crime is if money or valuable goods are making their way toward the carding ring. The old law enforcement maxim "follow the money" works.

Forged Cards

One of the ways that phishing gangs have been turning stolen credit card numbers into cash is to create fake ATM cards. Until recently, this has been possible using low-cost equipment readily available through the Internet. This is the criminal's ideal means of turning a stolen card number into cash. ATMs are numerous, provide 24 hours of service, and are frequently situated in locations that make any surveillance attempt easy to detect.

In response, most banks now use additional information (called the **CVV code**) that is encoded on the magnetic stripe in the card but does not appear on the card itself. This means that the phishing gangs must obtain more information than a consumer tricked into entering his details into a Web page is able to supply. There is also a second number called the **CVV2 code,** which appears on the back of the card but not on the magnetic stripe. This is used to detect a forged card created using a recording of the magnetic stripe.

These codes were introduced by the credit card companies in the mid 1990s after a spate of incidents in which carding rings used credit card receipts recovered from garbage to create fake cards. Most credit card transactions use the CVV code as part of the authentication process. The same is increasingly true of ATM transactions, although making any changes to the financial services networks is difficult and time consuming, particularly when they affect multiple banks.

It is a bit like treating a bear for a toothache without using anesthetic. In principle, the process of removing the decay and replacing it with a filling is no different from the same operation performed on a human. In practice, we must account for the likelihood of objections from the bear.

The introduction of CVV codes led to the carding gangs using handheld magnetic swipe card readers to **skim** a credit card when it was being used for a legitimate transaction such as paying for the bill in a restaurant. Some of the skimming devices are so small that they easily fit into the palm of the hand.

Carding gangs have also been known to create fake ATM machines to steal credit card numbers, or more subtly, attach a camouflaged card reader to an existing ATM. The gangs will sometimes include a wireless video camera to observe the customer entering his PIN number if they don't have a means of extracting the PIN from the card.

Making a forged credit card is time consuming, and the person using it in person runs a significant risk of being caught. A forgery created using data obtained by phishing will lack the CVV code and is therefore likely to be detected. Carding gangs who make forged credit cards are much more likely to use data obtained from skimming or a fake ATM than from phishing.

Package Reshippers and Money Movers

Criminals were stealing credit card numbers long before the Internet was invented. The Internet allows the phishing gangs to steal very large numbers of credit card numbers. There would be no point in doing this unless the carding gangs had found a way to turn large numbers of credit cards numbers into cash.

The solution that the gangs have found is to use **mules**, the package reshippers and money movers mentioned in Chapter 1, "Motive." Some are dupes; many are willing accomplices. In either case, the recruit is in for a nasty shock when he discovers that his real job is to be the person who gets caught.

The fraud detection schemes put in place by the banks, brokerages, and card associations are accountability based: They don't prevent fraud, but they make it much more likely that the perpetrators will suffer consequences.

The carding gangs circumvent the accountability schemes by recruiting mules to take the consequences while they take most of the money. The mules don't get to wear smart uniforms or carve out the inside of a volcano like Blöfeld's minions in *You Only Live Twice*, but they are just as expendable.

When the mules get caught, they face the probability of prison time. They are also likely to be required to repay all the money that they have transferred out of their account. The transfers of stolen money into their account will be cancelled, but not the transfers out of the account. The recruit is usually left with a huge debt.

Some gangs even use the personal information they obtained while recruiting to perform an identity theft on the mule after he has stopped working for them.

The recruits receive a triple-whammy: prosecution, debt, and ruined credit.

The carding gangs behave in ways that should make their employees suspicious. All contact is through e-mail; the gangs avoid accepting mail or making a telephone call that could be traced. Despite this peculiar behavior, some carding mules are genuinely fooled; they only realize that what they thought was their great new job has gotten them involved in organized crime when the police knock on their door. Others understand that they are involved in something "dodgy" but don't realize that they are risking jail and bankruptcy.

Some carding rings use a "chocolate and flowers" approach. The carder finds a lonely heart online, befriends her, and after gaining her trust, asks if she could forward a package to him as a favor.

Auction Fraud

Bank phishing is an attack against a trusted brand. Online auction fraud applies the same principle but targets a reputation feedback score, the brand of a private individual rather than the brand of a well known bank.

I discovered a fraudulent auction placed by a criminal gang a few weeks after Motorola launched its RAZR phone.

The seller had 39 positive feedback responses with no complaints, apparently a trustworthy vendor. Looking more closely, this was the first time the seller was selling something; in the previous auctions, he had always been the buyer. This is not necessarily proof of fraud—everyone has to start sometime—but most people do not begin their career dealing in cell phones, and those who do are unlikely to be able to offer a model so hard to get that the established dealers had not received their stock yet. And if they were a genuine dealer, they would certainly want to receive close to the $499 list price for a model with such high demand rather than offer it brand new for $160.

The seller's profile said that he lived in the U.S., but the cell phone was being offered priced in Australian dollars, and the description of the goods stated they were being shipped from Eastern Europe.

Suspicious, I contacted the seller and received a rapid reply that confirmed my suspicions (see Figure 8-5). Not only had the price jumped up (although still a good deal), but the seller was now proposing to sell the phone direct, avoiding the auctioneer completely, and wanted to be paid by wire transfer rather than the payment mechanism supported by the auction house, which would be guarded by fraud protection measures. This would allow the "seller" to collect his payment from the wire transfer office, and there would be no way to catch him after he left the building.

First I want to tell you that my items are brand new, unopened box
all accessories included and also an international warranty.
My price is the best you could get 350$unit, including the
shipping and insurance taxes. We will pay them because the package
will be delivered from Europe.
We have also a %10 discount if you'll buy it from us in less than 24
hours from now on.
As delivery service we use FedEx air service (with insurance and
15 days return policy), because it's the faster. And if you will have
a quick payment, we must also have a quick delivery. So that's why we
use as a payment method Western Union money transfer, the fastest and
also very secure way of sending money.
So, if you agree with my terms I'm sure that we can close the deal as
soon as possible.
Waiting your quick answer right now,

Figure 8-5   *Reply from fraudulent auction offer*

Stopping Carding

If carding is stopped, there will be no demand for phished credit card numbers. The first step in stopping carding is to make as many people as possible aware of how the carding gangs work, and that anyone who gets involved in one of their schemes is going to find out that it's the job from hell.

The next step is to do what law enforcement has always done when investigating serious financial crimes: Follow the money.

The activities of carding mules leave a distinctive pattern if we learn how to look for it. Whenever a package reshipper is recruited, he will suddenly start to receive deliveries of goods bought using a large number of credit cards, all with different billing addresses. This is a pattern of activity that the businesses that support Internet payments can look for and investigate.

Sting operations are already proving effective in tracking the activities of phishing gangs. The phishing gangs are given active credit card numbers with spending limits carefully chosen to allow enforcement by the FBI. Each time one of the cards is used, the alarm bells go off.

Schemes of this type have the potential to provide a process that law enforcement can apply repeatedly with a success rate that is both measurable and predictable.

It would be interesting to take the process a stage further and infiltrate the carding operations with undercover money movers and package reshippers. The most productive approach to this type of investigation would be a collaboration between law enforcement who have the powers to do this type of work and the businesses involved in Internet commerce, the merchants who sell the merchandise, the payment services that process the payments, and the shippers who transport the packages. Similar collaborations between law enforcement and banks have led to arrests in money laundering cases; it is time to apply the same techniques in this field.

Anything that can be done to make the carding gangs suspicious of and distrustful of the mules they recruit adds to their cost of doing business. The higher the cost of doing business, the less attractive the crime becomes. Let the carding gang receiving a shipment wonder whether the packages contain the digital cameras and computers they ordered or another GPS homing device and a couple of bricks to make up the weight like the last one.

Conditions for Success

Phishing is a tactic; bank fraud is the goal. We have identified responses that are effective against specific phishing tactics such as the e-mail lure.

- Disrupt attacks in progress.
- Prevent theft of credentials.
- Prevent use of stolen credentials.

All we need to do to stop phishing is to establish a condition where another form of bank fraud is more profitable to the perpetrators. To stop bank fraud, we must apply these techniques across the whole Internet infrastructure and not just the parts that the criminals target today.

To succeed, we must understand that although no bank likes to lose money, it is the indirect losses due to Internet crime rather than the direct loss that most are worried about. In particular, the bankers I work with ask me for ways to

- Reduce calls to customer service centers
- Justifiably restore confidence in Internet security
- Reduce the profits made by the perpetrators

The last point is particularly important; many banks are quite prepared to spend $2 to recover a $1 fraud loss. Equally important is the fact that no banker has ever demanded an antiphishing solution that is guaranteed to be 100 percent effective. Banks are in the business of risk management; they do not demand a perfect solution.

Disrupting Attacks in Progress

Disrupting attacks in progress increases costs and lowers rewards for the attacker. Even modest efforts to disrupt attacks in progress can result in disproportionate benefits as attackers switch to more profitable targets.

- **Detect planning for attacks**—The ideal outcome is to stop an attack before it has started by detecting tell-tale signs of planning, such as registering domain names or running a Web crawler on target Web sites.
- **Block contact mechanism**—Most phishing attacks involve a large number of contact attempts made in a short period of time. If the contact attempts can be detected and characterized as such, it might be possible to cause further contact attempts to be blocked.
- **Takedown capture sites**—The longer a capture site is active, the more credentials the attacker can steal and the greater his profit. Contacting the ISP hosting the capture site and persuading him to take it down reduces losses.
- **Block capture sites**—Getting an ISP to take down a capture site can take too long. Circulating blacklists of active phishing sites allows attempts to access the sites to be blocked in the browser or in the network infrastructure until the capture site itself is taken down.

Preventing Theft of Credentials

Phishing is generally presented as a problem caused by the Internet, but the real root cause is the inadequate authentication mechanisms used by the banks, credit card systems, brokerages, and so on. Strengthening both infrastructures to make it harder to steal credentials is necessary.

- **Prevent platform compromise**—Spyware is only possible because the software platforms we use have flaws. Web browsers, e-mail clients, and operating systems are all written in ways that allow them to be compromised. In addition to making these platforms resistant to attack, we must reduce the propagation of the attacks themselves.

- **Prevent impersonation of trusted party**—E-mail phishing is effective because e-mail allows the attacker to easily impersonate a party that the target already trusts. Preventing such impersonation through strong authentication infrastructure is essential.

- **Use theft-resistant credentials**—Phishing is credential theft. Phishing becomes impossible if it is not practical or possible to steal a usable credential, as the strong authentication technologies such as One Time Password tokens (OTP) and smartcard described in Chapter 14, "Secure Identity." are designed to ensure.

Preventing Use of Stolen Credentials

Even if the credential is stolen, all is not lost. The (direct) loss occurs only when the credential is used successfully.

- **Fraud intelligence networks**—To use a credential, the criminal must in most cases use a compromised machine. Because the number of compromised machines is finite, the same machines are used in attack after attack. Sharing of fraud intelligence data allows compromised machines to be identified more rapidly, allowing use of stolen credentials and possible man-in-the-middle attacks to be detected.

- **Multilevel security**—Any access to an online bank account is a potential confidentiality compromise, but only specific types of behavior (transfers out of the account, adding a new payee, and so on) result in a profit to the attacker. **Two-level access schemes**, in which a password is sufficient to read the account but a second password or a stronger means of authentication is required to perform riskier operations, provide greater security when it is required.

- **Risk management**—For decades, credit card companies have used risk scoring systems that detect suspicious behavior. Modern computing and network infrastructure allows risk management systems to be tailored to the individual account holder, detecting patterns of activity that are unusual for the particular customer.

Adapting to Survive

A final component of our solution must be constant review and constant vigilance so that emerging threats such as telephone phishing do not need to become a major problem before remedial action is taken.

Key Points

- The objective is to steal the money.
  - Impersonation spam is only one tactic.
- Phishing and carding are processes.
  - The details change, but the basic elements are constant.
  - We must focus on disrupting the process.
- Tactical and Strategic approaches must be balanced.
  - Tactical approaches have immediate benefit and commercial potential.
  - Strategic approaches change the environment.

CHAPTER 9

Stopping Botnets

In computer security, a **Trojan** is a program that contains hidden malicious code. Tools circulating on the Net allow code to be added to any program file to turn it into a Trojan. When the modified program is run, the extra code runs in the background.

Before the Internet, the worst a Trojan (aka virus) could do was to "trash" the infected machine: delete a few files, write rude messages, make some noise. Machines with access to the Internet provide the attacker with much more scope for exploiting the captured machine. Installing a "backdoor" program allows the attacker to control the machine remotely. He can install any program he wants, open or close the CD drawer, or even turn on a video camera to watch the user if there is one.

A machine under control of an attacker is known as a **bot**. Controlling a bot allows a range of malicious actions to be performed.

- Cover their tracks.
- Attempt to take over other machines.
- Perform a denial-of-service attack.
- Send spam.
- Perform premium rate fraud.

The scope for malice increases considerably with the ability to control multiple bots. A network of bots is known as a **botnet**. A problem such as breaking a password that might take a year on one machine can be completed in half a week on a botnet with 100 machines.

Self-described "elite hackers" claim control over networks of thousands or even tens of thousands of machines. Such claims need to be taken with some caution: Although there are certainly some large botnets in existence, most are small, and it is not a trivial matter to create or manage a large botnet.

Gaining control over a machine is only the start. The attacker must fend off attacks from others as well as the owner's efforts to restore control of his own property. Wars between botnet operators are common.

The commands supported by a common botnet control program give a good indication of their use.

- Check a credit card number.
- Perform denial-of-service attack on another machine.
- Scan another machine for vulnerabilities.
- Create an encrypted connection to control another compromised machine.

The use of botnets makes tracing an attacker more challenging. An attack might be distributed over a series of machines rather than coming from a single source. For example, the attacker might try a "port scan," attempting to connect to each TCP/IP port reserved for system use (port numbers 1 through 1023). An attack coming from a single location is easily detected, and the firewall protecting the target can block further connection attempts from a source after a certain number of failures. The attacker can bypass a limit of 10 connection failures by making the attack through a network of 100 machines (see Figure 9-1).

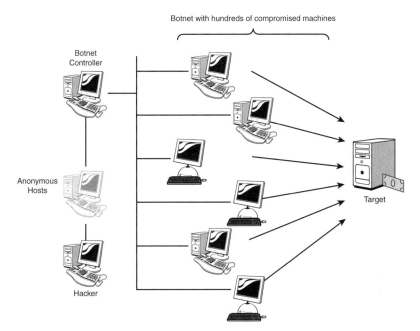

Figure 9-1   *Making an attack harder to identify by disguising the source*

Where Biological Analogies Fail

Biological diversity is an effective protection against biological disease. My parent's house is on a wooded riverbank. The woods once had horse chestnuts and elms. The horse chestnuts still stand, but there are no elms anymore. Almost every elm in Europe died in less than a decade, killed by Dutch elm, a fungus growing underneath the bark. Unlike most trees, elms do not produce nuts; they spread through shoots that emerge from the roots. This allows the shoots to concentrate on outgrowing their competitors for the light at the roof of the forest. Unlike a tree that grows from a seed, each shoot contains an exact copy of the genetic material of the parent. If one member of an identical population is vulnerable to a disease, then so is every other.

More than nine out of ten computers in use today run a version of the Windows operating system. There is almost no diversity in the computing gene pool, a fact that is sometimes pointed to by advocates of one of the platforms making up the minority 10 percent as being a security issue.

Like many advocacy arguments, the diversity argument is superficial. Every organism produced by sexual reproduction is genetically unique (except for identical twins). Every computer system with the same operating system software installed is essentially identical. A hundred operating system platforms would not come close to matching the diversity of biological systems. The advocates want to move from one platform to two or three, an insignificant change.

Nor is diversity particularly successful as a survival strategy for the individual organism. We get sick; we die. Diversity serves the survival of the species, not the individual. Biological viruses adapt their attack strategies slowly through the process of Darwinian evolution. Computers are not biological organisms, and viruses are the product of human intellect and follow the Lamarkian pattern of evolution, otherwise known as **intelligent design**.

There is, however, an advantage to using a minority platform, albeit a small and diminishing one. Platforms with few users are a less attractive target for the professional criminal than those with many users.

This was particularly the case with old-style viruses, which spread through the power of exponential growth. A virus infecting twice the number of machines with each successive generation will grow rapidly, reaching a million machines in 20 generations. A virus that spreads to an average of less than one machine per generation will quickly become extinct. A virus attacking a minority platform with one-tenth the market share of the market leader must be ten times more potent.

Modern viruses do not spread exponentially; indeed, they are not analogous to a biological virus in any meaningful sense. Modern virus attacks are blasted out from a botnet at rates of ten million an hour or more. An attacker who targets a minority platform will capture fewer machines, but the machines caught might be more valuable. Users of minority platforms are more likely to have high-power machines connected to fast Internet pipes. After they are captured, it is less likely that the attacker will face competition from another attacker.

Stopping Infection

Prevention is better than cure. If the botnet problem is to be controlled, we must make it as difficult as possible for the criminals to recruit new machines.

There are two principal strategies for infecting a machine: The attacker can look for a bug that allows him to bamboozle the machine into running code that it should not, or he can try to bamboozle the user into causing the code to run by disguising it as a Trojan.

Blocking Bug Exploits

"Let he who is without sin among you cast the first stone."
—John 8:7

Computer systems always had bugs and probably always will. Advanced programming techniques called **formal methods** allow a program to be proven correct with respect to a specification. But this leaves us with the problem of bugs in the specification.

The Internet criminal requires a specific type of bug, a bug that allows him to gain control of a machine by sending it a particular stream of data, not merely the type of error that results in a minor annoyance such as the £2.3 trillion ($4.4 trillion) electricity bill one man recently received in the UK.[1]

Engineers argue over which computer, which editor, which operating system is best the way sports fans argue over their teams. Inevitably, security is recruited as an argument.

We trust what is familiar to us. I remember when traditional mainframe folk would criticize VMS as lacking the security features necessary for "serious corporate computing." Later VMS folk derided UNIX in the same terms. The current argument between UNIX and Windows advocates does not differ in either form or substance.

The number of security vulnerabilities is irrelevant; the attacker only needs one to succeed. Much more important is how widely the vulnerability is known and how quickly a vendor fixes known security issues.

Many bugs could compromise security in principle but, in practice, one class of programming error has dominated reports of security vulnerabilities for more than a decade: the buffer overrun.

The basic principle of the buffer overrun was described by Aleph1 in a 1996 article in the hacker magazine *Phrack* called "Smashing the Stack for Fun and Profit."[2] The basic idea is to send the targeted computer an unexpectedly long sequence of data. If the programmer has not handled this properly, the sequence of data can be written right past the end of the data storage area, corrupting the memory location where the computer stores a particularly important piece of information, the address of the next program instruction to execute. This allows the attacker to gain control over the machine.

Bugs might be inevitable, but buffer overrun bugs are not. FORTRAN, the programming language of the 1960s and 1970s, had bounds checking built in to prevent buffer overrun conditions. State-of-the-art programming languages such as Java and C# have memory management techniques that prevent buffer overrun conditions.

What is now understood to be common sense was largely ignored during the 1980s until Java appeared in the mid 1990s. All the major operating systems in use today are written in either C or C++, languages that regard preventing buffer overruns to be the task of the programmer rather than the computer.

None of the computer systems we use today has really been designed for use on a global computer network that can be accessed by anyone in the world.

Although buffer overruns are the most common type of exploit, they are not the only type. Programmers like to add features to programs, particularly features that appeal to programmers, such as the ability to write programs. This is the reason that I can in theory write a chess program in Excel or Word, a capability that I find entirely mystifying. Nor is this an area where UNIX fans can claim superiority. It is not only possible to write a chess program in the UNIX program editor emacs, but there are people who consider emacs a natural platform for writing a chess playing program, and emacs users have several to choose from. You can even have two copies of emacs play each other over the Internet.

The problem with programs that provide this level of flexibility is that it is difficult to be sure that it does not provide an entry point for a Trojan. It is a bad thing if you open a spreadsheet and find that everything on your hard disk has been erased.

Firewalls

The only way to be certain that a machine is never compromised by a network attack is to disconnect it from the network entirely and make sure it never sees a USB memory stick or CD-ROM. This provides a high level of security at the cost of significantly reduced functionality. Machines used for exceptionally security-sensitive tasks are often configured this way, but most users need the network to do their jobs.

A firewall provides a better compromise; unnecessary network functionality is disabled and only functions that are necessary and acceptably safe are allowed.

Firewalls use a variety of techniques, but one of the most useful is to differentiate between communications that are initiated inside the protected network and those that are initiated outside.

Acting as an initiator is inherently less risky than acting as a responder. If you are the initiator, you control when you communicate and who you communicate with. If you are the responder, you lose that control. Blocking incoming communications significantly reduces the degree of risk for the user.

Today there are two basic types of firewall in common use. A **border firewall** is a device that patrols the connection between a local network and the Internet. A **personal firewall** is a program that runs on a computer and controls the network connections of just that machine (see Figure 9-2).

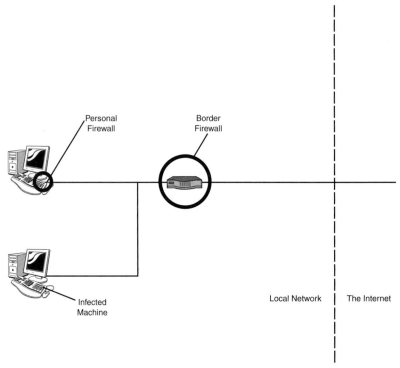

Figure 9-2   *Border and personal firewalls*

Firewalls are an effective but not infallible security measure. Some people treat a firewall as if it was a magical amulet that makes the wearer invincible. These people tend to end up in the same sort of situation that a lot of drivers of 4-wheel drive vehicles end up in each winter here in Massachusetts. Each winter, half the cars I pass buried in snow drifts are 4-wheel drive machines driven by overconfident drivers.

Firewalls are a perimeter security measure. A fence can stop the bad guys from getting out (or in) but cannot do anything about the bad guy who manages to sneak around it. Many of the most serious enterprise security problems come from inside the network. The biggest security threat for an enterprise is almost always the disgruntled (or merely corrupt) employee who is upset about not getting a promotion or having alimony deducted from his paycheck or for any other reason he might choose, justified or not.

A firewall is not even a fence; it is more like a gate with a gatekeeper. A gate is only as good as its gatekeeper.

Managing enterprise firewalls is a complex task that is increasingly being outsourced to specialist "Managed Security Services" providers. It is unusual but not exceptional for an engineer auditing the existing firewall configuration at a new customer site prior to bringing the systems under management to discover that a firewall has been configured to allow any traffic through in either direction. Instead of buying a hundred thousand dollar firewall, the customer could have achieved the same effect with a five dollar cable. This is usually the result of the firewall being "temporarily" short circuited to diagnose some sort of network problem, such as deployment of a new project. After the project is up and running, victory is declared, and nobody remembers to restore the firewall.

A high-capacity enterprise firewall installation can cost hundreds of thousands of dollars. For home use, a device called a **cable/DSL router**, also known as a **NAT box**, does an adequate if less than ideal job for $50. Most "WiFi" access points used to set up a wireless network support this feature.

If you have a high-speed Internet connection, you should get a NAT box. A NAT box does not provide perfect security, but there is no other security tool that costs less than $50 that does as much. If you have a laptop computer, you can pay a few dollars more for a wireless router that allows you access to the Internet from any room in your house. Just make sure you turn on the encryption feature, for reasons we will return to shortly.

The primary purpose for which cable/DSL routers are sold is to share one high-speed Internet connection among several computers. It is still a good idea to buy one even if you only intend to connect up one machine. When these devices first appeared, several cable Internet providers saw them as a threat to their revenues and tried to discourage use. After a short time, however, the companies realized that reducing the risk of machines being compromised reduced their customer support costs. Most cable companies and virtually all DSL companies in the U.S. now allow them, and many are beginning to encourage use.

E-Mail

With the benefit of hindsight, it is easy to see that it is a bad idea for an e-mail program to run a program file attached to an e-mail message at the click of a mouse.

Unfortunately, hindsight does not fix the millions and millions of e-mail programs still in use that work this way. Even a pop-up message to warn the user against running a program from an unknown source only protects those who take notice of it.

The virus problem would virtually disappear if only we could persuade users not to run programs sent to them as e-mail attachments. But user education is not going to provide a solution to this problem. The dangers of e-mail attachments will never be as readily apparent as, say, the risk of deep frying a turkey in highly inflammable oil using a gas burner on a wooden deck attached to a house. America has a new thanksgiving tradition that has led to several Americans burning their house down each year.

The warning on Martha Stewart's Web site[3] neatly illustrates the problem with user education, "This recipe should be made outdoors; making it in the kitchen is too dangerous." The warning does not give the reason for the danger, so a reader who is aware of the risk of carbon monoxide poisoning might reasonably assume this is the only risk and that the wooden deck attached to his house is a suitably ventilated location and thus overlook the risk that hot oil would spill over the edge of the cooking pot, to be ignited by the burner and set fire to first the deck and then the house.

As e-mail programs have tried to close this loophole, the attackers have looked for ways to reopen it. The "Bagel" virus spread itself as an encrypted file attached to a message giving the decryption key. This represents a measure of success because even though this tactic allowed the virus to evade the antivirus filtering mechanisms in place, the method it used to do so made it harder for the intended target to turn himself into a victim.

Blocking Executable Code

If it is a bad idea for e-mail programs to allow users to execute programs sent in mail, one would think it a good idea to block executable code in mail. Until recently, the consensus was that this is an excessively draconian measure, which is somewhat odd because I can only remember three occasions in which I have done anything of this sort in the past 30 years. I would not expect most users to try this, let alone decide that they need it. More oddly still, many of the people making the objection work for companies that already have filters in place that block executable programs of any sort and don't seem to be aware that they have them.

The current default corporate security setting is to scan e-mail using an antivirus product that attempts to detect malicious code using pattern recognition techniques. When the antivirus company engineers detect a new virus, they publish a new virus **signature** that tells their filtering products how to detect it.

Like the battle between the spammers and the blacklist maintainers, pattern matching is a never-ending game of whack-a-mole. The virus writers are always developing new tricks and techniques to evade the antivirus filters. To be effective, an antivirus filter must be updated with details of the latest attacks. Selling subscriptions for updates is a profitable business model for the antivirus vendors but means that only a small proportion of machines have up-to-date filters.

Business users are generally willing to pay for state-of-the-art antivirus systems. A Trojan that infects a machine in their network is likely to attack their network from within. Persuading consumers to pay for antivirus scanning is much harder. The users who are willing to pay to protect themselves against viruses are the ones who are least likely to cause a problem.

An antivirus filter can help prevent my machine from being infected by a virus but cannot protect me against a denial-of-service attack or spam or a phishing attack from somebody else's machine that was recruited into a botnet because it had no filtering. If we are going to deal effectively with the botnet problem, we must do more than simply protect our own machines against Trojan infection; we must find a way to protect almost every machine against infection. This is not going to be possible unless the protection is practically free.

As we just saw, old-style viruses spread exponentially. If the virus was identified quickly enough, a pattern could be distributed before the trickle of attacks became a torrent. Modern viruses harness the power of botnets. The attack starts without warning at full strength. By the time a signature is published, the attack is over. We must find a new approach.

Blocking *every* message that contains a program file is simpler, cheaper, and more effective than trying to distinguish good code from bad. This approach requires no subscriptions, no updates, and provides protection even when the virus has never been seen before.

As Marcus Ranum puts it, we must stop looking for badness and start looking for goodness instead.[4] Only e-mail that is known to be safe should be accepted.

If every ISP made blocking e-mails with executable attachments their default configuration, the virus problem would be limited to code exploits. The blocking system would require minimal maintenance after it was deployed.

I do not accept the objection that blocking program files is an unacceptable restriction on the use of e-mail. Most users never notice. The tiny number of users who notice and object might be allowed to receive program files after paying for a subscription to an antivirus scanning service.

Most forms of executable program are easy to block outright. The mail message has a label called "Content Type" that describes the type of data being transmitted. Unfortunately, there are a number of what protocol designers call "corner cases" because solving them is a bit like the problem of how to cut a tile to fit in the odd-shaped space in the corner of a room.

Document data formats that allow embedded programs create one class of corner case. We can all manage without sending programs in e-mail. Without the ability to send word processor documents, spreadsheets, and presentations, we lose much of the power of e-mail.

Part of the solution is already in place. Most applications that support scripting (programs embedded in a document) warn the user before running a program. Future versions of these programs will support a "sandbox" type of security model allowing scripts that are potentially harmful to be distinguished from those that are harmless.

The robustness of these controls could be improved if the e-mail message processor stamped each potentially hazardous incoming message attachment with a label that signified "received through e-mail; treat with caution." In a corporate scenario, where users are expected to run only the latest, known-to-be-secure versions of programs, it would not be a problem if adding this label rendered the file unreadable by legacy application programs. This would be so much the better because it would force employees with older programs to upgrade to versions that enforced the restrictions.

Another class of corner case is created by file formats that take a whole collection of files and turn them into a single unit. The main file format used for this purpose on Windows is called ZIP. There is also a UNIX equivalent called tar.

Both the ZIP and tar formats are well-defined standards supported by a large number of software producers. Unpacking the files and examining each one in turn to see if it is a suspicious executable program is only a matter of including the necessary code in the blocking software.

E-mail encryption presents a challenge regardless of whether we are looking for goodness or badness. No filtering system can block dangerous content in content that it cannot read. This is a problem that we will return to when we consider e-mail security in Chapter 13, "Secure Messaging."

Shared Folders

Another trick that viruses use to spread is to copy themselves into any place they can find that is shared between machines. This allows a Trojan that has compromised one machine in a corporate network to spread to other machines. The same trick can also be used on a small scale to compromise a home system through an insecure wireless network—another reason for people to turn on encryption on their wireless network.

Another charming tactic of the shared folder virus is the pornographic filename. It's not just porn-hound Bob who might look at a file named hotlesbians.sci. When Alice, his boss, finds the file, she is pretty certain that it should not be there, and she opens it to check.

A shared folder virus is like a landmine—it might be days or years before it is triggered. Antivirus scanners provide a measure of protection, but we are still stuck looking for badness.

To deal with the shared folder virus effectively, we need to completely rethink how we go about computer security. Instead of looking for bad code, we need more effective means of identifying legitimate code. We return to this issue in Chapter 17, "Secure Platforms."

Curing the Disease

When prevention fails, we must cure the patient.

One of the biggest problems many computer specialists face today is the number of their friends and relatives asking them to clean spyware off their machine. At one time, people assumed the most likely explanation for a computer that was behaving oddly was faulty hardware or buggy software. Today, any computer problem that does not involve black smoke pouring out the sides of the machine is immediately put down to a virus or spyware. If black smoke is involved, a perfunctory examination is performed before spyware is blamed.

Traditional security approaches have considered compromise of the machine to be the worst possible thing that could happen. If the machine is compromised, it is "game over," and there is no point in considering the situation further.

The typical consumer does not know any state secrets let alone store them on his home computer. Compromise of the machine is not "game over"; it is a recoverable situation if we have the right tools.

Crimeware Removal

When spyware first appeared, it occupied a middle ground between the outright criminal virus and the programs that the user actually wanted to install on his machine. At first, the antivirus vendors did not realize that their customers required them to remove all the unwanted programs from their machines, not just the ones they classified as viruses. This led to a new class of security program called **antispyware**, which removes unwanted programs after they have installed themselves. Today we recognize no ambiguity; spyware is just another form of crimeware, and the term **malware removal** is more appropriate.

Antispyware programs have two major challenges. The first is to determine whether a machine is infected. The second is to remove any infection that is found.

The problem of finding out if a machine is compromised became apparent after the notorious hacker Kevin Mitnick attacked Digital Equipment Corporation (DEC) in the late 1980s. DEC had a large corporate network with tens of thousands of machines. Mitnick found a way into DEC's network before the first firewalls were developed. The only way to be sure that Mitnick had not left a nasty surprise behind was to reinstall the operating system on every machine in the company that was connected to the network. This meant that several thousand DEC system administrators had to spend about a week reinstalling operating systems and dealing with the resulting problems. DEC estimated the cost of this exercise at $4 million, considerably more than the $160,000 cost of direct damage and tracking Mitnick down.

The Mitnick episode led to the development of security architectures that created internal partitions within the corporate network so that an attacker who breached perimeter security would not compromise the whole corporate network.

The episode also led to development of technologies to determine whether a machine had been tampered with. The best known of these programs was *Tripwire*[5] developed by Dr. Eugene Spafford and Gene Kim at Purdue University. Starting with the system in a known secure state (or at least presumed secure state), the tripwire program is run and calculates a "fingerprint" of every sensitive file on the machine. The tripwire program is then rerun every day or so, and the system manager is warned about any differences in the fingerprints. If an attacker has managed to leave a surprise, the daily status report catches it.

Realizing the idea in practice requires us to deal with the fact that many sensitive files on a computer system have a habit of changing. Few files are as sensitive as the list of usernames and passwords, but this is expected to change on a daily basis as new users are added, old ones deleted, and existing users change their passwords.

Tripwire was designed for use on large computers with full-time system managers running operating systems with security mechanisms that created a sharp separation between system management tasks and ordinary user activities. This separation is much less distinct on a personal computer, where the user is the system administrator. All the major personal computer operating systems—Windows XP, Linux, Mac—allow for separate user and system accounts. Getting nontechnical users to use this feature is rather hard.

On a 1980s-style minicomputer operating system, most if not all of the programs used by the typical user would be installed by the system manager. The only exceptions would be programs that the user wrote himself—if this was even permitted. At my first job writing code for a machine of this type, I would have to call up a system manager to load a magnetic tape containing mere data, let alone a program. Home users are not going to call up their system manager to ask them to load up the CD-ROM to play *World of Warcraft*.

Spyware detection programs have a much harder job to do than the minicomputer era programs. Modern operating systems provide a lot of places to hide. Fortunately, many powerful antispyware packages are available, each of which scans programs running on the computer and stored on the computer disk looking for the following:

- Known malicious programs
- Signs of modifications to program files
- Unexpected changes to previously detected files
- Changes to critical system files such as the registry in Windows

After we have detected the spyware, the next challenge is to get rid of it. This can be hard, because successful spyware programs have many tricks, including corrupting parts of the operating system.

Antispyware programs have a second advantage: They provide an effective means of ridding a machine of unwanted code of any type. There are several programs that are not exactly spyware but refuse to leave after they have outstayed their welcome. A well-known program that plays sound and music clips has a habit of pestering the user to upgrade it to the latest version. After refusing this request, I discovered a blinking icon in the taskbar. Clicking on the icon gave two options: Upgrade now, or be reminded in two weeks. I decided on the third option: Remove the program from the machine, and block access to the distribution site for the software at the firewall to prevent anyone from downloading it again.

Stopping Transmission

If all else fails and the patient cannot be saved, stop the infection from spreading.

If we have failed to protect our own computer, then let's make sure it is not used to attack the rest of the community. This is not just a courtesy to the rest of the Internet community; reducing the value of a compromised machine to a criminal encourages him to attack a different target.

Stopping transmission can also avoid legal entanglements resulting from a compromise of a machine. There have been several occasions in which the full might of the law has been poised to crush a "hacker" who has turned out to be an entirely innocent home user with a faulty security configuration. At some point, a company that has suffered major damage as a result of an Internet attack is going to file a lawsuit alleging that allowing a machine to be taken over constitutes negligence.

It is much nicer living in a world where people don't need to lock their doors. Unfortunately, it only takes a few criminals to make locking doors necessary. At one point, it was quite common for people to leave their wireless Internet access points open as a courtesy to people who might just be in the neighborhood and looking to download their e-mail. I used to have an open configuration, but I decided this was a bad idea after reading about the Toronto pederast mentioned in Chapter 1, "Motive." who was caught using open wireless access points to surf child pornography Web sites.[6] If the police investigation had started with the seizure of log files kept by the Web site, the innocent owner of the access point might have found himself with some difficult explaining to do to the police.

Reverse Firewalls

The Great Wall of China remains the world's most monumental building feat, requiring more manpower than any other before or since. Hadrian's wall in Britain marking the northernmost effective extent of the Roman empire is 80 miles long and required a permanent garrison of 9,000 soldiers. The Great Wall is 50 times longer—more than 4,100 miles—and if garrisoned in the same manner as Hadrian's wall, it would have required almost half a million troops.

The Great Wall began as three separate walls in the third century B.C., which were only joined to form a single fortification several centuries later. The remains that can be seen today are of the wall built during the Ming dynasty in the thirteenth century onward, when the imperial army had only 80,000 troops. Even by committing every soldier in the army to sentry duty and assuming a four-watch rotation, there would be only five soldiers for each mile of wall. The wall could not have been permanently garrisoned, but construction would not have continued over several centuries if it was merely one ruler's egotistical whim.

The Great Wall had more than one purpose, but it is unlikely that blocking an actual invasion by a foreign army was one of them. The Chinese military classic *The Art of War* advises commanders not to rely on static defenses. Even a garrison of half a million men would only be enough for one soldier every 40 feet or so—hardly enough to repulse an invasion force.

The likely defensive purpose of the Great Wall was to deter raiding parties that would charge in from the north, pillage a town or city close to the border, and then escape with the loot. The wall could not prevent the raiding parties from entering China, but it could stop them from escaping with the loot. It is one thing for a few hundred bandits to sneak over an unwatched stretch of wall in the middle of the night, but it's quite another to escape back over a fully guarded wall carrying large quantities of loot with an army in pursuit.

The conventional firewall configuration protects the internal network from external attack. Preventing attacks in the reverse direction reduces the value of a captured machine to an attacker. Botnet "herders" rent out machines according to utility: how powerful the machine is, how fast its network connection is, and whether there are ISP-enforced restrictions on use. The objective of a reverse firewall is to minimize the value of a machine without interfering with normal use.

Fortunately, there is no conflict. Machines in normal use do not remotely resemble a hacked machine. Normal users do not attempt to send a million e-mail messages an hour or send out packets with false source address information or send ten thousand connection requests per second to the same machine or repeatedly perform DNS lookups without trying to establish a connection.

Implementing these types of control does not require a lot of processing power, which is in any case abundant these days. The "cable router" box I bought for $50 contains a 200Mhz RISC processor, which is as fast as the fastest engineering workstations available in the early days of the Web. Adding a reverse firewall feature to the software would have negligible impact on performance. There are also spare cycles that could be put to use in cable and DSL modems. Deployment of reverse firewalls need not add to the cost of setting up a home network.

Inevitably, some people will complain about any limitations on their use of the Net, just as people complain about the fact that most high-performance sports cars have a top speed that is electronically limited to 155 mph. Almost nobody who complains about the speed limiter has the slightest intention of driving close to that speed, and even if they wanted to drive that fast, they probably couldn't. The objection is not to what they *will* do; what counts is what they *might* want to do.

There is an easy solution to this objection: Enable the reverse firewall by default, but let people who really want to turn it off do so. The vast majority of people will leave the reverse firewall enabled. Even most of the people who would otherwise complain about the infringement of their Internet liberties will leave it enabled.

An easy way to make sure that an attacker cannot disable the reverse firewall is to require the user to type in the serial number stamped on the bottom of the device when he disables it. This is easy for the owner but hard for an attacker.

The big difficulty with deploying reverse firewalls is that they are a measure whose principal benefit is to the Internet community rather than to the individual buying a cable modem or router. It is difficult to convince the companies who make networking hardware that the investment is worthwhile.

There are two constituencies with the power to drive deployment of reverse firewalls. The first is broadband ISPs who buy most of the broadband modems and effectively dictate their standards to the manufacturers. The second constituency is government regulators. It is not desirable for governments to micromanage Internet security measures in general, but governments should take a role in encouraging the adoption of measures such as reverse firewalls that are in the general public interest but might not otherwise be adopted.

Intelligence and Control

Securing the local network is the first part of the problem; our next challenge is to provide security at the level of the **internetwork**, the network of networks that make up the Internet.

If you are in a traffic jam, it is often difficult to see the extent of the problem or its cause. You might be stuck for a few minutes or an hour. If a friend calls to ask what the traffic is like, all you can tell him is that you are stuck; the alternative route might be better or even worse. To understand what is really going on, you need to see more information than is visible from a single point of view.

Responding to an Internet security incident poses the same problem. It is one thing to see a suspicious pattern of activity that might indicate that an attack is in progress, but it's quite another to be able to do anything about it. Sometimes an impending problem is only visible in a global view.

What we need is a way to communicate intelligence on attacks in progress so that information from the target of an attack can be automatically routed to a party that is capable of cutting off the source.

A recent study estimated that there are more than a million zombie computers on the Internet. It is not difficult to identify a zombie machine with some confidence; a machine that is scanning another system for vulnerabilities is almost certainly compromised but might just be a legitimate security check that the target requested. Only the target knows for sure.

Most of the information needed to identify botnet members already exists at one or more of the companies that provide security services. The problem is that these companies can only use the information to protect their customers when what they would prefer to do is to prevent the machines from being used for further mischief.

Today, the Internet response system works through e-mail and the telephone. Taking down a phishing capture site is expensive, time consuming, and can easily take several hours. A more efficient system is needed, one that takes the human out of the loop for routine reports.

INCH

Work on building such a system is currently focused on the IETF incident handling protocol (INCH). As often happens in Internet protocol design, this work is a repurposing of an infrastructure originally designed to meet a different need.

The original INCH working group was set up to allow for automated reports of computer security "incidents" to be reported to a response coordination center such as the CERT at Carnegie Mellon University. CERT was originally set up to coordinate response to computer security incidents in the wake of the Morris worm, which brought down a significant proportion of the Internet in 1988. There are now 170 similar incident response teams around the world.

The emergency response center model works well for the emergencies it was designed to deal with but does not come close to having the resources necessary to track down every attack reported. Most of the "incident response" turns into collecting and analyzing statistics. This is important work—it is the raw material that drives computer security research—but it is not the type of response we require.

We must have an immediate response. This requires the incident report to reach the ISP or other party capable of responding to it. If a bank is targeted by a phishing attack, the incident notification must reach the ISPs hosting the capture site and the botnet sending out the spam.

Meeting this need presents us with a common problem in computer networking. The information we need to solve our task exists somewhere, but we don't know where. We need to find out which ISP is responsible for a particular IP address or DNS domain name.

Fortunately, we already have an infrastructure that is designed to meet precisely this need: the DNS.

Although the main function of the DNS is to map domain names such as example.com to IP addresses such as 10.2.3.1, we can also use the DNS to state where the INCH server for reporting security incidents involving example.com is to be found.

The DNS also works in reverse, allowing the IP address 10.2.3.1 to be mapped back to the domain name example.com. This aspect of DNS is known as the reverse DNS and allows us to advertise the location of the INCH server for reporting security incidents by IP address.

These mechanisms would be sufficient if every packet sent over the Internet had an authentic source IP address or domain name. Unfortunately, the lax approach to Internet security in the early days means that this is not the case. Most ISPs will route any Internet traffic that their customers present to them unchecked, including packets that have a false "spoofed" source address.

When a message is sent with a spoofed source address, any response will be sent to the spoofed address rather than the actual origin. This does not make a lot of sense unless the objective is to perform a denial-of-service attack against either (or both of) the spoofed source or destination address given.

As we saw in Chapter 1, denial-of-service attacks are used to extort money from businesses that rely on their Internet connection. Spoofed source addresses are almost always used.

Even though the source address of the packet might be forged, there is no such thing as a false destination address. Internet routers always try to forward packets to the destination specified.

When we come under this type of attack, we can't know where the attack is coming from. However, we do know which of our immediate neighbors is forwarding the traffic to us, and we can notify them. Those neighbors can in turn determine which of their neighbors is forwarding the attack traffic and notify them. If a sufficient number of Internet backbone providers support the notification protocol, the source(s) of the attack can be run to the ground and appropriate measures taken to stop it.

The final piece needed to complete the puzzle is a business model that provides ISPs with an incentive to accept incident notifications. The incentives are clear; responding to security incidents is a major customer support cost for ISPs, automating the response reduces these costs. Vigilance reduces the incentive to attack a network because any bots established will likely be short lived.

Some people worry that ISPs will refuse to accept incident notifications because this would make them liable for responding to them. If this is the case, we need to educate judges to reject this "head in the sand" defense as clearly contrary to the public good. It is, in any case, not a new requirement, because the Internet protocol standards already require ISPs to accept notification of computer abuse via e-mail. All that is being proposed is a means to make it easier and cheaper to act on the information provided.

Pre-Emptive Data Escrow

INCH and protocols like it might also provide an answer to one of the biggest difficulties when tracking down a computer criminal: unraveling the network of zombies that they are hiding behind. Obtaining log files from an ISP almost always requires a subpoena. When e-mail messages are involved, the law might require an ISP to demand a subpoena before providing the information.

Obtaining subpoenas takes time, particularly when multiple jurisdictions are involved. Often the trail leads from one compromised machine to another. If it has taken too long to get the subpoena that identifies a particular link in the chain, the ISP might have already erased the information that is needed. The next ISP in the chain is also a victim of the attacker and also has an interest in catching them and preserving the evidence. But there is nothing they can do until they know about the problem.

What we need is a protocol to allow ISPs to warn the previous link in the chain that an attack has been detected and that they should 1) preserve data relating to the use of specific machines and Internet addresses and 2) if possible, send a notification to the link prior to them. This would allow attacks to be traced back to their source, making it harder for the attacker to wear the cloak of anonymity, which makes Internet crime so hard to police.

Key Points

- Botnets are established by Trojan applications.
  - There is no longer a useful distinction between Trojans, worms, and viruses.
  - Computer viruses do not act like biological viruses.
    - Diversity is not an effective defense.
    - Evolution is Lamarkian, not Darwinian.
    - Multiplatform viruses have existed for many years.
    - Trojans are distributed en-masse through botnets.
    - Millions of attacks are sent out before an antivirus signature can be compiled.
- Bug exploits are a major cause of infection.
  - Buffer overrun bugs are particularly common.
  - All platforms are vulnerable.
- Executable e-mail attachments are the other major cause of infection.
  - ISPs should block executable attachments by default.
- Reverse firewalls protect the rest of the Internet even if a machine is compromised.
  - They remove the incentive for the criminal.
- We need a mechanism to exchange intelligence peer-to-peer while attacks are in progress.
  - INCH/RID is currently the most promising candidate.

Cryptography

If I had written this book ten years ago, cryptography would have been the topic of the first chapter. The terms *network security* and *cryptography* were considered to be synonymous. Today, we understand that cryptography is merely a useful tool, not a panacea.

What makes network security different from traditional computer security is that without cryptography, each machine in the network is essentially alone; there is no way for a machine to know with any confidence where any information came from unless it was obtained from a direct, physical connection to another machine. The attacker exploits this isolation. Cryptography provides "cement" that allows us to establish durable, trustworthy connections between machines regardless of their physical connectivity.

Like cement, cryptography is a powerful tool that almost every architect will employ in some fashion in almost every building, but there is much more to architecture than the correct use of cement, and few buildings that are constructed entirely out of cement have won public praise and affection.

Cryptography allows us to remove some of the differences between Internet crime and traditional methods that are stacked in favor of the Internet criminal. We must, however, remember that the similarities are at least as important as the differences.

Historical Use of Cryptography

Cryptography was used to keep secrets in ancient Rome. Suetonius describes Julius Caesar's use of a simple cipher in which every letter in a word was replaced by the letter that appears three letters before it in the alphabet:

"If he had anything confidential to say, he wrote it in cipher, that is, by so changing the order of the letters of the alphabet, that not a word could be made out. If anyone wishes to decipher these, and get at their meaning, he must substitute the fourth letter of the alphabet, namely D, for A, and so with the others."
—*Suetonius, Life of Julius Caesar, v56*

The problem with this approach became apparent in the civil war following Caesar's assassination. When Romans fought against Romans, everyone knew the code. This led his successor, Augustus Caesar, to change the imperial cipher to use a one letter shift. In cryptography terms, he changed the *key* from 3 to 1.

"Whenever he wrote in cipher, he wrote B for A, C for B, and the rest of the letters on the same principle, using AA for X."
—*Suetonius, Life of Augustus, v88*

This scheme is easily broken by trial and error because the Latin alphabet in Caesar's day only had 24 letters and thus only 23 possible Caesar ciphers. The **ROT-13** encryption that is sometimes used on the Internet to hide punch lines to jokes or answers to quizzes is a Caesar cipher with a shift of 13 letters. Encrypting twice results in a shift of 26 letters, and the text returns to its original form.

Shifting letters by a fixed number of places does not provide enough variations to be interesting. If we allow any letter to be substituted for any other, we have more than 10^{25} possibilities, a respectable number of variations for any cipher. This is known as a **substitution cipher**; whereby each message is encrypted using the same basic technique (substitute one letter for another), but this technique allows a large number of variations. Our new (larger) key is the substitution table.

The substitution cipher is easily broken, despite the vast number of possibilities, by noting the frequency with which letters appear in the encrypted text. If the letter *r* appears most often in the encrypted text, it is almost certainly being used to substitute for a commonly occurring letter such as *e*.

Solving a substitution cipher is a bit like solving a crossword puzzle. If you enjoy solving crossword puzzles, you might like to try decrypting the message in Figure 10-1.

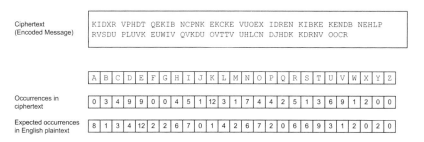

Ciphertext (Encoded Message)	KIDXR VPHDT QEKIB NCPNK EKCKE VUOEX IDREN KIBKE KENDB NEHLP
	RVSDU PLUVK EUWIV QVKDU OVTTV UHLCN DJHDK KDRNV OOCR

	A	B	C	D	E	F	G	H	I	J	K	L	M	N	O	P	Q	R	S	T	U	V	W	X	Y	Z
Occurrences in ciphertext	0	3	4	9	9	0	0	4	5	1	12	3	1	7	4	4	2	5	1	3	6	9	1	2	0	0
Expected occurrences in English plaintext	8	1	3	4	12	2	2	6	7	0	1	4	2	6	7	2	0	6	6	9	3	1	2	0	2	0

Figure 10-1 *Decrypt the secret message*

The substitution cipher can be made much stronger if the substitution table is changed each time a letter is encoded. This type of cipher is known as a **stream cipher** because the text that is encrypted is combined with a stream of data that is ideally random but is known as the **cipherstream**. For example, we might use the Caesar cipher technique of shifting letters by a certain number of spaces but shift the first letter by 23 places, the second by 12, the third by 2, the fourth by 0, and so on.

The strength of this scheme depends on how we arrive at the sequence of shift values and whether we ever use the same sequence twice. If the sequence is genuinely random and used only once, the scheme is known as a **one-time pad** and is provably unbreakable *if the pad is only used once*. If the sequence is not random, the code can be broken by guessing the sequence.

A simple way to generate a sequence of apparently random letter shift values is to use another text. For example, we might use the Declaration of Independence to provide our sequence. The first letter W is the twenty-third letter of the alphabet, the second e is the fifth. "We the People ..." gives us the sequence 23, 5, 20, 8, 5, 16, 5, 15, 16, 12, 5 ... as our cipher stream (see Figure 10-2).

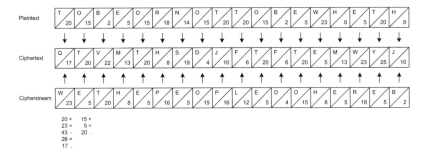

Figure 10-2   *Using a text to provide a stream cipher key*

Using another document to provide cipherstream isn't random enough to be secure. The letter *e* occurs four times in the first three words of the Declaration of Independence. This type of cipher can be broken even when both texts are unknown by combing our knowledge of the frequency with which certain letters appear with knowledge about the frequency with which one letter follows another.

If the one-time pad is simple and provably unbreakable, why do we hear about ciphers being broken? Unfortunately, a system can be both simple and secure without being practical.

Alice and Bob can only use a one-time pad to communicate their secrets securely if they have a secure means of communicating the one-time pad. The one-time pad must be at least as long as the message they want to exchange, and *they must never use the pad a second time.*

If an attacker is able to get hold of two messages that are encoded using the same pad, he can subtract one message from another, and the cipherstream cancels out. The unbreakable code is now reduced to the difficult but breakable two texts problem we just saw. Instead of the two plaintexts being added, one is subtracted from the other, but this is essentially the same problem to the cryptanalyst. Instead of having a signal that is entirely masked by a completely random signal, we have two signals with a regular pattern mixed together (see Figure10-3).

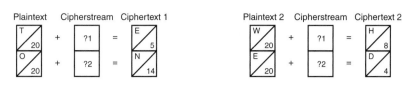

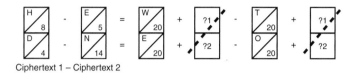

Ciphertext 1 − Ciphertext 2

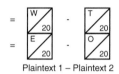

Plaintext 1 − Plaintext 2

Figure 10-3   *Breaking the "unbreakable" one-time pad*

The lesson here is that cryptographic security schemes can be secure in theory but brittle in practice. The unbreakable security of the one-time pad is entirely dependent on the feature that makes it so inconvenient to use.

Before computers became cheap, the only practical way to create a reliably random cipherstream was to use a physical process such as throwing a large number of dice many times. This might be why the KGB reused some of the one-time pads they had used to encrypt diplomatic traffic in the early 1940s. What appears to be an elementary cryptographic mistake is perhaps understandable when it is considered that in 1941 the German army had reached Moscow.

The mistake was spotted by a group of U.S. cryptanalysts who produced a series of intelligence decrypts known by the code name VENONA. The VENONA intelligence led to the discovery and execution of the U.S. atomic spy Julius Rosenberg and his wife Ethel mentioned in Chapter 3, "Learning from Mistakes." It also led to the unmasking of Alger Hiss, Klaus Fuchs, and Donald Mclean as Soviet spies.

Machine Encryption

The art of cryptography was essentially in a stalemate until the arrival of mechanical computers. With the important exception of the cumbersome one-time pad system, every cipher that could be applied using a paper and pencil could be broken using a paper and pencil.

The ability to automate the process of encrypting and decrypting messages allowed the use of ciphers that were not only much stronger than the paper-and-pencil schemes but could present almost any desired degree of difficulty to an attacker by building a big enough machine. Machine cryptography demonstrates the power of exponential growth. A small incremental increase in the complexity of the encryption machine can multiply the effort required for an attack many times. Two small increases gives the square, three the third power, and so on.

Modern computer ciphers generally use a large number expressed as a series of binary digits (bits) as a key. For a secure symmetric cipher, each additional bit in the key doubles the difficulty of breaking the cipher. If a 56-bit cipher takes a purpose-built computer a day to break a key, then a 57-bit cipher will take two days, a 59-bit cipher more than a week, a 61-bit cipher a month, a 65-bit cipher more than a year, and a 72-bit cipher a century. Computer security protocols generally use ciphers that have 128 bits, and the purpose-built computer would take approximately 13 billion, billion years, or about a billion times the age of the universe.

The German Enigma machine has become the best-known mechanical encryption system because of the work done by Alan Turing and his colleagues at Bletchley Park to break it during World War II. Intelligence from the Enigma decrypts provided the critical edge that allowed Britain to win the Battle of Britain and prevent Hitler's planned invasion.

The Enigma machine consists of a keyboard with a series of lights mounted above (see Figure 10-4). To encrypt a character, the operator presses a key, and the corresponding encrypted character appears on the light board. The heart of the machine consists of a set of three or four rotors, which are metal disks with a sequence of electrical contacts on either side. Inside the disk, the contacts are wired so that each contact on the left side of the disk is connected to a contact at a different position on the right. The circuitry inside the machine connects the keys to the lights on the light board in such a way that the current flows through each rotor twice. Each time the operator presses the key, the rotors advance one position, in effect changing the code. The difficulty of breaking the code was further increased by a plug-board, which superimposed a fixed substitution cipher onto the varying substitution cipher implemented by the rotors.

Figure 10-4   *Enigma machine (Photo courtesy NSA)*

The achievement of Turing's team is all the more remarkable when it is understood that the Nazi confidence in the Enigma system was largely justified. The three-rotor Enigma has approximately 10^{23} different rotor and plugboard settings. This is equivalent to breaking a 76-bit cipher and would take the hypothetical purpose-built modern computer approximately 2,800 years to break.

The reason that the codes were breakable was that the machine had a small number of flaws that allowed the problem to be reduced to a series of smaller problems that could be solved separately.

Even so, breaking the Enigma codes required an unprecedented amount of computing power that was far beyond the capabilities of any mechanical apparatus and required the invention of the modern electronic computer to break.

A mechanical encryption machine similar in appearance to the Enigma is stolen from a Soviet Embassy in Istanbul in the second James Bond film, *From Russia with Love*, where it is called the Lector. Even though both Fleming and the KGB knew that the Enigma machines had been broken, it is quite believable that a Soviet embassy would have used a mechanical machine for low-sensitivity diplomatic traffic as late as the 1960s.

The Keying Problem

Let us return to the unbreakable one-time pad. The system is unbreakable, but only if you have a secure means of distributing the cipher stream to your correspondents. This means that the use of a one-time pad to secure diplomatic communications requires secure distribution of large quantities of cipherstream. A one-time pad might contain 25 rows of 15 numbers, 375 in all. Each time the embassy cipher clerk encrypts or decrypts a letter, a number is crossed off the pad. This paragraph contains 617 letters (not counting spaces), and encrypting it would require almost two pages from a pad. A busy embassy communicating large amounts of sensitive information could easily run through dictionary-sized quantities of cipherstream.

Distribution of cipherstream was a major headache for security agencies during the peak years of the Cold War even without enemy tanks outside their gates. Large numbers of young men were dispatched to visit world capitals with briefcases strapped to their wrists.

Use of one-time pads could only be afforded for the most sensitive communications. Bulk traffic was sent using **cipher machines**, which allowed a message of any length to be encrypted using a fixed-length secret key. This made the problem of key distribution much easier; even if the keys were changed several times a day, a single sheet of paper could list enough keys to last a month. But the problem was not eliminated; use of encryption was only possible if the parties had planned in advance.

A New Direction

The arrival of the minicomputer in the 1970s resulted in a dramatic rise in the amount of data being created, which in turn resulted in a rise in the quantity of data that needed to be moved securely. The rising demand for cipherstream was in particular felt by the British cryptographers at GCHQ. Transporting cipherstream to foreign embassies was requiring the British Navy to commit a large part of its remaining fleet to touring foreign ports engaging in that quaint diplomatic euphemism "flying the flag."

This problem led a GCHQ cryptographer named James Ellis to propose a new type of cryptography system he called **no-secret encryption**. But it seems unfair to have to use a secret to encrypt a message; what we really want is a system where the information required to encrypt the message is public knowledge and the only information that needs to be secret is the key used to *decrypt* the message. It is easy to build a mechanical system that provides this property. I can put a letter in a post box even though I don't have the key to open it. The problem of realizing a secure mathematical no-secret encryption scheme resisted solution for several years until it was solved in 1973 by Clifford Cocks.

The GCHQ system was developed in a world where use of cryptography was considered the exclusive prerogative of governments. No-secret encryption was a technology that might have changed the world but was instead kept a closely guarded secret, a mathematical oddity known only by a handful of cryptographers in Britain and the U.S.

Fortunately for the Internet, the principle of no-secret cryptography was rediscovered by Whitfield Diffie and Martin Hellman, who called their idea **public key cryptography.**[1] Diffie and Hellman proposed an encryption scheme with two keys: a public key used to encrypt the message, and a private key to decrypt the message that the holder would keep secret.

To send an encrypted message to a person using public key cryptography, you could look up his public key in a directory that looked like a telephone book with very, very long telephone numbers. If the directory was accurate, the message could only be decrypted by the intended recipient, who would be the only person with access to the secret private key. Like Ellis before them, Diffie and Hellman were unable to realize a scheme that had all the properties they proposed for a public key encryption scheme known, but they did come up with a system that comes very close, known as **Diffie-Hellman,** which allows two people to use their own private key in combination with the public key of the other to securely create a common cryptographic key (see Figure 10-5).

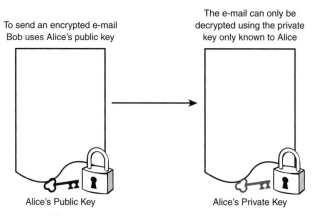

To send an encrypted e-mail
Bob uses Alice's public key

The e-mail can only be
decrypted using the private
key only known to Alice

Alice's Public Key   Alice's Private Key

Figure 10-5 *Public key encryption*

No-secret cryptography had little effect on military communication until after its reinvention as public key cryptography revolutionized the academic field. Diffie and Hellman clearly defined a mathematical challenge unlike any before it, to discover a problem that was

- Easy to compute in one direction (that is, it should be easy to encrypt the message)
- **But** very hard to compute in the reverse direction (that is, it should be difficult for an attacker to decrypt the message)
- **Unless** the person had available a particular piece of information that made it easy to compute in the reverse direction (that is, it should be easy for the intended recipient to decrypt the message using the private key)

Many mathematical puzzles are easy to create but hard to solve. If you choose two prime numbers at random, you can multiply them using a pocket calculator in a fraction of a second. But reversing the process (factoring) takes a lot more effort. If the numbers chosen are large enough, factoring would take the largest computers ever built millions of years.

In 1977, Ron Rivest, Adi Shamir, and Len Adleman, three professors at MIT, used the factoring problem to create a public key cryptography scheme known as **RSA** after the authors' initials. RSA is the de facto standard public key algorithm in use today securing e-commerce transactions and the chip-and-pin credit cards used in Europe.

Public key cryptography uses different keys for the encryption and decryption operations. For this reason, it is often referred to as **asymmetric key cryptography**. Traditional cryptography, in which the same key is used to encrypt and decrypt, is known as **symmetric key cryptography**.

Session Keys

Besides the use of two keys instead of one, there are two other important differences between asymmetric and symmetric key cryptography. The first is that asymmetric keys must be much longer to achieve the same degree of security as symmetric keys. Using current techniques, breaking an RSA key of 1024 bits requires approximately the same degree of computational effort as breaking an 80-bit symmetric key.[2] Although this has in the past generally been considered to provide an adequate degree of security, the use of 2048-bit RSA keys is greatly preferred, which provides a more comfortable safety margin equivalent to 112 bits in a symmetric scheme. Achieving a level of security equivalent to a 128-bit cipher requires a 3072-bit key.

The second important difference is speed. A moderately fast PC with a 2MHz Pentium 4 processor can encrypt or decrypt a stream of data using **AES**, the standard single key (symmetric) cipher, at 60Mbps (megabits per second).[3] This is faster than the typical computer can read information from a disk drive. The same machine takes about 30 milliseconds to perform a single 2048-bit RSA decryption operation. That means it takes the machine about the same time to perform one 2048-bit RSA operation or encrypt the entire text of this book using AES.

Encrypting an entire book using RSA would be completely impractical without special-purpose hardware designed to perform

RSA calculations very quickly, and the result could only be decrypted by another computer equipped with special hardware.

To avoid the need for special hardware, we combine the use of symmetric and asymmetric cryptography to get the best features of both—the speed of symmetric key cryptography and the flexibility of public key cryptography. We do this by first encrypting a document under a randomly chosen key called a **session key**. Then we encrypt the session key under the public key of each intended recipient.

Digital Signatures

Having described the invention and rediscovery of public key cryptography, it is time to remember that throughout this book, we have identified authentication rather than confidentiality as our primary security concern. Unless we get authentication right, we cannot solve the confidentiality problem, because we could end up encrypting the data for the wrong person's key.

In e-mail phishing, the attacker gains access to confidential information (the credit card number) by impersonating the bank. To block this type of attack, we need to be able to securely authenticate messages from the bank.

What we need is a cryptographic system that allows the sender of a message to add a "digital signature" to the message such that

- The signature can only be created by the sender of the message.
- The signature can be verified by any person receiving the message.
- The verification process allows any modification of the message to be detected.

The RSA public key cryptography scheme can also be used to create a digital signature (see Figure 10-6). A digital signature is a blob of data added to the message that is created using the private key and verified using the public key. Any modification of the message will cause verification of the signature to fail.

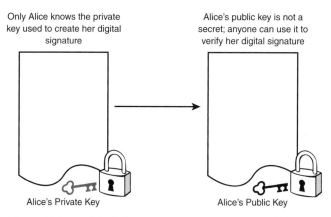

Only Alice knows the private key used to create her digital signature

Alice's public key is not a secret; anyone can use it to verify her digital signature

Alice's Private Key

Alice's Public Key

Figure 10-6 *Using a digital signature to authenticate and validate e-mail*

As with public key encryption, a practical implementation of an RSA digital signature scheme requires the public key encryption scheme to be combined with a faster cipher that can be performed at high speed. This is called a **message digest function**. Because all we want to do is to authenticate the message, the message digest does not need a key. The message digest takes all the bits in our document, applies what amounts to a "digital shuffle," and emits a fixed-length string of 160 or so bits of data.

A message digest function is sometimes referred to as a **one-way function** because a good message digest is easy to calculate in one direction but prohibitively difficult to calculate in the opposite one. Unlike a public key cryptography system, there is no private key that allows the holder to take a shortcut.

Smartcards

Passwords provide a paradoxical form of authentication. If Alice knows the password, then she can authenticate herself to Bob by telling him the password. But this only works if Bob also knows the password. If Alice tells Mallet the password, mistaking him for Bob, it is no longer secret, and the whole system collapses.

Public key cryptography provides a convenient and secure method of authentication, where Alice can authenticate herself to anyone at all using her private key without ever revealing it.

This particular property of public key cryptography makes it the queen of authentication techniques. It is quite likely that you already carry one or more private keys around with you today without even knowing it. If you have an American Express Blue credit card or a card issued by a European bank, there is a private key in the chip hidden beneath the gold contact pads. Most cell phones have a private key embedded in either the phone itself or a chip that is inserted into the phone before use.

A true smartcard has a microprocessor embedded in it that performs all the public key cryptography operations involving the private key. The private key cannot be read using ordinary techniques, although it is possible for a well-funded attacker equipped with an electron microscope to obtain it from the card.

The main drawback of using smartcards for Internet authentication is that few computers come with a reader. If every computer keyboard had a smartcard reader, those readers could replace passwords, and credit card numbers and the phishing problem would be eliminated.

Fortunately, smartcard technology is now becoming available in a form factor that plugs directly into a standard USB port. These smartcards are similar in size to a door key and are designed to be carried on a key fob (see Figure 10-7).

Figure 10-7   *Smart token*

Equations Alone Do Not Make a Solution

"God forbid that Truth should be confined to
Mathematical Demonstration!"
—William Blake, circa 1808,
"Notes on Reynold's Discourses"

Public key cryptography provides an elegant mathematical solution to a precisely stated problem. She is a seductive mistress, and it is easy to fall in love with her beauty and believe that every security problem can be reduced to mathematics until the real world intrudes to remind us forcefully that she is unattainable.

I am reminded of the phrase "the crystalline purity of logic" that Wittgenstein used in *Philosophical Investigations* when he realized that language could not be reduced to pure logic. The philosopher continued, "We have got on to slippery ice where there is no friction and so in a certain sense the conditions are ideal, but also, just because of that, we are unable to walk. We want to walk: so we need friction. Back to the rough ground!"

To secure e-mail against phishing attacks, we must do more than make use of cryptography possible; we must make it ubiquitous and accessible. A digital signature does not tell a consumer that an e-mail has come from a bank unless every single e-mail from that bank is signed, and this information is conveyed to the consumer in a manner that is effective, unobtrusive, and unforgeable.

Key Points

- Cryptography is a key tool of network security.
  - It is only one tool, and it is easy to be overconfident.
- Symmetric ciphers have the following characteristics:
  - They use the same key to encrypt and decrypt.
  - They are fast but require a key distribution mechanism.
  - 128-bit ciphers offer a sufficient degree of security for most purposes.
- Public key cryptography (asymmetric cryptography) is characterized by the following:
  - It uses two keys: public and private.
  - Public key is used to encrypt; private key is used to decrypt.
  - Private key is used to sign; public key to verify a signature.

- It is slow, but it can be used in a hybrid system where public key cryptography is used for key distribution and symmetric cryptography is used for the bulk cipher.
- In the RSA scheme, 2048 bits is a preferred size; larger is better.

C H A P T E R 1 1

Establishing Trust

Public key cryptography allows us to protect the confidentiality, integrity, and authenticity of any type of digital communication *provided that we know the public key of the party we are to communicate with.*

If we receive a signed message that claims to have been sent by Alice, we need to do two things to verify the claim:

- Use the public key to verify the signature.
- Make sure the public key really belongs to Alice.

An attacker could try to fool us in two different ways:

- Break the encryption mechanism.
- Fool us into trusting a different key as belonging to Alice.

Unless the protocol designer has made a serious mistake (it happens), the first type of attack is very difficult, like trying to move the Sahara desert with a pair of tweezers, one grain of sand at a time.

From time to time, a new cryptanalytic attack receives some attention, and for the next few weeks, I have to spend time explaining to customers and the press that there is no immediate danger. Even if the discovery replaces the tweezers with a shovel, they still have the Sahara to move.

The design of cryptographic algorithms is still something of a black art, but one that is practiced extremely conservatively. Modern computers allow us to choose almost any margin of safety. Unless there is good reason not to be, we are exceptionally conservative in our choices so that even when an algorithm is "broken," a very large margin of error remains. We begin planning for a replacement at the first signs of weakness.

We are conservative because we can afford to be. Choosing the strength of a symmetric cipher presents a curious problem: knowing when to stop. A strong symmetric cipher with 101 bits is twice as hard to break as a symmetric cipher with 100 bits. A cipher that is twice as good costs only 1 percent more. Public key cryptography systems pose a somewhat trickier problem: A 2048-bit RSA key does not offer quite as much security as a 128-bit symmetric one but is large enough to cause some inconvenience.

Choosing a cipher strength is the easy part; a cryptographic system using a 101-bit cipher is still only as secure as its weakest link. Unless the designers and reviewers have made a serious mistake, the weakest link is not going to be the cipher.

The link that is hardest to secure is the point where the cryptographic system meets the real world. If Alice and Bob each know the other's public key, they can communicate securely in spite of Mallet's attempts to interfere. All is lost if Mallet can persuade Alice that his key belongs to Bob. Here the economics are much less favorable: Making it twice as difficult for Mallet to attack might double the cost to Alice and Bob as well.

Knowing that we have the right key is a hard problem. It raises the question of identity. Who is Alice anyway? Is it the Alice that works for Aardvark Bank or some other Alice? Is Aardvark Bank the same as Aardvark Financial?

The problem becomes even more complex when time is considered. If we are going to use a digital signature to authenticate a contract, we may need to check a signature several years after it was created. By this time, Aardvark Bank might have been sold, and Alice might not work for the new company.

Public Key Infrastructure (PKI) is designed to meet these requirements. It is a means of using public keys to represent the trust relationships between organizations and between people. That is a hard problem because trust relationships are complex and change significantly over time.

PKI has been around since the mid 1980s. It is at the core of SSL, the principal security measure used in the Internet today. SSL and PKI made the 1990s e-commerce boom possible. Every day billions of dollars are transferred safely and securely over the Internet using SSL.

You use SSL every time you visit your bank or shop at Amazon or Overstock. You probably didn't even notice you were using it.

And that is a big part of the problem: SSL exists to provide you with the security information you need to be safe online, and *you didn't notice it.*

How can we hope to control Internet crime when the security mechanism is unnoticed? We will return to this problem in Chapter 12, "Secure Transport." If end-to-end security means anything, we must recognize the fact that the real ends of the communications are people and businesses, not machines.

The Problem of Identity

PKI is designed around the problem of how Alice can be sure she really knows Bob's key and how Bob can really be sure he knows Alice's key. But this is a false reduction; we are asking how Bob can be sure he is dealing with Alice. But what Bob really wants to know is this: *Is it safe? Can I trust her?* Even if Bob is completely sure that the Alice he is communicating with is the "real" Alice, this does not guarantee that she is not an axe murderer.

Security is the effective management of risks. **Trust** is having confidence in the ability to accurately predict risk. I trust the chair I am sitting in not to break; I trust my bank not to steal my money. I know that either risk might be realized, but I accept them because I am confident that they are unlikely.

One way that Alice and Bob could exchange their public keys is to meet in person and swap business cards carrying their public key. This is somewhat inconvenient; it forces us to deal in the world of atoms and not (as we want) the world of bits. It also means that the security of our system depends on the difficulty of forging a business card. Requiring a passport or driving license would reduce but not eliminate the possibility of impersonation.

The number of business cards that need to be exchanged increases with the square of the network size. Pretty soon everyone would be doing nothing but exchanging business cards and managing the public keys.

If PKI is going to work on a global scale, a broker is required. Instead of exchanging business cards with Bob, Carol, … Zachary, et. al., Alice visits a PKI broker, who verifies that she is in fact the person she claims to be and issues a universal **digital passport** that tells Bob, Carol, … and anyone else who might need to know what Alice's public key is.

If the world was simple, a scheme of this sort would have been completed long ago. Instead, attempts to realize this design have led to rediscovery of the fact that the world is complex and that different parties have different trust needs for different purposes.

Separating the business of authenticating keys from the business of using them requires us to introduce some additional terminology:

- **Subject**—The subject is the party to whom an issued credential refers. The subject of Alice's passport is Alice.
- **Relying party**—The relying party is the party that relies on the issued credential for a particular purpose. When Alice presents her passport to passport control, the relying party is passport control.
- **Issuer**—The issuer is the party that issued the credential. In the case of Alice's passport, the issuer is the passport office.

Delegating the task of authenticating public keys to specialist third parties has another important property: It becomes practical to demand more than just a business card as a means of authentication. A credential that can be presented to many relying parties has a much higher value to the subject than one that only serves a single subject. It is worth investing more time and effort to obtain a higher-quality credential.

The Problem of Bits

In their original paper proposing public key cryptography, Diffie and Hellman proposed that the trust broker would create a "directory" of public keys. This would look like a telephone book with amazingly long telephone numbers (more than 300 digits each). To find out Bob's public key, Alice (or rather the program sending the message) would look up Bob's public key in the directory (see Figure 11-1). Bob could check Alice's signature by looking up her public key in the same directory.

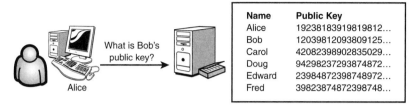

Figure 11-1 *Public key directory*

The directory model was proposed long before the Internet had become a reliable infrastructure. The principal means of transferring information from one computer to another was magnetic tape; the 5¼-inch floppy disk was the bleeding edge. The directory model could only work if the sender and receiver of the message had access to a ubiquitous computer network, which in 1977 did not yet exist.

Digital Certificates

The difficulty of realizing the directory model in 1979 led Lauren Kohnfelder, an MSc. student at MIT, to propose that the trust broker sign each entry in the directory with his public key to create what he called a **digital certificate**[1] (see Figure 11-2). A trust broker issuing certificates is known as a **Certificate Authority (CA)**.

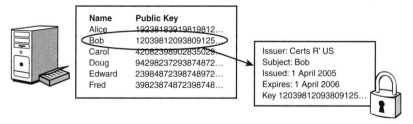

Figure 11-2 *A digital certificate*

The Kohnfelder certificate model was quickly adopted as *the* way to make PKI work in practice even as the constraints that it was designed to overcome were becoming irrelevant. Meanwhile, attempts to make the certificate model work in practice led to the need for a series of complex additions and embellishments.

Revocation

One of the most problematic embellishments is the need to support revocation. However careful we are making sure that the certificate is issued to the right person, there is always a possibility of a mistake. People make mistakes as well; they might lose their key in any number of ways, or important information contained in the certificate might no longer be valid. If the bank decides to fire Alice, it does not want her to be able to sign e-mails on its behalf until the certificate expires the next year.

When credit cards first appeared, the principal fraud control measure was a list of stolen cards circulated by the credit card companies. A copy of the list was usually taped to each register, where credit cards were accepted and the cashier would (in theory) check each credit card against the list in the hope of a modest bonus from the card company.

Kohnfelder proposed a similar scheme. Each day the CA would issue a Certificate Revocation List (CRL) giving the serial number of every certificate that had been revoked.

The problem with this scheme is that the number of revoked certificates tends to get rather large. If a CA issues a million certificates, and only 2 percent need to be revoked before they expire, the list will have 20,000 entries. If each entry requires 100 bytes, the list will be 2Mb long. Even with a high-speed Internet connection, the file will take up to a minute to download. Users with dialup connections would be waiting a very long time.

By the early 1980s, the credit card companies faced the same problem. The list of stolen credit cards had become a large book, and looking up numbers could take quite a while. Cashiers tended to use it only for the major sales.

This problem was solved by a small company founded in Hawaii called Verifone. If you have used a credit card, you have almost certainly seen a **Verifone terminal** in use; it is the little box that your credit card is swiped against in a store. The box connects to a central computer that approves or rejects the transaction. The PKI equivalent of the Verifone box is a protocol called **Online Certificate Status Protocol (OCSP)**.

Topology of Trust

As PKI was deployed in the real world, it was quickly realized that there would need to be more than one level of trust and certainly more than one trust broker.

This led to the problem of how to verify the signature of the CA, which in turn led to the idea of certificate chains in which one certificate would be signed by a key, which was in turn certified by another certificate.

The collection of certificate chains would in turn chain up to a single **root key** (see Figure 11-3).

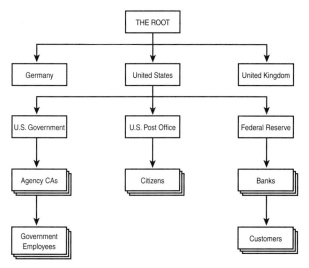

Figure 11-3   *CA hierarchy*

Modern PKI systems have root keys but their role is deliberately limited and controlled to prevent either an abuse of the power or the personal risk that having such a degree of power would entail. The single master root is a completely different proposition, it is not merely a root, it is THE ROOT, a singular point of control for every information system in the world. Outside of a spy or science fiction novel, THE ROOT cannot exist.

For THE ROOT to be acceptable as an international solution, it would have to be established by treaty and probably run by the United Nations, a nontrivial exercise in diplomacy.

The idea of establishing an international root quickly collapsed after the U.S. civil service discovered that it could not even agree on a single agency to be responsible for THE ROOT at the national level. The National Security Agency would never surrender control of such a critical cryptographic resource to a civilian agency. The Government Services Agency would never allow a military agency to control the civilian infrastructure and so on.

The antithesis of the hierarchical approach was Phil Zimmermann's e-mail encryption program pretty good privacy (PGP), where every public key holder is in effect a certificate issuer, and the total collection of certificates creates a **Web of Trust**. PGP began as a breakaway from the then-hierarchical certificate-based world of PKI, but the only real changes are that everyone is a trust provider and everyone can choose the trust providers they rely on. PGP does not expect a hierarchical structure (see Figure 11-4).

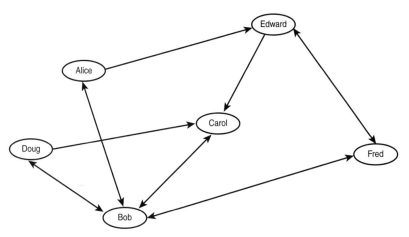

Figure 11-4   *Web of Trust*

The Web of Trust is certainly a better means of meeting Zimmermann's goal of pretty good privacy than a monolithic hierarchy. The Web of Trust can deliver a high degree of privacy protection in a small community that is tightly interconnected, and the maximum distance between members of the Web is no more than two or three hops.

As the Web becomes larger, the problem of discovering a trusted path becomes harder. A computer with access to the necessary data can easily find a connection between two people; working out what that connection means and whether it is trustworthy is much harder.

The Web of Trust is difficult to ground. What might appear to be a highly reliable key signer might be a facsimile created by an attacker who collects genuinely trustworthy data from a large number of sources and then repackages it along with a few of his own malicious entries.

Synthesis

Over time, elements of the Web of Trust model found their way into the certificate world. Fitting the whole world into a single hierarchical structure turned out to be impossible. Managing a PKI with a billion trust providers was impractical.

The solution was a two-level system in which there could be more than one root of trust. Each root of trust would issue certificates to end users according to whatever certificate practices they choose, and trust relationships could be established between roots in Web of Trust fashion if the managers of the roots decided to do so (see Figure 11-5).

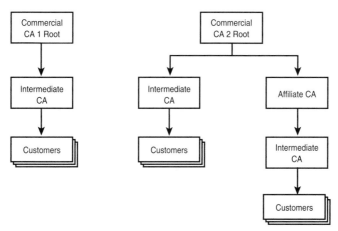

Figure 11-5 *Multiple roots of trust*

The multiple roots of trust model allows each user to set his own trust criteria by deciding which roots to trust, while keeping the number of separate roots to a manageable number. Anyone can decide to become a trust provider, but unlike in PGP, they are required to decide that this is what they want to do.

We still have a path discovery problem, but it is tractable. A small number of specialist trust providers can be held accountable for their issuing practices more easily than a large number.

We still have something of a path discovery problem, however. We can easily find a path after we have the necessary data, but the problem is compiling and maintaining the data in the first place. A global scale PKI would require tens of thousands of trust roots, and these would change over time.

The solution adopted is to establish one or more Webs of Trust to express the trust relationships between the roots of trust themselves. Establishing trust between trust providers is a complex and expensive task, one that will only be undertaken if there is a solid business reason to do so. In some parts of the Web of Trust, the need for interconnectivity between the trust networks will be sufficiently great to justify establishing cost-saving policies and structures, but this is currently the exception rather that the general case.

An infrastructure that might set the pattern for trust interconnection is the U.S. Federal Government Bridge CA. Early attempts to deploy PKI in the federal government led to argument over which government agency should be in charge of THE ROOT. The "bridge CA" allows each government agency to recognize every other agency as a peer. Each government agency recognizes its own certificate hierarchy as its unique root of trust and delegates the authority to recognize other agencies to the bridge CA, which in return recognizes every government agency that is a member of the bridge.

The bridge CA allows every government agency that is a member to securely interact with every other government agency without ceding control. Similar structures have been established to serve higher education and by other governments.

Bridge CAs allow the cost of establishing credentials between CAs to be addressed but do not supply enough regularity to eliminate the path discovery problem. The number of trust providers is still large and the trust relationships between the providers inescapably complex, the type of complexity that design for deployment tells us should be kept out of the client at all costs. We need an architecture that has more flexibility, an online service we can ask to perform a path discovery operation for us whenever we might need it.

Simple Certificate Validation Protocol (SCVP) is an emerging IETF standard that attempts to address this problem by allowing a client to delegate the task of path discovery or validating the path discovered.

XKMS

When access to network services is required for path discovery and certificate status information, we can greatly reduce the complexity of the system by returning to the original directory model where one lookup serves all our needs. This realization led to the XML Key Management Specification, or XKMS for short.

If a program wants to connect to another system, it can obtain the appropriate cryptographic keys from an XKMS service. The query specifies the address of the party to be contacted, the protocol to be used, and the type of cryptographic information required.

XKMS is useful because it allows the simplest possible client to connect to the most complicated PKI imaginable. All the complexity of the PKI is implemented in the XKMS service. This approach also allows the PKI to be modified without the need to deploy new clients (see Figure 11-6).

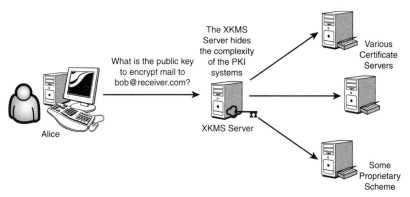

Figure 11-6 *An XKMS service acting as a gateway to a complex PKI*

It is quite easy to write an XKMS server that provides information on a few tens or hundreds of keys, but the architecture was designed to make it possible to support millions of users or more. If you are planning to manage more than about five public keys, you need to carefully consider how to get information *into* the system as well as out, and the larger part of the XKMS protocol is concerned with this part of the problem.

We still have the problem of how to secure the communication to the XKMS service. But this is a tractable problem. All we need to start from is a means of knowing the public key of our XKMS service. We can do that by using a message digest of the public key of the service.

The Problem of Trust

Having described the technology of trust, it is almost time to discuss how we establish trust in actual applications. To do so, we must first look at the applications and the risks that must be controlled, which is the topic of the remainder of this book.

Key Points

- Public key cryptography allows the confidentiality and integrity of any communication to be protected, provided that the public keys of the parties are known to each other. PKI provides the necessary keys.
- The directory of keys was impractical in 1977, but now it is practical. XKMS implements this model.
- Certificates are more flexible than the directory approach, but they do not require online access. Flexibility comes at the cost of complexity
- Both the monolithic hierarchy and the Web of Trust models have disadvantages. Practical PKIs employ a hybrid model that combines these approaches.

Secure Transport

Cryptography allows us to secure the network, but this effort is wasted unless we also secure the last two feet between the screen and the user's eyeballs. Strong cryptographic protocols are only the starting point for securing the system.

We have spent enough time reviewing past failures. It is time to look at the one unqualified success story of Internet security. SSL has performed beyond its original expectations for more than a decade. SSL does not meet every security need we recognize today, and the user experience falls short of what we want. Like any important infrastructure, SSL needs ongoing maintenance so that it meets the needs it serves today that are above and beyond the original design brief. If we understand what works in SSL and how to extend it to meet our current needs, we can apply the same principles to e-mail, blogs, instant messaging, and new forms of Internet communication as they emerge.

Secure Sockets Layer (SSL) was originally designed by Netscape, then known as Mosaic Communications Corporation, and later submitted to the IETF for standards work, where the name was changed to Transport Layer Security (TLS).

The original design was shaky, but it was fixed in the end. Today SSL/TLS is the most widely used and trusted Internet security protocol.

SSL is the technology behind the padlock icon that appears in Internet Explorer or Firefox when you are visiting an online bank or store.

How SSL Works

SSL is built on public key cryptography and PKI. The original design principle of SSL was to allow any Internet protocol to be "secured" by simply replacing the standard code library used to send data over the Internet with equivalent calls to the SSL library.

To establish a network connection on a UNIX system, a programmer writes something that looks like Figure 12-1.

```
struct sockaddr_in local, mask;
SOCKET s;

local.sin_port        = htons (port);
local.sin_family      = AF_INET;
local.sin_addr.s_addr = inet_addr(address);

// Create a socket
s = socket (AF_INET, SOCK_STREAM, 0);
Assert (s != INVALID_SOCKET, -1, ("Could not allocate socket"));

// Bind the socket to the TCP interface and port
int b = bind(s, (struct sockaddr*)&local, sizeof(local));
Assert (b != SOCKET_ERROR, -1, ("Could not bind to socket"));

// Put the socket into listener mode (i.e. we are a server)
int r = listen(s, SOMAXCONN);
Assert (r != SOCKET_ERROR, -1, ("Could not listen to socket"));
```

Figure 12-1 *Creating a UNIX network connection*

From the programmer's point of view, the code creates a communication socket, configures it for use with TCP/IP, and sets it up to listen for data. Under the covers, a lot more is taking place, but the programmer does not need to worry about this. The work is done for him by the operating system.

According to the original concept, the programmer would create a "secure" Internet socket by replacing calls to socket, bind, listen, and so on with similarly structured calls to secure_socket, secure_bind, secure_listen, and so on. Security would then be just another task that takes place under the covers that the programmer does not need to think about.

As a programming abstraction, this approach works well. Programming is an enormously complex task, and keeping control of complexity is the key to building large systems that work well. Abstraction is simply the practice of ignoring unnecessary details.

As with TCP/IP, a lot of work is taking place. To establish a secure communication, the browser performs a handshake with the Web server. In a typical session, the browser does the following:

1. Checks to see if it can reuse a master secret established in a previous communication session with that server
2. Sends a ClientHello message to the server
   - This contains random information known as a *nonce.*
   - If a previous session was stored, the browser asks if the server is willing to resume it.
   - This specifies the cryptographic algorithms that the browser is willing to use.
3. Receives a ServerHello message from the server
   - If the browser asked to restart a previously established session, the server message might accept the response, in which case the handshake is complete.
   - Otherwise the server returns the following:
     - An X.509v3 certificate that is compatible with the cipher suites specified in the ClientHello message
     - Cryptographic parameters, including a server nonce
4. Verifies that the X.509v3 certificate returned by the server meets its built-in acceptance criteria

   The browser attempts to find a trust chain to the server certificate that begins at one of the embedded roots of trust in the browser.
5. Sends a message to the server containing a randomly generated secret key known as the **pre_master_secret** encrypted under the certificate returned by the server
6. Tells the user that a secure connection has been established

If everything is correct, the browser and server (and only the browser and server) can calculate a value known as the **master secret**. The master secret is generated by mixing the pre_master_secret value and the two nonces into a cryptographically secure one-way function. The browser knows the pre_master_secret because it originally generated it. The server knows the value because it knows the private key necessary to decrypt the encrypted value sent by the browser in step 5.

The SSL protocol is as complete and correct as the state of the art in cryptography allows. It is steps 4 and 6 that give rise to real-world security problems. The security of SSL depends on the acceptance criteria for the Web browser being sufficient to ensure the trustworthiness of the certificate. As we saw in Chapter 11, "Establishing Trust," this is a difficult problem. And as we saw in Chapter 3, "Learning from Mistakes," one of the biggest security challenges we face is how to secure the last couple of feet between the screen and the user's eyeballs.

The full specification has a number of additional bells and whistles that allow various attacks to be thwarted. The most important points for our purposes are these:

- Both the browser and server can avoid computationally intensive public key operations entirely if it is possible to restart a previous session.
- The browser needs to perform one public key encryption operation to encrypt the pre_master_secret and one or more public key signature verification operations to validate the certificate chain.
- The server needs to perform one private key operation to decrypt the pre_master_secret when a new session must be established.
- After the master secret is established, the overhead incurred by encrypting and authenticating actual data packets is negligible.

TLS Restart

When SSL was introduced, a decent personal computer came with a 50MHz processor and a 28.8Kbps dialup modem. Using SSL could delay loading of a Web page by several seconds. Today, computers are a thousand times faster, dialup is twice as fast, and most users have access to broadband. Except in rare instances, the impact of SSL on the Web browser is negligible.

The same does not quite hold for Web servers. A personal computer typically has one user visiting one Web page at a time. A Web server, on the other hand, might serve thousands of requests at a time.

When SSL was introduced, the client and server had to go through the whole master-secret establishment process every time a Web connection was made. The protocol has since been changed to allow reuse of a previously established master secret, so the calculation-intensive SSL handshake process need only be decided once per session.

There are two important reasons for drawing attention to this particular detail of the SSL protocol.

The first is at the direct request of a friend who is responsible for Internet security at one of the world's 50 largest banks. For several years, he has unsuccessfully attempted to convince the administrators responsible for maintaining the bank's Web servers that they should use SSL to protect every page on the bank Web site. In particular, he wants to secure the first page the customer sees. Because the vast majority of visits to the bank Web site are to use the home banking service, the server will perform one SSL handshake for every user visiting the Web site. It costs no more to secure the page where users enter their username and password as the next page where the data is accepted.

The second reason for calling this feature to attention is that it allows us to use SSL to secure communications to the lowest cost, most feeble microprocessor-based devices imaginable—provided, that is, we don't mind using a master secret that might have been negotiated a year or so earlier.

This type of flexibility is particularly useful when dealing with an embedded device such as an intelligent light switch, which we would like to be able to control using a cheap 8-bit microprocessor of the type that powered the computers that began the microcomputer revolution in the late 1970s.

Gap Analysis

The SSL protocol is widely deployed and used. The protocol itself has survived numerous expert reviews, and there is a great deal of confidence in its design. The same is not true of the way that applications implement SSL. The user experience is unsatisfactory in many respects:

- **The padlock icon is practically invisible**—Most users don't know it exists, and of the few who do know it's there, even fewer remember to look for it.

- **The browser does not answer the question the user is asking**—The questions the user cares about are "Can I trust this site" on first contact and "Is this really the party I know" on subsequent visits. What the padlock actually says is, "This connection is encrypted."

- **Information is not presented in a form that typical users can understand**—The certificate information dialog in existing browsers is designed as a debugging tool for site administrators rather than a means of communication to the user. Interpreting the dialog correctly requires detailed knowledge that is beyond the typical Web administrator, let alone a typical user.

- **The user is bombarded with irrelevant queries**—Most browsers warn when a site contains a mixture of secure and insecure content (but not which is which!), when the user moves from an insecure page to a secure one and so on. These dialogs are intrusive, and most users quickly learn to turn them off. The only purpose that the dialogs serve is to allow the browser designer to blame the user for mistakes caused by the poor user experience.

- **The user is not told the identity of the trust provider**—The certificate issuer is not held accountable for errors or negligence. Reliable authentication processes cost time and money. Without accountability, new entrants to the certificate business have little incentive to invest in either.

- **Elements of the browser user interface allow an attacker to emulate a secure site**—One of the chief offenders in this regard is the "favorites icon" that appears in the address bar of some Web browsers. Many users assume that favorites icons are trustworthy because they appear in the part of the display that they assume to be reserved for verified information. In fact, these are displayed without authentication measures being taken.

In many cases, remedying the faults revealed by the gap analysis requires little more than recognizing them as such and applying the obvious fix. In particular, the user experience for security must be designed to center on the needs of the user and not on the Web site administrator.

In particular, *the user should not be warned about administrative security defects*. This might sound counterintuitive.

What is the point of having security if the user is not told when it fails? But in the Web today, the majority of Web sites have no security at all. Adding security measures should never reduce the quality of the user experience.

The only time the user should see an intrusive warning message is when he is about to do something that is unsafe. It is appropriate to display a warning if the browser has reason to suspect that the user has been directed to a phishing site.

Instead of warning the user that the site certificate is invalid, the browser should display the site as it would any other insecure page—that is, without the padlock icon or any other indication that the page is secure.

The need for administrators to check their own sites should be met by browser tools and extensions that are purposely designed for Web administrators, not by dialogs that pester every user.

Secure Chrome

Users cannot tell which information they can trust and which they cannot.

Current browsers present a mish-mash of secure and insecure content. The user is meant to know that a page is safe when he sees the padlock icon. But any Web site can present a "favorites icon" that is displayed more prominently.

Study after study tells me what I already know: that the existing user security experience is confusing. Are we measuring the innate capabilities of users here, or their reaction to lousy user experience design?

The tools are digital, but the outcomes are not binary. No matter what we do, there will be some users who are confused by some attacks. It makes a huge difference to me, to the users, and to the banks that pay for my services whether the failure rate is 90 percent, 50 percent, or 10 percent.

We are not going to achieve a 0 percent failure rate immediately, but we can significantly reduce the failure rate by beginning with a consistent idea of which parts of the browser display should be considered "trustworthy" and which are under control of the content provider.

In the early days of the Web, people would lecture me about how people wanted to have more control over the user experience, how they wanted pop-up windows and the ability to disable the navigation buttons, how they wanted the ability to display "rich content," and so on. They stopped inviting me to their meetings after I asked "which people" wanted this: the content providers, or the people visiting their sites? At that time, the browser was given away free as a loss leader to sell Web servers offering all the bells and whistles necessary to drive the user crazy.

Today, we have rediscovered the fact that the Web belongs to the users. It is *my* address bar, *my* back button, and *my* status bar, and nobody else gets to steal them.

In browser jargon, the control areas of the browser, the address bar, the status bar, the navigation button, and so on are called **chrome**. We need to decide which areas of the chrome are to be considered secure and ensure that only trustworthy information that has been verified by the browser appears there.

From a usability point of view, there can be only one answer to "What parts of the chrome should be secure?" The answer: *All of it.* The user cannot be expected to distinguish between chrome that is secure and chrome that the content provider can manipulate. All of the chrome must be secure down to the last pixel (see Figure 12-2).

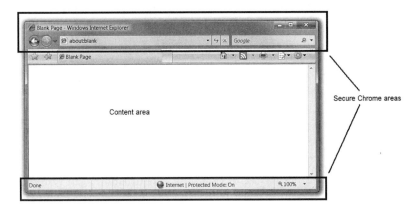

Figure 12-2   *Secure chrome*

Making the secure chrome secure is partly a matter of resisting unnecessary features and partly a bug-hunting exercise. For some reason, the designers of JavaScript decided that the content provider should be allowed to control the display of chrome in any way it saw fit: turning off any or all of it. After it is realized that the user, not the content provider, was the owner of the browser, and the user, not the content provider, should control the user experience, removing these features became straightforward.

Reclaiming some parts of the chrome will be a challenge. Prying some people's fingers off their favorites icons in particular will be hard. The challenge here is political, not technical.

The Problem of Trust

Having covered the basics of the most widely used PKI-based application, we can now continue our earlier discussion of the role of a Certificate Authority in particular and Trusted Third Parties (**TTPs**) in general.

When you shop online, you need to know whether you are dealing with a real merchant or a phony out to steal your card number.

Proof of identity is not sufficient to establish trust. I may be absolutely confident that the person applying for a loan is Al Capone. That does not mean I can trust him or want to do business with him. Just as the criminals don't really want to know the credit card number, I am not really interested in the name of an online business. What I care about is reputation and accountability. I want to know that the Web site I am dealing with online is the same business I already know by reputation. I want to know that the business should default in some way, there will be accountability.

To take full advantage of the global Internet economy, we need to be able to trust a business we don't already know. I might need to buy an obscure part for my 1977 MGB from a business I found through Google. Knowing with certainty that the Web site is run by "Obscure MGB Parts Co." is of little use unless I know I can trust the company.

What I need in this circumstance is not proof of identity or reputation but proof of accountability. I can trust the business if I know that it will be effectively deterred by the consequences of malpractice.

A PKI establishes identity, which in turn establishes reputation and accountability, which in turn establish trust.

Costs and Benefits

Establishing trust is expensive and time consuming. Unlike with cryptography, there is no technical magic that allows us to have twice the security for almost the same price.

Trust is expensive, so we must know exactly how much trust we need for a given application. We should not expect the same process to serve for the problem of establishing the trustworthiness of a bank and the problem of securing discussion on Johnny's personal Web site.

Until recently, the Web supported only two trust levels: either a padlock appeared, or it did not. The padlock was hard to see, and few people understood what it meant. Substantial quantities of advertising revenue went into telling consumers that the padlock icon meant "it is safe" when, in fact, all the padlock says is "communication to this site is encrypted."

To decide what level of trust is required, we must consider both the risk that is to be controlled and the information that the relying party is expected to understand.

If the relying party is a machine, we can have a hundred or more shades of trust between black and white. If the relying party is a human, our scope is limited. Ideally there would be three levels of trust:

- **Promiscuous encryption**—For routine interaction
- **Domain validated encryption**—Low-risk security-sensitive interaction
- **Accountability**—All interactions that present a criminal incentive

We might in time add more levels that go above and beyond accountability, but there is little advantage to be found in exploring the shades of gray between these three levels.

The lack of "no security" is deliberate. Although encryption is not quite free (CPU activity raises power consumption), the cost is negligible. Authentication, in particular authenticating key holders, is what costs money. If we are prepared to do encryption without authentication, we can do it for "free."

Promiscuous Security

Promiscuous security is encryption without authentication. Only two pieces of information are required:

- The purported domain name of the subject
- The purported public key of the subject

From a security point of view, using encryption without authenticating the keys is profoundly unsatisfactory.

In particular, the protocol is subject to a "man-in-the-middle" attack in which Mallet inserts himself into all communications between Alice and Bob. When Alice sends Bob her key (and vice versa), Mallet replaces it with his key. Every time Alice sends Bob a message, Mallet decrypts it with his key, keeps a copy, and re-encrypts it for Bob (and vice versa). Alice and Bob think they are communicating securely, but Mallet is reading every message.

Profoundly unsatisfactory is considerably better than nothing at all—provided, that is, the user is not encouraged to think that the system is more secure than it actually is. The default behavior of a Web browser should be to turn on encryption whenever possible but not tell the user.

From a technical point of view, we need a means of realizing this feature within the existing framework of deployed PKI infrastructure. The simplest way to do this is to create an ordinary digital certificate with an embedded comment to the effect, "If you don't trust the signer of this certificate, please accept it as is and turn on encryption without showing the padlock icon or otherwise notifying the user." Such a certificate need not be signed by a regular CA. It could even be "self-signed": signed with the key contained in the certificate.

Promiscuous security is better than nothing; it is also much less than we would want before making any indication that the user might interpret as "I am secure." As a practical matter, the padlock icon means much less today than was originally intended. In 1995, the padlock guaranteed *accountability*; today, the padlock only demonstrates that the domain name of the site has been authenticated.

Domain-Validated Encryption

Authenticating the domain name defeats the man-in-the-middle attack and provides a bare minimum of security that allows us to display a discreet security indicator such as the padlock icon. Domain name validation provides effective security for activities such as personal e-mail, blogs, and low-risk commercial interactions, provided the parties are already known and trusted. To achieve authenticated encryption by means of domain name validation, we require more information:

- The information required for promiscuous encryption
- Proof that the entity described in the subject name exists
- Proof that the applicant has control of the specified domain name
- Proof that the applicant has control of the specified public key

Domain name validation is perfectly adequate if all I need to know to be safe is "Am I at the right Web site? Is the communication encrypted? Is the communication authentic?" It works somewhat less well if I need to be certain I have the domain name right and does not work at all if I don't already know the site.

Accountability

Checking a domain name is relatively straightforward. Achieving accountability is rather harder. **Accountability** as far as I am concerned means legal accountability: If there is a problem, I can call either a lawyer or the police, and they will know where to serve either a writ or a search warrant. To achieve accountability, we require more information:

- Proof that the applicant has the right to apply for the certificate on behalf of the subject

- Proof that the entity described in the subject name is legally registered according to the governing law of the jurisdiction where it operates
- A verified address where legal process can be served

Re-Establishing Accountability

When VeriSign started the Internet CA business in 1995, three levels of authentication were defined. The lowest level of authentication, class 1, corresponds to domain name validation. The highest level, class 3, is designed to provide accountability. The definition of the criteria has been revised since then, but the criteria have remained essentially the same.

All certificates issued for SSL Web site authentication on the VeriSign label are class 3. Most other brands of SSL certificate (including brands such as Thawte and GeoTrust that VeriSign has since acquired) require only domain name validation. Until recently, however, all SSL certificates were equal as far as the user experience was concerned: All received the same padlock icon. The user experience designed to indicate the presence of accountability had been diluted.

This situation was widely recognized as unsatisfactory for many years. CAs offering a product designed to provide accountability were frustrated by competing products that diluted the value of the padlock indicator. Browser providers recognized that users were being led to believe that the padlock meant, "You are safe" when all it said in fact was, "This communication is encrypted." The situation was unstable, and something had to give; either authentication criteria would have to be raised industry wide, or the industry would engage in a "race to the bottom" that would doom it to extinction.

Despite the seriousness of the situation, some of the discount CAs rejected any attempt to raise the bar. As far as they were concerned, they should be able to issue certificates according to any criteria or none provided only they documented their criteria and passed an audit.

The deadlock was eventually broken by a combination of proposals for next-generation certificate products. Microsoft had decided that Internet Explorer 7 should differentiate between issuing practices that provided a high degree of assurance and those that had merely passed an audit. At the same time, I proposed Secure Internet Letterhead, which would require CAs to authenticate the brand logo as well as the domain name of the certificate holder.

Raising the issue criteria for existing padlock icon certificates was not an attractive proposition for bargain-basement CAs. Establishing a new market for high-assurance premium certificates and letterhead certificates was.

Extended Validation

The convergence of circumstances led to a meeting of CAs and the major browser providers in New York, which in turn led to the formation of the CA-Browser forum, which has produced a set of minimum issuing criteria for **Extended Validation** certificates.

Rules that a company defines for its own use can allow for a certain degree of discretion. When exceptional cases occur, they can be referred to the people responsible for drafting the rules in the first place.

Rules designed to set minimum standards for an industry cannot allow for discretion. Even though the processes designed to meet both VeriSign Class 3 and Extended Validation are designed to achieve accountability by applying the same basic principles, the details differ, and the details matter. The net result is that issuing Extended Validation certification requires more work than a traditional certificate.

The incentive offered to upgrade to Extended Validation is a new user experience in IE7. A similar experience is available for Firefox 3.0.

When a user visits a site secured with an Extended Validation certificate using IE7 and the antiphishing filter is enabled, the address bar is split into two parts, both of which turn green. The left side of the address bar presents the URI of the visited page as normal. The right side shows the subject name from the EV SSL certificate (see Figure 12-3).

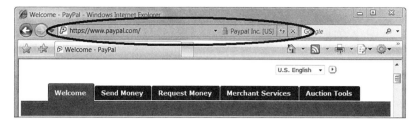

Figure 12-3   *Extended validation user experience*

From a security usability point of view, we may regard these visual cues as a work in progress rather than the final word. Color is the most effective cue for most users in most situations; it is less effective if the user is colorblind and not effective at all if the user is using a monochrome display.

What is important from a security perspective is that the Web browser displays the security status information prominently without being intrusive and that it provides the information the user needs to reliably decide whether the site is to be trusted.

Issuer Accountability

After a few seconds, the display of the Extended Validation subject name is replaced by the issuer name (see Figure 12-4). This represents a critical step toward holding certificate issuers accountable.

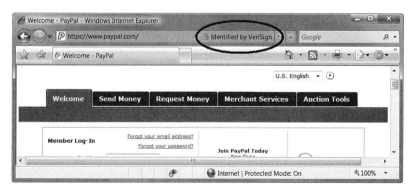

Figure 12-4   *Extended validation issuer name*

Substitution of inferior goods is a potential problem with almost every consumer product. That is why most consumer products from bleach and detergents to breakfast cereal are sold by brand. Even "generic" consumer products are sold by brand; in effect, the goods are sold under the store brand rather than a manufacturer's.

Issuer accountability will cause the market for CA services to become self-regulating over time. CAs that earn a reputation for issuing faulty certificates will quickly lose customers. Like the major credit card associations, the largest CAs will be required to invest heavily in promoting their brand, thus raising the stakes if a faulty certificate is issued.

Secure Internet Letterhead

Extended Validation has already succeeded in reversing the "race to the bottom." A new dynamic has been established that allows CAs to compete by offering authentication products with criteria that are stricter than those offered by their competitors rather than less.

Extended Validation began with a more ambitious purpose, however: to define criteria for authenticating the subject brand in the certificate (see Figure 12-5).

Figure 12-5   *Display of subject logo*

When a customer visits a bank branch, he recognizes it by the bank logo. The bank card in his pocket carries the bank logo, as does every letter from the bank. Banks already present their logo to customers on the Web and in e-mail; the problem is that the mechanism used to do this is easy for an attacker to copy.

It is unlikely that Secure Internet Letterhead will bring an end to the problem of phishing. But we can at least provide a trustworthy channel to the alert user.

Defining authentication criteria for a subject brand is certainly a challenge, but it is no more challenging in principle than authenticating the name of the subject as text. The only difference is that we are much more confident that the end user will take notice of a brand than text. After a decade in the business, I believe that anyone who is not prepared to put their authentication processes to this test should quit.

At the time of this writing, the CABForum has not agreed on authentication processes for letterhead certificates, and opinions differ as to the best way to proceed. It is generally agreed that any Secure Internet Letterhead certificate must as a minimum meet the Extended Validation criteria.

One approach to authenticating a brand is to require the applicant to provide proof that he owns a registered trademark in the brand. This is somewhat easier to do on a global basis than might be imagined due to a treaty on trademarks called the Madrid Protocol, which has been ratified by 61 countries, including practically every major industrial and nonindustrial country. The Madrid Protocol recognizes the need for an international trademark registration system to meet the needs of international trade.

Under the Madrid Protocol, the contracting parties agree to recognize trademarks filed with an international bureau. A useful side effect of the system is that it has established international standards for electronic exchange of trademark registration data.

What we care about most is not whether the brand is registered or even that it is unique. What matters is that the applicant is recognized by means of that brand and has a right to use it.

The Extended Validation criteria already define a mechanism that serves this need: the opinion letter.

An **opinion letter** is a formal legal opinion issued by a lawyer (or accountant) to a client. In the Extended Validation process, an opinion letter is one of the methods that an applicant can use to prove that he has the right to apply for a certificate on behalf of the specified subject name.

Because a brand is merely another aspect of the subject identity, an opinion letter stating that the applicant has the right to use the specified brand provides a satisfactory means of authentication for Secure Internet Letterhead.

Accessibility

One objection that is sometimes made to the use of letterhead is that it is not as useful for blind or visually impaired users. Accessibility is an important issue, but this concern is misplaced. X.509 certificates already contain the subject and issuer names as text strings that are fully compatible with World Wide Web Consortium Accessibility guidelines. Letterhead certificates must continue to contain this information for the X.509 PKI infrastructure to work.

Accessibility is an important concern even for sighted users. There is no visual channel on the telephone system today.

The logotype specification allows sounds to be included in certificates as an alternative to an image, but this feature does not appear to me to be as useful as simply reading out the existing certificate subject name.

Establishing "secure chrome" in the context of a voice browser is difficult but not impossible. For example, let us imagine that the user is using a voice browser while driving a vehicle (using a hands-free headset, naturally). The user asks for the daily stock report from "The Motley Fool," but an attacker has attempted to fool him by registering the voice tag "The Motley Pool," which will tell him that the hot stock pick of the day is something else (see Figure 12-6).

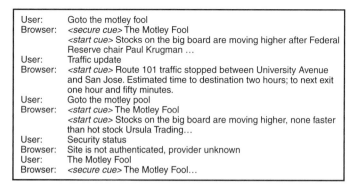

Figure 12-6   *Sample voice browser interaction with secure chrome*

To prevent emulation by an attacker, each user selects his own personal <cue>. One user might hear a lick from Jimi Hendrix's *Purple Haze*, another the chimes of Big Ben.

Alternatively, if the state of the art in voice-to-speech technology improves sufficiently, the voice browser might use different voices to render secure chrome. Normal text might be read by a newsreader voice, while secure chrome might be rendered by a more Churchillian tone.

Beyond Accountability

SSL and the VeriSign Class 3 authentication practices were designed to meet the needs of Internet retail. The design goal was to make shopping online at least as safe as shopping in a physical store.

Accountability is sufficient when Alice is looking to buy a dress online. If she is looking for a bank, it is rather more important to know that it is insured.

Accountability is good; assurance is better.

Authenticating Assurance

The credit card system has become the lynchpin of the online economy in the U.S. because it is safe as well as convenient. If fraud occurs in a credit card transaction, the consumer's loss is by law limited to a maximum of $50. In most cases, the issuing bank goes further and indemnifies the customer for the full loss.

The credit card system works because every transaction carries insurance. The merchant is charged a small percentage fee on each transaction, a small fraction of which goes to cover losses due to fraud.

The same principle operates in the U.S. financial system. Virtually every U.S. bank is insured by the Federal Deposit Insurance Corporation (FDIC). Virtually every U.S. brokerage house is insured by the Securities Investor Protection Corporation (SIPC).

If Alice wants to bank online, she needs to know that the bank she chooses is FDIC insured. She could check this herself at the FDIC Web site. But it is rather more convenient for a CA to do the verification for her.

Certificate Issuer Liability, Warranties, and Insurance

Issuing certificates is easy; standing behind them is hard. The X.509 PKI infrastructure makes this particularly difficult because the CA is required to issue a statement about the holder of a public key without control over who might rely on the certificate and in what situations.

In 1995, nobody had operated a commercial CA, and the whole business was surrounded by unknowns and uncertainties. VeriSign was founded before the great dot-com boom in an era when investors still asked awkward questions about profitability and the legal risks involved. The principal business question: the extent to which CAs would be liable for issue of a faulty certificate. A CA might be paid $350 for a certificate and then be held liable for its use in connection with a $10 million real estate transaction. Clearly, the CA must accept some risk. But if the CA accepts too much liability, the certificates will become too expensive or the CA will go out of business.

In 1995, part of the solution to this problem was to devise a legal strategy that replaced liability with insurance. Determining whether the CA was at fault in a particular situation would almost certainly cost more than compensation for the loss. From a business point of view, it makes much better sense to insure the certificate subject and relying parties against certain types of loss than to require them to prove that the loss was caused by negligence on the part of the CA.

The result met the needs of 1995 and the current needs of SSL, but not the needs of the next generation of the Web, the Semantic Web, driven by machine-machine interactions. Here we would like the CA to be able to accept risk on a commission basis and insure the transaction, or act as a broker for other insurance services.

The limited scope for control of liability in X.509v3 was one of the principal motivations behind my work on next-generation PKI infrastructures, such as XKMS, mentioned in Chapter 11, "Establishing Trust," and SAML, which will be addressed in Chapter 14, "Secure Identity." In SAML, an assertion may be directed at a particular audience, such as the person who paid for the insurance. The CA is liable to a specific relying party for a specific purpose and not the whole world.

Communicating Assurance

Identity is one important starting point for establishing reputation and trust, but not the only one we use when selecting a business partner.

If you walk into almost any bank branch in the U.S., you will see a sticker displayed prominently at every teller window to tell customers that the bank is FDIC insured. Most video games carry the logo of the ESRB. Stores that accept credit cards proudly display the Visa and MasterCard brands at their door.

Such brands might tell us useful compatibility information (the store accepts my credit card), but all serve as indicators of trust (my credit card company will provide me with certain protections against fraud if I use my card to shop there).

Such indications become even more important in the Internet, where the traditional accountability imposed by physical location is lost.

Many Web sites display the VeriSign SiteSeal to demonstrate that they are trustworthy. The site seal display scheme has certain countermeasures built in to make it resistant to spoofing but, ultimately, any material that is displayed in the content area can be simulated. To make something completely secure against this type of attack, display of the SiteSeal must be controlled by the browser security mechanism and the brand itself displayed in the secure chrome.

Community logos can be displayed alongside the subject logo or by means of a secondary popup dialog that appears when the user interacts in a particular way. In the prototype shown in Figure 12-7, the secondary dialog appears when the user holds the mouse cursor over the letterhead subject logo.

Figure 12-7   *Display of community and issuer logos*

Revocation and Reputation

So far, we have been looking at ways that a trusted third party can predict behavior on the basis of bona-fides presented by the applicant. To achieve full accountability, we would like to see reports that take past behavior into account as well.

Past behavior is a good, but not perfect, indicator of future behavior. In particular, we must always be on the lookout for scams in which a criminal operates a legitimate business for a short while and then defaults after a reputation has been established.

Blacklists

Antispam blacklists are a form of reputation service, albeit an imperfect one, as we have seen before. Reputation services such as better business bureaus and consumer rights centers perform an important role in both business-to-consumer and business-to-business transactions.

Trusted Agent

Reputation services based on third-party accounts of behavior are inevitably subjective. What if a trusted third party could provide an objective measure of reputation by directly observing the subject's actions?

Cryptographers tend to be particularly fond of schemes of this type. Unfortunately, I am rarely fond of their efforts, which tend to use exotic cryptography to meet a specific set of goals. The type of scheme that gains applause at cryptography conferences is rarely the one that best meets practical real-world needs.

The approach I prefer to use is **trustworthy hardware**, a computer that has been factory programmed to perform in a particular way that *cannot be overridden*. Trustworthy computing is an emerging technology that we return to for an in-depth look in Chapter 17, "Secure Platforms."

The best smartcards use trustworthy hardware; after a private key is installed on the card, it cannot be extracted from the card under any circumstance without considerable time and effort. Recently, a prison in Iowa had to change every lock after a set of warder's keys was auctioned on eBay.[1] Even if the prison had bid for the keys themselves, they could never be sure that someone hadn't made a copy. If a trustworthy smartcard is lost and then found, it is virtually certain that the key was not extracted and copied.

A **trusted agent** is a program that runs on trustworthy hardware that provides a reliable report of a particular behavior. Reports from the trusted agent are signed with a key certified by a trusted third party.

For example, we might have a trusted agent that reports the rate at which an e-mail server sends e-mail. E-mails received from a server that has sent less than a hundred e-mails in the past day are almost certainly not spam.

For a trusted agent to be trustworthy, we would like it to have as few moving parts as possible. Coding a trusted mail server would be a monumental task, and the result would probably fall short of a user's expectations for usability. When I started looking at trusted agents as a means of addressing the spam problem, I suddenly realized that it was not necessary to monitor the e-mail server code; all that was necessary was to sign the e-mail and monitor use of the signing key.[2]

Key Points

- SSL provides security at the transport layer.
  - SSL uses a combination of public key cryptography and symmetric key cryptography.
  - The performance overhead of SSL is no longer significant for clients.
  - The performance overhead might be significant for servers, but the processing overhead is per visitor to the site, not per page returned.
- The user experience of SSL is unsatisfactory.
  - Most users don't notice the padlock icon.
  - The Extended Validation user experience overcomes some of these concerns.
  - Secure Internet Letterhead provides the actual brand of the certificate subject.
    - Secondary accreditations such as Better Business Bureau approval can be expressed as community logos.
- There is a competitive market for CA services.
  - The level of authentication performed for some "padlock icon" certificates falls below the standards we should expect.
    - Extended Validation requires CAs to meet minimum standards.
    - Display of the issuer name in the user experience holds the issuer accountable and encourages him to go above and beyond the minimum requirements.

Secure Messaging

Secure Internet Letterhead applied to a bank Web site allows the alert customer to distinguish the genuine bank Web site from a capture site set up by a phishing gang. But the traditional e-mail-based phishing attack begins with an e-mail message, and the first trust decision the customer makes, therefore, is whether to trust that message. A comprehensive security solution must include e-mail.

As we saw earlier, the state of e-mail security leaves much to be desired. We have two powerful e-mail security protocols, one of which has a virtual monopoly of mindshare and another that has a virtual monopoly on deployment. Neither is widely used. The SenderID/SPF scheme described earlier provides a third authentication option, albeit one that is not cryptographically secure and only vouches for the last mail server that the message passed through.

Requirements

Before looking at solutions, we must decide our requirements and what deployment constraints we face. In particular, we need to start by considering the user experience and then work back to decide which technology platform is best suited to deliver that experience.

Authentication

As you have probably guessed, the authentication user experience should be based on Secure Internet Letterhead.

To apply Secure Internet Letterhead to e-mail, we must define our area of "Secure Chrome." The natural place for this is in the area where information from the message headers such as the Subject, Date, From, and To addresses is displayed (see Figure 13-1).

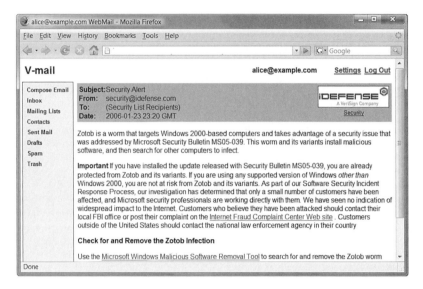

Figure 13-1   *E-mail message with signature logo*

As we saw in the discussion of SSL, the *entire* user experience must be considered, not just the success cases. Most S/MIME clients provide a satisfactory user experience when an e-mail has a valid, trusted signature, but the response to error conditions is poor to dreadful *without exception.*

For example, most S/MIME clients warn the user if the message is signed with a certificate that is no longer valid because it expired *even if the certificate was valid when the message was sent.* Unnecessary warnings are also given when the certificate is not trusted or the message is signed using a signature algorithm that is not supported.

None of these warnings serve a useful purpose when 99 percent of the messages that the user receives are unsigned. The signer cannot anticipate when the recipient will read the message, and he has a limited ability to anticipate which certificate issuers and signature algorithms he might trust.

Adding security to a communication should never degrade the user experience for either sender or receiver. *If a message is received that carries a signature that is unsatisfactory for any reason, that message should be treated as if it were unsigned.*

The Enterprise Dimension

Although the principal focus of this book is Internet crime, the principles of design for deployment require us to consider how to establish an early adopter market that can find value in Secure Internet Letterhead before a critical mass of senders and receivers is established.

If a sufficiently large Web-mail provider such as Yahoo!, Hotmail, AOL, or Google were to present Letterhead, a critical mass might be established at a stroke. This is certainly the best chance for rapid deployment, but the critical dependency on a small circle means that we need a backup plan.

The principal purchasers of Internet security products and services are enterprises. If we can find a way that enterprises benefit from Letterhead deployment *before a network effect has been established*, we have a second early adopter market.

As it turns out, there are two important benefits that should more than repay the (modest) cost of deployment.

The first benefit is that Letterhead provides a means of defeating a form of social engineering known as **pretexting**. In 2004, a prankster provided a humorous example of pretexting by registering the domain starbucks-inc.com and then impersonating the Starbucks CEO in an increasingly bizarre e-mail exchange with a recent hire.[1]

The same technique could have been used to obtain information that might affect the stock price, reveal corporate strategy to a rival, or divulge confidential client details. How common is this attack? I don't know, but I would certainly like a reliable means of measurement.

Displaying the company brand on every internal e-mail provides employees with an immediate means of determining whether an e-mail is from inside the company or outside.

The company I work for has 5,000 employees, five or six principal offices in the U.S., and maybe a hundred worldwide. I am actively engaged in many aspects of the company business, so on any given day, any of those employees might send me an e-mail. There is no way for me to know if someone is an employee or not without checking the organization chart each time. It should be the responsibility of the machine to give me this necessary information.

Letterhead is an authentication technology, so we might expect authentication to be a benefit. A second potential benefit is that Letterhead might discourage undesirable behavior.

Anyone who has managed an e-mail system in a large organization knows about the problem of "e-mails too stupid to write." Just what is it that causes people to use the company e-mail system to send insults, gossip, pornography, and intimate conversations? Supplies of stupidity are inexhaustible, but anything that makes people more likely to think before they click quickly pays for itself.

A good way to make people think is to remind them that every e-mail message they send is going out on company Letterhead. It is not unknown for an unfortunate letter to be sent out in the post, but I have never seen a message on official Letterhead remotely like the one I received from a U.S. Coastguard address after an (anonymous) experiment to determine whether it was feasible for Blöfeld to use Craigslist to recruit people to hollow out his volcano (see Figure 13-2).

Figure 13-2   *A (redacted) message from the U.S. Coastguard*

Confidentiality

Even though the need for authenticity must be our first concern, the need for confidentiality remains underserved. People who use e-mail for business need to be very concerned about confidentiality, especially when they are responsible for protecting customer's confidences. Doctors, lawyers, and engineers consider this to be a professional duty.

More importantly for our purposes, confidentiality is a need that is recognized by the enterprises we want to engage as early adopters for Letterhead. We cannot persuade them to deploy a new authenticity solution unless their confidentiality needs are also met.

As a minimum, Alice must be able to send e-mail to Bob confident in the knowledge that Mallet cannot intercept and read the contents. In some situations, we would like to go further, so that Alice can send a message to Bob in such a way that Alice maintains control over the contents so that Bob cannot forward the message to Careless Carol.

The much bigger problem we face is usability. Using the current generation of e-mail encryption standards requires the user to think before sending each message and expects him to notice when encrypted messages are received. That is too much effort.

No damage is caused if an e-mail that does not require confidentiality is sent encrypted. If an e-mail recipient is capable of receiving encrypted e-mails, all mail sent to that recipient should be encrypted by default.

The user does not need to know whether the e-mails he receives were sent encrypted. If the message was sent without encryption, the damage has already occurred and cannot be corrected.

The only time that user input is required is to identify cases where confidentiality is necessary.

Figure 13-3 shows an example of a user interface following these guidelines. The Compose Email dialog has options to allow the message priority (high, medium, low) set and mark the message confidential. Both options are presented in the context of the standard composition dialog and not as a separate pop-up screen.

The user is only ever warned about security if it is not possible to provide the specified or necessary level of security (see Figure 13-4).

Luxury

We could spend a great deal of time considering what an acceptable user experience for confidential e-mail would look like, but more than likely we would get it wrong. When we use the term "acceptable," we are asking, "What is good enough?" If the computer user experience is to improve, we have to stop asking that question and instead ask, "How can we achieve luxury?"

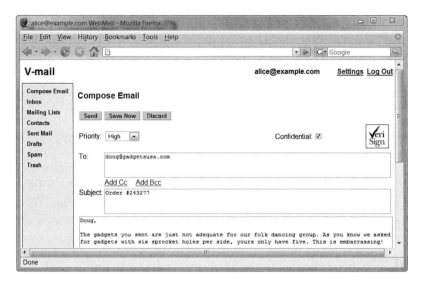

Figure 13-3   *E-mail sending security interface*

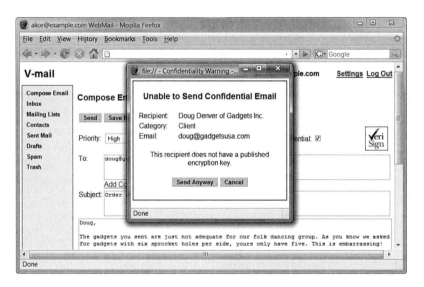

Figure 13-4   *Warning the user that a message cannot be encrypted*

You don't need to spend hours preparing a luxury car for a road trip; you just put the key in the ignition and go. If the car needs fuel, oil, or water, it will let you know. The same should be true of a security solution. Unless you are personally responsible for administering the system, you should not need to do anything to configure your e-mail to use encryption.

John Aravosis of Americablog, a blogger who has made something of a habit of annoying certain politicians, recently became somewhat concerned that someone might intercept his e-mail. After some investigation, he triumphantly advised his readers that he had installed an e-mail security program in a mere twenty minutes. Twenty minutes might be acceptable for a high-profile political blogger, but for most of us, it is twenty minutes too long. Six months later, he had only received encrypted e-mail from "about three people."[2]

Instead of giving the *user* instructions on how to configure his e-mail program to send and receive encrypted e-mail, the security provider should give the instructions directly to the *computer*. People find following instructions difficult; computers do nothing else but follow directions.

While we are at it, let's end the rest of the e-mail program configuration nonsense: entering the address of the incoming and outgoing e-mail servers. Why should the user be required to know what these are, let alone be required to hunt through his ISP's Web site to find out this information? All network configuration information, such as the address of incoming and outgoing e-mail servers, public key infrastructure, and so on should be obtained from the network infrastructure automatically.

The only security configuration that needs to be visible to the user is the ability to set a default security level for a given correspondent through the address book interface (see Figure 13-5). In a large company, this could be set by an external administrator. Making the process automatic for the individual or the smaller company is more challenging. It might be an application for the Semantic Web.

Alternatively, we might get to the point where deployment and use of confidential e-mail technology becomes so ubiquitous that its use becomes mandatory among professions and businesses where confidentiality is a concern.

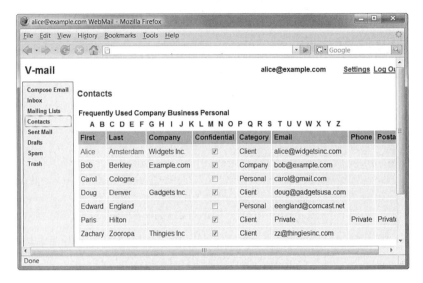

Figure 13-5   *E-mail address book security interface*

Gap Analysis

We have acquired a rather long list of requirements that the existing e-mail security standards do not meet:

- An e-mail authentication mechanism that can be applied to every message sent
  - The mechanism must not require end user configuration.
  - The mechanism must not have a detrimental effect if the receiving e-mail program does not support it.
- A means of applying secure Internet Letterhead to the e-mail authentication mechanism
- A means by which the receiver of an e-mail can determine if a signature should be expected on an authentic message
- An e-mail encryption mechanism that does not require user intervention
  - The mechanism must not require end user configuration.
  - Encryption keys for recipients should be acquired automatically.

In addition, we would like any new solution to be 100 percent backward compatible with the existing e-mail infrastructure.

Designing for Deployment

To provide secure e-mail, we need a strong authentication mechanism that can be applied to every message sent and an encryption mechanism that can be applied whenever the recipient can accept encrypted e-mail.

We want deployment to be as rapid as possible. Applying the principle of design for deployment discussed in Chapter 5, "Design for Deployment," this means that we should plan for deployment at the network edge rather than the endpoints (see Figure 13-6).

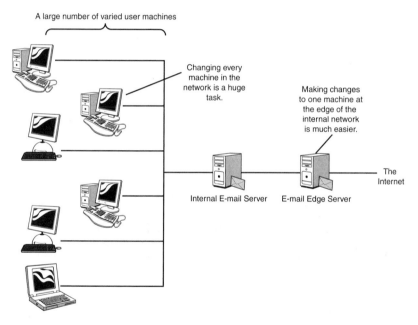

Figure 13-6   *E-mail edge server*

A pure edge-to-edge system is the quickest to deploy, but improving the user experience requires changes to the user agent.

We need to approach deployment in stages, first authenticating e-mails at the outgoing edge server and verifying the authentication data at the incoming edge. After we have a sufficiently large population of signers, there is value in modifying e-mail clients to present the authentication data (including Letterhead) to the user.

How E-Mail Is Different

Having decided on an edge approach, why can't we just apply SSL? If it is designed to support any network protocol and it works well on the Web, why not use it for e-mail?

Using SSL to secure e-mail is a good idea indeed. There is already an IETF standard that is widely supported. Unfortunately, applying SSL to e-mail achieves only some of our security goals and only in some situations.

SSL provides an effective, low-cost answer to some of our security needs, but not all of them. Like SenderID/SPF discussed in Chapter 7, "Stopping Spam," SSL only establishes a security context between machines that are in direct communication. E-mail is a store and forward protocol. Except in rare cases, the sender's machine does not communicate directly with the recipient's.

Users need to be able to send and receive e-mail using machines that only connect to the network intermittently. To meet these demands, a typical e-mail makes at least three hops moving from source to destination. The sender forwards the message to his outgoing mail server, where it is put in a queue waiting for delivery. When its turn comes, the message is sent on to the recipient's incoming mail server, from which the recipient will collect it at some point (see Figure 13-7).

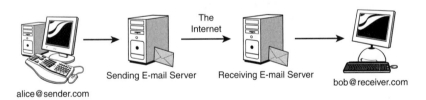

The Internet

alice@sender.com　　　Sending E-mail Server　　　Receiving E-mail Server　　　bob@receiver.com

Figure 13-7　*Direct mail transfer*

We can only establish a security context for one hop at a time. We cannot establish the security context between the sending edge server and the receiving endpoint that Secure Internet Letterhead requires.

As we saw in Chapter 7, the e-mail system is complex, and a message might take many detours on its travels, including alumni forwarders and mailing lists (see Figure 13-8).

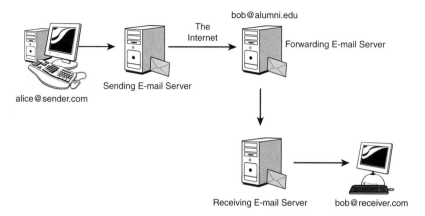

Figure 13-8   *Mail forwarders*

Damaged Goods

These detours make securing e-mail much more challenging than securing the Web. In addition to limiting the value we obtain from using SSL, each detour represents an opportunity for the e-mail message to become damaged.

If everyone followed the e-mail architecture as we now understand it, messages should never become damaged in transit. An e-mail message is like a snowman with two parts: a head and a body.[3] The message goes in the body. The head contains a sequence of headers that carry information about the message. These include who sent it, whom it was sent to, the subject, the date, and information describing the format of the message.

If we were writing a new e-mail specification, it would probably prohibit modifications to the message body. If I send a letter by postal mail, I do not expect the post office to open the letter, reformat it in a different font, and staple an advertisement to the end of it. Many governments that used to engage in practices of that type disappeared rather quickly.

Unfortunately, e-mail dates from the prehistory of the Internet, before the importance of such rules was understood. In those days, the Internet was one network among many, and exchanging mail between networks frequently required substantial changes to the message bodies.

Practically every machine produced today is designed to represent characters using both the ASCII character set, where characters are represented by 8 bit-bytes, and the larger UNICODE character set, which uses 16-bit words. When e-mail was being invented, 7-bit machines were common, and 9-bit machines were not unknown. IBM mainframes used the EBCDIC character encoding.

Translating between the formats used on the different systems required masses of complex, one-of-a kind code, the type of complexity that needed to be managed using edge architecture. Modifying messages was considered to be a core function of a mail server rather than damage.

Digital signatures are designed to detect the smallest possible change in a message. This means that a verified digital signature provides the strongest possible proof that the message has not been modified. It also makes the system brittle; a message that was slightly changed and an outright forgery give the same result.

Both S/MIME and PGP support a range of strategies for dealing with the problem of damage. The most powerful technique is to re-encode the entire message using only characters that are known to survive even the most abusive servers. This technique, **base64 encoding**, all but eliminates the possibility of damage, but it means that the message can only be read by a recipient with a compatible mail reader.

The need for client support is unavoidable in an end-to-end encryption scheme. It is impossible for the ultimate recipient to decrypt a message unless his client is capable of decryption. The same is *not* true for authentication. This is the root of why we cannot use PGP or S/MIME to support our authentication needs; it is simply not possible to sign every message sent if this will render it unreadable to an appreciable number of intended recipients.

PGP supports a mode that is somewhat less demanding on the recipient. You might have seen e-mail messages that look something like the following:

```
-----BEGIN PGP SIGNED MESSAGE-----
Hash: SHA1

Testing.

-----BEGIN PGP SIGNATURE-----
Version: PGP 8.0.2

Q29uZ3JhdHVsYXRpb25zLCBpZiB5b3UgYXJlIHJlY
WRpbmcgdGhpcyB5b3UgaGF2ZSB3YXkgdG9vIG11Y2
ggdGltZSBvbiB5b3VyIGhhbmRzLg==
-----END PGP SIGNATURE-----
```

The end user sees the PGP "armor." This approach allows a message to be read by anyone, regardless of whether that person has a special mail reader—provided that is, he is not confused by the additional gibberish.

In addition to confusion, the armor can create a false sense of security. Only a tiny proportion of the people who receive PGP signatures have the ability to check them and, of those, we can expect none to actually do so. PGP armor violates a core usability principle: A trust indicator is presented that is not trustworthy.

Authentication

We need a new message format if we are to apply strong authentication to every e-mail sent.

SenderID/SPF does not provide strong authentication and, like SSL, it only provides authentication to machines that are in direct communication. SenderID/SPF was designed to provide a quick fix for e-mail authentication, a system that had known limitations but could be deployed quickly and provide real value. Although SenderID/SPF provides a real benefit in the fight against spam, it is not designed to solve the problem of phishing, which only began to emerge after the deployment of SenderID/SPF had begun.

S/MIME and PGP provide strong authentication, but both have a significant impact on the end user experience, and both are designed for deployment at the network endpoints rather than the edge. If we try to adapt these solutions for the edge, we need to make significant changes. We lose the benefit of legacy deployment. Worse, it becomes a liability, because the change can result in unexpected behavior by legacy S/MIME clients.

Designing a new message format means that we lose the advantage of the existing infrastructure deployed to support S/MIME at a cost suggested by some to exceed $1 billion.[4] But even if the figure is accurate, we do not appear to have received value for money. If something is not a conspicuous success after a billion dollars of investment and a decade of effort, it is a sign that it is time to try something new and not a case to throw good money after bad.

In addition to a new message format, we need a new key distribution infrastructure that is lightweight, easy to deploy, and provides a compelling value to an early adopter community at no cost.

Confidentiality

Although none of the existing message formats precisely meets our authentication requirements, S/MIME and PGP both meet (most of) our encryption needs.

If this was a purely technical decision, we would simply pick one and move on.

From a political point of view, the problem is harder. S/MIME dominates deployment, but PGP dominates in terms of mindshare among system administrators. If we pick PGP, we lose the existing deployed base of more than a billion e-mail clients with built-in support for S/MIME. If we try to pick S/MIME, we lose the support of PGP supporters that we need to co-opt as advocates. And, regardless of which format we choose, both reflect the state of the art in confidentiality in the early 1990s. Neither provides the data-level security features that we would want in the next generation of confidentiality technology.

The political solution is clear: Support both message formats. PGP Inc. has taken this approach for many years. We need to persuade the S/MIME community to do likewise. The extra code required to support a second message format is not trivial, but it is not an unreasonable burden. Writing code is a lot easier than changing strongly held beliefs. The objective is to get people using strong e-mail security; which message encoding they use should be irrelevant.

Although the PGP and S/MIME message formats are adequate for our needs, their key distribution infrastructures need some work. In particular, the user experience requirements we have identified earlier commit us to supporting a transparent encryption mode in which the client automatically acquires and applies encryption keys. We also need to tweak the key distribution infrastructure to support encryption in an edge architecture to smooth the path for deployment.

User-Level Keying

Our first concern is to provide a domain-level security infrastructure that we hope matches the success of the domain-level SSL infrastructure, but many security specialists would reject any strategy outright unless it provides at least a transition strategy toward an end-to-end architecture in which individual end users hold their own personal signature and decryption keys.

Domain Keys Identified Mail

Domain Keys Identified Mail (DKIM) is a new e-mail authentication technology supported by a group of major providers of e-mail and security infrastructure that includes Alt-N Technologies, AOL, Brandenburg Internetworking, Cisco, EarthLink, IBM, Microsoft, PGP Corporation, Sendmail, StrongMail Systems, Tumbleweed, VeriSign, and Yahoo!. At the time of this writing, the first part of the DKIM specification has been approved as an IETF Proposed Standard,[5] and work continues on a second part.

DKIM grew out of the need for a simple, lightweight e-mail authentication protocol to fight spam. As people came around to the idea that authenticating the good mail would provide a real benefit when trying to eliminate the bad, two approaches emerged:

- **Path validation (SenderID/SPF)**—Publish the IP address of each authorized outbound mail server in the DNS.

- **Digital signature (DKIM)**—Add a header containing a digital signature to each message. Use the DNS to tell recipients to expect messages to be signed with a particular key.

As we saw in Chapter 7, the path validation technique of SenderID/SPF is expedient but limited. Digital signatures are considerably more powerful. The cryptography is practically unbreakable and, provided that the message manages to avoid damage, a signature can be verified by any e-mail server that is downstream of the signer, not just the next server in line.

Cryptographic security was clearly the better choice, so why did we choose the path validation option?

Although digital signatures were clearly the better long-term choice, it was also clear in 2003 that developing a standard that involved cryptography would take considerably longer than one that did not. Cryptography is a subtle art that needs time. With the spam tide rising, time was in short supply.

The digital signature approach was harder to sell. Public key cryptography had traditionally required large, complex support infrastructures. It was not generally understood that this complexity was a function of the assurances that the infrastructure was designed to deliver and that a simple PKI would be sufficient for the purposes of spam control. PKI is simple in principle; applying it to secure bank transactions made it hard. Another major concern was performance; many sites send millions of mail messages every day. It was not generally appreciated that modern servers could generate thousands of digital signatures a second even without recourse to special hardware.

The choice was clear: Do both. Begin work on a path validation scheme that could be deployed within a few months, and simultaneously begin work on a digital signature scheme.

Just in case you told your network administrator to immediately begin work on deploying SenderID/SPF at the end of Chapter 7, don't worry: The work has not been wasted. The work you have already done will greatly assist in your deployment of DKIM, and for the next few years at least, deployment of both systems will be necessary if you want to maximize the probability of your e-mail getting through the spam filters unmolested.

By late 2003, groups were forming to address both approaches. Several companies (including VeriSign) had floated digital signature approaches in private and even demonstrated code, but these had not yet gained critical mass. In December 2002, I met Jon Callas, CTO of PGP at the Aspen Institute. Joe Aladeff, CSO of Oracle, made an observation, "VeriSign and PGP together might be enough."

In the event, a collaboration that might have led to a press release to surprise Valley insiders never got a chance to get started. A few days later, Yahoo! announced its own digital signature–based e-mail authentication scheme called Domain Keys, followed shortly afterward by Cisco's announcement of Identified Internet Mail.

When four major companies arrive at essentially the same technical solution independently, it is time to put it to the test. Rather than put a third (or fourth) proposal on the table, it was time to focus efforts on arriving at a single standard.

Although all four proposals followed essentially the same approach, the provenance was critical. The fact that Yahoo! could propose signing every one of the hundreds of millions of e-mails it sends every day took the performance issue off the table. The fact that Yahoo! was not in the cryptography business provided reassurance that the proposal was not a plot designed to lead to deployment of an unnecessarily complex PKI.

Signing E-Mails with DKIM

Figure 13-9 shows an e-mail signed using DKIM. The first 16 lines of the message are the head, then comes a blank line followed by the body (Hi, we lost the game …).

There are seven separate headers. Each begins with a keyword (called a **tag**), followed by a colon, followed by data (called **parameters**).

Six of the headers contain information that is present in every Internet e-mail message. The From header specifies whom the message is from, the To header whom it is addressed to, and so on.

```
DKIM-Signature: v=1; a=rsa-sha256; s=brisbane; d=example.com;
        c=simple/simple; q=dns/txt; i=joe@football.example.com;
        h=Received : From : To : Subject : Date : Message-ID;
        bh=2jUSOH9NhtVGCQWNr9BrIAPreKQjO6Sn7XIkfJVOzv8=;
        b=AuUoFEfDxTDkHlLXSZEpZj79LICEps6eda7W3deTVFOk4yAUoqOB
        4nujc7YopdG5dWLSdNg6xNAZpOPr+kHxt1IrE+NahM6L/LbvaHut
        KVdkLLkpVaVVQPzeRDI009SO2Il5Lu7rDNH6mZckBdrIx0orEtZV
        4bmp/YzhwvcubU4=;
Received: from client1.football.example.com  [192.0.2.1]
        by submitserver.example.com with SUBMISSION;
        Fri, 11 Jul 2003 21:01:54 -0700 (PDT)
From: Joe SixPack <joe@football.example.com>
To: Suzie Q <suzie@shopping.example.net>
Subject: Is dinner ready?
Date: Fri, 11 Jul 2003 21:00:37 -0700 (PDT)
Message-ID: <20030712040037.46341.5F8J@football.example.com>

Hi.

We lost the game. Are you hungry yet?

Joe.
```

Figure 13-9   *DKIM signed e-mail*

The only header that is affected by DKIM is the DKIM-Signature header which, as you might expect, contains the digital signature information. This contains nine parameters that follow a `tag=value` syntax. The signature itself is the last parameter, the one that begins `b=bnUoMB` ...

The rules of the Internet e-mail protocol state that any program that sees a message header that it does not understand MUST ignore it. In Internet standards, the word MUST written in capitals has a very particular meaning. A program that does not meet the stated requirement is not compliant with the standard.

Although such instructions are not always observed, this particular instruction is. Many e-mail processing systems add message headers that are not part of the original e-mail protocol. E-mail applications that do not ignore unknown headers quickly break.

The use of a message header to carry the signature header means that we meet the first and most important of our e-mail authentication criteria: *Do no harm.* Users of legacy e-mail clients are safe; adding a DKIM signature should not result in a negative user experience for anyone.

Canonicalization

The second challenge we face is the problem of dealing with damage as the message takes detours. We do not insist that the message signature survive in every case, but we want as many messages to survive as possible, provided it neither compromises security nor imposes an excessive burden on implementers.

The solution is to sign what is known as a **canonical form** of the mail message rather than the original message. A canonical form is generally defined as a series of rules, such as, "Ignore all spaces at the end of lines." The technical challenge is to design a set of rules that produce a canonical form such that it is unaffected by the typical changes that may be inflicted on the message by a mail server while preventing an attacker from using it to change the meaning of a message (see Figure 13-10).

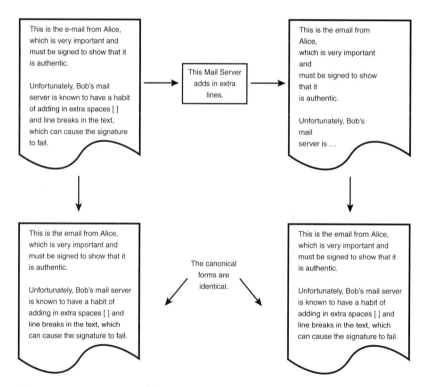

Figure 13-10   *Canonical form*

Getting the canonical form right is a black art. The base DKIM specification defines two canonical forms: simple and relaxed. The relaxed form is somewhat more tolerant of damage than the simple form.

Fortunately, the problem we face today is much less severe than the one faced in the early 1990s. We no longer need to deal with e-mail gateways serving other networks. (A few networks of this type survive, but most do not require support for e-mail, and those that do can make their own arrangements if they want to verify DKIM signatures on the other side.)

As DKIM is deployed, tolerance for mail forwarders that cause arbitrary damage will decrease.

One form of damage that is not likely to disappear is adding information to the end of a message. The legal departments of many companies insist on adding legal disclaimers to the end of every message sent. This particular case does not cause significant difficulty, because we can sign the message after adding the disclaimer. Disclaimers, advertisements, and other appendages do cause problems when they are added by mailing lists, however.

DKIM allows signers to avoid this problem by specifying the length of the message at the time it was signed. The solution is not ideal, not the least because it means that an attacker can add any information he chooses to the end of the message. Nor will it work if the appendage is added anywhere other than the end of the message. But it works well enough for most cases.

Key Distribution by DNS

We have applied the signature to the message. How is someone going to check it?

First, the verifier needs to know the signature algorithm used. The parameter a=RSA-SHA256 provides this information. That means that the RSA signature algorithm is used and the digest algorithm is SHA256. If the verifier does not understand either, it will not be able to verify the signature.

To locate the signing key, we look at the parameter q=dns/txt. This tells us that the signing key can be retrieved as a DNS TXT record (see Figure 13-11). The parameters s=brisbane and d=example.org contain the key selector and the signing domain, respectively. To obtain the signature key, we retrieve the DNS TXT record for the node brisbane._domainkey.example.org. The key record might look something like this:

```
brisbane IN TXT  ("v=DKIM1;
   p=MIGfMA0GCSqGSIb3DQEBAQUAA4GNADCBiQ"
                       "KBgQDwIRP/UC3SBsEmGqZ9ZJW3/
                       DkMoGeLnQg1fWn7/zYt"
```

```
"IxN2SnFCjxOCKG9v3b4jYfcTNh5ijSsq631uBItLa7od+v"
"/RtdC2UzJllWT947qR+Rcac2gbto/
NMqJ0fzfVjH4OuKhi"
"tdY9tf6mcwGjaNBcWToIMmPSPDdQPNUYckcQ2QIDAQAB")
```

The key record requires only two parameters. The `k` parameter tells us that the algorithm is RSA; the `p` parameter gives the value of the public key.

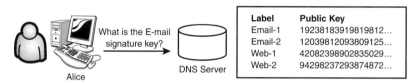

Label	Public Key
Email-1	19238183919819812...
Email-2	12039812093809125...
Web-1	42082398902835029...
Web-2	94298237293874872...

Figure 13-11 *Key lookup using DNS*

The DNS provides a perfectly adequate method of distributing a small number of public keys. If we try to use the DNS to manage a large number of public keys at each site, we start to run into problems. The DNS is large, complex, and critical. It is designed to serve one purpose: translating Internet names into addresses. It is not well suited for adaptability.

Our use of the DNS is reasonable because it relates to machines and not people. Configuring the DNS is a normal step that every network administrator performs when adding a new machine to a network or changing its function. Adding new users to a system does not normally require changes to the DNS unless they are being issued a personal machine, in which case the configuration is for the machine and not the person.

Secure Internet Letterhead

All we need to add Secure Internet Letterhead to our signature is a parameter to the key record to tell the verifier where he can obtain the certificate containing the authenticated letterhead logos:

```
   brisbane IN  TXT  ("v=DKIM1;
p=MIGfMA0GCSqGSIb3DQEBAQUAA4GNADCBiQ"
          "KBgQDwIRP/UC3SBsEmGqZ9ZJW3/
          DkMoGeLnQg1fWn7/zYt"
          "IxN2SnFCjxOCKG9v3b4jYfcTNh5ijSsq631uBItLa7od+v"
```

```
"/RtdC2UzJllWT947qR+Rcac2gbto/
NMqJOfzfVjH4OuKhi"
tdY9tf6mcwGjaNBcWToIMmPSPDdQPNUYckcQ2QIDAQAB;"
"x509cert=http://certs.example.com/Brisbane;")
```

Retrieving the certificate and verifying the certificate chain requires rather more work than just reading the key value, but we don't need to do this every time the signature is verified. We only need to do this at the ultimate destination, where the message is being presented to a human. Spam filters can continue to use the key record value.

We don't even need to fetch the certificate every time we show a message with Letterhead. We can keep a local copy of the certificate, or just the logos and the expiry date in a cache. Even in the largest deployments, the additional processing required is manageable.

Mail Sending Policy

The final piece we need in our puzzle is a mechanism that lets a mail server know to expect messages sent from a particular source to carry a signature.

Again, this is simply another task for the existing DNS system that translates Internet names into Internet addresses. In Chapter 7, the DNS was extended to allow an e-mail sender to write a rule that says, "Expect all e-mail from this domain to come from one of these mail servers." Now we need to write records such as, "E-mail from this domain might be signed with signature key X" and "Expect all e-mail from this domain to be signed."

At the time of this writing, we are deep in the design of this particular part of the system.

My contention is that the only mail-sending policy that is actionable and thus useful is one that states that every message sent is signed without exception. I would code this as a DNS TXT record as follows:

```
_smtp_outbound.example.com. IN TXT "DKIM"
```

This sending policy states that every outbound e-mail carries a DKIM signature header.

In certain rare cases, we might want to add more than one signature to each message. In this case, the policy might be this:

```
_smtp_outbound.example.com. IN TXT "DKIM=a DKIM=b"
```

This sending policy states that outbound e-mail carries two DKIM signature headers. One has a key selector with the suffix .a; the other has the suffix .b.

We can extend the e-mail sending policy to support other formats in the same way. We could use the policy SMIME to state that an S/MIME signature should be expected, PGP for PGP, and so on.

One particularly important piece of information we might want to put in an e-mail sender policy is to warn recipients that our domain is likely to be targeted by phishing gangs and that recipients should be extra vigilant in filtering unsigned messages.

Another piece of important information might be to tell a recipient how he can report unsigned messages and messages with signatures that fail verification. This might allow misconfiguration of our servers to be detected before too many messages have been lost or provide advance warning of a new phishing attack.

Providing Confidentiality

Having addressed authentication, it is time to turn our attention to confidentiality. As we have seen, the S/MIME and PGP message formats are perfectly adequate for the purpose of encrypting e-mail messages. What we need to do is to provide a few missing pieces of "glue" to make deployment easier.

In particular, we want to be able to make discovery of encryption keys easier and to support a mode in which messages are encrypted under a key that is assigned to the entire receiving domain rather than a single user. Creating and managing a separate encryption key for every one of the hundred million or so users of Hotmail would be prohibitively expensive and provide no real security advantage unless each user held his personal encryption key personally, a situation that is not really compatible with the concept of Web-hosted e-mail services such as Hotmail, at least in the form they exist today.

We also want to allow for the issue of user-level keys where they are available through a standards-based protocol such as an LDAP Directory, Web Repository, or XKMS service.

Mail Receipt Policy

We did most of our work when we defined our Mail Sending Policy. To support encryption, we need to define a Mail Receipt Policy to tell the senders what form(s) of encryption we will accept.

First, we need to specify what encryption formats we will accept:

```
_smtp_inbound.example.com. IN TXT "PGP SMIME XKMS"
```

This receipt policy states that the PGP and SMIME message formats and the XKMS key location service are supported.

If necessary, additional configuration information may be supplied for each protocol in a separate policy record:

```
_pgp.example.com    IN TXT "KEYSERVER=pgp.mit.edu"
_smime.example.com IN TXT ("XKMS=xkms.example.com;"
                           "LDAP=ldap.example.com")
```

We don't need to put every piece of information necessary to send encrypted mail to us in the DNS itself, but we do need to state where the information needed can be found.

If we decide we need new message formats to support the content rights management systems discussed in Chapter 16, "Secure Networks," or other new security applications, all we need to do is to define the appropriate tags.

Communicating with Perimeter Security

One of the consequences of this DNS policy-based key discovery scheme is that the sender does not need to know whether the encryption key he is using is a domain level or a user key.

This allows us to avoid the consequences of what has become the dirty secret of "end-to-end" security: Not only is it expensive, but end-to-end does not meet the user's real security needs.

In an enterprise environment, we want to be able to scan incoming messages to see if they contain spam, viruses, or other objectionable material. If spammers can bypass our filters by sending us encrypted mail, they will quickly learn how to do so, and within a short period of time, nobody will be accepting encrypted mail.

The other major limitation in the end-to-end principle is that the modern e-mail system has as many ends as a cat of nine tails. I regularly read my e-mail on four different machines. In addition, my cell phone is also an e-mail pager. Encryption is useless to me unless I can read incoming messages on whichever machine I happen to be using at the time.

Hop-by-hop encryption is less intellectually attractive than end-to-end security, but it meets the user's real needs much better.

If a user requires more control over his personal security than his network manager allows, he should get a domain name of his own.

Deploying DKIM

The process of deploying DKIM is essentially the same as the process for deploying SenderID/SPF, described in Chapter 7.

1. **Identify Resources**—Read the technical documentation on DKIM. Links to the latest versions of the specifications and the latest installation guides can be found in the "deployment" section of http://dotcrimemanifesto.com/.

2. **Identify your outgoing mail servers**—Identify each of the mail servers you use to send outgoing mail and the mail server software used. If you deployed SenderID/SPF, you will have this information already.

3. **Install DKIM signature module; create your signature keys and DNS records**—What you need to do in this step will depend on the mail server software you are using. Plug-ins are available for all popular mail servers.

4. **Publish your records**—To publish your records, you will
   need to be able to insert a TXT record into your DNS
   zone file. Consult your DNS administrator. If he doesn't
   know what a TXT record is, you need a new DNS
   administrator.

5. **Test**—Several Web sites provide testing services. The service provided by the E-Mail Service Provider Coalition
   tests for both SenderID/SPF and DKIM(http://senderid.
   espcoalition.org/).

Key Points

- The user experience is the key.
  - Security features are useless unless they are used.
    - Twenty minutes' effort is far too much.
    - Security must be automatic.
  - Adding security must never result in a worse result.
    - "Warning: This message is secure."
- Integrity is our principal concern.
  - Neither PGP nor S/MIME serve our need for a trans-
    parent authentication mechanism as currently defined.
  - DKIM, a standard being developed by the IETF, does
    meet our requirement for transparent authentication:
    - The message format is simple and does not break
      existing mail clients.
    - Lightweght key distribution is achieved using DNS.
  - We can add Secure Internet Letterhead with a simple
    modification.
- Confidentiality is important to gain adoption.
  - It must solve the key discovery and configuration issues.
  - Key-centric PKI meets these needs.
    - DNS key distribution supports edge-level security.
    - XKMS supports the full end-to-end model.

CHAPTER 14

Secure Identity

Poor authentication is the *leitmotif* of Internet insecurity: Alice is not sure she is really dealing with her bank, and the bank is not sure it is really dealing with Alice.

Reducing the probability that Alice will be tricked into giving her password to an attacker is good, but an authentication credential that Alice is unable to give away is better.

Today, we use passwords for practically every type of Internet transaction regardless of risk; whether we are reading an online newspaper or trading stock, and despite knowing that they provide terrible security and have significant hidden costs.

No end of new authentication technologies has been developed over the past 20 years: smartcards, smart tokens, fingerprint and iris scanners. Yet we remain stuck in the password age.

Smartcards are more secure and easier to use than passwords. In many applications, the total cost of ownership is less. But they don't do me any good on my PC without a smartcard slot to plug it into. I could plug a smart token into the USB port, but I don't have USB on my phone. Physical connectivity is the bane of smartcard deployment. Passwords survive because they are compatible with the existing infrastructure.

Inventing the wheel is not enough: Most ancient civilizations knew that round things roll more easily than square ones. The road, not the wheel, is the real innovation. It takes a lot of effort to build a road infrastructure for the wheels to run on.

Without ubiquitous hardware, there is no incentive to deploy the necessary software systems required to accept them. I have a European Chip and PIN credit card in my wallet and a card reader in my desk drawer. And that is where the card reader will stay until enough merchants accept Chip and PIN for Internet transactions to make it worth my while to take it out and plug it in.

To meet all the challenges of Internet insecurity, we need more than an authentication infrastructure; we need an identity infrastructure. An authentication infrastructure allows Alice to demonstrate that she is Alice; an identity infrastructure allows much more, in particular:

- Alice can demonstrate that she is Alice.
- Alice can demonstrate a fact about herself (for example, that she is over 18).
- Bob can contact Alice.

In particular, an identity infrastructure allows Alice to do some, all, or none of these things independently. If Alice is over 18, she can demonstrate this fact to a Web site without revealing either who she is or how she can be contacted.

The problem of identity is much bigger and harder than the problem of authentication. If we could wind the clock back to 1995, the prudent course would be to address authentication first and then look at the bigger picture. Design for deployment forces us to consider the wider picture at the start. As far as most Web applications are concerned, the problem of authentication is already solved. However bad the existing solution, they consider change worse. To build critical mass today, we must offer more.

The more we offer, the more difficult our technical task becomes. Developing an infrastructure that can describe Alice is no more difficult from a technical perspective than verifying her name, but an identity system that supports contact securely is much more complicated: We need to face the problem of spam once more. This we will defer to the next chapter.

Authentication Technologies

Passwords remain the Internet authentication standard despite their acknowledged flaws and despite the lack of many better alternatives. Every week, a new company sends me a glossy brochure to tell me about an exciting new authentication device.

Which technology will win? Most likely, there will be no single winner. The Internet has a million uses and a billion users. It is unlikely that one single technology will meet every need and, with authentication, more is usually better than less. We must build an infrastructure capable of supporting all of them.

New authentication technologies appear every week, but beneath the covers the same basic principles are applied:

- Something you know
- Something you carry
- Something you are

In security terminology, these principles are known as **factors**. Combining authentication technologies based on different factors usually provides better security. Chip and PIN is a two-factor authentication technology; it is based on something carried (the Chip) and something known (the PIN).

First Contact

Before we start, we need to remind ourselves that what the computer security field describes as "authentication technologies" are not. A password does not demonstrate that you are Alice, nor does a smartcard or even a biometric. All an authentication *technology* can do *at best* is to demonstrate that a person is the same person who was present in a previous encounter.

The real authentication usually takes place at *first contact*: the start of the relationship between an employer and employee, a doctor and a patient, a bank and a customer, a blog and a reader. If the information gathered at first contact is bogus, it will be equally bogus thereafter.

Presenting a passport or a driving license on each visit to the bank would be tedious in the extreme. Presenting an authoritative credential during first contact is generally acceptable when a significant relationship such as with a bank or an employer is being established.

Government credentials typically provide the best form of authentication available: not very good. Most U.S. college students know that forging a driving license is well within their capabilities. Holographic foils look pretty when the card is new but quickly wear away, rubbing up against other cards in the pocket. In Frederick Forsyth's novel *The Day of the Jackal*, the assassin obtains a genuine passport under a false name by requesting a copy of the birth certificate of a dead person.

Similar schemes still work today. As with any other authentication mechanism, government-issued credentials at best only demonstrate that the person who presents them is the person to whom they were issued.

Identity is a relative, not an absolute, value. If this conclusion appears to be unacceptably postmodern, it is. Computers follow logic blindly to its illogical conclusions and tend to puncture overconfident philosophical pretensions in passing.

It is not the name but the accountability that is important. If someone decides to live under the name of Mr. Saunders, it does not matter if *Saunders* is or is not his real name, only that it can be used to hold him accountable if necessary.

When a bank issues a credit card, it only needs to be confident that the applicant will pay his bill. Knowing the identity of the applicant is much less important than knowing his previous credit history.

Passwords and PINs

Passwords are a single factor authentication technology: something you know. The problem is that a password is disclosed every time it is used.

There is not really much to be said in favor of passwords except that everyone uses them, which in infrastructure terms is everything. As password-protected Web sites proliferate, they are not even easy to use.

It is not too difficult to remember a single password that is used every day. Nobody tries to remember a hundred different passwords. Either they write them down on a post-it note stuck to their monitor, or they do as I do and use the same password (almost) everywhere. I have (separate) strong passwords for my bank and brokerage accounts and for work, but I don't spend my time and effort protecting other people's property unless they are paying me to do so.

As the problems with passwords become ever more painfully apparent, Web sites demand increasingly complex combinations of letters, numbers, and special characters in a futile attempt to force the user to choose a new password that is hard to guess. As a result, I find myself forgetting passwords rather often or, more precisely, I find myself forgetting which particular variation of my password I used at the time.

I bank online, but I don't check my insurance policies online anymore. Remembering a username/password combination I use only once a year is more trouble than calling them on the telephone.

Knowledge-Based "Authentication"

Passwords cost almost nothing to register and almost nothing to use. The cost of passwords is hidden in the back end, in the customer service or help desk calls that result from inevitably forgotten passwords.

This brings us to the question of how to authenticate a password change request. The solution favored by many banks today is another password, one that is easier to remember: the name of your first pet or mother's maiden name—something that is easier to guess and quite likely a matter of public record.

This technique can provide an effective control of certain risks in limited situations. Dignified with the unjustified term **knowledge-based authentication**, it threatens to become a dangerous form of pseudo-security.

Some promoters suggest public awareness campaigns designed to persuade people to keep this public information secret. As efforts in futility go, telling people that the answers to life-long questions must be kept secret is a world-class effort; the MySpace generation has few secrets, and none are life-long. They have already blogged any information they are willing to give to a bank.

Callback

A stronger form of backup authentication is a **callback scheme**, such as the e-mail challenge response scheme we encountered earlier. Verifying the e-mail address, telephone number, or physical mailing address associated with the account provides a stronger means of authentication than a password alone.

Verifying an e-mail address is straightforward but makes the security of the bank dependent on the security of the e-mail service provider. This is a serious flaw if the customer uses a popular e-mail provider and has used the same username and password combination as for their bank account.

The telephone system is somewhat more secure; telephone service providers expect to provide a certain level of security. Unfortunately, the level of security actually provided is rather less than one would desire. And a telephone callback is useful only if the bank has the correct telephone number in the first place. Few customers tell their bank when they change their telephone number; many would rather not receive yet more telemarketing from their bank and give false information anyway.

Machine Verification

Callback provides stronger authentication but at the cost of convenience. Users of Internet banking want to be able to access their account from anywhere, not just from home, and they don't want to have to go through a callback procedure every time. Machine verification bridges the gap. The IP address from which the request is received and information stored on the computer on a previous visit are used to create a profile of the machine from which the request is made.

A request to log in to an account from a computer that has been used to access the account previously is less likely to be fraudulent than a request from a different machine. A request coming from a network address close to the customer's home is much less likely to be fraudulent than a request from a high-risk country such as Nigeria.

Many banks manage their fraud risk by profiling individual customers and looking for anomalies in their particular behavior pattern. A frequent traveler to Europe might be allowed to access his account from France, whereas a customer who has never traveled is asked to provide additional authentication such as respond to a callback request. A frequent traveler to Nigeria might be given a strong authentication token to use abroad.

One-Time Password Tokens

Passwords are expensive, inconvenient, and insecure, but they are the technology that the existing Internet infrastructure is designed to support. Few Internet protocols provide a smartcard "slot," but *every* successful protocol provides a password slot.

The chief security weakness of a password is that every time it is used, the other party knows the password. A password that changes every time it is used—a **one-time password**—allows less opportunity for the attackers.

Customers of some European banks already use a one-time password scheme. The bank sends the customer a sheet of cardboard with a series of numbered scratch-off panels. To log into their online bank account, the customer removes the next scratch-off panel to reveal the authentication code, which will be their next One-Time use Password (OTP).

The determined criminal intent on stealing from a particular individual might with some time and effort obtain their OTP password sheet. But doing so forces the perpetrator to return to the pre-Internet tactics used in traditional credit card frauds: stealing wallets, intercepting the mail and so forth. This in turn requires them to accept pre-Internet risks and profits, making the game considerably less appealing to them.

Using a one-time password in place of a traditional static password limits the damage caused by phishing attacks. The phishing gangs can still use phishing attacks to steal authentication codes, but they can only use each code once, and they have to use it before the consumer logs into his account.

The use of one-time passwords interferes with the criminal value chain of the phishing gangs, limiting the type of crime that they can perform. Stolen authentication codes have to be used almost immediately; a carding gang buying stolen codes has to be able to trust the supplier, which is somewhat difficult given that dishonesty is their trade.

Scratch-off cards provide an effective low-technology method of limiting the damage caused by phishing. Unfortunately, "low technology" does not mean "low cost." The bank has to track which card each of its customers is using and send out a new card before the old one is used up. For the scheme to be secure, every scratch-off card must contain a unique sequence of numbers. Production and distribution of the cards becomes a major effort.

More importantly, for banks that are trying to encourage their customers to use online banking services rather than costly to provide branch services, scratch-off cards encourage customers to ration their use of the online banking service. If they are on a business trip and they are coming close to the end of the card, they are less likely to use the online service.

OTP tokens provide an infinitely large scratch card. An OTP token is used in the same way as a scratch card, but there is no limit to the number of times the customer can visit his online banking site. Each time a button is pressed, the next password appears (see Figure 14-1).

Relying on the OTP token alone only provides a single authentication factor. Although the OTP token provides a password that is considerably stronger than a static password chosen by the user, the token itself might be lost or stolen. Using an OTP token and a password (or PIN number) in combination provides two factor authentication: Something known and something carried. Using two factor authentication means that an attacker must break two different types of puzzle to succeed.

Figure 14-1   *One-time password token*

OTP tokens were until recently an expensive proprietary technology guarded by a thicket of patents. An enterprise would typically pay $50 per user per year for a time-based token which, like the replicants in *Blade Runner*, came with a preprogrammed termination date.

The **Initiative for Open AuTHentication (OATH)**, an alliance of token manufacturers and security service providers, has since broken the proprietary lock. OTP tokens are now a commodity technology. Tokens based on the OATH open standards are readily available from a wide range of suppliers for less than $5 in volume, little more than the price of the CPU, battery, and display.

Over time, the cost of OATH tokens will fall even further. Most people already carry a CPU, battery, and display in their pocket: their cell phone. With open standards, any device can be turned into an OATH token for a few pennies (see Figure 14-2).

Figure 14-2   *Cell phone with OATH token support*

OTP tokens offer much better security than passwords alone, but less than we might like. A one-time password is still a password and still vulnerable to a man-in-the-middle or phishing attack. The successful attacker only gains limited access to the account, but that might be enough.

The most important impact of OTP tokens appears to be that they negate the tactics used in a traditional phishing approach. A customer who uses an OTP token to log in is much less likely to be fooled by an e-mail message demanding that he "verify his account."

Some one-time password tokens involve a time or challenge element. These make a man-in-the-middle attack somewhat harder and the results somewhat less useful. We can't eliminate the attack unless we can reliably train users to authenticate the source of the request before giving out their password.

Smartcards and Smart Tokens

PKI is the queen of authentication methods. Public key cryptography allows Alice to prove to Bob that she knows a secret without revealing the secret to anyone.

The main problem with PKI is storing the secret key; it is much too big for a person to remember. If he only ever uses one computer and the computer is sufficiently trustworthy, he could store his secret key on his machine.

Most people have machines that are far from being "trustworthy," although this is beginning to change. Making an entire operating system trustworthy is a colossal task; making just the part of the computer where secret keys are stored trustworthy is still difficult but achievable.

The simplest means of achieving a high degree of security for a secret key is to store it in a dedicated computer that is purposely built for performing public key calculations. Depending on the form factor, these are known as **smartcards** or **smart tokens**. The Chip and PIN credit cards issued in Europe are a type of smartcard.

Smartcards offer much better security than one-time password tokens, but they only work where there is a reader. USB smart tokens are slightly bulkier and work with practically any computer made since 1998.

At some point in the future, it is possible that wireless smart tokens based on the Bluetooth specification will become practical. Bluetooth is still a rarity on personal computers but commonplace on telephones. A particular advantage of using a wireless token in a corporate environment is that the wireless signal has a finite range so that it can act as a proximity device. The computer can be set to lock its keyboard whenever the user steps away from his desk for a minute or two and unlock automatically on his return.

Bluetooth keyboards are already starting to appear. It might not take more than a couple of years for the makers of computer monitors to realize that Bluetooth is a complementary technology to the USB hubs that they already offer as a built-in option.

Hybrid Tokens

OTP tokens work anywhere; smart tokens offer higher security but only work where there is a slot for them to plug into. How should we choose?

Fortunately, we don't need to. A hybrid token offering both authentication methods need not cost much more than a single-purpose token of either type (see Figure 14-3).

Figure 14-3 *One-time password token*

Biometrics

According to proponents, biometric authentication technologies offer the strongest possible demonstration that a person really is who he claims to be. After all, what could be more secure than examining a person's fingerprint or looking at a retina scan?

As it happens, plenty. The practice tends to fall far short of the claims.

Biometrics certainly provide an additional strong authentication factor *under carefully controlled conditions*. The U.S. government uses biometrics at border crossings to ensure that the person who is using a visa is the same person who applied for it. In the workplace, biometrics prevent workers from using a borrowed ID card or punching a time clock for a friend.

In August 2006, the popular science program *Mythbusters* demonstrated that it was possible to defeat a purportedly "high-security" fingerprint lock using distinctly low-technology methods.[1] In one test, a paper copy of the fingerprint was sufficient. It would be hard to use the Mythbusters' technique with a U.S. immigration officer watching, but fooling a fingerprint-based lock or safe is much easier.

Biometrics rely on the secrecy of something that isn't very secret. Every time a finger is presented to a fingerprint scanner, the reader has the opportunity to make a complete inventory of every single feature of the fingerprint. No matter how clever the communication protocol between the scanner and the analysis device, the subject gives away the whole secret every time.

Of the biometric identification techniques on offer today, iris scanning appears to be the most promising. Unlike earlier retinal scanning techniques using lasers, iris scanning is noninvasive. Under controlled circumstances, it is practically impossible for an impostor to present a substitute to the scanner in place of his eye without being noticed. If the circumstances are not controlled, we are back playing the game of determining whether the sample presented to the scanner is live tissue.

Although the iris scanner would probably require the Mythbusters to raise their game, I believe it can be beaten. Biometric techniques work well as a means of preventing employees sharing an authentication token. Current biometric techniques do not provide a good replacement for an authentication token, and it is unlikely that any ever will.

Another, more serious problem with biometrics is that the person's body becomes the key. What do you consider more important: your person or your property?

In 2005, a gang of Malaysian car thieves tried to steal a $75,000 Mercedes. When the thieves were unable to bypass the fingerprint-scanner activated immobilizer, they chopped off the owner's index finger to start the car.

User Experience

As with secure messaging, secure identity must begin with the user experience, or rather the user experiences. It is entirely appropriate to use three-factor authentication (for example, PIN, ID card, fingerprint scanner) to control access to a high-security data center, but not to post a comment on a blog.

An identity infrastructure must support a range of authentication techniques. A relying party must be able to set a minimum standard for authentication, but users should always have the option of going above and beyond the minimum and use a stronger means of authentication.

An identity infrastructure must respect the users' time and convenience. The current confusion of a hundred usernames and passwords is unacceptable. I have three credit cards, each of which is accepted at any one of a million or so places around the world. The Internet identity infrastructure should work the same way.

An identity infrastructure must be transparent and always inform the user what information is being disclosed and the consequences of doing so.

An identity infrastructure must allow a single person to maintain multiple online identities. The ability to be someone else is an important aspect of cyberspace, notably celebrated by Sherry Turkle in her book *Life on the Screen*.[2] It is also, as Roger Hurwitz suggested to me,[3] a historical tradition: Halloween, the Venetian Carnival, and *Twelfth Night* all celebrate the idea of being someone else. The idea that a person who has failed in Europe can move to America and reinvent himself is at the core of the "American dream." As we saw earlier, the boundary between the online and offline world is a crucial safety control in many Internet situations.

An identity infrastructure must allow a subject to establish an exclusive claim to an identity. Nobody else can claim to be me; nobody else can claim my pseudonymous identities.

An identity infrastructure must be open and unencumbered by artificial commercial relationships.

An identity infrastructure must clearly distinguish an identity that is subject to accountability from one that is not.

User Centric

For the past two decades or so, the principle question in "human computer interaction" has been how the human can provide the machine with the information it needs to do its job. The user-centric principle reverses this bias and demands that we make how the computer serves the user our primary concern.

The padlock icon is emblematic of the old approach. The user wants to know if he is safe, but the padlock icon only tells him that the communication is encrypted. In the old approach, the user was not given the information he needed in case he "became confused." The user is, however, bombarded with information he simply doesn't need, such as warning dialogs of the type that lawyers write to dump responsibility for security onto the user.

We can state a principle of user-centric security as follows: The user must be given exactly the knowledge he needs to make an informed trust decision and no more.

Registration

The user experience begins with the first contact between the user and the identity system, when the user registers the personal details he wants to share with the site.

The user who is asked to provide information must balance the benefit of disclosure against the disclosure risk. A user might respond to a Turing test to demonstrate that he is not a robot without much fear; anything else carries a disclosure risk.

We would like registration to be as infrequent as possible. If I have entered all my personal details to register for the *London Times*, I should not be required to enter them again for its sister paper, *The Sun*. I should not be required to enter them again anywhere, unless I want to establish a new pseudonymous identity.

Many Web sites collect this type of information so that they can tell their advertisers the type of person who reads the site. Accuracy is preferred but not essential. If someone claims that he is a millionaire rather than unemployed, he will receive advertisements targeted at the wrong audience. Other Web sites—particularly those offering financial services—do need to know if their customer is telling the truth, if not for their own purposes then to meet government regulations. The verification performed on the information provided, if any, should be appropriate for the level of risk.

Log In

As with registration, logging in should be as infrequent and as easy as possible. Authentication should be as lightweight and simple as possible. This means that if the user is visiting multiple sites, he should not normally be required to log in to each one individually unless there is a particular reason to require an additional authentication step.

Ubiquity

The user experience should be ubiquitous, available on any platform a user might use whether that is a computer (Windows, OS X, and so on), a mobile phone, or anything in between.

Roaming

Roaming is the ability to access an account from more than one machine. Depending on the application, roaming might be a requirement.

It is entirely reasonable for a bank to decide that customers will only be able to use a limited number of machines to perform a risky transaction such as adding a recipient for bill payment or requesting a wire transfer. Readers of a newspaper or a blog are going to expect to be able to read it from anywhere.

Card Space

The field of computer security usability is new, even by Web standards. The seminal papers in the field were published in 1999, and the first conferences held in 2005. Microsoft CardSpace, a component of Windows Vista that is also available for Windows XP, represents the first new major mainstream security application whose design has been shaped by security usability considerations.

A useful demonstration of the CardSpace user experience is the blog of its chief architect, Kim Cameron.

- **Only ask for authentication when necessary**—Readers of the blog are only asked to authenticate to post comments.

- **Design for deployment**—CardSpace is a new technology, and it might take as long as a decade before CardSpace infrastructure becomes ubiquitous. Posters are offered the choice of using CardSpace or responding to a Turing challenge (see Figure 14-4).

- **Employ distinctive and consistent cues whenever the user is asked to make a security decision**—CardSpace runs in a separate operating system partition that Microsoft refers to as the "secure desktop." Whenever the user is asked to make a security decision in Windows Vista, he is taken to the secure desktop, and the screen goes dark except for the dialog presenting the user with the security decision.

- **Present necessary information using familiar metaphors**— As its name suggests, CardSpace uses the metaphor of a set of cards (see Figure 14-5). Each card represents a different expression of identity.

Figure 14-4   *CardSpace or username/password*

Figure 14-5   *CardSpace card collection*

On my main computer, I have two cards: PHB and Phill. One has my work contact information, and the other has both my work and private contact information. A picture of my car helps me keep them apart.

- **Put the user in control**—The user decides which card to use to access a site, and he is told what information the card contains the first time the card is used at a particular site (see Figure 14-6).

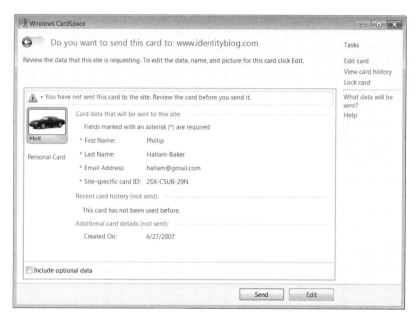

Figure 14-6   *Using a card for the first time*

- **Hide unnecessary technical details**—Underneath the covers, CardSpace employs the full arsenal of state-of-the-art computer security techniques, including PKI and trustworthy operating system technology.

We live in what I call the "Google Earth" era of user experiences. Google Earth was the first mainstream consumer application other than a game to present the user with an experience that was as compelling as those routinely presented in Hollywood movies. CardSpace is the first security user experience to cross that bar.

CardSpace 1.0 demonstrates that security is not incompatible with usability and meets all our requirements for the user experience except ubiquity and roaming.

Ubiquity is already being addressed: CardSpace is built on open standards including WS-Security and WS-Trust, and code implementing the protocol is already available from the Open Source Higgins project. Equivalent implementations should be available for all the major operating system platforms in a short time.

Roaming is supported in CardSpace 1.0, but the user experience is much worse than we would want. People who use multiple computers on a regular basis will have to transfer their CardSpace credentials from one machine to another using the limited import and export features supported by CardSpace. This particular limitation is much harder to remove without compromise to the security measures that protect CardSpace credentials from malicious code such as viruses. The most likely solution is to abandon the idea of transferring the credentials altogether and instead implement the CardSpace subsystem on some form of smart token.

OpenID

CardSpace is built to answer the question, "What is the best possible identity infrastructure we can build today if we begin from a completely clean slate?" OpenID is built to answer the question, "What is the best identity infrastructure we can build today if we begin from where we are?"

CardSpace represents a clean break with the past, a no-compromises approach designed to replace the existing infrastructure. OpenID 2.0 is the result of an organic, pragmatic approach combining the work of many different authors.

The difference in approach has proved to be complementary rather than disruptive. OpenID provides an approach that any Web user can use today; CardSpace provides the no-compromises architecture we want to arrive at in the future. The challenge is to ensure that these approaches eventually meet.

You might well have used OpenID already without even knowing it. OpenID is often used to allow a reader to post comments on different blogs without needing to register separately for each one.

The keystone of the OpenID system is an identity provider. Several identity providers exist, and a core article of faith in the OpenID system is that users can choose any identity provider they wish.

My identity provider is the VeriSign Labs personal identity provider (PIP), and my OpenID is hallam.pip.verisignlabs.com.

1. To create the identifier, I went to the PIP page at VeriSign Labs and followed the normal routine of setting up an account: username, password, and Turing test to discourage robots.

2. If a site supports OpenID, I can enter my OpenID into the login screen as the username. The site then redirects me to the identity provider.

3. If this is the first time I am logging into an OpenID site this day, I authenticate myself in the normal way. In this case, I am using a password, but I could use any authentication mechanism, including an OTP token or even Microsoft CardSpace. If I have already authenticated myself, I can skip this step.

As with CardSpace, OpenID allows me to control the information I reveal to a site. I can even manage independent personas for different sites.

The Architecture of Identity 2.0

From a technical perspective, both the architectures of OpenID and CardSpace share much of the technical architecture of Security Assertion Markup Language (SAML), an earlier attempt to define a next-generation identity architecture. OpenID, CardSpace, and SAML collectively form the technical basis for the movement known as Identity 2.0.

An identity infrastructure must address three important issues.

- **Identifier**—How are the personas that belong to an individual represented in human and machine-readable forms? What ownership rights does a user have over his identifier?

- **Access control**—How is a claim to an identity authenticated? How is reputation information relating to the identity represented and exchanged? How are decisions made based on the identity exchanged?
- **Discovery**—How do we locate the authentication service that is to be considered authoritative for a particular identifier?

Each part of the Identity 2.0 ecology makes an important and distinctive contribution. CardSpace contributes a no-compromise user experience integrated deep into the security systems of the operating system platform. OpenID provides the means of building critical mass. SAML lays the technical architecture for the common ground where OpenID and CardSpace meet and the means to take Identity 2.0 forward to the next generation of Web architecture, the Semantic Web. SAML is thus the natural choice for describing the technical architecture of Identity 2.0.

SAML: Access Control as Service

SAML was designed before the emergence of blogging and before the emergence of professional Internet crime had been widely acknowledged. The specification was designed to meet the concerns of enterprises that had made significant investments in IT infrastructures and were looking to make sense of them. In particular, the enterprises wanted to eliminate the error-prone process of managing authentication and authorization data separately for each IT system.

Single Sign On systems were available from many vendors, but deployment was a serious headache requiring each IT system to be individually "integrated" into the Single Sign On system, work that might need to be repeated if a system was upgraded. Instead of enabling the enterprise to become more flexible, the IT infrastructure was making it more difficult to change.

SAML was designed to provide a standards-based access control infrastructure that would allow enterprises and the vendors of Single Sign On systems to push the cost of integration onto the application providers. Enterprises with SAML deployed would insert the question, "Does the vendor's product support SAML?" in the Request For Proposals (RFP) they issued at the start of a purchasing process. A feature that is regularly requested in RFPs is likely to become part of a vendor's product roadmaps. And new versions of their products would come with a SAML "socket" for the customer to "plug" their enterprise SSO system into.

The concept of a network authentication service was not new; the RADIUS and Kerberos standards were introduced in the mid 1980s. LDAP and X.500 directory allowed for publication of attributes. Various proprietary schemes were being marketed for network authorization services. Each infrastructure served the limited set of functions it was designed to perform, but each worked in a completely different way.

SAML brought together all the component parts of the access control problem—authentication, attributes, and authorization—as consistent standards-based network-accessible service.

The principal building block in the SAML architecture is the assertion. An **assertion** has a specified issuer and contains three types of information: statements, conditions, and advice.

Issuer	The party making the claim
Statements	The set of claims made
Conditions	The conditions under which the claims are made
Advice	Additional information that can be used to support the claim, such as a formal proof

A SAML assertion is not simply a set of claims; it is a set of claims that can be subject to conditions. Conditions allow the scope of a claim to be bounded in time and by audience. This is important from a legal point of view. Many of the legal complications raised in X.509 are because an X.509 certificate is simply an assertion made to the world in general; the issuer in effect writes a statement headed "To whom it may concern." In SAML, the issuer can direct an assertion to a specific audience, thus limiting and possibly eliminating unintended liability to parties outside that audience.

SAML Identity Assertions

The core SAML specification defines three types of statement:

Authentication   A party purporting to be Alice was authenticated using credential X and may be reau-
thenticated by proof of possession of
credential Y.

Attributes   Alice is over 21, is licensed to drive, is an
employee of BobCorp, and is a member of
the BobCorp finance department.

Authorization   Alice has been granted read and write access
to the BobCorp Accounts folder.

In the classic SAML architecture, assertions containing these
assertion types are issued by separate services (see Figure 14-7).
These services allow each part of the infrastructure to obtain
exactly the information required to do its function.

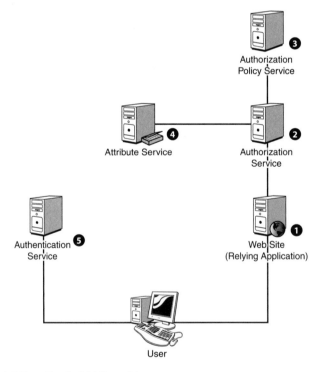

Figure 14-7   *Classic SAML architecture*

The relying application ❶ has a decision to make: Should it
permit access to a resource or not? The application does not

want to manage the information necessary to answer the question, so the question is handed to an authorization service, which answers it by means of an authorization statement ❷. To issue the authorization statement, the authorization service consults some form of authorization policy ❸ . The SAML specification does not address authorization policy, but the sister specification, eXtensible Access Control Markup Language[4] (XACML), does.

An authorization policy can be written using statements of the form, "Alice is allowed to access the accounts file," but working at this level of detail is time consuming, error prone and, in almost all cases, unnecessary. Security policies are easier to maintain in terms such as, "Members of the finance department may read files with the finance attribute" and "The accounts file has the finance attribute." To resolve a policy of this type, we need an assertion containing an attribute statement such as, "Alice is a member of the finance department." ❹

Before allowing "Alice" to access the accounts file, we do, of course, need to be sure the request actually comes from the real Alice. This decision must ultimately be taken by the application that controls the requested resource, but again the application does not want to have to support every possible method of authenticating Alice. This question is much better handled by an authentication service, ❺ which authenticates the party purporting to be "Alice" by any of the authentication mechanisms it supports and returns an authentication statement that states, "Alice was authenticated using mechanism X and may be reauthenticated by mechanism Y by proof of possession of credential Z."

Toward the Semantic Web

I intended the assertion structure of SAML to be both a critique of and a bridge toward the Semantic Web. The Semantic Web is a vast topic that demands at least a book in its own right.

Today, the Web provides vast quantities of raw information, much of which cannot be used. The aim of the Semantic Web is to build a Web of "knowledge," which I define as information that can be used.

In the "layer cake" model of the Semantic Web set out by Sir Tim Berners-Lee, trust is the apex of a pyramid built layer on layer, with logic at the base. In my view, trust must be the foundation; before we decide whether to read the statement, we first decide whether it is worth reading (see Figure 14-8).

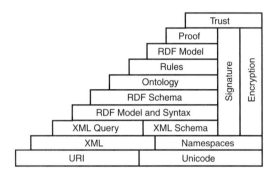

Figure 14-8   *Semantic Web layer cake model*

This conventional model is not entirely wrong; trust is not just the foundation. Trust is also one of the types of information we want to deduce using the Semantic Web. As children, we trust information provided by a small circle: our parents, teachers, and friends. Over a lifetime, our circle of trust changes as a result of our experiences.

Discovery: The Missing Piece

SAML 1.0 is agnostic on the subject of identifiers. This appeared to be a good idea at the time, but it has since proven to be a mistake.

Failing to commit to a particular identifier scheme has meant that SAML cannot commit to a discovery scheme which in turn means that SAML provides us with most of the necessary components to *build* identity systems but falls short of *providing* an identity system.

OpenID does define both an identifier format and a discovery mechanism. When I claim my OpenID hallam.pip.verisignlabs. com at a Web site, the site applies the rules set out in the OpenID specification to discover the location of the authentication server it should use.

Applied Identity

Design or programming errors can make a network protocol insecure but security is a property of a system, not a protocol. To understand how secure identity can be in practice, we must look at how it is applied.

Enterprise Authentication

When employees require access to valuable assets to perform their jobs, employers need reliable means of controlling access and establishing accountability. Strong authentication is an essential requirement in both cases.

SAML was originally designed to meet the expanding needs of enterprise authentication, authorization, and accountability. The cost of managing a proliferation of authentication systems was widely understood but, for most enterprises, "Single Sign On" (SSO) remained a pipe dream.

The problem was not a lack of SSO solutions; a cornucopia was on offer. But SSO was a moving target with new applications springing up as fast as the old were integrated. And the integration process began again whenever two enterprises with SSO solutions from different vendors merged.

As soon as it appeared that SSO was finally becoming a solved problem in the enterprise, the extranet hit. Each outsourced service required employees to manage a fresh set of accounts: telephone conferencing, Web conferencing, travel, 401K, stock options.

Secure identity based on CardSpace and SAML puts SSO within the reach of the enterprise once again: one employee, one account. Instead of starting with the authentication solution, enterprises can issue each employee with the credential that is most appropriate to manage cost, convenience, and risk.

Stopping Blogspam

Blogspam is the pain point that drove the evolution of OpenID, which is somewhat curious since we could eliminate 99% of current spam appearing on blogs without using any form of authentication at all.

Most spam appearing on blogs today is linkspam. Unlike e-mail spam, the target of linkspam is not the reader of the blog; it is the search engines that use Web links to rank the relevance of sites. In particular, the target is Google.

All we need to do to eliminate the incentive to post linkspam is to mark the Web page so that the search engines know which parts were written by the blogger and which contain third-party comments. The search engines can then either ignore the comments entirely when computing rankings or use the information to identify linkspam sources and apply appropriate penalties.

Of course, the day that the spammers stop targeting the search engines will be the same day they begin targeting the user. Dealing with the replacement spam will require the same accountability-based approach of authentication accreditation and consequences. Strong identity provides the tool we need to begin.

The necessary information could be encoded by extending the Web page markup language HTML. However, this would take a lot of time. A much better approach is to use a technology called RDFa, which allows an HTML document to be annotated with Resource Description Framework (RFF) attributes. RDFa is currently being developed by the World Wide Web Consortium as part of its Semantic Web initiative. It is a much better solution because it allows the information to be encoded without changes to the Web infrastructure.

Figure 14-9 shows an example of how RDFa markup might be applied to a blog. The objective is to encourage search engines to use only the parts marked in bold to calculate search rankings. The page is written in normal XHTML. The RDFa markup is contained in the <span> elements.

The first span element declares that all the markup in the comment area has come from an external source. There are two comments, each of which is marked with a span declaring it a separate contribution and a second span that identifies the poster. The first comment is linkspam from an unknown source. The second comment comes from an authenticated source and might be acceptable to the page ranking engine if both the blog hosting the comment and the individual commenter are considered trustworthy.

```
<html xmlns:ann="http://www.example.com/2007-06-28/ann#">
...
<body>
<h1>Phill's Blog</h1>

<h2>Post: Using RDFa to annotate blog posts</h2>

<p>Linkspam is a problem that affects every blogger today. Unlike traditional spam
which is aimed at the reader of a blog, linkspam is aimed at the robots which spider
the Web for the big search engines</p>

<h3>Comments</h3>
<span property="ann:external">

<span property="ann:contribution">
<h3><span property="ann:contributor" content="unknown">Linkspammer</span> said</h3>

<p>Great post! Take a look at <a href="http://fake-viagra.com/">this</a></p>
</span>

<span property="ann:contribution">
<h3><span property="ann:contributor"
content="openid:hallam.pip.verisignlabs.com">Phill</span> said</h3>

<p><a href="http://identityblog.com/">Kim Cameron</a> wrote about linkspam last
week.</p>
</span>

</span>
</body>
</html>
```

Figure 14-9   *RDFa markup*

Semantic markup allows us to do much more than control blogspam. Knowing the purported identity of the commenter and the means of authentication allows tools to be built that aggregate comments from multiple blogs in interesting ways. A personal blog might have a link to a page listing all the comments that the blogger had posted on other blogs.

Applying semantic markup also allows us to build moderation schemes that work across the blogosphere as a whole instead of being confined to individual sites.

Secure Online Banking

Secure identity provides the necessary authentication infrastructure to secure transactions.

Earlier in this chapter, we saw how banks today use machine verification techniques as a key input to their risk mitigation strategy. Today these systems rely on HTTP **cookies**—pieces of data that a Web server sends to a browser and the browser returns on its next visit. HTTP cookies are a notoriously problematic technology from the privacy point of view; they provide too much information on where a user has been. On the other hand, cookies offer much less than we would like from a security point of view. Although Web browser security architects take the need to protect cookie data very seriously, the application designer is always at a disadvantage to the authors of malware in all its forms.

You can think of CardSpace as providing a "super cookie" answering both the security and privacy concerns. Working within the security context of the platform, the CardSpace implementers start with an advantage over the providers of malware, which will become even stronger as technologies such as trustworthy computing are deployed. User-centric design addresses the principle privacy concerns that cookies raise. The user is always in control and must give explicit approval each time a card is used.

Secure Transactions

Customers want banks to protect their confidentiality, but their customers much bigger concern is for the banks to protect their money, which is also the principle concern of the banks.

A criminal market for confidential information certainly exists, but the opportunities for the criminal who steals money are considerably greater than the opportunities for the criminal who steals information.

The essential concern, therefore, is to control the means by which the criminals can transfer money out of the account:

- Send a check to themselves using bill payment
- Transfer money to an account from which they can make an ATM withdrawal
- Transfer money to a mule recruited through a "work at home" scam
- Wire transfer the money to an account they control
- Buy goods that can be easily resold

As we saw in Chapter 9, "Stopping Botnets," the emperors of ancient China understood this problem; the Great Wall did not stop barbarians from getting in, but it did prevent them from getting out with the loot.

The principal tools used to control transaction fraud today are risk assessment and velocity controls. The more that is known about the recipient of the transaction, the more effective these tools become.

In particular, most bill payment transactions are used to pay utilities for the telephone, gas, or electricity. The actual risk involved in this type of transaction is essentially nil: If a payment is made by mistake, the bank knows that the recipient is unlikely to disappear before the money can be recovered. The problem we face today is the lack of an effective and scalable mechanism for identifying the low-risk transactions from those that are potentially higher risk.

Extended Validation is likely to play a key role in developing a next-generation infrastructure for secure transactions, as are CardSpace-like protocols and platform infrastructures, which securely bind a transaction authorization to a specific recipient and a specific amount.

Ubiquitous Customization

Recently, I talked to an old friend who was complaining that the system which remembers the position of the seat on his BMW had only three positions. This would not be a problem for him as such, except that his wife often lends the car to her parents and, won't he please just fix it so that there is a fourth position?

A fourth button would meet the immediate need, but what will happen when the children want to drive? And the aunt from out of town?

In the future, we will increasingly expect and demand that machines accommodate themselves to us. Machines must anticipate and adjust to our needs.

An identity infrastructure would play a critical role in such an infrastructure. Instead of limiting the car to three, four, or even fifty seat positions, you could store each user's preference on his identity token. The same token would be used to start the car, to set the temperature preferences, and to tell the radio which stations the driver likes to listen to. If it was a preplanned trip, the satellite navigation system would be automatically programmed with the route and know which places it should suggest stopping at for a break.

Protecting Children

As we saw in Chapter 1, "Motive," the risks of online dating, or for that matter dating of any kind, do not stop when a child reaches the age of 18. Security education for children must teach lifelong skills, not just how to survive until adulthood. A 120-pound thirty-something woman must treat personal security with at least the same degree of concern as a 120-pound teen when meeting a six-foot tall, 250-pound male that she only knows through meeting in an Internet chat room. Does someone know where she is? Is the place where the couple is to meet public? Does she have an escape route planned?

The security concerns of kids are not very different from the security concerns of adults. The chief difference is the resources available to them. Adults are more likely to have a car or other means of personal transport that provides them with an escape route. Adults are more likely to have cash available in case of emergency.

Another difference between adult and child safety is that we consider consenting adults to be safe when they are only meeting online. A child who is chatting online with a person she believes to be a child but is in fact an adult pedophile is very much at risk.

A secure identity infrastructure would allow "children only" chat rooms to be established, where anyone posting as a minor must be accredited by his school or other trustworthy youth-centered organization. Such a scheme is hardly a panacea; children pose at least as great a threat to each other as adults do. But it does help control the risk of adult predators and does not appear to significantly increase other types of risk.

Schools are not in the business of operating an identity infrastructure, but the architecture of Identity 2.0 means that they can provide the necessary proof of age accreditation information without doing so. Extended Validation provides us with the necessary infrastructure to authenticate the schools as credential issuers. All we are lacking is the necessary political imperative to put the pieces together and deploy.

Identity 3.0

Deployment of Identity 2.0 infrastructure is already underway. OpenID, CardSpace, and SAML are already widely used and are rapidly approaching critical mass. We have not yet arrived at a common Identity 2.0 technology, but a common set of features and a common user experience is beginning to emerge.

As we start to build experience of using Identity 2.0 and begin to understand both its real benefits and practical limitations, it is time to start asking where we should go next. At this point, it is impossible to answer that question with any degree of certainty. I dislike futurology, but in accordance with Alan Kay's dictum "The best way to predict the future is to invent it," I can assert author's privilege and describe some of the Identity 3.0 ideas that I am working on.

My recent Identity 3.0 work has focused on the question, "What is the least amount of information we can require to be exchanged at any given point in the identity cycle?"

Deferred Registration

The proposed UK national identity card is officially estimated to cost $5.5 billion,[5] with realistic estimates running at up to three times that amount.[6] If past experience of IT project contracting is any guide, the actual costs will exceed even the most pessimistic estimates. Her Majesty's Government has not yet noticed that the minimum number of consultants required to implement an IT system is the square of the number contracted to design it.

Worse still, all the costs will be incurred up front before the government agencies see any of the purported cost savings and the entire project rests on a meager base of political support.

The biggest cost in the scheme is registering and authenticating the 45 million or so citizen cardholders. Every cardholder must be authenticated using a procedure that meets the needs of the agency with the most demanding needs. So 30 million citizens who will never draw unemployment benefits will have to be authenticated as if they will.

The SAML architecture allows the process of authenticating and registering identity claims to be deferred until they are needed. The citizen could receive the card in the mail or buy one over the counter from a supermarket as they would a SIM card for their mobile phone.

Authentication would only take place as and when required. If the citizen wanted proof of age accreditation, for example, he would present his card and proof of age at a post office. Biometric techniques only provide an effective control in limited areas such as preventing benefits fraud. It makes no sense to require millions of citizens who are unlikely to require these services to present themselves for a biometric registration process, which will inevitably be expensive as any process requiring millions of unwilling and uncooperative individuals to comply will be.

Attribute Only Authentication

If Alice enters a British pub, the barmaid only needs to know that Alice is over 18 to serve her. He does not need to know her name, address, or anything else about her.

The SAML architecture allows the identity of the party making the request to be concealed from the relying application. Only the attribute server and the authentication server need to know *who* is making the request; these services do not need to know *what* is being requested.

Unlinkable Identifiers

We can take the principle of minimizing the amount of information disclosure a stage further. Using traditional authentication approaches, we can hide Alice's name from the barmaid, but the barmaid can still keep a record of the number of times a person has visited previously. If we want to be serious about privacy, we should ensure that the barmaid *only* knows that Alice is over 18 and nothing more.

SAML does not support this type of interaction. We can replace the name "Alice" in an SAML assertion with a random string of bits, but the random string of bits is constant each time it is presented. We can eliminate the identifier altogether, using a fresh random string on each use, but this does not help us unless all the information that Alice presents to the relying party is random and unlinkable, including the authentication credentials.

This type of interaction has been studied at length by the cryptographers who have proposed a range of sophisticated schemes that simultaneously provide strong authentication and complete anonymity. The work of David Chaum and Stefan Brands is particularly interesting.

My approach to this problem is rather more pragmatic. I like the protections provided by exotic cryptography, but not the constraints they bring. In particular, every system I have ever built that has been successful has been used in ways that I never anticipated during the original design. Using exotic cryptography tends to result in a scheme without any "slack" necessary to adjust to real-world circumstances.

This is particularly the case in a national identity card scheme. Without the ability to adjust and adapt the scheme to the needs of preventing terrorism and emergency needs such as imposing rationing, an identity card scheme has little value. Her Majesty's Government is not going to accept a scheme that is expressly designed to shut the door on these requirements—not least because its members remember that terrorists attempted to murder the entire British cabinet in 1984.

A simpler solution to the problem is to use conventional cryptography to encrypt the information exchanged between the cardholder and the relying party such that only the authentication authority can determine the cardholder's identity. The communication between the authentication authority and attribute authorities is then carefully designed so that these interactions—including legally authorized exceptions—are effectively subject to civil accountability.

Key Points

- Many Internet crimes exploit inadequate authentication technology.
    - Passwords are insecure and increasingly impractical.
- An authentication technology merely tells us that the same person is presenting the credential.
    - The real authentication takes place at first contact.
    - Unfortunately, even government documents can be forged.
- Secure authentication technologies exist, but not the infrastructure necessary to support them widely.
    - OTP tokens can be used as a direct replacement for passwords, with fewer security concerns.
        - Phishing attacks are still possible, but the advantage to the attacker is more limited.

- The OATH initiative has established open standards for OTP tokens.
- Smartcards are secure, but they're useless without a card reader.
- USB smart tokens are secure and compatible with most computers (but not telephones).
- Hybrid tokens offer the best of both approaches.
- Identity 2.0 provides the infrastructure for strong authentication.
  - CardSpace is a no-compromise approach that offers strong security and good usability. Roaming is not supported well.
  - OpenID is a lightweight approach that does not require software installed on the user's machine.
  - SAML provides an architecture within which all the competing proposals may meet.
    - SAML is designed to provide a gateway to the Semantic Web.
    - The SAML assertion structure can be used to wrap Semantic Web assertions.
- Identity 3.0 requires us to look at even harder problems.
  - Unlinkable identifiers allow Alice to prove that she is over 18 without revealing that she has been to the pub before.

Secure Names

An identity infrastructure allows us to securely demonstrate who we are. A naming infrastructure allows others to contact us.

The best change that the Internet has made to our lives has been the ability to contact anyone, anywhere, anytime we want using any mode of communication we want. We can contact our friends from our homes, from our cars, from our work, and from our school, and we can use e-mail, instant messaging, voice, or video.

The worst change that the Internet has made to our lives is that it has given our friends, our colleagues, our acquaintances, and a billion people we have never met the ability to contact us anytime, anywhere.

The Internet has turned everyone into an electronic celebrity hounded by a gang of robotic paparazzi 24 hours a day.

The problem began with the telephone. When the telephone first arrived in the houses of the ultra-rich, it was usually kept in a closet and answered by servants. In those days, only servants answered to bells. Today, we are all servants of the telephone and must answer its call day or night.

Unified Communications

The first step toward a solution is to discard the idea of making it difficult for people to make contact by keeping our telephone number or e-mail address secret. In the age of Google, it only takes one accidental disclosure for that strategy to fail completely. The only reason we need more than one name is to maintain separate identities, not to stop someone who already knows who we are and what we have done from pestering us.

In the billion-user Internet, each of us is a celebrity, and each of us requires a gatekeeper so good that we will not receive unwanted communications if our Internet address is put on a billboard in Times Square, New York.

One Address

I have two principal identities: my work identity and my private identity. People can reach me at three telephone numbers, a fax line, two e-mail accounts, and three instant messaging accounts.

A single address should serve all modes of communication—e-mail, instant messaging, video, voice. The only reason to need more than one address should be to maintain more than one online identity. I should not need separate addresses for e-mail and instant messaging.

My private identity is mine alone; my identity as an employee is subject to claims by my employer. This distinction is particularly important in the financial services industry. Regulations in the U.S. and other parts of the world require all communications between customers and brokers to be logged and archived for three years or more.[1] When I send an e-mail to my broker, I am actually sending it to his firm, not my broker. His firm is responsible for securing and archiving the communication and directing it to another broker if he leaves the company.

Rights

My telephone company offers CallerID to tell me who is calling before I answer a call and CallerID blocking so that I can avoid giving other people my telephone number whenever I make a call. More than a few people use both services.

What might appear to be hypocrisy is not: I want to know who is calling me, not the ability to call them back at any time of the day or night that I might choose for years to come.

I don't use CallerID blocking because it would only stop my number from being given to people who I *want* to see it. The dirty little secret of CallerID blocking that the telephone companies don't tell their customers is that it does not work for toll-free calls, the type of call where their telephone number is most likely to end up placed on a telemarketing hit list. Technically, the telephone companies are telling the truth, as the calling number identification information is still suppressed. However, toll-free subscribers have access to a second system called Automatic number identification (ANI) that provides the same information.

Ownership

One of the most important rights is the right of ownership. A business cannot invest in advertising a telephone number or a domain name unless the ownership is clearly understood.

This concern gave rise to the modern telephone system. Almon Strowger, an undertaker, invented the automated telephone exchange after a competitor bribed operators at the telephone switchboard to direct calls to him.[2] His rival was profiting from the investment that Strowger had made in his telephone number.

Customers need more than logical security; they need ownership. Changing a telephone number or an e-mail address imposes significant costs if you are a business or a consumer. Unless the customer owns his contact name, the service provider has all the bargaining power in every negotiation. The introduction of telephone number portability in the U.S. reduced the cost of switching between service providers, causing prices to drop rapidly.

Gatekeepers

Celebrities, CEOs, and other busy people have gatekeepers to control access to them; a close personal friend is put through immediately; a salesperson making a cold call is put on permanent hold.

Most of us cannot afford human gatekeepers, so we use disclosure of our telephone number and e-mail addresses as a proxy. I have separate telephone numbers for my work and personal business even though I work at home and both call the same telephone. At the end of my business day, the work line automatically calls the answering machine.

The result is imperfect but better than nothing. I have colleagues in Europe, the Americas, and Asia. There is no hour of the day that I can be confident that nobody will try to reach me.

Sometimes someone who does not know I have a home office will try to call me knowing that it is 3 a.m. my time, with the intention of leaving a message on my voice mail and not talking to me directly.

Automated gatekeepers exist, but they don't have the information they need to be effective. They don't know who my friends and business partners are. They do not know that if Bill Gates calls me on the weekend, the call should be put through immediately.

Levels of Contact

An automated gatekeeper typically chooses between accepting the call immediately or directing it to e-mail. A human gatekeeper has a much wider repertoire; a caller might be asked to call again later at a specific time, to send an e-mail, or be directed to an entirely different person to contact.

I want my gatekeeper to allow anyone to make some form of contact if this person can show sufficient accountability to prove that his message is not spam. The mode of contact allowed depends on who is asking; the most intrusive modes are the most closely guarded.

A colleague might be allowed to send an instant message during normal business hours. At other times, the request might be automatically converted to an e-mail message. These settings might be reversed for a relative.

E-mail might be the lowest contact mode supported, or we might want to define a more restricted form of e-mail specifically for use in contact requests. Such a contact mode might allow only a few hundred words of text without tables, active content, or images other than secure letterhead. This would be sufficient for messages such as, "We met at the ABC conference. Would you like to discuss the project further?"

An intelligent contact manager would modify the permitted modes according to a person's schedule or location. Telephone call requests might be automatically directed to voice mail during a meeting. A call from a customer or other important caller might be directed to a software agent that would consult the diaries of both parties and schedule a future call.

Introductions

Designing a gatekeeper is the easy part. The hard part is keeping it fed with the necessary information required to do its job without its becoming more of a nuisance than the unwanted contact requests.

One way to compile the necessary information is to observe who the user makes contact with. If Alice calls Bob frequently, she is probably willing to accept his call.

Relying on this principle alone with a single communication mode such as e-mail results in a "first mover" deadlock. Alice can only call Bob if he calls her first, and he can only call her if she calls first.

Applying this principle only to the most intrusive communication modes allows the deadlock problem to be avoided; Alice can send Bob a contact request, and Bob can respond with an appointment for a telephone call, but this only goes partway to solve our information management problem and provides a loophole for spam.

To reduce the information management problem to a reasonable level, we need to have a mechanism for introductions.

Introductions have been the basis for communication for centuries. In the eighteenth century, aristocratic youths were dispatched for the grand tour of the continent, with letters of introduction from eminent men telling "whom it may concern" that the bearer is of family such and such, known to them since such and such a time and so on.

One of the functions of the grand tour was to establish cohesion among the European aristocracy. At the completion of their travels, the tourists would have established their own network of contacts and might sign letters of introduction for others.

Social Networking

The emergent introductions mechanism for the Web is social networking.

Social networking has recently become a hot topic with "Web 2.0" sites such as MySpace, LinkedIn, Plaxo, and Friends Reunited, each attempting to carve out their own niche.

Each social networking scheme works in a slightly different way, but LinkedIn is typical. If I access my LinkedIn account, I see a list of my existing contacts. I can then click on a contact to see his profile. This will usually contain information such as the person's name, contact addresses, and current employer. If the contact has opted to share his contacts, I can see that list.

The principle means of establishing contacts on LinkedIn is through e-mail. Whenever I make a new LinkedIn contact, I look at the person's contacts to see if I might want to connect to any of them. Usually, I find one or two. I can tell LinkedIn to send these people an e-mail inviting them to join my contact network. When the recipients receive the e-mail, they can decide whether to accept, decline, or simply ignore the invitation.

From a security point of view, my chief objection to these schemes is ownership. After six months of using LinkedIn, I have about a hundred contacts in my profile, or rather LinkedIn does, as I don't really own the LinkedIn identity I have been building.

From a usability point of view, what I want is less e-mail, not more. I should be able to add people to my contacts directory without pestering them; in turn, they should be able to add me without pestering me. LinkedIn insists that every link always resolve and every link must work in both directions, but that's a fundamental weakness.

The problem of managing link requests might be acceptable if there were only three proprietary social networking systems attempting to establish themselves. But the Web 2.0 bandwagon is already full, and there are plenty of latecomers trying to push their way on board. Some of these have proved to have sharp elbows indeed.

The LinkedIn approach allows me to build and navigate a social network, but it does not allow me to put it to work as a communication gatekeeper. And even if LinkedIn were to extend its service to offer this feature in the future, to use it would make me unacceptably dependent on them.

Friend of a Friend

Friend of a Friend (FOAF), a Semantic Web application designed by Libby Miller and Dan Brickley, provides a possible foundation for an open social networking structure.

In FOAF, I simply list my set of contacts and decide which of them I want to make public and on what terms.

My FOAF profile is shown in Figure 15-1.

```
<rdf:RDF
      xmlns:rdf="http://www.w3.org/1999/02/22-rdf-syntax-ns#"
      xmlns:rdfs="http://www.w3.org/2000/01/rdf-schema#"
      xmlns:foaf="http://xmlns.com/foaf/0.1/"
      xmlns:admin="http://webns.net/mvcb/">
<foaf:PersonalProfileDocument rdf:about="">
  <foaf:maker rdf:resource="#me"/>
  <foaf:primaryTopic rdf:resource="#me"/>
  <admin:generatorAgent rdf:resource="http://www.ldodds.com/foaf/foaf-
a-matic"/>
  <admin:errorReportsTo rdf:resource="mailto:leigh@ldodds.com"/>
</foaf:PersonalProfileDocument>
<foaf:Person rdf:ID="me">
<foaf:name>Phillip Hallam-Baker</foaf:name>
<foaf:title>Dr</foaf:title>
<foaf:givenname>Phillip</foaf:givenname>
<foaf:family_name>Hallam-Baker</foaf:family_name>
<foaf:nick>Phill</foaf:nick>
<foaf:mbox_sha1sum>e8385a5423bca512ddf3a12b9b40837d2218e188</foaf:mbox
_sha1sum>
<foaf:homepage
rdf:resource="http://dotfuturemanifesto.blogspot.com/"/>
<foaf:workplaceHomepage rdf:resource="http://dotfuturemanifesto.blogspot.com/"/>
<foaf:knows>
<foaf:Person>
<foaf:name>Tim Berners-Lee</foaf:name>
<foaf:mbox_sha1sum>965c47c5a70db7407210cef6e4e6f5374a525c5c</foaf:mbox
_sha1sum>
<rdfs:seeAlso rdf:resource="http://www.w3.org/People/Berners-
Lee/card"/></foaf:Person></foaf:knows></foaf:Person>
</rdf:RDF>
```

Figure 15-1 *My FOAF file*

The main problem with FOAF comes in the instructions given in the "FOAF-a-matic," which I used to generate my FOAF file. The instructions tell me to copy the text, save it in a file called foaf.rdf, and put it on my Web site. But how is anyone to find it?

To use FOAF as a social networking infrastructure, we need tools that anyone can use and a discovery mechanism for FOAF information that is integrated into the identity infrastructure described in the previous chapter.

FOAF gives us a static data structure, but not the network protocol infrastructure to build and animate it so that Alice can allow members of her FOAF network to grant introductions to her. This privilege is only going to be effective if there is a mechanism that allows Alice's contacts to be able to discover that they are in her FOAF file.

FOAF contains the information we need to make social network–gated contact work at an Internet-wide scale. What we lack are the standards-based protocols to share the address book on our own terms.

Done right, such a system would allow me to use rules such as, "Allow any contact I have marked as a friend to contact me by e-mail or instant messaging, and allow this person to see any of my other contacts marked as a friend."

Figure 15-2 shows an example of using social networking to control contact. Alice has listed Bob as a friend who is allowed to call her on her mobile phone and to introduce other friends. Alice has not listed Carol as a friend. Carol is not allowed to call Alice by telephone, but she can send her an e-mail because she is listed as Bob's friend.

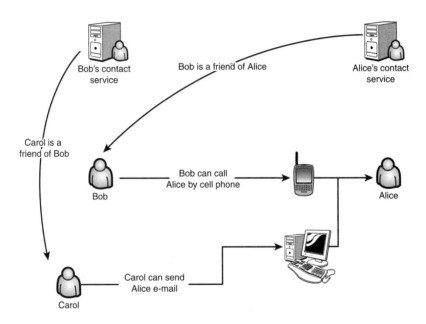

Figure 15-2 *Contact gated by social networking*

Scheduling a Meeting

To complete the picture, we would need a scheduling capability. If two people call me at the same time, I want the second caller to be told, "Ring back at time X," or for the system to automatically schedule a meeting when we are both free.

Moreover, an automated scheduling system should take account of the same information that my personal assistant does: my travel schedule and differences in time zones. This is information I am willing to make available, but only on my terms and under carefully controlled conditions.

If I need to set up a meeting with Microsoft, IBM, and myself, I want to allow their scheduling agents limited access to my calendar for the purpose of setting up the meeting. Today, we manage this type of problem by batting proposals backward and forward in e-mail. Letting an automated scheduling agent manage the appointment allows us to arrange meetings more quickly with fewer round-trips. For this automated scheduling to be possible, we must all be confident that the information we disclose to the agent is not going to be passed to any other party. All we want to do is to find a mutually agreeable meeting time.

Architecture

The principal challenges in a naming scheme are the identifier format and the discovery mechanism. Because we are talking about a naming infrastructure for the Internet, both choices are effectively made for us.

We can invent whatever fancy forms of identifier we like. If they are to be used as an e-mail address, users will expect them to look something like alice@example.com.

Equally, we can attempt to build whatever new infrastructure we like to interpret our identifiers, but we are not going to get the rest of the Internet to adopt it unless it is possible to obtain the same answers from the existing DNS infrastructure.

It takes a great deal to establish a new naming system for a communication infrastructure. We have international systems for postal addresses, telephone numbers, book numbers, product codes, and Internet names. Each infrastructure has evolved over many decades and is the result of complex diplomatic negotiations between governments.

DNS Service Specification

Most of us are familiar with the DNS names that appear at the start of a Web address. When the Web was being designed in the early 1990s, the primary function of the DNS was to provide an address for an actual physical machine connected to the Internet.

Today, the Web is a rather different place. When we point our browser to cnn.com or google.com, it is the service that we are interested in; which machine provides that service is irrelevant.

Maintainers of e-mail servers had come to a similar realization in the mid 1980s. Reliability became increasingly important as e-mail evolved into an infrastructure that academics were relying on to do their work. Directing mail to a specific machine meant that the mail service would be lost whenever the machine was out of service.

The solution to this problem was the DNS MX record, which allows a system administrator to provide a list of e-mail servers with information to indicate the order in which the servers should be tried and the proportion of traffic that each server with the same priority should receive.

The DNS Service (SRV) record is the general form of the MX record. Each service on offer is identified by a prefix. Figure 15-3 shows what a set of SRV service advertisements might look like for a site offering SAML and OpenID.

```
_samln._tcp.example.com.   IN SRV 10 60 80 saml1.example.com.
_samln._tcp.example.com.   IN SRV 10 20 80 saml2.example.com.
_openid._tcp.example.com.  IN SRV 10 20 80 openid1.example.com.
_openid._tcp.example.com.  IN SRV 10 20 80 openid2.example.com.
```

Figure 15-3   *DNS service announcement using SRV*

The main problem with using SRV in this way is that we have not to date agreed what the service-specific prefixes should be.

DNS Policy

Another problem with using SRV is that it only answers questions I *know* how to ask; it does not help me work out which questions I *should* be asking. Knowing what questions to ask becomes increasingly important as identity and authentication protocols proliferate.

We need an additional layer of protocol description that tells us which protocols a given site offers. This is the same requirement we arrived at in Chapter 13, "Secure Messaging," where we used a DNS policy record to announce the e-mail security protocols offered (see Figure 15-4).

```
_authorization.example.com. IN TXT "SAML OPENID"
```

Figure 15-4 *DNS policy announcement using TXT*

DNS Security

As with secure messaging, deployment of secure naming requires us to increase our reliance on the Internet DNS infrastructure. This causes some people to become nervous. Isn't this putting too much reliance on one piece of infrastructure?

The DNS is already a mission-critical infrastructure for the Internet. If the DNS is down, so is the Internet. Fortunately, the DNS is a remarkably robust infrastructure. The cost of running the DNS—in particular, the cost of defending the DNS against the daily barrage of cyberattacks—is huge. Fortunately, those costs are shared between the holders of more than 150 million domain names.

The DNS exists to be used. The cost of maintaining the DNS is entirely determined by the level of attack. Adding new legitimate uses will not increase costs by a measurable amount.

A more relevant concern is the fact that adding more functions to the DNS might offer additional opportunities to attackers, particularly because the DNS as originally designed has no cryptographic security.

This is where DNS Security (DNSSEC) comes in. As we increase our reliance on DNSSEC, we need to increase the security of the DNS infrastructure, applying digital signature technology to turn the DNS into a Public Key Infrastructure.

Key Points

- One address should serve all modes of communication.
  - The only reason that a separate address should be required is to maintain a separate identity.
  - The customer must control his own name to be independent.
  - Unwanted contact should be controlled through gatekeepers.
    - The level of contact available should depend on the likelihood that the contact is desired.

- Social networking infrastructure can be used to provide necessary data.
- FOAF offers an open, standards-based social networking infrastructure.
- The DNS is the naming platform for the Internet.
  - Efforts to supplant it are misguided and almost certain to fail.
  - We can use DNS without modification to deploy SRV and TXT records.
  - DNSSEC allows us to secure the DNS cryptographically.

CHAPTER 16

Secure Networks

For the past decade, the world of network security has been dominated by firewalls and the perimeter security model. Perimeter security is a good idea; every major corporate HQ has a staffed reception desk. Sneaky thieves do think twice about walking past a reception desk or a security guard with a stolen computer under their arm. But fences are only as secure as their weakest point. A reception desk is a much less effective deterrent if a thief can enter and leave by the fire escape.

As they have become ubiquitous as the first line of defense, firewalls have become increasingly ineffective as the last line of defense. In an extended enterprise, the idea of defining the perimeter of the corporate network becomes meaningless. Constant mergers, acquisitions, and occasional divestitures mean that the perimeter is always moving, never fixed. Business trends such as outsourcing and close supply chain coupling with customers and suppliers means that the perimeter is increasingly blurred. And even if the front door is protected with an effective firewall, it is increasingly difficult to ensure that the back doors created by laptops, flash memory drives, and PDAs are closed.

The term **deperimeterization** has been coined to refer to these changes. As a description of the problem, it is useful and self-explanatory: Perimeter security is eroding, and we need to apply new thinking.

Where I am less happy with the use of the term is to describe an architecture intended to meet the challenge of the failing perimeter security model. Using the same term to refer to both the cause and the solution implies that the solution to these problems is simply to let our defenses down and everything will be fine.

There is an emerging consensus on the three main components of a security architecture to address these challenges: ubiquitous authentication, ubiquitous policy enforcement, and data-level security. What we lack is a concise term that joins these three distinct approaches into a coherent sound-bite phrase.

While considering this problem, I reread Marcus Ranum's article *The Six Dumbest Ideas in Network Security*.[1] His first culprit is the concept of **default permit**: allowing anything that is not explicitly denied. Default permit neatly sums up what is most wrong about the typical enterprise network today: Once past the perimeter, anything goes. The opposite of default permit is **default deny**, a term that neatly describes the state that we want to achieve.

Default deny infrastructure is a network and application security architecture in which anything that is not explicitly allowed is prohibited.

Designing for Deployment

As always, the devil is in the deployment. Designing the architecture of default deny is the easy part; working out how to persuade the industry to back it is the real challenge. Modern network administration is already too complex before adding new security considerations.

The difficulty of network administration provides our opportunity. Few enterprises are willing to pay for network security, but every enterprise must pay for network administration whether it wants to or not. Fortunately, it is an area where there is no shortage of opportunities for improvement.

When the modern digital computer was introduced, programmers would write programs at the machine level, laboriously converting instruction sequences into number sequences by hand and entering them into the machine using punch cards or paper tape. Over time, programming was made easier with the introduction of assembly language and modern high-level programming languages. Today, *the computer serves almost all the needs of almost all the users without the user having to write any program code.*

Network administration is sadly stuck somewhere between the machine code and assembly stages. Instead of administering the network, we administer the individual machines connected to the network. As a result, any change that is to be made to the network almost invariably requires changes to be made at multiple points within the network. Inconsistency leads to error, which in turn leads to insecurity and unreliability.

IPv6

Design for deployment tells us to look beyond our immediate needs to others with needs that might align with our own. For much of the Internet standards community, the biggest concern is not security; it is the fact that when we originally built the Internet, we built it just slightly too small for our needs, and we are rapidly running out of room.

The Internet architecture was originally designed to connect a few hundred or a few thousand machines at the major research universities. As such, the decision to reserve 32 bits each for the source and destination address in every IPv4 data packet appeared far sighted at the time because it would allow for an almost unimaginable 4 billion Internet hosts. Today, with a billion people using the Internet and well over a billion connected Internet hosts, the old IPv4 address space is rapidly becoming exhausted.

IPv6 is designed to solve the IPv4 address space shortage by providing a 128-bit address space with more than 340 billion billion billion billion addresses (340 undecillion).

It seems clear that the Internet must "eventually" move from IPv4 to IPv6, but again the devil is in the deployment. I can set up an IPv6 network in my house, but none of the broadband providers in the area will provide me with an IPv6 Internet connection. And even if they did, the IPv6 Internet today is a lonely place.

For those of us who have spent the past 15 years building the Internet and the Web, it is easy to assume that others think as we do and believe that a problem for the Internet as a whole is a problem for the individuals who use the Internet. This is unfortunately not the case; in particular, an issue that is a problem for *one* Internet user (or would-be user who cannot get an address) is not a problem shared by *all* Internet users.

Merely running out of IPv4 address space is not going to be enough to force a transition. Today, the IPv4 Internet is the party everyone wants to go to. The party will continue without interruption long after the tickets have run out. Only those who did not get their ticket in time will be disappointed.

In a sense, we have already run out of IPv4 addresses, or we would have done so in the mid 1990s if we had not been rescued by the Network Address Translation (NAT) scheme described in Chapter 9, "Stopping Botnets."

If the incentives for IPv6 deployment are currently ambiguous, the costs are not. Managing the transition of a major network from IPv4 to IPv6 with current network management tools is for most network managers simply impossible.

To successfully manage the transition to the next generation IPv6 Internet, we must develop tools that make the transition simple and painless.

Again, the design of high-level programming languages provides a useful model. When I first started programming, I used an 8-bit microcomputer called a Commodore PET. Later I used a 32-bit VAX computer. Later still, I used 64-bit computers. The programs I wrote in machine code for the PET would have to be rewritten from scratch for the VAX. But the programs I wrote on the VAX still run on modern computers because they are written in a high-level language.

We need a high-level language for network administration so that, in the future, the network administrator neither needs to know or care whether his network is using IPv4 or IPv6. Let the machines take care of managing the transition.

We do not have to deploy IPv6 to deploy the next generation of Internet and network security, but we face the same core problem of how to change existing Internet infrastructure. We need to be strategic and work on finding ways that further both objectives, without creating dependencies that could hinder both.

Default Deny Infrastructure

Network administration costs are already reaching the saturation point in the enterprise. It will not be long before this point is also reached in the home.

The year is 2020, and you wake to find that your robot butler has brought you your usual breakfast of coffee, freshly squeezed orange juice, and toast. Your all-purpose tablet turns on instantly as you pick it up to read the international and national news headlines. Turning to your mail, you discover that you were unsuccessful in your bid for tickets for the Rolling Stones' latest final farewell tour, but you did get tickets for The Who.

Finally, you turn to the task you were looking forward to least: dealing with the domestic staff. The coffee maker appears to have been infected by a virus and has been hosting a phishing capture site. Meanwhile, the refrigerator and some of the light switches (you don't know which) have been acting as part of a botnet. One of the televisions is refusing to accept media from the storage server, warning that it might have been compromised. The list continues. As the poison causes you to slowly slip from consciousness, you wish you had read the report on the coffee maker before drinking its coffee.

Unless gadgets become easier to use, consumers are simply going to stop buying them. It is time to remember that the original point was to make life easier and simpler.

Applying the default deny principle in this scenario, we see that the coffee maker does not need the ability to talk to the Internet at all, let alone host a Web server. The security problem becomes much simpler if we only allow the coffee machine to access the local network, and *only for the purposes that are strictly necessary for its function*: to determine the current time, to receive a request to make coffee, to report that the coffee is ready and *no other purpose*.

Default deny allows us to realize the principle of least risk: Unless we need a feature, turn it off so it can't hurt us. Firewalls work by applying this principle at the perimeter. In default deny infrastructure, we want to apply the principle ubiquitously and at every level.

Ubiquitous Authentication

The first step toward simplifying administration is to have a simple, secure, and effective means of identifying the devices connecting to the network. In particular, we need a mechanism that allows a network manager to note that a new device is attempting to access the network and decide whether it should be allowed to join without leaving their desk.

The IEEE 802.1x standard provides some but not all of the tools we need. 802.1x defines a secure protocol for performing the actual authentication but is agnostic on the subject of the device credentials.

As a result, 802.1x does not by itself meet the "single desk administration" criterion. The administrator must install a credential before the device can be used. Installing the credential might only take a few minutes, but the device must be on the administrator's desk or the administrator must attend to the device to do this. The process of unpacking the device, powering it up, shutting it down, and repacking it for shipping to its final destination can easily take an hour or so. Even a few minutes of administration can mean a huge overhead when an enterprise has more than one site.

The simplest means of meeting the "single desk administration" criterion is to apply Public Key Infrastructure (PKI), described in Chapter 11, "Establishing Trust." Each device would have a public key pair and digital certificate installed during manufacture. The device can then present the digital certificate during 802.1x authentication to securely establish the device model and a unique device identifier.

A scheme of this type has already been deployed in the DOCSIS 2.0[2] and later specifications for cable modems. The costs of authenticating the device during manufacture and meeting the requirement are negligible.

The natural choice for a unique device identifier is the MAC/EUI address. This is a unique, stable, and already widely used network authentication measure. A MAC address is a unique 48-bit number that is assigned to every Ethernet and WiFi device during manufacture. Assignment of MAC addresses (since renamed EUI-48 addresses) is managed by the IEEE. Newer protocols such as Bluetooth use the EUI-64 scheme, which works in the same manner and provides 64 bits of address space.

802.1x was developed because network administrators had already begun to use MAC/EUI addresses as a means of authentication despite the fact that every network administrator knows that a MAC address is not secure.

The transition from using MAC addresses to 802.1x rests on the assumption that network managers will choose security over convenience. A support infrastructure already exists for use of MAC/EUI authentication. Many network devices have their MAC or EUI64 address printed on their case as a barcode, and distributors often list MAC addresses on shipping notices so the device can be added to the authorization database automatically or with a wave of a barcode scanner.

If anyone is going to chose security over convenience, it is network administrators. But it is much better to avoid forcing them to make the choice. Device certificates installed during manufacture provide the necessary glue to use the MAC/EUI address securely.

Device and Application Description

When a network administrator sitting at his desk notices that a new device is asking to join the network, he needs to know what services it offers and what services it requires to perform its function. For this, we need a device description language.

Like many topics in computer science, the design of device and protocol description languages can easily become an end in itself. For the purposes of security, simpler is usually better.

What we need is a language that allows a device to make statements such as these:

- I am a coffee pot, model number 8080, manufactured by Robobrew.
- I respond to the make coffee request.
- I raise the signal coffee.
- I provide the following status information: water level, coffee level, pots brewed, time since last brew.
- To present the current time on my display, I require access to the NTP protocol.

Encoding this type of information in XML requires us to deal with two types of information. The first is information related to the actual function of the machine. The second is information related to the network access required to perform that function.

Describing every aspect of every machine that might be connected to the network is a hard problem, one that will require us to apply semantic Web technologies such as **ontologies**— shared vocabularies of terms used with a specific meaning.

Describing just the network access requirements is a much simpler problem. We still need to build an ontology of network resources, but the set of concepts we need to describe is small, and for practical purposes, it's fixed for long periods of time. We know that we will need to express concepts such as "IP address," "IP port," "protocol," and so on. Although it is not a job that will be easy to get right, it is certainly an achievable goal.

Service and Policy Discovery

Just as the network needs to know which services the device requires to perform its task, the device needs to know which services the network offers that meet its needs. Here, the secure naming architecture described in Chapter 15, "Secure Names," is applied.

The choice of the DNS as the service and policy discovery mechanism is important because it allows us to distinguish the logical network from the physical one.

If Alice is connecting her employer-issued laptop to her employer-managed network at work, the logical and physical networks are the same. If Alice is working from home or staying overnight at a hotel, the physical network has changed, but the logical network should not.

If, on the other hand, Alice wants to become master of her own domain, she can buy her own domain name and set her policy exactly the way she wants it, *if* the provider of her physical network is prepared to allow a machine with her policy configuration to connect. This should not be a problem at home, where Alice is paying her ISP for the network connection, but it might be an issue at work, where her personal policy preferences might not be compatible.

Ubiquitous Policy Enforcement

The core principle of default deny is to prohibit everything that is not explicitly permitted. Ubiquitous authentication and the network security policy allow us to determine whether an action is permitted. The next question is how and where the policy is to be enforced. Should this be at the network interface, the network hub, the router, the firewall?

In practical terms: Should the coffee pot be responsible for enforcing network policy, the network hub serving the kitchen, or the cable modem connecting the house to the outside world?

The default deny answer is "All of the above." We do not want to rely on a single point of failure; the goal is to enforce policy at every point in the network where resources allow. As CPU costs continue to decline, it becomes practical to do this at every level in the network.

What this means is that no device that connects to the network is allowed to make any more use of network resources than its function requires, as decided by the owner of the network. If Alice decides she does not want the coffee pot to access the Network Time Protocol (NTP), she turns it off and the coffee pot does not display the time.

A printer connected to the network is allowed access to the resources appropriate for printers. If it is compromised by a Trojan that attempts to send spam or perform a SYN flood denial-of-service attack, the packets are rejected and the network control center notified that an incident has occurred.

Traditional firewalls are also a form of policy enforcement mechanism, but the range of enforcement options available at the network perimeter is more narrow than deep within the network, where fine-grained control is possible.

A firewall cannot stop a Trojan infection from spreading after an initial breach has occurred. Default deny cannot prevent the printer from being infected by a Trojan, but it can make it easier to detect the compromise, and it can help prevent the infection from spreading to the coffee pot.

Most network devices will have a need to access the local DNS and NTP services for naming and time information, but a need for access is not the same as a need for unlimited access. If a printer, coffee pot, or for that matter any device is making hundreds of NTP requests per second for the current time of day, something odd is happening; possibly the NTP requests are being used as some form of control channel.

The Death of Broadcast

Two features of current-day networks that disappear almost entirely in default deny infrastructure are broadcast communication and open listener configuration.

A broadcast message is a message that is sent indiscriminately to every device in a network. Because the whole point of default deny is to suppress indiscriminate communication, there is no choice but for broadcast to go.

We would like to eliminate broadcast in any case because any protocol that relies on indiscriminate communications will only work at the local level and cannot scale. Systems that depend on broadcast messages tend to stop working in unexpected ways when a new network hub or bridge splits what was previously a single physical network span.

Early Ethernet networks consisted of a coaxial cable strung from one machine to the next. Every data packet injected onto the network was seen by every other machine on the same loop. In an open listener configuration, a device snoops on packets directed for other machines.

Applying the default deny principle, we should only allow a machine to be configured in broadcast or open listener configuration if the network policy recognizes a need to do so. A network manager might have a machine authorized to operate as an open listener for tracing network faults.

Intelligence and Control

Operating a default deny infrastructure over any extended period requires the ability to detect and monitor internal and external threats and to adapt the network security policy accordingly.

No network security scheme will ever be so good that it is possible to ignore internal or external events with impunity. If a device suddenly starts behaving in a way that is inconsistent with policy, the network management needs to know. Equally, if the opposition has launched the next Code Red or Slammer, the management of even the most secure network needs to know what is about to (or has already) hit them.

Without intelligence and control, even the best security policy becomes an electronic Maginot Line. We still need the INCH protocol described in Chapter 9.

Data-Level Security

The third leg of the default deny stool is data-level security.

It is often said that the only way to protect yourself absolutely against an Internet attack is to cut the cord connecting you to the Internet. As we saw in Chapter 1, "Motive," this is not true, because cutting the cord does not prevent the criminals from using the Internet to conspire against you.

It is, however, possible to protect yourself against the risk of information disclosure by not having any information to disclose. If you never ask for your customer's social security number, it cannot be stolen from your computer systems. You can't lose what you never had.

Handling sensitive information is sometimes inescapable. Today, credit card transactions require a card number, and it will be some time before this is fixed. But merchants that store every credit card number they see are placing themselves at much greater risk than those that delete the information as soon as they no longer need it.

Applying the least-risk principle to data provides a three-step approach.

1. Only collect, accept, or otherwise obtain confidential data when there is a business need to do so.
2. Only continue to store confidential data when there is a business need to do so.
3. Use strong cryptography and procedural controls to enforce access controls on confidential data.

The key to implementing such an approach is again accountability. Many enterprises have appointed a chief information security officer (CISO). One of the primary roles of a CISO is to take responsibility for information security and, in particular, to ask questions such as, "Why are we collecting and storing all this sensitive data we never use?" An organization where these questions are raised by junior engineers is at a much greater risk than one where they are raised by a senior executive reporting to the CIO or CEO.

Enforcement of such controls in large-scale databases is becoming a generally understood problem with well-established solutions. Many data breaches occur when data is extracted onto a personal system. The extraction itself might be malicious; in some cases, spammers have paid employees for lists of e-mail addresses. In many cases, the original extraction was authorized. The problem is what happens to the data afterward; the stolen auditor's laptop containing sensitive personnel records has become cliché.

A good starting point would be to use existing security infrastructures. File encryption has been supported by premium versions of the Windows operating system since 2000 and is available on every other major operating system. An appropriate accountability control might be to bar any firm of auditors from performing security audits for some number of years should it be found after a breach that they failed to employ such measures.

Secure storage and secure transport only take us part of the way. We still rely on the (all-too-fallible) user remembering that secure transport must be used whenever the personnel spreadsheet is sent by e-mail. Our objective must be to take security to the data.

Content rights management (CRM) systems allow us to do just that. In a typical CRM system, the sensitive data is stored in encrypted form. The decryption key is only released when the CRM system receives sufficient assurance that certain constraints on the use of that data will be observed.

In the e-mail security schemes described in Chapter 13, "Secure Messaging," Alice can send an encrypted e-mail to Bob, but after Bob decrypts the message, he can use the information in the same way that Alice can. In a CRM system, Alice can send the message to Bob with strings attached. Bob might only be allowed to forward the message to a limited distribution list (for example, other company executives). Printing the document might only be allowed on specific printers or prohibited entirely. Bob might not be able to read the document at all after a certain date.

CRM is a form of digital rights management (DRM). More precisely, CRM is a euphemism that attempts to distinguish the use of DRM to protect privacy from the more controversial use of DRM for copyright enforcement. As such, the same objections that are made against copyright enforcement schemes tend to be thrown at CRM regardless of validity.

The technical difficulty of enforcing controls depends on the size of the distribution and the incentive to the attacker. Protecting copyright content such as a Hollywood blockbuster is difficult because the film must be playable on any of the billion-plus DVD players sold. A criminal who successfully breaks the protection scheme has a ready market and can make a fortune.

Protecting confidential documents that are distributed to a few hundred senior executives represents a much more manageable task. All we need to deter the professional criminal is to ensure that the expected cost exceeds the expected profit. In order to make money, an attacker must obtain one of the machines authorized to handle the protected material. To profit, the attacker must break the protection scheme while the confidential information still has value.

The current generation of CRM systems offers a level of security best described as "advisory." The CRM system prevents intentional and unintentional abuse by the typical user but is vulnerable to a compromise of the operating system platform and intentional abuse by a sophisticated insider. Future generations of the CRM system based on the trustworthy computing technology described in Chapter 17, "Secure Platforms," will offer considerably greater resistance to attack.

Network Administration

We already have most of the pieces we need to deploy default deny; all we lack is the necessary glue to join the existing pieces. The most important missing glue is the infrastructure necessary to simplify network administration.

Starting a Network

Setting up a new network or adding a device to an existing network should require as little operator input as possible.

The first thing a customer needs to know when buying a piece of network equipment is whether it supports the default deny standard. An industry conformance brand similar to the "WiFi" brand is required.

Let us imagine that Alice comes home from her shopping trip with a box labeled "network hub" and another box labeled "PC."

To install her network, she plugs the network hub into whatever socket brings high-speed broadband Internet into her home.

At this point, she is almost done. All she needs to do now is to connect her PC to the network hub and complete the installation. For the time being, let us pass over the additional complexity introduced if the network is wireless and assume that she is using Ethernet.

Alice plugs her new PC into the network hub and turns it on. After the machine has started, the network configuration dialog begins automatically. This requests the following information:

- Billing information for the Internet service provider (optional)
- The domain name for the network (optional; defaults to the domain provided by the Internet service provider)
- The means of authenticating the network administrator
- A DNS name for the machine currently in use

After the requested information is supplied, the network setup is complete.

What appears to be simple on the surface requires a significant amount of effort and choreography behind the scenes.

When the network hub is plugged in, it looks to see what other devices are available to talk to. At this point, the only device it can talk to is whatever machine is on the other end of the broadband connection, and this particular machine is not going to route packets beyond that point until it knows that it has a paid subscriber. Because the hub is just a box without either a keyboard or a display, it is not able to do anything more at this point.

When the PC connects to the network, it first obtains a network address and domain name from the network hub using a protocol called DHCP. It then registers the services it is able to offer. One of these services is providing a network administration console. The network hub can now request the additional information it needs to complete the setup.

Adding a Device to a Network

The same choreographed dance is repeated each time a new device is added to the network, except that from this point on, each new device that asks to join or rejoin the network will be required to authenticate itself via 802.1x.

When a new device asks to join the network, the request is routed to whichever machines are currently managing requests to join the network. A coffee pot requesting minimal network access might be added automatically; a machine such as a personal computer requesting comprehensive network access might require specific approval. The administrator might also want to qualify the approval, limiting the services to be offered or the network scope that is visible to the device.

We make the choreographed dance work by using the DNS-based service and policy mechanisms described earlier.

Adding Wireless Devices

Dealing with wireless devices is a little more complex, because there is frequently more than one wireless data network in a given location. We want to make sure that we connect to the right one and the wrong people do not.

If the device connecting to the network has a keyboard and a display, we can type in the domain name of the network we want to join. The problem is a little more difficult if the device is a network hub, a printer, or a light switch.

If the device has any sort of input and display capability, we might provide a list of the visible wireless networks and ask the user to select one. This is a somewhat clunky procedure, though.

The approach I prefer would make use of the fact that flash memory devices, in particular, USB "thumb" drives have become extremely cheap, as is the infrastructure to support them in silicon. If a device is to have a Bluetooth or WiFi capability, the cost of adding a USB or flash memory interface to the design is negligible. To connect a device to the network, the administrator would load a small configuration file onto a flash drive and plug it into the device he wanted to connect to the network and press the Setup/Reset button.

Coffee Shop Connection

Much of this book has been written at the local Panera. One of the main reasons for drinking coffee at Panera is that they provide free WiFi Internet.

The Panera WiFi service is among the best on offer today, but it still demonstrates the clunkiness that results from the fact that authentication was an afterthought in the WiFi specifications. As a result, the user experience falls far short of what it should be.

Using the Internet service in a hotel, airport, or coffee bar should be as simple and seamless as in the home. And, even though I am not at home, I should still be able to use my home printer, fax machine, and storage system.

DHCP makes no distinction between obtaining Internet service from a trusted local network and obtaining it from an untrusted public network. This is an important limitation. Just because I like the coffee at Panera does not mean that I want the company to take over administration of my computer, nor would Panera want to take the responsibility.

What Panera does care about is that I agree to its terms of service. In particular, I must agree not to hog bandwidth, surf porn sites, or sue the company if the connection goes down.

What I care about is that I am connecting to the real Panera network and not subject to an attack known as the "evil WiFi twin." The WiFi specification does not provide a means for the access point to authenticate itself to a user connecting to it. Anyone can set up a WiFi network that advertises itself as "Panera."

Dealing with these concerns is straightforward but time consuming. We need to revise the WiFi protocols without breaking any of the existing systems. EV certificates and Secure Internet Letterhead allow us to know the access point is genuine before we connect.

Securing the Internetwork

The end-to-end principle tells us to avoid all avoidable complexity in the Internet core. Securing the networks where Internet communications originate and terminate meets the bulk of our security requirements for addressing Internet crime.

This leaves the possibility of attacks against the internetwork infrastructure of the Internet. In particular, the Border Gateway Protocol (BGP) used to exchange routing information is vulnerable.

Attacks based on exploiting security weaknesses in BGP are seen today. Fortunately, they are not yet common. The attackers prefer to attack at the weakest point, which is today the two feet between the user and the screen. Social engineering attacks usually trump attacks based on technical sophistication.

Security measures protecting BGP are in place today. My concern is that they rely almost entirely on manual exception processing, and this approach might not scale in the face of a concerted criminal attack, the level of attack we might anticipate if we succeed in shutting down the simpler methods of attack.

BGP Security

Like most descriptions of how the Internet works, this book started with explaining how large messages are chopped up into smaller packets of data, which then pass from one Internet router to another until they finally arrive at their intended destination.

Like most such descriptions, I omitted one of the most important questions to be answered in any such system: How does the router know where to send the packets?

A full technical answer to this question requires at least a book in its own right.[3] A shorter explanation is that the machines that form the Internet backbone are constantly exchanging messages containing route advertisements using BGP.

When an ISP wants to start a network, it applies to its local registration authority to be issued a "block" of IP addresses. A typical allocation for a small network might be 192.168.69.0 through 192.168.69.63.[4]

The ISP connects its router to its upstream Internet provider and sends out a BGP route advertisement for the new network block. This, in effect, says, "I route to 192.168.69.0 through 64 with a distance of 0." The router for the upstream provider then sends out a message to each of the routers it is connected to saying something like, "I route packets to 192.168.69.0 through 64 with a distance of 10." Those routers then advertise a distance of 20 and so on.

When a router receives a packet with a destination address of 192.168.69.23, it looks up its table of known routes and chooses the one it considers "best," taking into account the bandwidth the various links support, how congested they are, and so on.

As the Internet grew, the number of IP address blocks became unmanageably large. Instead of advertising a route for an address block directly, groups of address blocks are mapped to an **Autonomous System** (AS). Providing BGP security between nearest neighbors is straightforward. Unusually for a routing protocol, BGP is layered on TCP, which means we can secure the communication between nearest neighbors using SSL.

The challenge in BGP security is that each router relies on the information provided by its neighbors, which in turn rely on the information provided by their neighbors, and so on. Securing a communication to the nearest neighbors does not provide accountability to the original source.

The problem is similar to a rumor circulating at a cocktail party. Knowing who told you the rumor is not the same as knowing who started it or why.

Another similarity with the cocktail party rumor problem is that the participants have an interest in concealing their sources. For understandable reasons, the companies that provide the Internet backbone are reluctant to fully describe the internal architecture of their networks to competitors.

So far, proposals to secure BGP have tended toward the access control model of "Decide what is bad; make sure it never happens." Some parts of the BGP security problem, in particular the mapping of IP address blocks to autonomous systems, are tractable using this approach. But the results are not encouraging when we attempt to rely on this approach alone. In many cases we can only decide what was bad after observing the consequences.

I believe that the key to deploying BGP security at the inter-network level is to apply an accountability approach. In other words, we accept that there will be problems and develop a mechanism that allows the culprit to be identified.

An event that should help pave the way for deployment of some form of accountability-based security architecture for BGP is that a PKI is currently being deployed that will allow the holders of IP address allocations to authenticate the route advertisements they advertise.

Key Points

- Deperimeterization means that the perimeter model is increasingly insufficient.
  - A fence is only as good as its weakest point.
  - USB flash memory and laptops create holes.
  - Outsourcing and supply chain integration make the perimeter ambiguous.
- Default deny infrastructure responds to the challenge of deperimeterization in three ways:
  - Ubiquitous authentication—every device, user and application is authenticated before they use the network.
  - Ubiquitous policy enforcement—nothing is allowed to happen in the network unless there is a policy rule to say that it is permitted.
  - Data-level security—wherever possible we apply security to the assets we wish to protect, not just the place where they are stored.
- The devil is in the deployment.
  - Network administration is already too costly.
    - Deployment of IPv6 faces the same challenge.
  - Domain-centric administration makes default deny practical.
    - Device authentication—every device authenticates itself to the network automatically.

- Device description—every device provides a description of the network services it provides and requires.
- DNS service advertisement—the DNS is used as the network and internetwork service discovery mechanism.

CHAPTER 1 7

Secure Platforms

In *The Matrix,* Neo faces a choice: Should he take the blue pill and continue to live as he is, or should he take the red pill, which offers "the truth"?

Neo takes the red pill (otherwise, the film would be rather short) and discovers that his life to date has been lived as a "brain in a vat," with every sensory input created by *The Matrix,* a vast computer infrastructure.

The Matrix provides a good analogy for what happens when a computer system is taken over by a rootkit. The rootkit allows the user to believe that he is working on a normal machine, but meanwhile, hidden in the depths of the machine, the rootkit is busy spying on the user's every key click and mouse movement.

The current generation of rootkit technology is not quite a blue pill, but it is close. To eliminate doubt, white hat security researcher Joanna Rutkowska has demonstrated proof of concept code for Blue Pill, an undetectable rootkit.[1]

Building a Secure Platform

According to a recent report, 61 percent of computers in the U.S. are infected with some form of malware.[2] Bad as this is, the question that we should perhaps be asking is, "How did the other 39 percent survive?"

All the computers currently connected to the Internet are *without exception* running operating systems based on original architectures that predate the era of ubiquitous global network connectivity.

Don't let partisan arguments fool you: No operating system on the market today is satisfactory where security is concerned. It isn't the number of brilliant minds that work on a system that matters where security bugs are concerned; it's the number of less than brilliant minds plugging away at caffeine-fueled late-night coding binges just before the code ships.

To bring computer security under control, we need to build on a base that we can have confidence in.

In the past, that base was the operating system: Windows, OS/X, VMS, UNIX. Today, we have the applications running on top of the operating system and applications running within the Web browser. All raise similar security issues, and it makes sense to talk about "platforms" to refer to all software systems that are designed to be built upon by other applications.

There is, however, one important difference: If the operating system is compromised, it is going to be difficult to tell.

Questions of Code

We cannot stop programmers from making mistakes, but we can do a great deal to stop the mistakes they make from mattering.

In his seminal Turing Award lecture *The Emperor's Old Clothes*,[3] Professor Tony Hoare made a prescient observation: Security had been a key principle in the design of the programming language Algol 60. Every time an array lookup was performed, the compiler would insert code to check that the index was inside the array.

When the lecture was given, the programming world had turned away from languages like Algol, which offered this security feature. Hoare believed that we might come to regret this as a mistake. The buffer overrun errors described in Chapter 9, "Stopping Botnets," have proven him right.

Algol 60 was designed during the mainframe era of computing. Programs were processed in batch mode. Performance was important, but getting the right answer was more important. If a program had an error, the whole batch would need to be run again. A whole day might be lost.

During the 1970s and 1980s, the interactive model replaced the batch approach. A delay of a few milliseconds became the difference between the user being happy or dissatisfied. Security and bounds checking were abandoned in favor of the programming language C, designed to allow the programmer to extract the full power of the machine (such as it was).

Today, security is once again the primary concern. Modern computer languages such as Java and C# perform extensive checking as the program runs.

Least Privilege, Least Risk

In feudal times, there was one law for the common people and another for the nobility. This **private law** gave us the word *privilege*.

Operating system privileges have a similar origin. Early computer security schemes were designed to protect the system from the common user. The less a user was allowed to do, the lower the risk that he might cause damage to the expensive system. System administrators (the nobility) were granted special privileges.

The **least privilege** principle states that every entity in the system should be granted the least level of access required to complete his function.

Strictly speaking, this is a mechanism rather than a principle, but it is the nomenclature of the field. If we strip away the mechanism, least privilege is the result of applying the principle of **least risk**: Never take a risk you do not need to take.

Today, our concern is to protect the user from the system, but this makes the least privilege principle even more useful and necessary. If you don't want the kids to install a Trojan on your computer, use the accounts feature that Mac OS/X and every version of Windows has had since Windows XP and don't give them the administrator privilege.

Windows Vista introduces a new security dialog "Allow or Deny," which is invoked each time a program is attempting to perform a privileged action. The dialog is deliberately intrusive and requires programmers to think about the privileges that their code requires to run.

To take "least risk" seriously, we need to add another option: isolation mode.

A program running in isolation mode would work in the same way as the "virtual machine" I use to run suspect programs without putting my own machine at risk. A program running in isolation mode would not be able to see or modify any programs, processes, or data running on the host.

Running a word processor or spreadsheet in isolation mode would severely limit its functionality. Files created by the word processor would not be visible to any other program on the machine.

Running a game or a Web browser in isolation mode is much less of a limitation. A game only needs to read files containing game data and "save game" files it wrote itself, not your tax records or word processing documents.

The Trusted Computing Base

The problem of controlling access to privileges in a complex system began to be a concern even in the 1970s when systems were considerably smaller and simpler than they are today. This concern led Butler Lampson to propose the concept of a reference monitor, an operating system within the operating system that would have exclusive responsibility for security related functions (at the time the term monitor was used for what we now call an operating system).

The reference monitor concept is another instance of the least risk principle. Concentrating all the security-related functions in the reference monitor makes it much easier to get both the design and implementation right. It might even be possible to apply formal methods to provide proofs of correctness for much of the reference monitor implementation.

As the reference monitor concept evolved, it became known as the Trusted Computing Base (**TCB**). Ideally, a TCB should be rigorously verified through each step of its development. For this to be possible, it is helpful if the TCB is as small as possible: tens of thousands of lines of code rather than millions. A key goal of the system security architect is to design the system in such a way that its security depends only on the correctness of the design and implementation of the TCB.

As with the development of programming languages, realization of the TCB concept was trumped by performance. All the popular operating systems in use today allow far too much code to bypass the TCB by running in the inner operating system "kernel."

The principal offenders in this respect are **device drivers**—small pieces of code that manage the shuffling of bits back and forth between the computer and devices such as keyboards and printers that are connected to it.

If good security design principles had been followed, the operating system designs would have rigorously isolated the device drivers from the operating system kernel. But 1980s vintage machines had barely enough CPU processing oomph for their intended purpose. The operating system was pure overhead, and every CPU cycle spent on housekeeping was time the user would be kept waiting. Walking away from this legacy has proven difficult.

Trustworthy Computing

Today, we trust computers with our secrets, our wealth, and even from time to time our lives. Computer systems today are trust*ed*. We need systems that are trust*worthy*.

Extending the *Matrix* analogy, we have a minimal definition of a trustworthy platform.

- We can tell if we swallowed a blue pill.
- There is always a red pill available that will reverse the effects of the blue pill—without loss of data or other assets.

If we are to achieve our data-level security goals, we further require the following:

- The ability to demonstrate to a third party that we are not acting under the influence of a blue pill
- The ability to demonstrate to a third party that an application is running on a machine in a state that the third party can consider trustworthy

This second set of requirements is somewhat more controversial because it provides a foundation for strong copyright enforcement mechanisms that some find objectionable.

We can't secure the Internet if we have to worry about providing systems that are *too* secure. Any system that allows a doctor to view a medical history with controlled redistribution rights is going to provide features that might prove useful to someone developing a copyright enforcement scheme.

A software vendor could use trustworthy computing mechanisms to lock his program so that it will only run a particular machine. A filmmaker could use trustworthy computing mechanisms to ensure that his movie would only be displayed on secure hardware that guarantees that it will not copy it.

Having sat through a sales pitch from a promoter of this type of scheme a few years ago, I can understand these concerns. At the start of the demonstration, the hypothetical user paid $3.99 to "buy" the right to listen to a 4-minute song for the next 30 days. Each time the song was played, the user would be bombarded by pop-up ads offering to sell T-shirts, mugs, a biography of the band, and the full album on CD.

Strong copyright enforcement does allow record labels and film distributors to attempt to abuse their customers in new ways if they are daft enough to want to; however, it does not compel the customer to buy.

Strong copyright enforcement does allow copyright owners to protect their revenues by discouraging widespread unpaid use, but there is no real risk of the copyright owners being able to extinguish fair use or reversion to the public domain after the copyright expires, as some have claimed. Any system that depends on the security of a billion end user devices has a billion potential points of vulnerability and is going to fail on frequent occasions.

In any case, the choice we face is not whether copyright enforcement mechanisms will be employed but whether they will be transparent or clunky. Most games sold today insist that the user insert the game disk into the machine before it will run. This provides an effective means of copyright enforcement but an inconvenient one for a five-year-old child with sticky fingers.

Trustworthy platforms provide tools that we can use to make copyright enforcement much less of a bother. Instead of locking a game or a utility such as a word processor to a particular machine, it could be locked to an identity managed through an online service. The user could then use the program on any machine he owned or happened to be using, and the rights management infrastructure would prevent it from being used in more places than the license allowed.

Trustworthy Bootstrap

When a computer system starts, it runs a program called the **bootstrap**. On a personal computer, the bootstrap is one of the functions of the BIOS (Basic Input/Output System) installed during manufacture.

The bootstrap program performs some system checks to see if the hardware is working; then it looks for an operating system to load. The bootstrap transfers control to the operating system after it is loaded.

The first step toward making an operating system trustworthy is to make sure that the bootstrap loads the real, unadulterated operating system and not something else.

The solution to this problem is straightforward (at least in principle). The operating system image is signed using a digital signature. The bootstrap verifies the signature before transferring control. If verification fails, the machine does not start until the operating system is repaired.

Trustworthy Operating System

Knowing that we had loaded the correct operating system would have been sufficient if the operating system had been designed using trustworthy architectural principles from the ground up. In practice, the operating systems we want to run on personal computers are far too large and too complex for this to be sufficient.

Instead, we need to establish a "secure partition" within the operating system within which we can build a new TCB.

Implementing this approach is considerably more involved. The **Trusted Computing Group** (**TCG**), an industry consortium supported by more than 100 leading technology companies, has proposed an architecture in which an additional chip called the **Trusted Platform Module** (**TPM**) is added to the computer motherboard.

The TPM is in effect a computer in its own right that is designed to provide a new TCB that is genuinely trustworthy. The TPM implements a range of basic cryptographic functions such as encryption, decryption, digital signatures, the ability to generate random numbers that are genuinely random, and secure storage for cryptographic keys.

The TPM is tightly coupled to the main processor so that when the processor receives a request to load a specially privileged piece of code (which Microsoft calls the **nexus**), the TPM first checks the integrity before telling the processor that it is safe to execute. After it's loaded, the nexus runs in a parallel memory space that is independent of both the regular kernel and application programs.

Although the nexus contains a small amount of code, it has exclusive access to the cryptographic keys stored in the TPM. These keys are in turn used to control access to additional cryptographic keys stored outside the TPM, which in turn can be used to control access to data.

The nexus can inspect and report on other processes running on the system. Because the nexus has exclusive access to the cryptographic keys stored in the TPM, the nexus can provide a trustworthy attestation of the security measures that a process has employed.

In particular, the nexus can provide an attestation that a process is running in **curtained memory**. Curtained memory is a memory partition that is not visible to any other process running on the machine.

Secure Code

A secure foundation is good, but we don't want to spend all our time sulking in the basement. We need to secure what we build on the secure foundation, and do so in a way that users can understand and use. A trustworthy operating system is useless without trustworthy applications.

Signed Code

As with the operating system, all code that runs on the platform should be signed, and the platform should verify the signature on the code before it is run. It must not be possible for a virus to attach itself to other program files so that it can reinfect the machine in the future.

If the machine is infected (or merely suspected of being infected), we can easily restore it to its original state. We don't need to know anything about the latest tricks that the malware writers use to hide their code; all we need to do is to decide whether the program files stored on the machine have been tampered with.

If the code has not been signed by the original author, it should be signed during installation. In an enterprise setting, signing would probably be performed by a central service under the control of the IT department.

Accreditation

Ideally, the code would be signed by an accredited, accountable software publisher that has been vetted through a process such as Extended Validation. This is not always possible, however; many software publishers cannot afford accreditation, and a large number could not possibly qualify for accreditation. Code that is still being developed should *not* be accredited, but it should still be signed.

The range of privileges available to a program might depend on who signed it and the accreditations that the signer has received. If the signer has no accreditations, a consumer might be strongly advised to install the program to run in isolation mode. In an enterprise, the site policy might require such a program to run in isolation mode, if the user is allowed to run it at all.

Secure Drivers

Operating systems must be designed to protect themselves against malicious device driver code. No device driver code should run in the kernel.

Ideally, the need for most manufacturer-written device driver code would be eliminated. Every printer I have in the house uses the same set of print commands, and every one requires a slightly different device driver. My latest computer came with 300 printer device drivers from a single manufacturer.

There is no need for such complexity. It is not the case that all printers are exactly alike, but they are not entirely different either. The printer knows how many paper trays it has, which page description languages it supports, whether it offers color, and so on. We should abandon the driver-per-printer-model approach and instead use a small number of generic drivers that configure themselves to the capabilities of each available printer.

We can apply the same approach to most devices that currently demand their own special driver. There will inevitably be some exceptions, of course. Cutting-edge video games will always put a premium on high-speed communication to the video display driver. But these should become exceptions rather than the rule.

Revocation and Patches

Occasionally, a piece of software will be found to be a security risk. The risk might be caused by an accidental oversight or a deliberate attack.

Knowing what software is installed on the machine makes it much easier to determine whether the machine is at risk. Software identified as being a security risk might be replaced by a patched version—only allowed to run in isolation mode or disabled entirely.

Current Technology

Most Web browsers support a form of code signing today. The Microsoft Authenticode scheme is typical.

Authenticode was designed to provide a user who downloaded a program from the Internet with the same degree of assurance that he would receive if he were to buy the program in a shrink-wrapped box from a traditional store.

Authenticode more than meets its original design goals, but ten years later, we need the system to do more. In particular, we need to sign the actual program code that will run on the machine as opposed to just the distribution package.

Another area where adjustments are necessary is in the "Authenticode pledge," an undertaking that software publishers must agree to before receiving a certificate (see Figure 17-1).

The pledge seems clear enough to me, but some have claimed that despite admitting that their software is designed to spy on the user, bombard him with pop-up adverts, and resist removal by the owner, it is somehow not interfering with the use of data, systems, or operations.

In addition to the other representations, obligations, and warranties contained or referenced in the certificate application, the [individual] [commercial] software publisher certificate applicant represents and warrants that he, she, or it shall exercise reasonable care consistent with prevailing industry standards to exclude programs, extraneous code, viruses, or data that may be reasonably expected to damage, misappropriate, or interfere with the use of data, software, systems, or operations of the other party.

Figure 17-1 *The Authenticode pledge*

Key Points

- Secure platforms are essential if Internet security is to have a secure foundation.
  - None of the existing platforms is satisfactory.
  - Modern programming environments such as Java and C# perform many code safety checks automatically.
  - We still rely on a lot of code written in bug-prone languages such as C.
- Systems should be built on the principle of least risk.
  - All programs should execute at the lowest privilege level required.
  - All security actions should be mediated by the Trusted Computing Base.
- Trustworthy computing provides systems that are always able to vouch for their integrity.
- Code signing is the key to securing the application layer.
  - All code should be signed.
  - Critical code should be accredited.
  - As little code should run in kernel mode as is possible.

CHAPTER 18

Law

> *The mills of justice grind slowly, but they*
> *grind exceedingly fine.*
>
> —*FBI proverb after Friedrich von Logau*

In his address to the first World Wide Web Conference in CERN in 1994, Tim Berners-Lee described the Web project as "the chance to build a whole new world." Today, the Web is no longer a frontier town but a world inhabited by a billion people who use it to obtain news and information; to communicate with their family, friends, and business partners; to buy, sell, and advertise; and a hundred other uses. The Web is a world of people, not technology, and no human society has endured without law and order.

The law is like a massive siege gun used to batter the walls of a baroque fortress. It is a powerful weapon, but one that takes time and care to aim and can only be moved with considerable difficulty. We have limited ammunition and must ensure that it is well spent.

Deterring Crime

It is often said that only the stupid criminals are caught. The corollary is that even the cleverest criminal only needs to be stupid once.

Investigation, prosecution, and imprisonment of perpetrators is expensive, and the cost falls on the public purse. But a small investment of resources in law enforcement can greatly increase the deterrent effect of technical security measures. Police are no substitute for door locks or a burglar alarm, but the knowledge that a police patrol will respond quickly to an alarm significantly amplifies its deterrent effect.

Let us imagine metaphorically that technical security measures allow us to raise the bar for attackers from knee height to chest height. This is high enough to prevent the typical attacker from jumping over, but the fittest and the most athletic can still do so. The number of attackers jumping over the bar has dropped from a flood to a trickle.

Now imagine that we place a pair of guard dogs on the far side of the bar. If the bar is low, there are too many attackers jumping over it for the dogs to provide an effective deterrent. Each attacker knows that the chances are good that the dogs will pick a different target. As the bar is raised, the number of successful jumpers falls, and the risk of being bitten becomes serious. The risk/reward ratio is significantly less tempting to the attacker, and far fewer are willing to risk trying.

We can do much more applying technology *and* law than we can achieve with either on its own.

Setting the Agenda

It used to be a truism among members of the antispam community that legal approaches to stopping spam were hopeless. Then, in 2003, Jon Praed of the Internet law group introduced himself at the annual Spam Conference at MIT as follows, "I am a lawyer, and I sue spammers." He provided the facts and figures to back his claim, and minds were changed.

At the time, it was not unusual to open a newspaper and find a story describing in breathless prose the antisocial but exceptionally profitable business of sending spam. A typical example of the genre consisted of a long interview with a spammer describing his expensive house, car, jewelry, and so on, with a couple of "balancing" comments at the end from an antispam activist that made him appear to be some sort of communist.

Only two years later, in the introduction to his book *Spam Kings*, Brian Williams wrote, "Most businesses jump at the opportunity for free publicity. But none of the email marketers, or spammers, profiled in this book were eager to see their stories in print. In fact some even threatened lawsuits over its publication."

Spammers became averse to publicity because their trade began to have consequences. Spammers face a real risk of either being sent to jail or losing everything they own in a lawsuit. In one recent case, an ISP won a judgment of more than a billion dollars against a spammer. Several judgments of more than a million dollars have been won against spammers, and a spammer in Virginia recently received a nine-year jail sentence for sending spam. Nobody expects such judgments to be paid in full, but the ex-spammers face a lifetime in bankruptcy.

The Internet is not a purely virtual world. Physical jurisdiction matters. Moving a criminal enterprise offshore is not easy. Few countries welcome organized criminals seeking a new base of operations.

Lawsuits against spammers have not caused the spam "kings" to stop, but they do appear to have had a significant effect on the small- to medium-sized spammers, so-called **chickenboners** whose profits are not high enough to justify risking personal bankruptcy. The flood of opportunists seized by the idea that spam was the new Klondike has become a trickle.

To be effective, criminal sanctions must be backed by effective law enforcement so that the would-be criminals believe that they face a significant risk of being caught. Few criminals are indifferent to this risk, and even if they are able to successfully evade detection, the measures they must take to do so can impose significant costs in terms of effort and lost opportunities.

To Make the Punishment Fit the Crime

Gilbert and Sullivan's *Mikado* would have found a fitting punishment for spammers. In these more enlightened days, the range of criminal sanctions available is less imaginative.

From a security perspective, the point of putting criminals in jail is either to deter crime or to prevent the offender from reoffending. Although I would like to see condign punishments for Internet criminals, it is important to bear in mind that prisons are expensive, and the cost falls on the taxpayer. Incarceration at a low-security prison costs around $20,000 per prisoner per year; maximum-security prisons cost upward of $60,000.

A five-year sentence is probably sufficient for purposes of incapacitation in respect of computer-related crimes. Unlike the common criminal, the burglar or mugger, the Internet criminal must be constantly learning new techniques and adapting to the countermeasures that are used against them. Every prison has plenty of shoplifters and car thieves who are ready to pass on their skills to others. Relatively few have inmates with advanced technical knowledge, and it is not difficult to discourage interaction by situating such in different parts of the prison. Programming skills in particular must be practiced regularly to be kept sharp.

By the time an inmate has completed a five-year sentence, it is unlikely that he will be able to return to his previous occupation. It is certainly interesting to note that even the arch recidivist hacker, Kevin Mitnick, appears to have finally given up criminal hacking after serving a sentence just one month short of five years followed by a year of probation during which all computer use was prohibited.

It might be possible to reform hackers at even lower cost to the taxpayer. Kevin Poulsen, aka Dark Dante, once won a Porsche 944 S2 in a telephone call-in program by tying up all the telephone lines in the Los Angeles area. He went straight after serving three years in prison followed by three years' probation. Probation restrictions on computer use have been widely ridiculed in technophile discussion groups but appear to be effective, both as a punishment and in preventing reoffending.

Would a five-year sentence be sufficient to deter a master spammer making $5 million a year? Perhaps not, but most spammers do not make anything like as much. The possibility of five years in jail or more is likely to be a significant deterrent to the entry-level chickenboners.

Successful Cases

Until 2000, Internet crime consisted almost entirely of juvenile delinquents and the occasional recidivist. The subsequent rise in Internet crime went almost unnoticed by the public until the spam flood reached crisis proportions in 2002. The rate of criminal prosecutions of professional Internet crime is still low, but much of the slowness is explained in the time taken for legislation and law enforcement techniques to come up to speed with the new circumstances, and the fact that almost every criminal fraud investigation takes years.

The pace of Internet crime prosecutions will increase steadily as older investigations mature and investigators learn which techniques bring them the most success. It is important to remember that an investigation that is quietly collecting information might in the long run be more successful than one that hits the headlines with the arrest of a large number of relatively unimportant players.

Vladimir Levin

One of the earliest professional computer criminals was Vladimir Levin, a Russian national who was part of a gang believed to have stolen more than $10 million from Citigroup in 1995 using a method that has never been made public. Arrested at Heathrow airport in London, Levin spent two years unsuccessfully fighting extradition to the U.S. and served a further three years in U.S. prison.

The Jeremy Jaynes Gang

Jeremy Jaynes, also known as Gaven Stubberfield, ranked as the world's eighth-largest spammer until his arrest in August 2003. In November 2004, Jaynes received a nine-year prison term for sending e-mail with fraudulent and untraceable routing information. His sister, Jessica DeGroot, was also found guilty and fined $7,500. A third defendant was acquitted. The judge later overturned the conviction of Jessica DeGroot but confirmed the nine-year sentence on Jaynes.

During the trial, prosecutors claimed that Jaynes was making between $400,000 and $750,000 a month from his activities and had estimated his net worth at more than $24 million.

One of Jaynes "products" was a so-called FedEx refund processor kit, which was claimed to allow the buyer to make $75 an hour working at home. The software Jaynes provided would in theory allow a purchaser to provide a service claiming refunds for packages that had been delivered late. The software was worthless because no company that shipped enough packages to make the service worthwhile was likely to pay an agent a 50-percent commission to do the job when an employee could do the same job in minutes using the FedEx Web site.

Zachary Keith Hill

In May 2004, Zachary Keith Hill was sentenced to 46 months in prison for sending out phishing spams. Hill was caught with 471 credit card numbers, 152 bank account numbers, and 541 other usernames and passwords.

Hill's phishing scheme was unsophisticated; he appears to have been an unsuccessful spammer attempting to make more money by launching a copycat phishing scheme.

The International Dimension and the Nigeria Effect

The Internet is a global communication network, and a significant fraction of Internet crime is global. This leads many defeatists to conclude that certain third-world countries have no interest in protecting foreigners and will do nothing to prosecute Internet crime.

This view overlooks that fact that even though some Internet crime is international, the perpetrator and victim often live in the same country. Internet crimes are most frequently new variations of old confidence tricks, and few confidence tricks work as well across cultural boundaries.

Even though some Internet crime has a foreign source, this does not mean that the host country has no interest in policing it. Internet crime is in some ways a bigger threat to third-world and emerging states than the developed world.

In 1999, Nigeria held its first elections in 16 years. Foreign investment that had avoided the country during the kleptocracy of General Sani Abacha began to return. Then the advance-fee fraudsters began sending hundreds of millions of spams a day carrying the clear message, "Corruption is rife in Nigeria! Avoid! Avoid!"

When I visited Brazil to give a keynote at Comdex, I was impressed by the determination of local officials to defeat Internet crime. Since then, the authorities have announced four large Internet crime operations, the latest of which resulted in 115 arrests in one day.

Few governments do not realize the importance of preventing their country from becoming a haven for Internet crime. Even **tax-havens**, countries whose economies are built around the creation of loopholes in the tax laws of the major economies, realize the need to protect their reputation.

Every country needs to guard its reputation carefully. When the U.S. Federal Trade Commission held a hearing on antispam legislation, it was clear that new legislation was inevitable regardless of whether it could be made effective. At the time, the vast majority of Internet spam that could be traced had originated in the U.S. and was clearly dishonest. Every spam message sent was making a statement about the ability of the U.S. government to prosecute corruption.

Most governments want to tell the criminals that they are not welcome. This is not easy, particularly in societies where the rule of law is taken seriously and it is not acceptable to simply arrest a group of plausible suspects and convict them without paying much attention to issues such as evidence or guilt. Lawless Internet criminals are bad; lawless governments are worse.

One way that a country can send a signal to both criminals and investors is to put law enforcement resources into detecting and prosecuting Internet crimes, but it is hard to provide convincing evidence that Internet crime is being investigated diligently. In addition to being complex and requiring sophisticated investigation techniques, computer crimes tend to be volume frauds in which a relatively small amount of money is stolen from a large number of victims.

Another more visible way that a signal can be sent is to establish an Internet crime research center in a country. When the U.S. government wanted to send the message that it would treat cybersecurity attacks seriously in the wake of the Morris Internet Worm in 1988, it established the Computer Emergency Response Team (CERT) at CMU. Currently, 170 international response teams follow the CERT model.

Legislating Internet Crime

In the early days of the computer industry, there was a real concern that existing laws might not cover the new medium. Concern that copyright laws might apply only to works in a physical media led to the now familiar "shrink-wrap" software license. Before laws were introduced to criminalize electronic trespass, computer criminals in the UK were charged with "theft of electricity."

Today, Internet law is understood as a continuation of traditional legal principles. The correct means of applying these principles is not always immediately understood, but a consistent approach has emerged over time.

Almost every Internet crime is merely an old scam in a new form. The advance fee frauds are variations of a con trick started in the Middle Ages. Most spam is merely consumer fraud, and most phishing is little different from "skimming" by waiters in restaurants. Practically every form of Internet crime is already criminal, but some Internet crimes cannot be effectively policed.

Internet crimes create new challenges for law enforcement. Although the Internet crimes are almost without exception offenses under existing legislation, there are many questions that remain to be answered. Which branch of law enforcement should take primary responsibility for particular types of Internet crime? What powers do they need to effectively investigate and prosecute cases? What powers should not be granted?

Jurisdiction

There is no difference in principle between stealing $100 by picking a pocket and stealing $100 through an online scam. The pickpocket is clearly the responsibility of local law enforcement in the jurisdiction where the offense occurred. But responsibility for the online scam is harder to define.

In the U.S., Internet crimes fall within the jurisdiction of multiple federal law enforcement agencies (the FBI, the Secret Service, or the Postal Inspectorate) and any number of state or local offices. In practice, law enforcement agencies at every level have limited resources, and the policies that determine the allocation of resources tend to reflect existing priorities that have yet to adapt to the Internet crime wave.

Nor is Internet crime the only important emerging threat facing law enforcement. In the wake of the Oklahoma City bombing and the attacks on the World Trade Center, the threat from domestic and international terrorism is the top priority for the

FBI. The Secret Service, originally created to investigate counterfeiting operations, is facing a new form of counterfeit threat from low-cost color printers. Internet crime is an important new priority, but not the only one. The strategy that seems most effective in treating Internet crime with the concern it deserves is to focus attention on the use of the Internet to raise and distribute terrorist funds. The link between organized crime and terrorism is strong; many of the major organized crime syndicates have their origins in some form of irredentist struggle.

The U.S. agencies whose work is closest to the problem of Internet crime are the Federal Trade Commission (FTC) and the U.S. Postal Inspection Service. The FTC acts as an able guardian for the interests of the consumer, but it is a civilian agency and lacks the power to bring criminal prosecutions.

The U.S. Postal Inspection Service was founded by Ben Franklin and is the oldest federal law enforcement service. In addition to protecting the postal service from criminal activities such as theft of mail and attacks against postal workers, the Postal Inspection Service polices the use of the postal service for criminal purposes. Many Internet crimes are simply online variations of the crimes that the Postal Inspection Service has policed for centuries.

The main limitation of the Postal Inspection Service in policing Internet crime is that its charter remains fixed in what Nicholas Negroponte and the MIT Media Lab would call the world of atoms and not the world of bits. Today, the Postal Inspection Service can only begin investigation of an offense if there is a connection to either the U.S. postal service or a courier service.

Deemed Losses

Federal agencies use loss thresholds to decide if a case is important enough to merit their attention. This approach provides a loophole that is often exploited by domestic Internet criminals; they avoid attention by making many thefts of small amounts that are below the level that leads to action by the FBI or Secret Service. The Internet criminal who steals $100 from a large number of victims can perform a large fraud while remaining below the investigation threshold.

The actual loss in an Internet crime might be difficult to prove until it is too late for an investigation to succeed. Even when a perpetrator is arrested, it might be difficult to connect the crime to an actual loss and hence ensure that the appropriate sentence is applied.

The theft of a credit card creates the potential for theft but does not in itself cause the cardholder or card issuer to suffer an actual loss. Even if fraudulent charges have been made to the stolen card number, it is likely to be difficult to demonstrate that these were the result of one specific phishing attack.

A suspect who has been arrested in possession of a large number of stolen card numbers almost certainly had criminal intent in acquiring them, and the theft has almost certainly led to significant actual losses. It is an unnecessary waste of law enforcement effort to spend time proving and quantifying these losses, so law enforcement agencies and the courts apply a standard formula to arrive at an amount that is deemed to have been lost as a result of the theft. A convict arrested with 1,000 stolen credit card numbers in his possession is assumed to have stolen $50 from each one, resulting in a "deemed loss" for sentencing purposes of $50,000, which in U.S. federal court works out to roughly four years.

The assumed losses for theft of credit card numbers predate the appearance of large-scale Internet phishing fraud. In a phishing attack, the evidence problem is moved forward. We would like a demonstration that a certain volume of phishing spam was sent to provide sufficient evidence to arrest and imprison perpetrators for an appropriately long time. It is time to define deemed losses for activities that are preparation for Internet frauds, such as sending phishing spams or establishing control over a botnet of stolen zombie computers.

Tripwire Offenses

Sending phishing spam and botnet herding are criminal offenses under existing law. Sending a message that impersonates another party for the purpose of committing fraud is a crime, as is unauthorized use of a computer system. The purpose of defining a deemed level of loss is to ensure that the crimes are treated with the seriousness they deserve as preparation for serious theft without having to prove that a serious theft actually occurred.

Tripwire offenses are also used to deal with actions that are not themselves criminal but are most likely to indicate planning for criminal activity. An old English law prohibited "carrying housebreaking tools after dark." A well-chosen tripwire offense allows planning for criminal activity to be investigated and prosecuted in cases where it is difficult to legislate against or prosecute the crime itself.

The U.S. CAN-SPAM act is a good example of successful tripwire legislation. CAN-SPAM does not prohibit sending of unsolicited e-mail. It does not even prohibit sending of large volumes of unsolicited email. Instead, CAN-SPAM prohibits the tricks and deceptions used by spammers to get their messages through spam filters. The CAN-SPAM prohibitions are wide enough to make it effectively impossible for the bulk spammers to operate legally.

Some of the companies that sell hijacked software through the Internet claim to be operating legally, reselling software that they claim, but are unable to prove, has been legally acquired. A tripwire offense should be created to require dealers selling large quantities of software to verify its provenance with the copyright holder.

Clarification

Most Internet criminals operate in the shadows, avoiding attention. A small number, such as the sellers of hijacked software, operate as if they were legitimate businesses, blatantly violating the law under the pretext that their behavior is permitted through some obscure loophole.

In most cases, the loophole is closed when the first prosecution occurs. The courts tend to be intolerant of sophisticated arguments to excuse conspicuously corrupt behavior. In other cases where existing law is genuinely unclear or results in unexpected consequences, it might be necessary to provide clarification.

Agency

Some companies have discovered that they can benefit from spam without sending the spam themselves by marketing their products through "affiliate programs." The affiliate purchases a bottle of pills for $5 and sells it for $30 through extravagant (and illegal) claims made in (equally illegal) spam messages. The manufacturer avoids direct criminal involvement by recruiting others but profits handsomely, selling many bottles of pills costing a few cents for $5 a time.

Legislation might be needed to ensure that businesses that encourage others to act in a criminal manner on their behalf are held criminally accountable.

Spyware

Spyware is rapidly becoming the number-one Internet security nuisance. Personal information is clearly valuable, and using deception to obtain something of value is a crime called **fraud**. The pressure to legislate is likely to become irresistible even so.

Many spyware businesses operate openly. Accusations of malpractice result in flat denials or occasionally lawsuits against the accuser. Some companies have been sued or threatened with lawsuits for providing tools to remove unwanted spyware.

The legislative proposals circulating as I write this, attempt to outlaw spyware by enumerating the objectionable behaviors such as unauthorized communication of information. Drafting a statute of this type that is effective against all the objectionable behaviors without prohibiting desirable behavior is difficult. It is easy for antispyware legislation to end up unintentionally targeting antispyware software. Some spyware companies already pass off their spyware as spyware removal tools, so making an exception for antispyware is an invitation to abuse.

If we try to address spyware head-on, we face the problem of establishing intent. Intent tends to be difficult to prove, and lawmakers usually look to avoid creating statutes where this is necessary. Fortunately, we have two potential tripwire offenses that are easily defined and which virtually all spyware breaks but legitimate programs do not:

- Misleading the user as to the purpose when the program is installed or attempting to install itself without permission
- Resisting attempts either to detect the presence of the program or to remove it

CAN-SPAM made the wise decision of not attempting to define spam according to the annoyance caused. Bills to control spyware should take the same approach. It is probably impossible to draft a cast-iron definition of spyware behavior. It is much easier to define and thus criminalize tactics that spyware vendors have found are essential to make a profit.

Arms Suppliers

A journalist recently asked me to comment on the legality of a new e-mail-sending program that allowed spammers to send out e-mail from a botnet using a new twist on an old technique. Not being a lawyer and in view of strict company policy that prevents comment of that type, I simply stated that it was certainly illegal to use a machine for any purpose without the consent of the owner.

Thinking about the answer afterward, I realized that I might have misled. Use of the program to send e-mail through a botnet acquired by sending out a virus would be unambiguously criminal. But the question asked was whether the seller of the program was breaking the law, and it was entirely possible that a court might believe that it was not.

I believe that someone supplying tools whose primary purpose is to break the law should face the same consequences as those who use them. The author of a virus-writing kit is equally culpable as the "script-kiddie" who uses it to launch a virus.

The problem with legislating against arms-suppliers is that the dividing line between the white hat security specialist and the black hat perpetrator is the problematic question of intent.

Antihacking statutes are prone to abuse. In particular, they have been used to suppress legitimate discussion of the effectiveness of a security technology or product on several occasions. We are not going to bring Internet crime under control if the law prevents companies from being held accountable for providing faulty security technologies.

There is, however, a major difference between identifying a security vulnerability and providing the tools to exploit it. There is a big difference between pointing out that the door locks on a particular model of car can be defeated with a cunningly shaped piece of metal and making the piece of metal for sale. In the same way, there is a major difference between reporting the existence of a buffer overflow and releasing a tool that exploits the vulnerability to launch a phishing attack.

To be useful to the criminal, an exploit has to be properly assembled and packaged. A white hat does not need to create a complete virus or create a full function phishing package to demonstrate that vulnerability exists. The only reasons to go that far are an inflated ego or to sell his work to criminals.

Civil Law

The law is a form of security control; it mitigates risks resulting from human behavior. Criminal law imposes consequences. Civil law determines responsibility.

Responsibility

The cost of law enforcement, courts, and prisons falls on the public purse. It is, therefore, a proper concern of government to avoid unnecessary expenditure by ensuring that appropriate crime prevention steps are taken whenever it is practical and economic to do so.

Modern cars are safer because governments decided that manufacturers should be required to provide features such as seat belts, safety glass, and air bags.

Internet safety is a concern for every Internet user, every service provider, every application provider. In most cases, we have tried to design security measures that have an immediate benefit for the party that must act. We have tried to design the technology to align the ability to act with the benefit. In some cases, that is not possible, and regulation is required to align responsibility with the ability to act.

The botnet problem provides a good illustration. A bot is a minor inconvenience for the ISP managing the network it is connected to; the principal damage is caused to the rest of the Net. Measures such as filtering spoofed source address packets and controling channel rate capping can prevent a bot from becoming a problem to the rest of the Internet. However, the responsibility to act is not aligned with the ability to act.

Appropriate allocation of risk can eliminate the need for complex technical standards. Early in 1995, when I left CERN to work at the Web Consortium at MIT, I spent a great deal of time working on the problem of secure payments. The visible concern was the risk that an attacker might steal credit card numbers while they were being transmitted over the Internet. Although this was a significant concern for the banks, the banks were much more concerned that criminals would crack the systems of Internet merchants and obtain databases containing hundreds of thousands of card numbers at a time.

The proposed technical solution to this problem was a complex protocol called Secure Electronic Payments (SET). SET provided a secure payment mechanism that ensured that Internet merchants would never see their customer's credit card number except in encrypted form. By the time that SET was ready for deployment, the simpler SSL encryption scheme was already in place. SSL provided protection for the risk that concerned the consumer: the risk of having his credit card number stolen. But SSL only encrypts the communication between the customer and the merchant. The merchant sees the unencrypted credit card number and is not prevented from storing it in a database, where it is vulnerable.

The solution that the banks found to the delay in adoption of SET was to charge merchants a hefty fee for the replacement of any credit cards they were responsible for compromising. Reissue of compromised credit cards costs a bank approximately $50 per card. A merchant who lets an attacker get access to details on 20,000 cards faces a $1 million charge. As a result, most online merchants have learned the importance of treating credit card numbers with great care.

Risk allocation is not a cost-free panacea. It only works if the party made responsible is in fact able to act. The fact that a party appears to be causing a problem does not necessarily mean that it is the one at fault.

It is often suggested that the way to solve the Internet crime problem is to make software vendors responsible for the cost of their bugs. Certainly, regulation can make software vendors responsible for bugs, but that does not make them any more able to eliminate them.

The argument for liability is often raised by self-proclaimed advocates of open source software. This seems unwise; open source software would cease to exist if contributors faced the risk of unlimited liability from lawsuits. As one open source programmer put it to me, it is an argument heard from people who "say much but write little code."

As we saw earlier, the number of security bugs reported is not a good indicator of the quality of a product. Internet criminals choose their targets in the same manner as software developers; they choose platforms that are widely used. The larger the number of machines, the larger their potential "market" is. Security problems are reported for every one of the commonly used operating systems. Keystroke loggers have been deployed to steal credit card numbers on Windows, Mac, and Linux machines. Scripting attacks have been released attacking security holes in Internet Explorer, Firefox, and Opera.

If criminals are not trying to attack your software, it is because too few people use it to make it worth their while. If you want to have security through obscurity of your operating system choice, Microsoft Bob is the best choice imaginable.

On second thought, even Microsoft Bob might not be completely safe because it is layered on Windows 3.1 and MSDOS, both of which have known security issues and, in any case, security flaws frequently result from unexpected interactions between two independent systems. If a problem is found in the Windows 3.1 code, is it the fault of Windows 3.1, or is it the fault of Bob for using Windows 3.1 in an unexpected way? At least in this case, both pieces of software are provided by the same company, but what if there were two companies? How much will litigating the question of who is at fault cost?

Software systems are among the most complex human achievements. Real software systems consist of hundreds, even thousands of different modules that interact in ways that are rarely completely understood. Testing software systems is a major cost in itself. In 1995, Bill Gates made a presentation at MIT where he stated that for every programmer at Microsoft, there was another person whose full-time job was testing. In addition, the programmers spent half their time writing and performing tests. In other words, three times as much effort was going into testing than to original development. Today, it is not atypical for the ratio to be five to one or even ten to one.

Software engineering has not yet reached a point where it is possible to guarantee development of code free of all security bugs. Even modern programming languages such as Java and C#—where some of the most common types of security errors are eliminated—are far from infallible.

U.S. law has a legal standard for negligence, the **Judge Hands formula**:

Burden of	<	Probability	×	Gravity
Avoidance		of Injury		of Injury

The same formula has emerged independently in jurisdictions around the world, including some jurisdictions that apply Continental Law. We do not need to create a new formula for software.

The Hands formula is essentially a generalization of the **risk evaluation formula** used by insurers and security specialists:

Cost of	<	Probability	×	Amount
Control		of Loss		of Loss

By this analysis, it is reasonable to expect the manufacturers of cable modems and other Internet access devices to include features such as reverse firewalls because the cost of providing the protection measure is low, and the probability of a loss and the potential amount of the loss are high.

The cost of providing software that is guaranteed to be bug free, on the other hand, is extremely high. Tens of billions of dollars is spent each year on the development of operating systems and network applications. Software providers already face significant incentives to deal with program errors; the cost of testing and fixing bugs is many times the cost of developing the original program.

Making software providers liable might make sense if new software engineering methodology were to be discovered that allowed software errors to be excluded at a sufficiently low cost to meet the Hands test. That technology does not exist today.

Eliminating Perverse Liabilities

Civil law should encourage socially desirable behavior by establishing the correct alignment of responsibilities and liabilities. Occasionally, however, liability becomes so entangled that a counterproductive incentive is created.

Many states have enacted "Good Samaritan" laws that offer a medic certain protections against a lawsuit if they provide assistance in an emergency. The Good Samaritan laws became necessary after some doctors began to refuse to treat accident victims in these cases for fear of lawsuits.

This issue is often raised as an objection to schemes such as INCH/RID, described in Chapter 9, "Stopping Botnets." Does an ISP put itself at risk by allowing others to tell it of a security issue? Fortunately, the Internet standards already define an e-mail mechanism for reporting abuse, so defining an additional protocol does not affect the liability issue.

I strongly suspect that fears of similar perverse liabilities in the Internet security world are not well founded, but if they impede deployment, a cyber equivalent of the Good Samaritan law might be required.

Maintaining Pressure

There are no silver bullets guaranteed to stop Internet crime in its tracks without the possibility of an evasive measure. Battling Internet crime requires a pragmatic approach. Even an initiative that has a relatively obvious countermeasure can provide a real benefit, albeit short term, if it causes enough inconvenience to the criminal.

Internet criminals operate under many constraints. They have to avoid being detected, they have to run their schemes profitably, they have to pay accomplices for technology and services, they have to worry about competition from other criminals, some of whom might be in the habit of settling arguments with violence. Increasing the rate at which they must update their technology increases the pressure on them and gives them more opportunities to make a mistake.

In the physical world, there is no lock that is unpickable, no safe that is unbreakable, no accounting system that is unfoolable. But in most cases, the good guys do win. Law enforcement is effective despite having crime prevention tools that are flawed at best. Law enforcement has a set of techniques for dealing with organized crime, none of which provides a silver bullet, but used together they wear the criminals down.

Follow the Money

Phishing is a highly visible crime. The criminals go to great lengths to insulate themselves from the phishing capture sites and the botnets used to spam out advertisements for them. Tracking down the source of a phishing spam is hard indeed; by the time the spam has been received, the sender has covered his traces. Tracking down a capture site to the perpetrator is somewhat easier in principle because the information has to reach him somehow. But this is still a difficult proposition because there are many ways to hide a flow of information.

Hiding flows of money is a considerably harder problem, one that requires considerable knowledge and expertise on the part of the perpetrator. Each step in a money-laundering scheme moves the money closer to the perpetrator. Each step costs money, which means that the criminals must pay to reduce their risk of being caught.

Internet Currencies

The Internet money trail frequently stops at one of a number of schemes that purport to offer an Internet currency backed by either a hard currency or a precious metal such as gold.

The principal attraction of these schemes for the legitimate users appears to be ideological. Distrusting governments and government regulation, the account holders instead place their trust in what is effectively an unregulated and uninsured offshore bank registered in a country chosen for the opacity of its banking laws.

Internet currencies are attractive to criminals because transactions are instantaneous and irrevocable. A bank wire transfer can be reversed out if it is discovered to be fraudulent; an Internet currency transaction is final and purports to be untraceable.

If Internet currencies are to be permitted trade, they must be considerably more transparent than they are today and provide the same ability to trace fraudulent transactions and money laundering as the traditional banks. If they do not, they will be either legislated out of existence or fall victim to the common fate of unregulated, uninsured banks: the bank run.

A run has already occurred against the OSGold "High Yield Investment" scheme after the founder of the program disappeared just before the date on which investments in the scheme were due to mature. Investors are currently attempting to recover $250 million in a U.S. lawsuit that alleges OSGold to be a Ponzi scheme.

Government regulations can be inconvenient, but they provide protection for investors and prevent tax evasion. The Internet currency schemes talk a fine game on the subject of investor protection, claiming their reserves to be 100 percent backed by gold bullion. Whether these claims are actually true is another matter. The claim that some gold bullion is held might or might not be true, but there is no means of independent verification, and even if the assets can be verified, there is no way of knowing what liabilities stand against them.

In July 2006, the principals of Internet currency exchange service *Gold Age* were arrested and charged with transferring money without a license.[1] In April 2007, E-Gold Ltd and its owners were indicted on charges that included money laundering and operating an unlicensed money transmitting business.[2]

Key Points

- Law must be considered in a strategy to control Internet crime.
  - We must remember that this is a problem caused by technology, not law.
  - The legislative process takes time and should not be a first resort.
- Criminal law provides the ultimate consequences in an accountability scheme.
  - The law also helps set the agenda.
    - CAN-SPAM ended the idea that spam is a business.
  - Successful prosecutions are brought, including international cases.
  - States that are permissive of Internet crime risk becoming failed states.
- Legislation should apply established principles to the Internet.
  - Ensure that there is effective jurisdiction.
  - Sentencing policy establishes priorities for investigators and prosecutors.

- Deemed losses help set priorities correctly, facilitate convictions, and appropriate sentencing.
- Tripwire offenses make investigation and prosecution
easier.
- The law should prohibit agents and arms merchants,
not just the crime.
- Where the intent of the behavior is subjective, criminal-
ize tactics instead.
  - Criminalize software designed to resist removal, not
  "spyware."
- Civil law should be used to align responsibility with the
ability to act.
  - This alignment works if the party has the ability to act.
    - ISPs can deploy reverse firewalls.
  - Software vendors cannot be expected at this point to
  produce bug-free code.
- Follow the money.
  - Prosecute financial services designed to help launder the
  proceeds of Internet crime.

CHAPTER 19

The dotCrime Manifesto

This is not the book I started to write. It became the book I *had* to write so that I could write the one I started. When I began writing, security was to be one chapter in a book that was to chart new ways of using the Web. Instead, I have had to spend time my time trying to protect what we have already.

We will certainly reclaim the Internet. That should never be in doubt. Internet criminals of every type are being caught and prosecuted. Many of the technical proposals described in this manifesto are already being deployed in some form. But will we have the nerve to go forward and claim the future possibilities that are our right?

We face so many challenges that should have a much more urgent claim on our attention. Climate change and competition for the finite supply of cheap fossil fuels demand that we rethink our energy strategy. The rest of the world expects and demands Western living standards, whereas the West asks how it might be maintained after the retirement of the baby boomer generation. If we are going to meet these challenges, we must do more with less. The supply chain efficiencies that the Internet enables will play a critical role.

Early in 2002, I divided my time between two projects: stopping spam and securing Web Services, the next generation of the Web. The objective of Web Services is to allow businesses to make their information systems and thus their business processes much more efficient by allowing computers to talk to computers with the same ease that the Web allows humans to talk to computers. Security was already a major concern; no company was going to put its business infrastructure on the Internet until it was convinced that it was safe to do so. My catchphrase at the time was, "Without security and trust, Web Services are dead on arrival."

Five years later, I still believe that this is the case, but I have since come to understand that it is not enough to provide a security infrastructure for the new world of Web Services. I cannot persuade businesses to trust that infrastructure while Internet criminals appear to run amok unimpeded. I hope that this book has at least convinced you that we can tip the scales back in our favor and that the fight is a winnable one.

Design Rules

Winston Churchill wrote his 1945 election manifesto in 6,123 words, I have used more than 120,000. Moreover, Churchill was defeated by the Labour party, whose manifesto was 20 percent shorter at a mere 5,010 words.

Since then, the trend has been toward verbosity until Newt Gingrich successfully campaigned on his 10-point Contract with America. The 2005 Labour party manifesto set out Tony Blair's program for government in 6 phrases described in 20 words or less.

Internet crime is a complex problem, but not as complex as running a country. Here then is my five-point plan for reclaiming the Internet.

1. **Design to realistic goals**—Proposals must be designed to meet realistic goals that address the real and immediate problems of Internet crimes.

2. **Design for accountability**—Proposals must be designed to re-establish the accountability that existed in the original Internet.

3. **Design for usability**—Proposals must be designed to be used by the ordinary user with no intention of becoming a computer expert.

4. **Design for infrastructure**—Security must be part of the Internet infrastructure; the Internet infrastructure must therefore be changed.

5. **Design for deployment**—Proposals must be designed to rapidly establish the critical mass necessary to drive deployment.

We all have a part to play. Software vendors must produce applications that are designed to be secure when used in the way that ordinary users can be expected to use them. ISPs need to take more responsibility for dealing with the problem of botnets. Governments need to work out how to align ability to act against Internet crime with responsibility to do so. Users need to become aware of the types of scam that might be directed at them and the steps they can take to protect themselves.

Broken Windows and the Tipping Point

In this book, I have set out a plan for stopping the Internet crime wave. The plan is at least extensive if not comprehensive. Two important questions remain: What might success look like, and what is its probability?

One answer to what success looks like is to convince enough people that there are answers to the Internet crime problem and that they are being seriously pursued. This book might not provide the *final* answer to Internet crime, but I believe that I have at least provided *one* answer. Our opponents are cunning and tenacious. We must expect to have to change our plan as they respond, but we must always remember that this is a world that we, not they, created. Also, it is a world in which we, not they, will always have the upper hand if we choose to raise it.

We cannot surrender to the criminals, nor can we wait forever, paralyzed by the fear that no solution is guaranteed or that any action might have unforeseen consequences. Action must become the benchmark applied to every proposed solution. I would count this book a success even if none of the measures I proposed was deployed but it prompted someone to propose a better solution or a more deployable one.

Defeatism is never a solution. The New York subway system once suffered from defeatism. The outward symptoms of the defeatism were trains covered in graffiti, thugs and petty criminals jumping the turnstiles to avoid paying their fare, and dirty, dilapidated stations.

Much has been written about William Bratton's impact on the New York subway system and the application of the broken windows theory that environment is a powerful influence on crime. The essential point is that failure breeds failure; success breeds success. The subway system gained a reputation for being dangerous, which in turn drove away passengers, which in turn led to a loss of revenue, which in turn led to lower maintenance budgets, which in turn led to stations becoming dirtier and more dilapidated, which in turn confirmed the perception of danger. The key to reversing the spiral was proving that somebody cared and was committed to reversing the decline. Removing the graffiti, arresting the petty criminals, and cleaning up the station might not have reduced crime, but they did prove that someone cared.

It is harder to judge whether the broken windows theory played a leading role in the decline of crime when applied to New York City as a whole. Social programs do not allow for the type of controlled experiment performed in physics. The reduction in crime in New York City coincided with a rapid fall in the number of juveniles and the end of the nationwide crack epidemic. It is also possible that a reduction in mortality rates due to gunshot wounds due to improved trauma care played a role in reducing deaths from gunshot wounds and hence the murder rate.

Science is a method of thinking; politics is a plan of action. Politics must take place in the real world, not in a science laboratory, and those who engage in it must act on information that is never perfect.

The Internet has also suffered from the perception that it is a permissive environment. The World Wide Web has been the World Wild West, an environment dominated by a frontier mentality that it is beyond the boundaries of law and order. The people on the Register of Known Spam Operators list of top spammers began spamming believing that it was a quick and easy way to make a lot of money. Every one of the top phishing gangs believes that it can operate the most brazen of frauds with impunity because the Internet is a weakly policed environment.

I cannot know what the same individuals would have done if they had believed that the Internet was not a permissive environment, but it seems most likely to me that at least some current Internet crime kingpins would never have gotten started.

Existing antispam measures demonstrate what we might expect success to look like. Small-time spammers are already being squeezed out. The passing of CAN-SPAM and the effective criminalization of the main techniques used to circumvent spam filters have reduced what had once been a flood of new entrants into the game to a trickle.

The elimination of the entry-level spammers has not had a marked effect on the volume of spam. The remaining high-volume spammers have responded to filters by increasing their message volume and switching to scams that provide the highest margin when successful. The short-term effect of filtering is that the kingpins have responded with more and worse spam.

Spam filtering alone could never eliminate the spam problem; filtering has closed the ramp for new entry-level spammers, but the kingpin spammers respond by sending more spam. Nor can the law solve the problem alone. Each spammer eliminated is quickly replaced. But the combination of technology and law is more powerful than either on its own. The spammers that are eliminated are replaced at a much lower rate, and the number of spammers steadily declines.

Eventually, a tipping point will be reached; the pool of active spammers will be reduced to the point where the remaining criminals realize that their own day of reckoning is likely to come soon. There are signs that some spammers are already starting to avoid targeting the largest ISPs, which have been aggressively prosecuting cases against spammers.

I believe that deployment of countercrime security infrastructure will also see a tipping point effect. Early adopters of e-mail authentication will look for improved reliability of e-mail delivery as the benefit. As the proportion of authenticated and accredited e-mail rises to a significant level, spam filters will be able to raise the discrimination criteria for unauthenticated e-mail without resulting in unacceptable rejection rates for legitimate e-mail. This in turn will increase the incentive to authenticate outgoing e-mail, which in turn will drive further deployment.

Similar tipping point effects, or **positive feedback** in engineering terms, should be seen through technological effects in the deployment of the INCH incident notification infrastructure and reverse firewalls described in Chapter 9, "Stopping Botnets." ISPs that deploy these measures will effectively cause the criminals to switch their attention to ISPs that have not deployed. If your car is the only one parked in a street without a burglar alarm, it is the one most likely to be stolen.

Whatever the chance of success, we must try. Even if we believe we are certain to fail, we must try, or nobody will make the mistakes for the next generation of security specialists to learn from.

What is at stake here is not merely the Internet and the trillion-dollar Web economy, but what we might have in the future.

When the Internet began, nobody wrote a research proposal for inventing e-mail, but e-mail has proven to be immensely more valuable than anything that was planned. When CERN authorized the initial work that led to the World Wide Web, the objective was to produce a simple utility for use in the physics community, not to create the definitive information system of the twentieth century.

Web Services promise to revolutionize machine-to-machine communications as dramatically as the Web revolutionized human–to-machine interactions. Radio Frequency Identification tags (RFID) promise to revolutionize retail and manufacturing industries. The Semantic Web might allow us to change our understanding of knowledge itself.

Yet all these future benefits depend on our ability to secure the Internet as it stands today. We cannot convince businesses that they should move their entire information supply chain to the Internet until a convincing answer is given to the Internet crime problems we face here and now.

Further Reading

There are many books on Internet security. Rather than provide an exhaustive list, I have tried to select books that readers are likely to find particularly useful.

On Security Principles

Secrets and Lies, Bruce Schneier, Wiley (August 14, 2000)

When I first read *Secrets and Lies*, I found it difficult to understand why Bruce described his realization that security was a process of risk mitigation and not risk elimination as an epiphany. It was something that many of us had been saying for years. Later when I reread it, I realized that this was the problem: It is easy to talk about risk management, but much harder to apply it.

Security Engineering, Ross Anderson, Wiley (January 22, 2001)

For several years, I taught a course on computer security. At the time, the only textbooks available were essentially books describing cryptography. This is the book that I wish I had had then.

History of Cryptography

The Code Book, Simon Singh, Anchor (August 29, 2000)

If you are looking for a popular introduction to cryptography, *The Code Book* provides a more comprehensive account of this fascinating subject.

On Cryptography

Applied Cryptography, Bruce Schneier, Wiley (October 18, 1995)

Handbook of Applied Cryptography, Alfred J. Menezes, Paul C. van Oorschot, Scott A. Vanstone, CRC (October 16, 1996)

If you are looking for a more comprehensive treatment of cryptography, you should consider either or both of these books. Schneier's book is stronger on the use of cryptography within a system, whereas the mathematical background is stronger in Menezes'.

On Internet Safety

Look Both Ways: Help Protect Your Family on the Internet, Linda Criddle, Microsoft Press (October 18, 2006)

Internet Dates from Hell, Trisha Ventker, iUniverse, Inc. (August 29, 2006)

I found Ventker's cautionary tales and Criddle's safety manual rather more informative on the topic of Internet dating than any of the how-to guides.

History of Internet Crime

The Cuckoo's Egg, Clifford Stoll, Pocket (September 13, 2005)

Stoll's classic tale of computer espionage is about how a 75 cent billing error led to the arrest of eight hackers selling Western military secrets to the KGB. It is still a good read.

The Hacker Crackdown, Bruce Sterling, Bantam (November 1, 1993)

Sterling accurately describes the early history of Internet crime in the days when the biggest threat to Net users came from the teenage vandal and law enforcement was frequently another source of problems. The only caveat to bear in mind is that the situation is very different today.

On Security Usability

Security and Usability: Designing Secure Systems That People Can Use, Editors: Lorrie Cranor and Simson Garfinkel, O'Reilly Media, Inc.; 1 edition (August 25, 2005)

Security and Usability is a selection of 34 essays on different aspects of security and usability written by leading experts in this emerging field.

On Internet Crime, Phishing, and Countermeasures, Editors: Markus Jakobsson, Steven Myers, Wiley-Interscience (December 15, 2006)

Phishing and Countermeasures is an edited volume providing a comprehensive survey of the state of the art in antiphishing technology. It is a useful reference work for the researcher, but it might be overwhelming for the student or casual reader.

References

Chapter 1

1 Swindle, Orin. Keynote address to the Federal Trade Commission Spam Forum, April 2003.

2 Kelling, George, and Catherine Coles. *Fixing Broken Windows: Restoring Order and Reducing Crime in Our Communities* 1998.

3 Vaxbuster. "Safe and Easy Carding." *Phrack* Vol. 44, www.phrack.org/phrack/44/P44-20

4 Best, Jo. *Ireland Launches Phone Fraud Crackdown.* CNET-News, September 22, 2004, http://news.com.com/Ireland+launches+phone+fraud+crackdown/2100-1036_3-5377387.html

5 BBC News. *Bookies Extortion Gang Caught*, July 21, 2004, http://news.bbc.co.uk/2/hi/business/3914363.stm

6 KARE 11 TV. *Minnesota Attorney General Issues Fraud Alert*, June 1, 2007, www.kare11.com/news/news_article.aspx?storyid=255786.

7 *Stings, Busts, Arrests and Convictions of Nigerian Scammers*, www.crimes-of-persuasion.com/Nigerian/nigerian_busts.htm

8 van Beynen, Martin. *Key Man in $4m Hunt Dies*, The Press (New Zealand), November 22, 2002.

9 U.S. Secret Service. *USSS Operation 4-1-9*, http://www.secretservice.gov/alert419.htm

10 ibid.

11 www.state.gov/s/ct/c14151.htm

12 VeriSign iDefense. *Uncovering Online Fraud Rings: The Russian Business Network*, Webcast, http://labs.idefense. com/about/contactus/?reportRequest= Webcast%2520%2520Uncovering+Online+Fraud+ Rings%253A+The+Russian+Business+Network

13 Padgett Paige M., *Personal Safety and Sexual Safety for Women Using Online Personal Ads*, Sexuality Research and Social Policy: *Journal of NSRC*, June 2007, Vol. 4, No. 2, pp. 27–37, http://caliber.ucpress.net/doi/pdf/10.1525/ srsp.2007.4.2.27

14 There are some cases in which it is better not to give a citation; this is one of them. Anyone who really wants to find this book should have no difficulty locating it.

Chapter 2

1 CNN News Report: *Hacked CIA Web Site Still Down.* September 20, 1996, www.cnn.com/TECH/9609/20/ cia.hackers/index.html

2 See: "A Walk on the Dark Side," *The Economist*, August 30, 2007, www.economist.com/displaystory.cfm?story_id=9723768

3 McIntosh, Neil. "Mail Out of Order," *The Guardian*, February 27, 2003, www.guardian.co.uk/technology/ 2003/feb/27/spam.onlinesupplement

4 Peterson, T. F. *Nightwork: A History of Hacks and Pranks at MIT*, MIT Press 2003.

5 Sterling, Bruce. *The Hacker Crackdown: Law and Disorder on the Electronic Frontier*, Bantam Press, 1993.

6 The 9-11 Commission. "The 9-11 Commission Report," July 2004, Section 7.

7 ibid., Section 6.

8 See, for example, "Afghanistan: Five Years After 9/11," Committee on International Relations, House of Representatives, September 20, 2006 Serial No. 109–230, http://commdocs.house.gov/committees/intlrel/ hfa29973.000/hfa29973_0.HTM

9 Litan, Avivah. "Banks Must Act Urgently to Stop Account Hijackers," Gartner Group, June 2004.

10 TRUST e. "U.S. Consumer Loss of Phishing Fraud to Reach $500 Million," Press Release www.truste.org/about/ press_release/09_29_04.php

Chapter 3

1 Snider, L. B., and D. S. Seikaly. *Improper Handling of Classified Information by John M. Deutch,* CIA Inspector General, 2000, www.cia.gov/cia/reports/deutch/deutch.pdf

2 Welchman, Gordon. *The Hut 6 Story,* McGraw-Hill, 1997.

3 The 9-11 Commission. "The 9-11 Commission Report," July 2004, p. 77.

4 Saltzer, Jerome H., David. P. Reed, and David D. Clark. *End-to-End Arguments in System Design. ACM Transactions on Computer Systems 2,* 4 (November 1984) pp. 277–288. An earlier version appeared in the *Second International Conference on Distributed Computing Systems* (April, 1981) pp. 509–512.

5 Shim, Richard. *Wi-Fi Arrest Highlights Security Dangers.* CNET News.com http://news.com.com/ Wi-Fi+arrest+highlights+security+dangers/ 2100-1039_3-5112000.html

Chapter 4

1 Marx, Karl. *Theses on Feuerbach,* 1845.

2 Covington, Edward J., and Alfred Swan. http://home. frognet.net/~ejcov/alfredswan.html

3 Libowitz, S.J., and Stephen E. Margolis. "The Fable of the Keys." *Journal of Law & Economics,* Vol. XXXIII (April 1990) www.utdallas.edu/~liebowit/keys1.html

4 Kafka, Franz. *The Trial,* 1925.

5   Dunbar, R. I. M. "Neocortex Size as a Constraint on Group Size in Primates." *Journal of Human Evolution* (1992), Vol. 20, pp. 469–493.

6   Malthus, Thomas. *An Essay on the Principle of Population,* 1798.

Chapter 5

1   Brooks, Fred. *The Mythical Man-Month: Essays on Software Engineering,* Addison-Wesley, 1975.

Chapter 6

1   Federal Trade Commission. *False Claims in Spam,* FTC Report 2003, www.ftc.gov/reports/spam/ 030429spamreport.pdf

2   Hulten, Geoff. *Filtering Junk Mail on a Global Scale,* Talk at Spam Conference 2004.

3   For a typical example, see Mylene Mangalindan, "For Bulk E-Mailer, Pestering Millions Offers Path to Profit," *Wall Street Journal,* November 13, 2002, http://online.wsj.com/ article_email/SB1037138679220447148.html

4   Sobel, Dava. *Longitude,* Fourth Estate, 1995.

5   von Ahn, Luis, Manuel Blum, and John Langford. "Telling Humans and Computers Apart Automatically," *Communications of the ACM,* Volume 47, Issue 2 (February 2004), http://www.captcha.net/captcha_cacm.pdf

6   Hurwitz, Roger, and John Mallery. "The Open Meeting: A Web Based System for Conferencing and Collaboration," in Proceedings of the Fourth International Conference on the World Wide Web, December 1995, http://www.cl-http. org:8001/cl-http/ai/projects/iiip/doc/open-meeting/ abstract.html

Chapter 7

[1] Microsoft Open Specification Promise. October 23, 2006, www.microsoft.com/interop/osp/default.mspx

Chapter 8

[1] U.S. Dept. Homeland Security and the Antiphishing Working Group. "The Crimeware Landscape: Malware, Phishing, Identity Theft and Beyond," http://www. antiphishing.org/reports/APWG_CrimewareReport.pdf

Chapter 9

[1] "Computer Error Means £2.3 Trillion Electricity Bill," www.ananova.com/news/story/sm_756911.html

[2] Aleph1. "Smashing the Stack for Fun and Profit," *Phrack*, Vol. 49, 1996, www.phrack.org/phrack/49/P49-14

[3] Stewart, Martha. "Deep Fried Turkey," www.marthastewart.com/portal/site/mslo/menuitem. fc77a0dbc44dd1611e3bf410b5900aa0/?vgnextoid= 9a9040ee0c90f010VgnVCM1000003d370a0aRCRD&vgne xtfmt=default

[4] Ranum, Marcus. "The Six Dumbest Ideas in Computer Security," September 2005, www.ranum.com/security/ computer_security/editorials/dumb/

[5] Kim, Gene, and E. H. Spafford. *The Design of a System Integrity Monitor: Tripwire*, Department of Computer Sciences, Purdue University, CSD-TR-93-071, Coast TR 93-01, 1993.

[6] CTV.ca. "Police Warn of Wi-Fi Theft by Porn Downloaders," www.ctv.ca/servlet/ArticleNews/story/ CTVNews/1069439746264_64848946///?hub=Canada

Chapter 10

[1] Diffie, W., and M. E. Hellman. *New Directions in Cryptography*, IEEE Transactions on Information Theory, Vol. IT-22, Nov. 1976, pp. 644–654.

[2] Kaliski, Burt. "TWIRL and RSA Key Size," RSA Labs, May 6, 2003, www.rsasecurity.com/rsalabs/node.asp?id=2004

[3] Dei, Wei. "Crypto++ 5.2.1 Benchmarks," www.eskimo.com/~weidai/benchmarks.html

Chapter 11

[1] Kohnfelder, Lauren. Thesis, MIT, LCS 1979.

Chapter 12

[1] BBC News. "US Prison Sees Keys Sold Online," May 4, 2007, http://news.bbc.co.uk/2/hi/americas/6624831.stm

[2] Hallam-Baker, Phillip. "Control and Management of Electronic Messaging," U.S. Patent Application 2004/020513.

Chapter 13

[1] Shizzy, Joyce. "Shizzy's Mailbag," www.bobfromaccounting.com/shizzypage40.html

[2] Aravosis, John. Personal communication, June 26, 2007.

[3] I am obliged to Henryk Frystyk Nielsen for this particular aphorism.

[4] The $1 billion figure comes from an industry meeting where it was used by one of the participants to argue against abandoning S/MIME. Although no citation was provided, it is certainly consistent with the sums that I know to have been involved in certain U.S. government S/MIME deployment efforts. Not only do people fail to check signatures, many fail to check references as well.

5   Allman, E., et al. "DomainKeys Identified Mail (DKIM)
    Signatures," RFC 4871, May 2007, www.ietf.org/
    rfc/rfc4871.txt

Chapter 14

1   *Mythbusters*, "Episode 59: Crimes and Myth-Demeanors
    2," Aired August 23, 2006.

2   Turkle, Sherry. *Life on the Screen*, Simon and Schuster,
    1997.

3   Hurwitz, Roger. Personal conversation.

4   Moses, Tim. "OASIS eXtensible Access Control Markup
    Language Version 2.0," OASIS Standard, Feb 1, 2005,
    http://docs.oasis-open.org/xacml/2.0/access_control-
    xacml-2.0-core-spec-os.pdf

5   UK Government Home Office. "Identity Cards Scheme Cost
    Report," May 2007, www.identitycards.gov.uk/downloads/
    2007-05-10CostReport.pdf

6   London School of Economics. "The Identity Project: An
    Assessment of the UK Identity Cards Bill and Its
    Implications," June 2005, http://is2.lse.ac.uk/IDcard/
    identityreport.pdf

Chapter 15

1   SEC Interpretation. "Electronic Storage of Broker-Dealer
    Records," Securities and Exchange Commission, 17 CFR
    Part 241, www.sec.gov/rules/interp/34-47806.htm

2   Strowger, Almon B. "Automated Telephone Exchange," U.S.
    Patent 447918, March 12, 1889, www.google.com/
    patents?id=PShCAAAAEBAJ&dq=447918

Chapter 16

1   Ranum, Marcus. "The Six Dumbest Ideas in Computer
    Security," www.ranum.com/security/computer_security/
    editorials/dumb/

2   CableLabs. "DOCSIS 2.0 Interface," http://www. cablemodem.com/specifications/specifications20.html

3   For example, see Huitema, Christian, *Routing in the Internet*, Prentice Hall, January 2000.

4   Actually, this particular allocation is one that would never be issued because it is part of a block reserved for local network use and for use in examples like this one.

Chapter 17

1   Rutkowska, Joanna. "Introducing Blue Pill," http:// theinvisiblethings.blogspot.com/2006/06/ introducing-blue-pill.html

2   Thomas, Rob, and Jerry Martin. "The Underground Economy: Priceless," www.usenix.org/publications/ login/2006-12/openpdfs/cymru.pdf

3   Hoare, Tony. "The Emperor's Old Clothes," *Communications of the ACM*, Volume 24, Issue 2 (February 1981) pp. 75–83.

Chapter 18

1   Press Release. New York County District Attorney, July 27 2006, www.manhattanda.org/whatsnew/press/ 2006-07-27.html

2   Press Release. U.S. Department of Justice, April 27, 2007, www.usdoj.gov/opa/pr/2007/April/07_crm_301.html

I N D E X

B

T

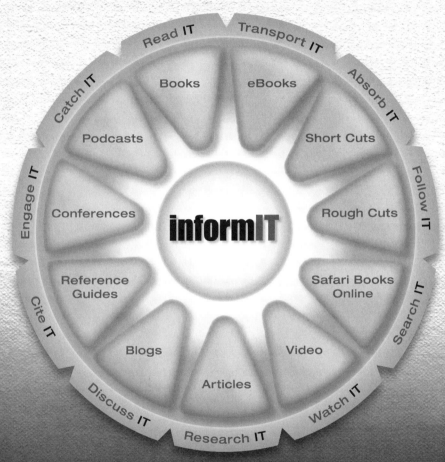

Safari Library
Subscribe Now!
http://safari.informit.com/library

Safari's entire technology collection is now available with no restrictions. Imagine the value of being able to search and access thousands of books, videos and articles from leading technology authors whenever you wish.

EXPLORE TOPICS MORE FULLY

Gain a more robust understanding of related issues by using Safari as your research tool. With Safari Library you can leverage the knowledge of the world's technology gurus. For one flat monthly fee, you'll have unrestricted access to a reference collection offered nowhere else in the world -- all at your fingertips.

With a Safari Library subscription you'll get the following premium services:

- **Immediate access to the newest, cutting-edge books** - Approximately 80 new titles are added per month in conjunction with, or in advance of, their print publication.

- **Chapter downloads** - Download five chapters per month so you can work offline when you need to.

- **Rough Cuts** - A service that provides online access to pre-published information on advanced technologies updated as the author writes the book. You can also download Rough Cuts for offline reference.

- **Videos** - Premier design and development videos from training and e-learning expert lynda.com and other publishers you trust.

- **Cut and paste code** - Cut and paste code directly from Safari. Save time. Eliminate errors.

- **Save up to 35% on print books** - Safari Subscribers receive a discount of up to 35% on publishers' print books.

  Addison Wesley

AdobePress

 ALPHA

Cisco Press

 Press FINANCIAL TIMES

 lynda.com

Microsoft Press

New Riders

O'REILLY

 Peachpit Press

PRENTICE HALL

QUE

Wharton School Publishing

 Redbooks

SAMS

IBM Press

The Terrifying Cost of Insecure, Badly Written Software...
and How to Finally Fix the Problem, Once and for All!

David Rice
ISBN 978-0-32-147789-7

Software has become crucial to the very survival of civilization. But badly written, insecure software is hurting people—and costing businesses and individuals billions of dollars every year. This must change. In *Geekonomics*, David Rice shows how we can change it.

Rice reveals why the software industry is rewarded for carelessness, and how we can revamp the industry's incentives to get the reliability and security we desperately need and deserve. You'll discover why the software industry still has shockingly little accountability—and what we must do to fix that.

Brilliantly written, utterly compelling, and backed by real-world data, *Geekonomics* is a long-overdue call to arms. Whether you're a software user, decision maker, developer, or manager, this book will change your life...or even the entire industry.

David Rice is an internationally recognized information security professional and an accomplished educator and visionary. For a decade he has advised, counseled, and defended global IT networks for government and private industry. David has been awarded by the U.S. Department of Defense for "significant contributions" advancing security of critical national infrastructure and global networks. Additionally, David has authored numerous IT security courses and publications, teaches for the prestigious SANS Institute, and has served as adjunct faculty at James Madison University. He is a frequent speaker at information security conferences and currently Director of The Monterey Group.